TRADITIONS

THEOLOGY IN A POSTCRITICAL KEY

SERIES EDITORS

*Stanley M. Hauerwas, Duke University,
and Peter Ochs, University of Virginia*

RADICAL TRADITIONS cuts new lines of inquiry across a confused array of debates concerning the place of theology in modernity and, more generally, the status and role of scriptural faith in contemporary life. Charged with a rejuvenated confidence, spawned in part by the rediscovery of reason as inescapably tradition constituted, a new generation of theologians and religious scholars is returning to scriptural traditions with the hope of retrieving resources long ignored, depreciated, and in many cases ideologically suppressed by modern habits of thought. RADICAL TRADITIONS assembles a promising matrix of strategies, disciplines, and lines of thought that invites Jewish, Christian, and Islamic theologians back to the word, recovering and articulating modes of scriptural reasoning as that which always underlies modernist reasoning and therefore has the capacity — and authority — to correct it.

Far from despairing over modernity's failings, postcritical theologies rediscover resources for renewal and self-correction within the disciplines of academic study themselves. Postcritical theologies open up the possibility of participating once again in the living relationship that binds together God, text, and community of interpretation. RADICAL TRADITIONS thus advocates a "return to the text," which means a commitment to displaying the richness and wisdom of traditions that are at once text based, hermeneutical, and oriented to communal practice.

Books in this series offer the opportunity to speak openly with practitioners of other faiths or even with those who profess no (or limited) faith, both academics and nonacademics, about the ways religious traditions address pivotal issues of the day. Unfettered by foundationalist preoccupations, these books represent a call for new paradigms of reason — a thinking and rationality that are more responsive than originative. By embracing a postcritical posture, they are able to speak unapologetically out of scriptural traditions manifest in the practices of believing communities (Jewish, Christian, and others); articulate those practices through disciplines of philosophic, textual, and cultural criticism; and engage intellectual, social, and political practices that for too long have been insulated from theological evaluation. RADICAL TRADITIONS is radical not only in its confidence in non-apologetic theological speech but also in how the practice of such speech challenges the current social and political arrangements of modernity.

AFTER THE SPIRIT

A Constructive Pneumatology from Resources
Outside the Modern West

Eugene F. Rogers, Jr.

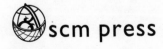

© Eugene F. Rogers, Jr. 2006

First published in the United States in 2005 by
Wm. B. Eerdmans Publishing Co., Michigan.

Published in 2006 by SCM Press
9–17 St Albans Place
London N1 0NX

www.scm-canterburypress.co.uk

British Library Cataloguing in Publication data

A catalogue record for this book is available
from the British Library

0 334 04046 9
978 0 334 04046 0

Printed and bound in Great Britain by
William Clowes Ltd, Beccles, Suffolk

Contents

A royal portrait is painted with visible colours,
and with oil that all can see is the hidden portrait
      of our hidden King portrayed
on those who have been signed . . .
This oil is the dear friend of the Holy Spirit, it serves him,
following him like a disciple. . . .
the hidden seal of the Spirit is imprinted by oil on the bodies
of those who are anointed in baptism: thus they are marked
      in the baptismal mystery. . . .
The face that gazes on a vessel filled with oil
sees its reflection there, and he who gazes hard sets his spiritual gaze thereon
and sees in its symbols Christ. And as the beauty of Christ is manifold,
so the olive's symbols are manifold.
Christ has many facets, and the oil acts as a mirror to them all:
from whatever angle I look at the oil, Christ looks out at me from it.

Ephrem the Syrian,
Hymn on Virginity, no. 7,
in Brock, *Harp of the Spirit*,
pp. 48-49, 51

Acknowledgments

In 1998-99 I received a grant from the National Humanities Center (specifically funded by the National Endowment for the Humanities) to finish the Aquinas chapters of *Sexuality and the Christian Body*. As it happened, I found myself, after that was done and the book was in press, with an unusual amount of time for answering copyeditor's queries. I had argued that the congregation at a wedding found itself caught up in the office appropriated to the Spirit, that of celebrating and rejoicing in the love of two. I wanted to add a footnote to some previous instance of such an application. Although I still liked the application, and no reviewer has objected to it — not even a reviewer objecting to lots of other things — I never found a previous usage. But I had the luxury to read about the Holy Spirit from morning to night most days of the week. Thanks to the National Humanities Center, the footnote that never was became this book. There I would like to thank especially the Director, Robert Connor; the Deputy Director, Kent Mullikin; the librarians, especially Alan Tuttle, Eliza Robertson, and Jean Houston, who were tremendously helpful when my research was most exploratory and I needed books on Syriac Christianity published in India. At that time I also spent many happy weekends at Dumbarton Oaks in Washington, D.C.; I would like to thank Alice-Mary Talbot, the Director of Byzantine Studies, for allowing a reader's card to a non-specialist.

In 2002-03 I was Eli Lilly Visiting Associate Professor of Christian Thought and Practice in the Department of Religion at Princeton University. I would like to thank the members of the Department of Religion there for making that administratively possible, especially Martha Himmelfarb and Jeffrey Stout, who were chairs before and during my time there, and John Gager, for conversation. This was made financially possible by the Eli Lilly

Foundation and Robert Wuthnow of Princeton's Center for the Study of Religion, to whom also thanks, as well as to Cleo McNally Kearns, another fellow at that Center, for conversation.

In 2002-03 I was also a Member of the Center of Theological Inquiry in Princeton, which provided not only an office within a minute's walk of Speer Library, but a townhouse with a fireplace and even firewood, and best of all lots of useful conversation. I wish to thank Wallace Alston, the Director; Robert W. Jenson, the Senior Scholar; Kathi Morley, Maureen Montgomery, Mary Rae Rogers, and Marion Gibson, administrators; and the members for gifts of companionship and conversation, including Steven Webb, Kevin Hughes, and above all John Muddiman. It was splendid to be in the intellectual and hospitable presence of Robert and Blanche Jenson.

I gave papers on this material for which I thank the Duodecim Society, especially Robert Jenson (again) and Richard Norris, for gifts of texts, questions, reading, and paraphrase. The faculty of the Department of Religious Studies at Brown University, especially Stanley Stowers and Susan Harvey, offered gifts of reading, listening, and conversation.

I thank the University of Virginia for topping up my leave support on both those occasions, and for summer research grants in 1999, 2001, and 2002. I also want to thank the staff of Alderman Library, and especially that of Library Express on Grounds, the book delivery service, including Winston Barham and Lew Purifoy. An award of $2500 from the University's Dean of Arts and Sciences subvened the publication of the plates.

I thank the editors of Radical Traditions, Stanley Hauerwas and Peter Ochs, also a colleague. They supported this project when it was only a two-page abstract, and they provided some of the best feedback on the penultimate draft, as did Anthony Baker and Lewis Ayres.

Thanks also to Annemarie Weyl Carr, Glenn Peers, and Warren T. Woodfin for art historical advice, although they are not responsible for any irresponsible flights of fancy or failures of taste.

I thank the students in my seminar on the Holy Spirit, especially Aaron Riches, Joel Marie Cabrita, Keith Starkenberg, Angel Méndez, Jenny McBride, Nathan Jennings, and Jacqueline Kamara, as well as two other graduate students, Tony Baker and Willis Jenkins, many of whom read the penultimate draft, and Keith Sterling Cox, who prepared the index.

Finally, I thank Derek Krueger, for his willingness to share a leave in Princeton, as well as for his willingness to share a life with me, and the Department of Religious Studies at the University of North Carolina at Greensboro, especially Charlie Orzech and Ben Ramsey, and Dean Timothy Johnston, for making a place for both of us there.

*   *   *

A portion of the Introduction has previously appeared as "Introduction," in Eugene F. Rogers, ed., *Theology and Sexuality: Classic and Contemporary Readings* (Oxford: Blackwell, 2002).

Portions of Part I, Chapters 1 and 3 appeared in much longer forms in "The Mystery of the Spirit in Three Traditions: Calvin, Rahner, Florensky: Or, You *Keep* Wondering Where the Spirit Went," *Modern Theology* 19 (2003): 243-60; and "The Eclipse of the Spirit in Karl Barth," in *Conversing with Barth*, ed. John McDowell and Michael Higton (London: Ashgate, 2004), pp. 173-90.

A portion of Part II, Chapter II, section 5 appeared as "Isaac in the Eucharist," *Journal for Scriptural Reasoning* 1:2 (2001/02). The journal is available online at http://etext.lib.virginia.edu/journals/ssr/.

A portion of Part II, Chapter III, section 2 appeared in "Water and the Spirit," *Scottish Journal of Theology* 56:1 (2003): 89-100.

A portion of Part II, Chapter IV, section 7 appears in "Faith and Reason Follow Glory: The Spirit in Aquinas," in Joseph Wawrykrow and Rik van Nieuwenhove, eds., *The Theology of Thomas Aquinas* (Notre Dame, Ind.: University of Notre Dame Press, 2005), pp. 442-59.

The Epilogue previously appeared in somewhat longer form as "The Eclipse of the Spirit in Thomas Aquinas," in *Grammar and Grace: Aquinas and Wittgenstein: Essays in Memory of Victor Preller,* ed. Robert MacSwain and Jeffrey Stout (London: SCM, May 2004) pp. 136-53.

INTRODUCTION

After the Body, After the Spirit

As I was putting together the collection *Theology and Sexuality*, I was also planning this book, *After the Spirit*. It treats the continual lip service and equally continual lack of substance accorded the Holy Spirit in modern Christian thought. Committed to talk of the Spirit by multiple traditions, modern Christian thought has less and less to say about it. Spirit-talk in the last hundred years has been ever more evoked, and ever more substance-free. The Spirit, who in classical Christian discourse "pours out on all flesh," had, in modern Christian discourse, floated free of bodies altogether.

What if the Spirit had grown boring because it no longer had anything to do with the body? And what if appeals to bodily experience in cases of sexual controversy led to mutual dismissal because they had become too individualist, because appealers failed to argue in terms of a common Spirit?

Thanks to a leave at the National Humanities Center in 1999-2000, I had enjoyed the leisure to dabble in Greek and Syriac texts of earlier centuries of the Christian era, where I noticed that — unlike in the twentieth century — talk of the Holy Spirit seemed, to a non-specialist at least, almost always strictly tied to talk of holy places, holy people, and holy things. It did not float free of bodily existence as it does in modern North Atlantic Christian discourse and worship. Indeed, it was embodied. One locus was baptism, in which the Spirit descended upon a person. Another was the Eucharist, in which it dwelt as a fire in consecrated bread and the wine. A third was unction,

---

This section appeared in slightly different form, and with a different context and purpose, in my introduction to Eugene F. Rogers, Jr., *Theology and Sexuality: Classic and Contemporary Readings* (Oxford: Blackwell, 2002), pp. xx-xxi. That shows the relation of spirit and matter.

in which "oil is the dear friend of the Holy Spirit," as Ephrem the Syrian wrote. It breathed on the water at creation; it moved in Mary's womb; it animated the churches; it appealed to the senses as light, fire, incense, wine, and song. The Spirit was not merely transcendent; it was immanent in bodily things.

In response to reviews of *Sexuality and the Christian Body*,[1] I found myself arguing in terms of human body and Holy Spirit at once: it seemed to me that Christian worship constructs the body liturgically. Liturgy is at once the place in which Christians bring their bodies into worship — even traditions that think of themselves as non-liturgical bow their heads in prayer or raise their voices in song — and also the site in which the Nicene definition of the Holy Spirit locates it: "with the Father and Son He is worshipped and glorified." So, for example, the notorious asceticisms of Symeon the Stylite — one of a number of such saints who spent years standing atop a pillar — turn out to be keyed to the mass and the calendar. Symeon's own ecclesiastical superiors, worrying lest his self-denial would lead to death, persuaded him to put them at the service of others. So he was induced to preach from his pillar, the people processing in and out as if at mass — and restricting his homilies to reasonable length. He was encouraged to save his greatest austerities for penitential seasons: he must eat more in ordinary time so as to eat less during Lent. One hagiographer even suggested that in standing on pillar-top he made of his body a living sacrifice rising like incense up to God. His body becomes a communicative sign, a liturgical formation — or as the traditional language would put it, imbued with the Spirit.[2] I went on to argue that the same kind of liturgical construction of the body is going on when modern Christian groups decide who may marry, who may offer themselves as communicative signs to the community. And yet this liturgical construction does not stop with human bodies: it is a cosmic liturgy.

As Aaron Riches has written,

> The outpouring of God's mercy in Joel refers to the coming of peace where all of material creation is raised up in God: the soil is told to be glad and rejoice (2:21), the animals of the field are told not to fear (2:22), the people are told that God has "given the early rain for your vindication" (2:23), that the threshing floor will be full of grain (2:24), and "You shall eat in plenty and be satisfied" (2:26). It is against this physicality that God says, "I will pour

1. Eugene F. Rogers, Jr., *Sexuality and the Christian Body: Their Way into the Triune God* (Oxford: Blackwell Publishers, 1999).

2. See Susan A. Harvey, "The Stylite's Liturgy: Ritual and Religious Identity in Late Antiquity," *Journal of Early Christian Studies* 6 (1998): 523-39 and "The Sense of a Stylite: Perspectives on Simeon the Elder," *Vigiliae Christianae* 42 (1988): 376-94.

out my spirit on all flesh; your sons and your daughters shall prophesy" (Joel 2:28).[3]

That the Spirit had grown dull because unembodied, and bodily experience unpersuasive because un-Spirited, was one of the initial insights for this book.

This book can be read in different ways by different audiences. From a Religious Studies point of view, you might regard the book as a reflection on indigenous (or naturalized) Christian accounts of matters very important to our discipline: community, experience, identity formation, ritual practice, economic activity, material culture. But because it seeks to remain adequate to those naturalized Christian accounts, it does not allow modern Western patterns of analysis to set the structure.[4] Rather it uses them heuristically, transgressively, and ad hoc.

Part of that transgression is that I have treated all parties as if they shared an orthodoxy. This is part of a humanistic conviction that authors are read best when read *in optimam partem,* in the best light. It is also part of a theological conviction that "given the persistence of the sin of others . . . as well as our own . . . there is only one way to respond to them which would not itself be sinful and domineering, and that is to anticipate heaven, and act as if their sin was not there, by offering reconciliation. [For] virtue cannot operate properly except when collectively possessed."[5] Therefore I have stared past two disputes that generate more heat than light, and that are, in any case, beginning to be overcome in ecumenical dialogue: the Filioque controversy[6]

3. P. Aaron Riches, "On Robert Jenson's Critique of the Spirit in Barth," unpublished typescript, p. 3.

4. For an account of how the study of religion can colonize indigenous cultures, see David Chidester, *Savage Systems: Colonialism and Comparative Religion in Southern Africa* (Charlottesville and London: University Press of Virginia, 1996). For a brief reflection on the relation between theology and Religious Studies, see Eugene F. Rogers, Jr., "Theology in the Curriculum of a Secular Religious Studies Department," in *Reflections on the Study of Religion,* ed. Jeffrey Stout and Randall Balmer (Princeton, N.J.: Princeton University Press, forthcoming).

5. John Milbank, *Theology and Social Theory: Beyond Secular Reason* (Oxford: Blackwell Publishers, 1990), p. 411.

6. The *Filioque* controversy asks whether the Spirit proceeds from the Father or from the Father and the Son. "Resting on the Son" is a version accepted by both sides. For good essays on the ecumenical state of the question, see Lukas Vischer, ed., *Spirit of God, Spirit of Christ: Ecumenical Reflections on the* Filioque *Controversy,* Faith and Order Paper 103 (London: SPCK and Geneva: World Council of Churches, 1981), of which the most interesting article systematically is Dumitru Staniloae, "The Procession of the Holy Spirit from the Father and His Relation to the Son, as the Basis of Our Deification and Adoption," pp. 174-86.

and the insights of the non-Chalcedonian churches. I have tried to eliminate sterilizing interrogations of formulae and to practice what German theologians call *kontroverstheologische Harmonielehre*, the acuity of the theology of controversy converted to irenic purpose. There is enough sterility in treatments of the Spirit without ruling large swaths of Christian insight out of court. As in any other work in theology or Christian thought, the burden is on the reader to show that a claim leads to bad consequences and why those consequences are bad. It is not enough to point out that a thinker accepts or rejects the *Filioque* or is revered in the churches of India. If Ephrem the Syrian, for example, is revered most in Kerala, that has not prevented him from being revered also by Wesley. If the goal is to expand the field of vision and enlarge the background assumptions, any other procedure would be self-insulating and prone to perpetuate the problem.

It is perhaps odd for a book concerned with body and Spirit to take little explicit account of the charismatic movement. Many charismatic texts are devotional; many studies of the charismatic movement are sociological:[7] neither genre tends to be primarily interested in the naturalized disciplines by which Christian communities reflect critically and constructively on their practices. That is, both devotional and sociological accounts are *data* that naturalized Christian patterns of reflection — or theology — might form. These pages tend to operate on another level of reflection, considering the intellectual adequacy of the patterns already formed. Fortunately two essays fill the gap. Thomas Weinandy's elegant account in *The Father's Spirit of Sonship*[8] is a theology largely compatible with the approach taken in this book, which however explicitly takes account of charismatic experience as a concrete, bodily way in which the Spirit rests on the body of the Son. Sarah Coakley's essay for the Doctrine Commission of the Church of England[9] instantiates that rarest of forms, sociological fieldwork combined with doctrinal reflection. There she distinguishes two kinds of charismatic reflection on practice

7. Good historical accounts include Grant Wacker, *Heaven Below: Early Pentecostals and American Culture* (Cambridge, Mass.: Harvard University Press, 2001) and David Martin, *Tongues on Fire: The Explosion of Protestantism in Latin America* (Oxford: Basil Blackwell, 1989). For a more popular account, see Adolf Holl, *The Left Hand of God: A Biography of the Holy Spirit*, trans. John Cullen (New York: Doubleday, 1998).

8. Thomas G. Weinandy, *The Father's Spirit of Sonship: Reconceiving the Trinity* (Edinburgh: T&T Clark, 1995).

9. Sarah Coakley, "Charismatic Experience: Praying 'In the Spirit,'" in *We Believe in the Holy Spirit* by the Church of England Doctrine Commission (London: Church House Publications, 1991), pp. 17-36. The Lutheran Church in America also put out a book of essays in response to the charismatic movement, Paul D. Opsahl, ed., *The Holy Spirit in the Life of the Church* (Minneapolis: Augsburg, 1978).

according to two ways in which participants relate Son and Spirit. In one kind of reflection, participants see themselves as moving from an economy of the Spirit into an economy of the Son, in a linear if ascending pattern. In another kind of reflection, participants see themselves as moving into the relationship between the Son and the Spirit. The second mode of reflection is compatible with Weinandy's account and mine.

Related to my reticence about the charismatic movement is the influence on me of Hans Frei. Frei learned from Barth to be suspicious of nineteenth-century subjectivism. It came in many forms. There was a turn to the intro-spective human subject in Schleiermacher's "feeling of absolute dependence"; there was a turn to the christological human subject in the quest of the histor-ical Jesus; there was a turn to the sociological human subject in *The Elemen-tary Forms of the Religious Life.* These multiple turns to the human subject also affected the doctrine of God: the Persons of the Trinity became centers of consciousness — rather than agents of a single activity.[10] The human con-sciousness and the divine consciousness might meld. Idealists and Romantics alike longed for Jesus to be present to consciousness. In that longing, theology made itself susceptible to Feuerbach's critique, and Jesus became a creature of human manipulation, so that a German *Leben Jesu* and a French *Vie de Jésus* could be quite nationally colored[11] (not a good thing in time of war).

In *The Identity of Jesus Christ,*[12] Frei argued that it undermined the indige-nous logic of Christian dogmatic claims to seek first for Christ's presence. The quest of the historical Jesus had its obverse in a quest of Christ's presence, and the quest of presence led to a loss of particularity and a washing out of the dis-tinctive features of the narrative. For example, the quest of the historical Jesus ended in the crucifixion, while the quest of Christ's presence focused on the resurrection: but in the narrative those events happen to one character, not

10. See Phillip Cary, "On Behalf of Classical Trinitarianism: A Critique of Rahner on the Trinity," *The Thomist* 30 (1992), esp. pp. 390-93, which may or may not be right about Rahner, but is right about ancient and modern notions of persons; André de Halleux, "'Hypostase' et 'Personne' dans la formation du dogme trinitaire," *Revue d'histoire ecclésiastique* 79 (1984): 313-69; Halleux, "Personnalisme ou essentialisme trinitaire chez les Pères cappadociens? Une mauvaise controverse," in two parts, *Revue théologique de Louvain* 17 (1986): 129-55 and 265-92; David Brown, "Trinitarian Personhood and Individuality," in *Trinity, Incarnation, and Atone-ment: Philosophical and Theological Essays,* ed. Ronald J. Feenstra and Cornelius Plantinga, Jr. (Notre Dame, Ind.: University of Notre Dame Press, 1989); and now Andrew Rouner, "Persona Non Grata," Ph.D. dissertation, the University of Virginia, 2004.

11. See Albert Schweitzer, *The Quest of the Historical Jesus,* ed. John Bowdin, trans. W. Mont-gomery et al. (Minneapolis: Fortress Press, 2001).

12. Hans W. Frei, *The Identity of Jesus Christ: The Hermeneutical Bases of Dogmatic Theology* (Philadelphia: Fortress Press, 1975).

two. Rather, the logic of Christian intellectual practice favored the depiction of character in narrative, so that the character of Jesus could be identified by what he undertook and underwent — by the interplay of plot and circumstance in the depiction of character — so that it was the one crucified who was raised. After a reader had grasped the identity of Jesus Christ — or had been grasped by it in the reading — she might or might not, by grace, recognize him as present. In a variation of the ontological argument, to know *who* Jesus was involved the reader in the conclusion that, as depicted, Jesus could not fail to be present. Luke's angel in the empty tomb portrayed Jesus as the ever-living one, the one who could not be sought among the dead. In that unique case, according to Frei, the logic of Christian doctrine was that Christ's identity brought his presence with it. That logic was almost sacramental: the narratives, like the bread and wine, brought what they proclaimed. Talk of Christ's presence, on the other hand, might not bring his true identity, but all manner of idols. The important thing, therefore, was to attend to the narrative description in the Gospels (or, according to Gerard Loughlin's formulation, in the lectionary and the liturgy[13]) in which action conveys identity.

Frei cited Strawson's *Individuals*,[14] but he might have cited Aristotle or Aquinas, both of whom were able to identify character long before the nineteenth century discovered centers of consciousness or Descartes abstracted minds from bodies. Earlier theologians from multiple traditions nursed suspicions of pneumatologies of presence. I use the Orthodox theologian Pavel Florensky, but one might use a Protestant (Calvin) or a Catholic (Rahner) just as well.[15] On the other hand, one might argue that the priority of identity over presence is simply counterintuitive. Getting to know human persons often involves being first in their presence and only then the observation of the acts that convey their identity. The answer to that objection will have to be practical: The accounts of the Spirit that start with presence are boring, and fail to portray the Spirit with much distinctiveness: they are part of the problem. The hypothesis that identity descriptions work better will have to be tested. Is the book that follows any improvement?

Frei's account considers "the identity of Jesus Christ," and not the identity of the Spirit. It leaves open two possibilities for a pneumatology. On the one

13. Gerard Loughlin, *Telling God's Story: Bible, Church, and Narrative Theology* (Cambridge and New York: Cambridge University Press, 1996).

14. P. F. Strawson, *Individuals: An Essay in Descriptive Metaphysics* (London: Methuen, 1964).

15. For accounts of Calvin and Rahner omitted here, see Eugene F. Rogers, Jr., "The Mystery of the Spirit in Three Traditions: Calvin, Rahner, Florensky: Or, You *Keep* Wondering Where the Spirit Went," *Modern Theology* 19 (2003): 243-60.

hand, a pneumatology might simply apply the same procedure to the Spirit that Frei applies to the Son. In that case, an account would seek to give a thick description of the character of the Spirit, by observing how the Spirit interacts with plot and circumstance in the Gospels. On the other hand, a pneumatology might claim that the "presence" brought with Christ's identity is not separate from the Holy Spirit: Christ's presence, on that view, *just is* his Spirit. In that case, it might be a mistake to seek an identity of the Spirit apart from the identity of the Son.

The procedure followed here leaves that alternative open. Because the acts of the Trinity toward the world are indivisible, the only time one could distinguish the Spirit from the Son would be when the narratives give glimpses of their *intratrinitarian* interaction. That means that, following the first option, the only interaction of the Spirit with plot and circumstance that could *distinguish* the Spirit from the Son, will be the Spirit's interactions *with* the Son. That means that, in accord with the second option, the theologian is never seeking the identity of the Spirit apart from that of the Son. In short, the two options coincide. Narratively, the Spirit is identified in her interactions with Jesus, and is so neither identical with him, nor apart from him: doctrinally, the Spirit alights, abides, or comes to rest on the Son.

In that regard it is interesting that in one of the most important places where Christian practice brings narrative and doctrine together — namely, in the creeds — the narrative about the Spirit has borne a difficult relation to the narrative about the Son. The standard form of the Nicene Creed clearly tells a story about the Son:

> I believe in one God, . . .
> And in one Lord Jesus Christ . . .
> who for us human beings and for our salvation came down from heaven,
> was incarnate by the Holy Spirit of the virgin Mary,
> and was made human:
> who for us, too, was crucified under Pontius Pilate,
> suffered,
> died,
> and was buried:
> the third day he rose according to the Scriptures,
> ascended into heaven,
> and is seated on the right hand of the Father:
> he shall come again with glory
> to judge the living and the dead,
> and his kingdom will have no end.

As clearly as that article is deeply narrative, this article about the Spirit is hardly narrative, unless the last clause counts as the barest of narratives:

And in the Holy Spirit
the lord and giver of life,
who proceeds from the Father
who together with the Father and the Son is worshipped and glorified:
who spoke by the prophets.

And yet there are other forms of the article on the Spirit that seem much more parallel in narrative form and detail to the article on the Son. In the anaphora of the Liturgy of St. James we find:

Have mercy upon us,
God the Father almighty,
and send upon us
and upon these gifts set before thee
thine Holy Spirit
the Lord and giver of life . . .
who descended in the likeness of a dove
upon our Lord Jesus Christ
in the river Jordan,
who descended upon the holy apostles
in the likeness of fiery tongues.[16]

And in the Armenian version of the Creed, we read:

We also believe in the Holy Ghost
uncreated and perfect
who spake in the law
and in the prophets
and in the gospels,
who came down upon the Jordan,
proclaimed the One Sent,
and dwelt in the saints.[17]

16. F. E. Brightman, ed., *Eastern Liturgies, Being the Texts Original or Translated of the Principal Liturgies of the Church* (Piscataway, N.J.: Gorgias Press, 2002), facsimile reprint of *Liturgies Eastern and Western*, vol. I, Eastern Liturgies (Oxford: Clarendon Press, 1896), p. 88.

17. Brightman, *Eastern Liturgies*, p. 427, modified in accord with Gabriele Winkler, "Eine bemerkenswerte Stelle im armenischen Glaubenserkenntnis: Credimus et in Sanctum Spiritum qui descendit in Jordanem proclamavit missum," *Oriens Christianus* 63 (1973): 130-62, esp. p. 143.

Why does the narrative of the Spirit survive only in Armenian? According to Gabriele Winkler, in the competition between christologies that place the Spirit at Jesus' conception, and those that place the Spirit first at his baptism, the version of the Creed that survives in Armenian was heard as adoptionist.[18] It was heard as tainted with the losing view that God the Father adopted a previously existing, non-divine human being to be his son at the baptism. It could, I think, also be interpreted in ways that did not lead to adoptionism. But that is not the important point for us here. The important point is more formal, about whose narrative this is. Here a narrative about the Spirit was not in fact heard as a narrative about the Spirit. It was heard as an alternative narrative about the Son.[19] The Armenian version of the Creed is thus an exception that proves the rule: Even when we have narratives about the Spirit — whether they are retained or whether they are suppressed, whether they remain local or whether they spread abroad, whether one favors or opposes them — they make sense precisely by reference to the Son.

The purpose is not exactly to find something distinctive for the Spirit to *do*, since *opera Trinitatis ad extra indivisa sunt*. But by "appropriation" theologians mean the assignment by human thought of specific aspects of the indivisible work of God in the world to trinitarian Persons according to their biblical characters. So I *do* want a livelier *appropriation* of God-talk to the Spirit, to overcome the tendency in modern theology by which, to put it crudely, any way of talking appropriated to the Spirit might be better appropriated to the Son. It's as if the ditty from *Annie Get Your Gun* were an unacknowledged premise like this:

Anything Spirit can do, Son can do better,
Son can do anything better than She.

In the foreground, I want to recover the way in which some Christian doctrines speak of the destiny of the human being as fellowship with God, variously called vocation (among Protestants), consummation (among Catholics), or deification (among the Eastern Orthodox): the sense in which human beings become "participants in the divine nature" (II Pet. 1:4), or, as the first question of the Westminster Catechism puts the same thing, that the chief end of the human being is "to glorify God and enjoy Him forever." I think a recovery of deification or consummation is not possible without a livelier doctrine of the Spirit, whose intratrinitarian office it is not just statically to represent but personally to witness or glorify the love between the Father and the Son.

18. Winkler, "Eine bemerkenswerte Stelle," pp. 151-52.
19. Cf. Winkler, "Eine bemerkenswerte Stelle," p. 156.

In the background, Barth is both the model and the disappointment here. The sense in which he is the disappointment is laid out in Robert Jenson's article "You Wonder Where the Spirit Went."[20] "The personal agent of [the church] in fact turns out at every step of Barth's argument to be *not* the Spirit, as advertised, but Christ; the Spirit is denoted invariably by impersonal terms," often "the power of Jesus Christ."[21]

Without going into how fair or unfair the characterization may be, I want to go on to the way in which Barth is the model. He has a wonderful way of linking without collapsing the immanent and the economic Trinity when he speaks of the *Second* Person. So for example this thesis from *Dogmatics in Outline:*

> In that God became human, it has also become manifest and worthy of belief that He did not wish to exist for Himself only and therefore to be alone. . . .[22]

so that the incarnation becomes grounds for believing that the Father of Jesus Christ is (with Son and Spirit) the Creator of the world. Similarly we read in the same place something about the goal of the world, that "God creates, sustains, and rules [creation] as the theatre of His glory — and in its midst, the human being also, as the witness of His glory." We expect this consummation of the human being to be grounded in work appropriated to the Spirit in the same way; we expect to read something like this: "In that God the Spirit blows at Pentecost, it has also become manifest and worthy of belief that He does not wish to enjoy and glorify Himself only and therefore to be without a witness." But we read no such thing. The end of the human being gets discussed without the Spirit who makes it possible for the human being to reach that end. I will be making such moves all the time, moves that Barth showed me how to make.

---

20. *Pro Ecclesia* 2 (1993): 296-304. For an account that does not take Barth as central, see D. Lyle Dabney, "Why Should the Last Be First? The Priority of Pneumatology in Recent Theological Discussion," in *Advents of the Spirit: An Introduction to the Current Study of Pneumatology,* ed. Bradford E. Hinze and D. Lyle Dabney (Milwaukee, Wis.: Marquette University Press, 2001), pp. 240-61.

21. Jenson, "You Wonder Where the Spirit Went," p. 303, citing *CD* IV/3.

22. Barth, *Dogmatics in Outline,* trans. G. T. Thompson (London: SCM Press, 1949), p. 50, *Leitsatz.*

Preliminary Theses

I take theologian's license to argue in theses. These are meant to be anticipatory and exemplary, not exhaustive.

1. *Opera trinitatis ad extra indivisa sunt.* The works of the Trinity toward creation are indivisible. That means that not only is the Father the Creator, but so is the Spirit; not only is the Son the Redeemer, but the Spirit also. This axiom gives us lots of scope to talk about the Spirit as the Creator God, the Redeemer God, and so on. Again Jenson paves the way here, with his Barth-inspired theologoumenon that the Spirit is the electing God.[23] The Persons are differentiated by their actions among themselves, not their actions toward us.[24]

2. Interactions among the Persons recorded in the New Testament give glimpses of the intratrinitarian life as it dilates — delays and opens up — to include human beings within it.[25] These interactions occur at the annunciation, baptism, temptation, and crucifixion of Jesus, and at the institution of the Lord's Supper. Most important among them is the resurrection of Jesus as described in Romans 8.

At the *annunciation,* the angel comes from the Father, and the Spirit over-

23. Robert Jenson, "The Holy Spirit," in Robert W. Jenson and Carl Braaten, *Christian Dogmatics,* 2 vols. (Philadelphia: Fortress, 1984), vol. 2, pp. 101-82. In personal correspondence my student Michael Barton Renner has traced apporoaches to that thesis in Barth, *CD* II/2, pp. 315, 317, 318, 321-22, 345-36, 414.

24. Lewis Ayres notes that this principle recalls a practice. "The doctrine of inseparability of operation sets bounds to or shapes how we envisage the diversity of the persons by shaping habits of speech that keep us attentive to the mystery of God's unity and diversity. Learning to speak of Father, Son, and Spirit as inseparably operating . . . does not so much lead us to an easy imagining . . . as it defers our comprehension and draws our minds to the constantly failing even as constantly growing character of our interpretation. . . . [Thus] the text of Scripture is understood to shape a movement of the intellect and imagination beyond (or into) its language and towards the divine mystery." *Nicaea and Its Legacy: An Approach to Fourth-Century Trinitarian Theology* (Oxford: Oxford University Press, 2004), pp. 297, 299.

25. The most persistent practitioner of this approach in modern theology has been Hans Urs von Balthasar, in his *Theodramatik* (Einsiedeln: Johannes-Verlag, 1973-83). For a comprehensive account, see Paolo Martinelli, *La Morte di Cristo come rivelazione dell'amore trinitario nella teologia di Hans Urs von Balthasar* (Milan: Editoriale Jaca Book, 1995), esp. pp. 154-96. I first paid attention to it at the suggestion of David Yeago. In particular, Martinelli (pp. 160-69) calls attention to a procedure that von Balthasar calls "trinitarian inversion," in which the Spirit precedes the Son in economic activity in the New Testament; see esp. Hans Urs von Balthasar, *Theodramatik,* 4 vols. in 5 (Einsiedeln: Johannes-Verlag, 1973-83), vol. 3, pp. 172-80. J. J. O'Donnell, "In Him and under Him: The Holy Spirit in the Life of Jesus," *Gregorianum* 70 (1989): 25-45 is primarily interested in the development of Jesus' self-consciousness, an issue not addressed here. Raniero Cantalamessa, *Lo Spirito Santo nella vita di Gesú: il mistero dell'unzione,* 2d ed. (Milan: Editrice Ancora, 1983) focuses on the baptism and temptation of Jesus.

shadows Mary in the conception of the Son, three Persons taking characteristic roles in the one indivisible *opus ad extra* of the incarnation. "And the angel said to her, 'The Holy Spirit will come upon you, and the power of the Most High will overshadow you; therefore the child to be born will be called holy, the Son of God'" (Luke 1:26).

At the *baptism,* the voice of the Father identifies the Son as his beloved — *agapetos* — while the Holy Spirit in the form of a dove alights on him: "Now when all the people were baptized, and when Jesus also had been baptized and was praying, the heaven was opened, and the Holy Spirit descended upon him in bodily form, as a dove, and a voice came from heaven, 'Thou art my Son, my beloved; with thee I am well pleased'" (Luke 3:21, Mark 1:10-11, Matt. 3:16-17).

At the *transfiguration,* similarly, the Son is again identified as the beloved of the Father, while traditional exegesis and Eastern iconography sees the Spirit in the cloud and in the pregnant word "overshadowed"; significantly, this occurs, in Luke, while Jesus is praying (Luke 9:28-36). For the orthodox tradition, the transfiguration represents the Taboric light, available to other human beings, that manifests the beginning of deification in this life. Jesus "went up to pray. . . . A cloud came and overshadowed them; . . . And a voice came out of the cloud, saying, 'This is my son, my beloved; listen to him'" (Luke 9:34-35; cf. Mark 9:7, Matt. 17:6).

In Paul's version of the *resurrection,* all three Persons are present; indeed, the resurrection identifies them and their relations, starting with the Spirit: "If the Spirit of the One Who raised Jesus from the dead dwells in you, the One Who raised Christ Jesus from the dead will give life to your mortal bodies also through his Spirit which dwells in you" (Rom. 8:11).

But this glimpsing of the trinitarian life does not mean, according to Christian contemplative practice, that human beings thereby gain certainty concerning divine things *(scientia in divinis)* or that they come to comprehend God in Trinity or in unity. Rather such glimpses occur as part of a human practice of reflecting upon scripture by which the Persons may begin to comprehend or embrace human beings — that is, catch them up into a divine life that increases in mystery even as it enfolds them.

I do not want a social theory of the Trinity in the sense that some theologians object to.[26] I do not want to give each of the persons his own depth psychology, or locate suffering and loss in the divine nature of the Trinity rather

---

26. See Philip Cary, "On Behalf of Classical Trinitarianism: A Critique of Rahner on the Trinity," *The Thomist* 30 (1992): 365-406; Karen E. Kilby, "Perichoresis and Projection: Problems with the Social Doctrines of the Trinity," *New Blackfriars* 81 (2000): 432-45; Lewis Ayres, *Nicaea and Its Legacy,* pp. 296-97, 384-429.

than in the human nature of Jesus. In that case Father, Son, and Spirit may no longer be one God except accidentally, and all three of them may be so much in the same boat with human beings as to seem unable to save them. But I am attracted to the Balthasarian idea that the New Testament gives occasional glimpses into intratrinitarian activity in the various theophanies. So I do not want to treat the baptism, say, as merely appropriating the words to the Father or the alighting to the Spirit. I want to say that at baptism human beings are in the process of moving to the inside of the trinitarian life. So they get a true glimpse. But on the other hand they do not understand what they are glimpsing. Human beings are only on the way, by anagogy, and even when they arrive they will be comprehended rather than comprehending. Any nineteenth-century center-of-consciousness psychology of the Persons would be less real, on this interpretation, than (say) baptism or transfiguration, not least because baptism and transfiguration are more nearly what human beings need to be led into by anagogy than into Hegel or Freud.

3. When intratrinitarian relations are glimpsed because the Holy Spirit reveals them in Scripture, the Holy Spirit also manifests (I Cor. 12:7) them in human beings as the conditions for the possibility of human participation in the trinitarian life.

One advantage of this approach is that it furthers anagogic practices of contemplation and scriptural interpretation that lead both into the narrative and into the mystery of the Trinity.[27] Since contemplation is a practice, it matters what virtues or vices it develops in the practitioner. Christian rational and contemplative practices do not have to float free from stories and ascend into ontological speculation in order to remain robustly trinitarian. The trick is not so much to eschew speculation (even ontological speculation, if ontology is at root a reflection on the conditions implied in a story) as to site it differently, in a narrative, scriptural place. If we took the narratives in one direction, we might claim to know how Father, Son, and Spirit *are* with one another, in a way that would reinforce tendencies in Christian theology to hubris (claiming to know too much), tritheism (treating the threeness so as to exclude unity), or idolatry (reducing divine Persons to mere humanoids). If we discipline the contemplation of the narratives in another way, the stories may invite us to enter more deeply without losing their mystery (their unexhausted goodness), somewhat as human persons become more rather than less mysterious the better we know them. Mystery, after all, is something that many Christians may associate primarily with the Spirit as the one they think they least understand — perhaps mistakenly, since the Father and the Son

27. See Ayres, *Nicaea and Its Legacy,* esp. pp. 284-85, 297-300, 321-24, 326, 328, 332, 343.

also share in the divine mystery. How could the Spirit be more mysterious than the Son? Or how could the Son speak more directly than the Spirit? As Thomas Aquinas repeats many times, "we are joined to God as to One Unknown,"[28] where the word for "joining," *coniugamur,* recalls the knowing in mystery of marriage or the being comprehended by another of sex.

4. In the New Testament we see human beings *in transition* from being exterior to being interior to the trinitarian life. This explains why it is sometimes hard to keep straight principles (1) and (2). Christians say both that God's actions toward human beings are indivisible, and that the trinitarian Persons are distinguished among themselves. In the New Testament it is sometimes hard to tell whether the action belongs to the first or the second category. The narrative is fluid and continuous and does not care for theologians' categories. The reason why it is hard to distinguish the Persons' distinct *internal* actions from their indivisible *external* actions is that in the New Testament the perspective is constantly changing. Or better, it is in transition. Everything that Jesus undertakes and undergoes *changes* the relation of the human being to the Trinity, because in him God is reconciling the world to Godself. As a gift to the Son, the Spirit is constantly incorporating observers, not excluding the writer and the reader, into the trinitarian life, *moving* them from an external to an internal relation, teaching them to say "Father," to take on the identity of the Son, to join in the Spirit's own celebration. Under those circumstances, instability is to be expected.

5. The Spirit proceeds from the Father to rest on the Son. This happens (1) in the life of Jesus as recorded in the New Testament, (2) in the life of his body the Church, as recorded in the liturgy, and (3) in the bodies of his members, as they are liturgically constructed in sacraments and prayer.

Many readers have objected that "resting" sounds static. I do not mean it that way; neither did John of Damascus or Dumitru Staniloae. Some of the same readers have suggested that "alighting" might avoid the static connotation of "rest." But "alighting," in turn, could imply that the resting is temporary, shortly to be succeeded by flight — and no one would want to say (would they?) that the Spirit flew from the Son. Rather, God rests in pure act, in unimpeded activity. The point here is not, however, to find the best word. The point is to illustrate the practice of proposal and negation in a concrete case, a practice that does not lead so much to the best word as into such interpreters' virtues as humility, temperance, justice, or love.

6. Because the Spirit hovers over the waters at creation and rests on the body of the Son in the incarnation, the Spirit rests on bodies in excess of na-

---

28. *Summa Theologiae* I.12.13 *ad* 1; *In Rom.* 1:19.

ture, or "paraphysically," to coin a word out of Romans 11:24: not just in a way that re-befriends the physical, but also in a way that redeems, transfigures, elevates, and exceeds it.

7. Either the Holy Spirit crosses the last bit of a *distance* between God and the human being, by entering into the heart; or the Holy Spirit *incorporates* the human being into the triune community. The distance-crossing metaphor works well precisely and only as a special case of the incorporation metaphor. Even the distance between God and creation is contained within the trinitarian embrace.

> Christians do not "worship" the Trinity in the sense that they stand, as it were, off from it and gawk reverently from a safe distance. On the contrary, their worship is a kind of participation in the relations among the members of the Trinity. Otherwise, what is to be made of the words of one reasonably representative eucharistic prayer, which has believers ascribe "all honor and glory" to God the Father "through Christ and with Christ and in Christ" and "in the unity of the Holy Spirit"?[29]

8. As "the Lord, the Giver of Life," the Holy Spirit rests on the elect of the Father. For that reason the Spirit witnesses and celebrates this election not only in God but also in the baptism of Jesus and finally in us, electing further witnesses to the good pleasure of the Father in the Son.

9. The Holy Spirit rests on the begotten of the Father. For that reason the Spirit does this not only in God but also in the world, hovering over the face of the waters at creation, overshadowing the waters of the womb of Mary, and putting fire in the waters of baptism.

10. In that the Holy Spirit guarantees (II Cor. 5:5) the promises to Abraham, the Spirit rests on the Israel of the Father as the consummator of Israel and therefore also of the Gentiles.

11. In that the Spirit of faithfulness reunites the Father and the Son, the Spirit rests on the Israel of the Father as the goal of Israel and therefore also of the Gentiles.

12. In that the cloud of the Spirit overshadowed Jesus at the transfiguration, "when we cry 'Abba! Father!' it is the Spirit himself bearing witness with our spirit . . . for we do not know how to pray as we ought, but the Spirit himself intercedes for us with sighs too deep for words" (Rom. 8:15-16, 26), so the Spirit may take human prayer up into the mutual praying and giving that takes place in the trinitarian life.

29. Richard Norris, "Trinity," unpublished ms., quoting the Episcopal Church (USA), *The Book of Common Prayer* (New York: Church Hymnal Corporation and the Seabury Press, 1979), p. 375.

13. In that the Holy Spirit witnesses the love within the Trinity between the Father and the Son, it can take human beings up also into that office in the created world, so that their chief end becomes "to glorify God and enjoy God forever," as the Westminster Catechism has it.

14. The intratrinitarian witness of the Holy Spirit to the love between the Father and the Son enables the victory of love over death in the resurrection.

15. When the Father "gives life to our mortal bodies also through the Spirit that dwells in us" (Rom. 8:11), human beings partake of the Spirit's proper office of celebrating the love of the Father for the Son and become guests at the wedding of the Lamb, for "the kingdom of heaven is like a Father who gave a wedding feast for his son" (Matt. 22:2, Rev. 19:9).

One could generate more theses like these, infinitely more. Part I of this book attempts to answer the question, Why not? Part II attempts to answer the question, How so?

I   You Wonder Where the Spirit Went

1 Is There Nothing the Spirit Can Do That the Son Can't Do Better?

Or, How the Spirit Puzzles a Trinitarian Revival

i. Barth Fumbles

It's become a commonplace of recent scholarship that successive trinitarian revivals have slighted the Holy Spirit. Whether a theologian has anything interesting to say about the Spirit has emerged as a heuristic. The chief puzzle has been Karl Barth. Leader of the twentieth century's most successful trinitarian revival, author of more than one book with "Spirit" in the title, and of some 2100 pages with "Spirit" in bold-face theses,[1] Barth nevertheless pro-

---

1. In books: Karl Barth, *Come Holy Spirit* (Grand Rapids: Eerdmans, 1978) and *The Holy Spirit and Christian Life: The Theological Basis of Ethics*, trans. Birch Hoyle (Louisville: Westminster/John Knox, 1993). In the *Church Dogmatics*: §12, "God the Holy Spirit," I/1, 448-90; Chapter II, Part III, "The Outpouring of the Holy Spirit," §§16-18, I/1, 203-456; §62, "The Holy Spirit and the Gathering of the Christian Community," IV/1, 643-739; §63, "The Holy Spirit and Christian Faith," IV/1, 740-79; §67, "The Holy Spirit and the Upbuilding of the Christian Community," IV/2, 614-726; §68, "The Holy Spirit and Christian Love," IV/2, 727-840; §72, "The Holy Spirit and the Sending of the Christian Community," IV/3/2, 681-901; §73, "The Holy Spirit and Christian Hope," IV/3/2, 903-42. The Holy Spirit is also announced in the *Leitsätze* or thesis statements of §9, "The Triunity of God," I/1, 348-83; §15, "The Mystery of Revelation," I/2, 122-201; §16, "The Freedom of Man for God," I/2, 203-79; §17, "The Revelation of God as the Abolition of Religion," I/2, 280-361; §18, "The Life of the Children of God," I/2, 362-456; §19, "The Word of God for the Church," I/2, 457-537; §25, "The Fulfilment of the Knowledge of God," II/1, 3-62; §26, "The Knowability of God," II/1, 63-178; §28, "The Being of God as the One Who Loves in Freedom," II/1, 257-322; §64, "The Exaltation of the Son of Man," IV/2, 3-377; and §[74], "The Foundation of the Christian Life," IV/4, 2-218. At least two secondary books are devoted to Barth on the Spirit: John Thompson, *The Holy Spirit in the Theology of Karl Barth* (Allison Park, Pa.: Pickwick Publications, 1991); Philip J. Rosato, *The Spirit as Lord: The Pneumatology of Karl Barth* (Edinburgh: T&T Clark, 1981). And yet to read all this is to be persuaded of the basic justice of Jenson's critique (cited in the next note).

vokes some consensus that his doctrine of the Spirit subsides into christology, as if there's nothing the Spirit can do that Christ can't do better.[2] As Robert Jenson writes, "The personal agent of [the community's] work in fact turns out at every step of Barth's argument to be *not* the Spirit, as advertised, but Christ; the Spirit is denoted invariably by impersonal terms," chiefly the "power" of Jesus Christ.[3]

Now, everywhere in Barth the Spirit makes possible any human response to God. The *Dogmatics* begins and ends with highly promising pneumato- logical insights.[4] In I/1 as decades later in IV/4, "it is the Spirit who constitutes revelation as historical, capable of being responded to by individuals in spe- cific contexts."[5] In the middle of the *Dogmatics*, however, Barth eclipses the il- lumination of the Spirit with the material objectivity of the Son. The Son be- comes a "ray of darkness,"[6] the Spirit mere penumbra.[7] In seven *thousand* pages Barth lodges this single protest against Christ-statements without Spirit-statements:

> Both statements denote one and the same reality. But neither renders the other superfluous. Neither can be reduced to the other. Hence neither is dis- pensable. Again, neither can be separated from the other. Neither can be understood except as elucidated by the other.[8]

And yet that is just what happens from I/2 straight through to IV/3. Christ-statements render Spirit-statements superfluous. Spirit-statements are reduced to Christ-statements. Pneumatological statements prove dispensable.

2. Above all and very elegantly, Robert W. Jenson, "You Wonder Where the Spirit Went," *Pro Ecclesia* 2 (1993): 296-304; Rowan Williams, "Word and Spirit," in *On Christian Theology* (Ox- ford: Blackwell, 2000), pp. 107-27, esp. pp. 107, 117-18, 120-21; Rowan Williams, "Barth on the Tri- une God," in Stephen Sykes, ed., *Karl Barth: Studies of His Theological Method* (Oxford: Claren- don, 1979), pp. 147-93; Eugene F. Rogers, Jr., "Supplementing Barth on Jews and Gender: Identifying God by Anagogy and the Spirit," *Modern Theology* 14 (1998): 43-81; Rogers, "The Eclipse of the Spirit in Karl Barth," in *Conversing with Barth*, ed. John McDowell and Michael Higton (Aldershot, Hampshire: Ashgate, 2002), pp. 173-90.

3. Jenson, "You Wonder Where the Spirit Went," p. 303, in reference to *CD* IV/3.

4. In IV/4, as in I/1 §12, 1, the illumination of the Spirit is more than a penumbra bearing witness to the objectivity of Jesus Christ; there it has something "not automatically given with the fact that Jesus is present as the revelation of the Father," something "added to the givenness of the revelation," a "special element" "not identical with Jesus Christ, with the Son or Word of God." *CD* I/1 (1975), pp. 449, 451.

5. Williams, "Barth on the Triune God," p. 118, citing I/1, 330. See also *CD* IV/4, 27.

6. In a phrase that Rowan Williams has used to title a book.

7. There is a mention of the Spirit as the creator of history in III/1.

8. *CD* IV/3/2, 759.

Christ-statements are separated from Spirit-statements for hundreds of pages. Christ-statements are understood as true without elucidation by Spirit-statements. With few exceptions, the middle of the *Dogmatics* does render the Spirit automatically given or identical with Jesus, or percussively reduces her[9] to his "power" or "promise."[10]

Calling the Spirit "the power of Jesus Christ" recalls Gregory Nazianzen's warning, which Barth had certainly read, that one should not "give Essence to the Father and deny Personality to the Others, and make Them only Powers of God."[11] Calling the Spirit the "act of communion" between the Father and the Son[12] recalls Gregory's claim that "act" language reduces the Spirit to an accident of God.[13] Gregory even anticipates a false reserve "out of reverence to Scripture."[14]

A thesis statement of I/1 announces the Spirit as an agent, "the Lord who sets us free." But when Barth comes to deliver on the claim, he does so in christological terms: "*Christ* has 'set us free' for freedom." Now, there's nothing wrong with bringing in the other Persons, whose act toward the world is indi-

---

9. It is well known that the Spirit takes masculine pronouns in Latin, neuter in Greek, and feminine in early Syriac. I follow Jerome's remark that this variety shows that God is beyond gender, in Harvey, below, p. 121, citing Jerome, *In Isa.* XI, on 40:9-11, ed. M. Adriaen and F. Glorie, CCL 73.1 (1963), p. 459. Accordingly, I vary the pronouns for the Spirit, using feminine ones especially when the words "Father" and "Son" put a confusing number of masculine ones in the context. See Sebastian Brock, "The Holy Spirit as Feminine in Early Syriac Literature," in *After Eve*, ed. Janet Martin Soskice (London: Marshall-Pickering, 1990); Susan Ashbrook Harvey, "Feminine Imagery for the Divine: The Holy Spirit, the Odes of Solomon, and Early Syriac Tradition," *St. Vladimir's Seminary Quarterly* 37 (1993): 111-39; and Gabriele Winkler, "Further Observations in Connection with the Early Form of the Epiklesis," in *Studies in Early Christian Liturgy and Its Context*, Variorum Collected Studies Series 593 (Aldershot, U.K.: Ashgate, 1997), pp. IV, 66-80, esp. pp. 69-73, 79-80, on invocations of "the Mother, the Spirit of holiness," p. 69.

10. Rosato argues differently. Counting the sections from III onwards that announce the Spirit, as actually about the Spirit, and noting programmatic statements in favor of pneumatology from 1947 onwards, Rosato charts a pneumatological turn from 1947 or so. It is a reading *in optimam partem*. What remains to be explained is why those treatments are remarkably un-pneumatological for another twenty years.

11. Gregory Nazianzen, *Fifth Theological Oration*, paragraph 32, NPNF translation. Barth's defenders might note that Gregory's warning applies only to the Spirit as a power of the Father. But we read earlier in Gregory, "Give [the Holy Spirit] to the Son, and number Him among the creatures. . . . [The Son] is not the Maker of a Fellow Servant, but he is glorified with One of co-equal honour" (*Fifth Theological Oration*, paragraph 12).

12. *CD* I/1, 470-71.

13. Gregory Nazianzen, *Fifth Theological Oration*, paragraph 6. It might be all right if each of the Persons was the act of the others, but we don't get that.

14. Gregory Nazianzen, *Fifth Theological Oration*, paragraph 5.

visible, and certainly nothing wrong with quoting Galatians. But Barth leaves the reader no reason to think you couldn't unpack the setting free in terms of Christ alone. The exposition abandons the Spirit to the rubrics. Another apparent treatment of the Spirit runs seven hundred pages, of which it shows up on fourteen.[15] One wonders if Spirit-talk appears for variety or ornament.

Barth is aware that the early trinitarians did not have the nineteenth-century German notion of "person" to go by, did not conceive of the trinitarian Persons as Idealist centers of consciousness. He knows that the Latin *persona* comes from *personare,* to sound through, as a dramatic mask. Correctively therefore he writes,

> [E]ven if the Father and the Son might be called "person" . . . the Holy Spirit could not possibly be regarded as the third "person." . . . He is not a third spiritual Subject, a third I, a third Lord side by side with two others. He is a third mode of being of the one divine Subject of [the] Lord.[16]

But this goes too far. The early trinitarians did not need the nineteenth-century notion of person to recognize characters in the biblical story, characters who interact among themselves. Aristotle, for example, could conceive of characters without an Idealist theory of interiority. If Father, Son, and Spirit appear on the New Testament stage, that alone is enough to see that, at least among themselves, they interact, even if toward the world they have a single indivisible action. Gregory's correction belongs here: Not a single sun in three forms, but three suns aligned to give a single light. One can even refer to the metaphor of the dramatic mask without modalism. Aristotle would not have imagined that three masks mark three roles of a single actor in modalist fashion, especially if they appear on stage together. Rather the three masks simply mark — as we see now in von Balthasar — three *dramatis personae,* three characters in the drama.[17] This language need *not* mean that the masks mark some reality hidden behind them, some *deus absconditus* or modalist hiddenness. They merely mean that a certain ancient literary analysis is going on, an obvious result of reading: in the narratives of the New Testament, three characters are one God. So while Barth is correct to reject nineteenth-century centers of consciousness, he is a poor reader of the New Testament if he denies that the Spirit is a character in the story, one who precedes the Son at the

15. For another example, "The Promise of the Spirit," in IV/3, 1 (pp. 274-367) takes twenty pages to mention the Spirit, abandons it for another fifty pages, and finally reaches the title topic on page 351, just for 18 pages out of 93, or less than 20%.

16. *CD* I/1, 469. I owe my renewed attention to this passage to Aaron Riches.

17. *Dramatis Personae* is the title of two part-volumes of *Theo-Drama.*

incarnation, hovers over him at the baptism, drives him into the wilderness, overshadows him at the transfiguration, anoints him at burial, indwells his body at the resurrection, and continues his mission at Pentecost. These acts of the Spirit do not follow automatically, as a power. Often they precede, anticipate, prevene, as grace. And when they follow, they do so with independent or unexpected initiative, as a gift.

Jenson diagnoses the problem like this: "[I]n Barth's theology, Western trinitarianism's common difficulty in conceiving the Spirit's specific immanent initiative in God must become a difficulty in conceiving the Spirit's entire salvation-historical initiative."[18]

An intratrinitarian problem looms: the Spirit has no gift to give the creature, which is not Christ, because the Spirit has no gift to give Christ.

ii. Florensky Shrugs

It is also a familiar theme in all Christian traditions that the Spirit does not always flaunt itself. "An evil and adulterous generation seeks for a sign"; their only sign will be christological (Matt. 12:38-41). Hunger for the Spirit can mask self-aggrandizement; the Spirit speaks in a "still, small voice" (I Kings 19:12); the Spirit initiates Christians into Christ's experiences of abandonment. Some suggest that such apophaticism is as it should be, including John Calvin, the sixteenth-century Reformer; Karl Rahner, the Kantian Catholic; and Pavel Florensky, the early twentieth-century Russian Orthodox polymath from whom both Sophiological and Neopatristic streams flow. We'll head straight for Florensky.

You might suppose that Calvin and Rahner have something in common to account for a retiring Spirit — namely, they are Western. The hiding of the Spirit behind the Son, a reader of Eastern polemics might confess, is a Western problem, a symptom of the *Filioque* and a tendency to subordinate the Spirit to the Son. But you would be wrong. The strongest case for an apophatic theology of the Spirit comes from the East.

Pavel Florensky's *Pillar and Ground of the Truth*[19] (published in Russian in 1914) makes a stronger case than either Calvin or Rahner for the anonymity of the Spirit, because he — the Easterner — makes it explicitly. He makes it from

18. Jenson, "You Wonder Where the Spirit Went," p. 300.

19. Pavel Florensky, "Letter Five: The Comforter" (= chapter 6), in *The Pillar and Ground of the Truth*, trans. Boris Jakim (Princeton: Princeton University Press, 1997), pp. 80-105. Original: *Stolp I utverzhdenie istiny* (Moscow: Put', 1914). Pavel Florensky (1882-1937) is different from the historian Georges Florovsky, whose works have been available in English for a long time.

the Cappadocians, the ascetics, and the liturgy: from the very sources in which Orientalist Western theologians expect to see an unreconstructed Pneumatic golden age. Furthermore, he finds the anonymity of the Spirit not a flaw, but an ascetic virtue.[20]

For Florensky, the Spirit's job is to foster asceticism. Since the work of the Trinity in the world reflects character of God *in se,* he expects the Spirit to practice ascetic discipline precisely in regard to herself.[21] Ascetic practice and the revelation of the Spirit are alike "only a betrothal," "a kiss of the Bride," "given in view of . . . the many torments."[22] The Spirit like the Kingdom appears only fleetingly before the End, even if truth and the ascetic run before it.[23] For Florensky, "Come, Holy Spirit!" and "Thy Kingdom come!" pray the same prayer, even after Pentecost.[24]

Florensky too "finds it strange" that a theologian should "speak of the importance of the . . . Spirit . . . but hardly . . . [give] a clear and precise explanation of anything."[25] He too applies this lack "chiefly to dogmatists, . . . the ones who have to speak decisively and to the heart of the matter." As Barth's critics would complain after him, "It is they who turn out to be almost mute, or clearly confused."[26]

Only this strangeness does not apply to twentieth-century theologians in successive trinitarian revivals (Barth, Rahner, von Balthasar): Florensky comes too soon for any of them. Nor does it specify the nineteenth-century trinitarian revivals of Hegel, Schelling, or Scheeben. Florensky has in his sights the theological tradition *tout court.* He aims his puzzled phrases at "all the holy fathers and mystical philosophers"! He concedes no more than a "false window" for symmetry's sake.[27]

Preceding Barth's critics by some eighty years, he says that even among the ascetics the Spirit becomes "a kind of sanctifying and impersonal *power* of God."[28] The ascetic fathers "began unnoticeably and gradually to speak of 'grace,' . . . something completely impersonal,"[29] another failure of nerve usu-

20. "Knowledge of the Holy Spirit would give . . . perfect deification to all Creation," p. 81.

21. Florensky, *Pillar,* p. 81.

22. Florensky, *Pillar,* p. 81.

23. Florensky, *Pillar,* p. 82.

24. Florensky, *Pillar,* pp. 101-104, with references to an old version of Luke 11:12, in which the Lord's Prayer goes, "Our Father . . . Thy Holy Spirit come down upon us," as well as to Gregory of Nyssa, Irenaeus of Lyon, and Maximus the Confessor.

25. Florensky, *Pillar,* p. 83.

26. Florensky, *Pillar,* p. 83.

27. Florensky, *Pillar,* p. 84.

28. Florensky, *Pillar,* p. 90.

29. Florensky, *Pillar,* p. 90.

ally noted elsewhere.[30] Words like "spiritual" and "spirit-bearing" abound, because "what is usually known is not the Holy Spirit but His grace-giving energies, His powers, His acts and activities"[31] on human beings. The more this happens, Florensky dryly observes, the harder it becomes to distinguish the Holy Spirit from the human spirit.[32] He sums up: "If, by their indecisiveness or silence, the dogmatist fathers show their inner uncertainty concerning . . . the Holy Spirit . . . the ascetic fathers by their copious words reveal the same state of consciousness even more clearly."[33]

The real test for Florensky is the liturgy, "the most reliable witness."[34] He turns to "the point where the very celebration [sought to glorify] all three Hypostases"[35] at Pentecost.[36] The tone keeps up gentle bemusement as he narrows his eyes at the three kneeling prayers.

The first prayer addresses God the Father: "We pray to You and we beseech you, Lord who loves the human being, *Father* of our Lord and God and Savior Jesus Christ."[37]

---

30. Robert W. Jenson, *Systematic Theology* I (New York: Oxford, 1997), p. 149.

31. Florensky, *Pillar,* p. 90.

32. Is that a problem? Florensky puts it this way: one might also say that our sonship comes from the Son — and yet no one entertains as much uncertainty as to "whether a particular passage is talking about the Son or a son." "In essence, the holy fathers speak much not about the Holy Spirit but about a holy spirit." If features of a personal perception of the Holy Spirit do emerge from the ascetic fathers, they are "preliminary and incomplete." *Pillar,* p. 90.

33. Florensky, *Pillar,* p. 90.

34. Florensky, *Pillar,* p. 87.

35. Florensky, *Pillar,* p. 87, sentence and paragraph boundary elided.

36. See now Miguel Arranz, "Les prières de la Gonyklisia ou de la Génuflexion du jour de la Pentecôte dans l'ancien Euchologe byzantin," *Orientalia Christiana Periodica* 48 (1982): 92-123. I am grateful to Paul Meyendorff for this reference.

37. Florensky, *Pillar,* p. 87. This is Boris Jakim's translation of Florensky's quotations. Florensky quotes *Bol'shoi Trebnik Dopolnitel'nyi,* ch. 78: The office of the Holy Pentecost, ed. of the Kiev-Pech. Labra, 1875. The service is perhaps most easily available in a slightly different English translation in Hapgood: *Service Book of the Holy Orthodox-Catholic Apostolic Church, Compiled, Translated, and Arranged from the Old Church-Slavonic Service Books of the Russian Church, and Collated with the Service Books of the Greek Church,* 6th rev. ed., trans. by Isabel Florence Hapgood (Englewood, N.J.: Antiochian Orthodox Christian Archdiocese, 1983), "Pentecost (Whitsunday)," pp. 245-57; here, pp. 249-50. I follow Jakim's version of Florensky's quotations, since it is best calculated to make Florensky's points.

The authoritative source for the underlying Greek is still Jacques Goar, *Euchologion, sive Rituale Graecorum complectens ritus et ordines divinae liturgiae, officiorum, sacramentorum . . . ,* 2d ed. (Venice: Typographia Bartholomaei Javarina, 1730; reprint ed. Graz: Akademische Druck-u. Verlagsanstalt, 1960), with Greek and Latin in parallel columns.

For an edition taking account of the Old Church Slavonic, cf. Michael Rajewsky, *Euchologion der orthodox-katholischen Kirche aus dem griechischen Original-Text mit durch-*

The second prayer belongs just as explicitly to the Son: "Lord *Jesus Christ* our God, who gave your peace to human beings and the gift of the Most Holy Spirit when you were still with us in life."[38]

The third prayer, "which occupies in the office a place that precisely corresponds to that of the two previous prayers, . . . their liturgical analogue, opens with the address: 'Eternally *flowing, living, and illuminating Source,* consubstantial with the Father, *enabling* Power, You Who wonderfully *accomplished* the economy of human salvation.'"[39]

Here Florensky's analysis deserves quotation at length.

According to the meaning of the feast itself (the Day of the "Trinity"), according to the liturgical place of this third prayer, and finally, according to the epithets it uses for the Person to Whom it is addressed, it is natural to expect the following continuation: "O Holy Spirit" or "Comforter" or "King of Truth" or some other name of the Third Hypostasis of the Holy Trinity. This expectation is so natural that, in listening to this prayer, one inevitably hears something like this and remains convinced that it is addressed to the Holy Spirit. But this is not in fact the case. Here is the immediate continuation of the prayer which we interrupted: "*O Christ our God;* You Who have broken the indestructible chains of death and the unbreakable bonds of hell. . . ."[40]

It is so shocking that one wishes for a historian to examine the transmission history.[41]

---

gängiger Berücksichtigung der altslavischen Übersetzung ins Deutsche übertragen (Vienna: L. C. Zamarski & C. Dittmarsch, 1861), Part 3, pp. 29-37.

38. Florensky, *Pillar,* p. 87, translation modified; cf. Hapgood, pp. 252-53.

39. Florensky, *Pillar,* p. 87; cf. Hapgood, pp. 254-55.

40. Florensky, *Pillar,* pp. 87-88; cf. Hapgood, pp. 254-55. The translation in Hapgood makes the surprise not quite so dramatic, as the "O Christ our God" comes a little earlier in the prayer. Cf. also Rajewsky, p. 37.

41. The ordinary eucharistic rite has of course been exhaustively studied, and scholars characteristically find in it a trinitarian shape lacking in the West. So Taft, speaking of the precommunion rites: "The Byzantine liturgy takes the shape it has in form and formula, text and symbol, because of its radically trinitarian shape and theology, a shape and theology quite different from the radically Christological emphasis of the ancient Roman *Canon Missae,* largely unaffected by the trinitarian controversies that embroiled the Christian East from the late fourth century on. This trinitarian eucharistic theology of the Byzantine rite, and its symbolic expression in details like the *zeon* [the dropping of water into the chalice to symbolize the descent of the Spirit], are nevertheless integral to a total *Symbolgestalt,* and there is no way that any of its elements can be understood or judged in isolation, apart from this integrated eucharistic pneumatology as expressed by the Liturgy of St. John Chrysostom in the anaphora and in the

Since Florensky, liturgiologist Miguel Arranz has argued that the third prayer was "unknown by the most ancient Greek euchologia."[42] The Great Church at Constantinople may have adopted it at the beginning of the eleventh century, amalgamating a variety of forms.

Although Arranz describes the third prayer as "also" addressed to Jesus Christ, he does not otherwise suggest what seems obvious to Florensky, that the third prayer somehow ought to be addressed to the Spirit instead, leaving Florensky's concerns no direct answer. And yet for one who has read him they do not go away; but recur in different forms. Is not the trinitarianism of this community sufficient to discipline sequences with tendencies as aggressively binitarian as that? What can the amalgamators have been thinking? Did the prayers really survive from the eleventh century to the twentieth without comment or reform? Even if, on account of the indivisibility of the acts of the Trinity *ad extra*, it is not actually wrong to appropriate power, illumination, and management of the economy to the Son, how can this be liturgically fitting?

Here too Florensky sounds more bemused than alarmed: "ridiculous to see in this incompleteness . . . a defect attributable to some deficiency of profundity."[43]

If anything is predictable about Florensky's argument, it's that the East has something right that the West has overlooked. But reversing the usual claim of Orthodox polemic — in which preoccupations with nature and grace, and subordination of Spirit to Son, have led Western Christians to know too little of the Spirit — Florensky worries that Western Christians have sought to know too much.

The apophaticisms of Calvin, Rahner, and Florensky raise a question for scholars like me who wonder where the Spirit went. Do they seek to know too much? What if the tendency of Barth, to announce the Spirit and expound the Son, is the tendency of the Christian community (almost) always and everywhere? What if even the Eastern liturgy of Pentecost, in the third of three prayers, announces the Spirit and addresses the Son? What if the missions of the Spirit and the Son are such that this is just as it should be?

---

prayers immediately before and after it." Robert F. Taft, *A History of the Liturgy of St. John Chrysostom, Vol. V The Precommunion Rites*, Orientalia Christiana Analecta 261 (Rome: Pontificio Istituto Orientale, 2000), pp. 495-96. See also Juan Metéos, "L'action du Saint-Esprit dans la liturgie dite de s. Jean Chrysostome," *Proche-Orient Chrétien: Revue d'études et d'informations* 9 (1959): 193-208.

42. Arranz, "Les prières," p. 102. On the basis of the earliest manuscripts he also argues that the first prayer may have Semitic roots, perhaps in Jerusalem, and that for the second prayer "we would have less trouble in recognizing a Basilian paternity."

43. Florensky, *Pillar*, p. 91.

Does the Father send the Son and the Spirit into the world always together, in a pair? Then *can* we see theological practices as different as that of Athanasius in the *Letters to Serapion* (naming Son and Spirit always together), Barth (announcing one and speaking of the other), and Bulgakov (making the yoking, or *dvoica,* itself the subject of reflective exposition)[44] as variations upon a theme, instead of rivalrous alternatives?[45]

Or are all three authors really objecting to something that late twentieth- and early twenty-first-century theologians hardly exhibit at all, and even tend to ignore: enthusiastic movements? After all, Calvin like Luther was afraid of the *Schwärmer;* Rahner dismisses charismatic movements as "elitist" in favor of the "everyday"; Florensky castigates the "new consciousness," which sought fresh revelations and social utopia.[46]

Perhaps this is the place to say how Christian practices of apophaticism, or Christian reflections about the human mode of language about God, qualify a book like this one. By the inseparability of divine operations toward the world, the mystery of the Spirit cannot leave out the Father and the Son. The mystery of the Spirit is also the mystery of the Father and the Son. The practice of apophaticism that leads Christians into the mystery of God is appropriated by Florensky to the Spirit because the Bible and the liturgy locate it there. Resistance to the anonymity he appropriates to the Spirit can be resistance to the practices of apophaticism that purify the mind for the triune God. Conversely, appreciation of the anonymity of the Spirit can foster the practices of apophaticism that lead into the triune God. The Spirit is among other things one of the scripturally appropriate sites for practices of reticence and silence before God. The reserve of the Spirit is the reserve of the triune God, somewhat as the incarnation of the Son is the incarnation of God, or creation by the Father includes the Spirit and the Son.

Both the refusal to separate God's operations *ad extra* and the appropriation of operations to a particular person are practices of contemplation and scriptural interpretation. In Part II of the book, I will often be following an

44. E.g., Serge Boulgakov, *Le Paraclet,* trans. Constantin Andronikof (Paris: Aubier, 1944) and Sergius Bulgakov, *The Bride of the Lamb,* trans. Boris Jakim (Grand Rapids: Eerdmans and Edinburgh: T&T Clark, 2002), e.g., pp. 97-98. See also, compendiously, Charles Graves, *The Holy Spirit in the Theology of Sergius Bulgakov* (Geneva: Word Council of Churches, 1972).

45. Again, is the Spirit — with the Creed — a "hypostasis," only we don't know what that is? Can "hypostasis" work so analogously, and so trinitarianly, that it comes out differently for each of the "Persons"? Is a hypostasis, perhaps, a "Person" whom we can recognize as such in the case of Jesus Christ, but more barely a narrative character in the case of the Father, and above all, a hypostasis in some third, more apophatic way in the case of the Spirit?

46. Florensky, *Pillar,* p. 91, translator's note *b.*

interpretive practice of inseparability: looking to see how the Spirit is not left out of the life of Jesus. But here in Part I, I will often be following a contemplative practice of appropriation: looking to see, for example, how the unnameability appropriately applied to the Spirit can recall the unnameability of God. In the next chapter, I look to see how the superfluity appropriately located under the Spirit reflects the superfluity of the triune God. To put it provocatively, if the Spirit is dispensable to the world, so is the triune God. And if the Spirit is gratuitous to the world, so is the triune God.[47]

iii. How Barth's love for Athanasius can cast out his fear of Schleiermacher

Both sides in the debate about Barth's pneumatology have neglected a salient fact: Barth does this kind of thing elsewhere, too, announcing one topic and pursuing another. He does it deliberately and with a certain mischievous delight. Take another famous case. In Christian doctrines of election, readers expect to hear about the predestination of the individual. But Barth finds the question "Am I predestined?" or worse "Is she?" a terrifically bad one. By turns narcissistic and voyeuristic, the question distracts anyone entertaining it from Christ. It's a when-did-you-stop-beating-your-wife question. The defense attorney can object; the judge sustain; the court reporter strike the question; but once voiced it infects the jury, and the defense attorney must *distract* the jury, in order effectively and successfully to unask it. In the doctrine of election, Barth first distracts the reader from "What about me?" with a hundred pages on God, as the one who elects first of all God's own self for the human being. Barth then treats the reader to a second hundred pages on "Jesus Christ the rejected One elected." Now that he has recast election as a doctrine about God's self-determination and Christ's atonement, one expects finally to reach the individual. But no, now we get a third hundred pages on the election of Israel and the Church, which for all its supersessionism at least teaches Christians that they are goyim. By this time the jury has pretty well forgotten the "have you stopped beating your wife" question, and at last we meet "the Individual." But no. Under that title we get again nothing about present-day individuals, but rather biblical typology: Cain and Abel, Saul and David, Judas and Paul, the scapegoat and the offered goat, the bird slain and the bird flown. The reader who perseveres has not only forgotten the original question, but completed Barth's *therapy* against it. She has been not just ad-

---

47. These paragraphs occurred to me on reading Lewis Ayres's *Nicea*.

vised — as Augustine, Luther, and Calvin all suggest — to seek the mirror of election not in herself but in Christ: she has been *caused* to do so.[48]

It is not too hard to see that something similar is going on with the Holy Spirit. Here too Barth wants to unask what he thinks is a terrifically bad question. No matter that Schleiermacher is resolutely christocentric in explicit statements; Barth diagnoses them as covertly anthropocentric, and that for a pneumatological reason: the Spirit of the Lord has gotten identified with the spirit of the human.

Barth himself makes the Holy Spirit indeed the root in God of the human response, which exists as God's taking the human being up into the trinitarian dance and thus, though Barth doesn't say so, as the beginning of theosis. For Barth, only God can properly respond to God; only God the Spirit can appropriately celebrate the love between the Father and the Son. *If* the human being should do so *too*, it is already a participation in the Spirit's proper work.[49]

But even the Spirit-borne human response is also, after Schleiermacher, susceptible of reversal, so that the Spirit becomes a human projection and Feuerbach wins. Better, in that case, deliberately and forcibly and therapeutically to turn every question about the Spirit into one about Christ, because the doctrine of Christ has an objective density that better (Barth thinks) resists attempts of nineteenth-century human beings to assume that theology is about themselves.[50] But if the flight from Schleiermacher also leads away from the Trinity, then by Barth's own principles it's out of the frying pan and into the fire.

Just as Barth names Athanasius as his only predecessor in his doctrine of election, so too Barth names Athanasius as again the one "who spoke the decisive word" on the Spirit.[51] In Athanasius we find a more musical execution of Barth's *intention,* to articulate "the deity and autonomy" of the Spirit, *simultaneous with* a defense of Barth's *practice,* never to speak of the Spirit

---

48. *CD* II/2, 3-506.

49. *CD* IV/4, 76.

50. Thus Rosato finds it not a flaw that the *Church Dogmatics* does not so much describe the Spirit as display its work. See note 3.

51. For more on Barth and Athanasius, see Willie Jennings, "Reclaiming the Creature: Anthropological Vision in the Thought of Athanasius of Alexandria and Karl Barth," Ph.D. dissertation, Duke University, 1993. The turn to Athanasius seems the more important when we consider Rowan Williams's claim that Barth's importance in twentieth-century theology comes because Barth plays Athanasius to the Deutsche Christen's Arius ("Postscript: Theological" to *Arius: Heresy and Tradition,* rev. ed. [Grand Rapids: Eerdmans, 2002]). Note too that in accusing Calvin, in his doctrine of election, of substituting a metaphysical principle for Jesus Christ as "the beginning of all God's ways and works," Barth recalls Calvin to the debate between Athanasius and Arius over the interpretation of that psalm, and places him — although Barth is uncharacteristically too polite to say so — on the Arian side.

apart from the Son.[52] In Athanasius we may see what Barth was trying to do. In this formula Father, Word, and Spirit all do one work by exercising in the world an intratrinitarian pattern:

> For what the Word has by nature . . . in the Father, . . . He wishes to *be given* to us through the Spirit.[53]

Note the passive voice. The Son does not give, but the Son wishes the Father to give through the Spirit. Even *God's* self-giving involves a dance of courtesy, bidding, and gratitude. God's self-giving characteristically incorporates human beings into that dance or pattern. In another passage Athanasius presents his argument as a prayer by the Son to the Father about the Spirit. He displays the pattern as an intratrinitarian conversation overheard in the Gospel of John.

> As Thou hast given to Me to bear this body, grant to them Thy Spirit.[54]

Or in a mariological version, from Jacob of Serugh:

> Mary gave a body for the Word to become incarnate,
> while Baptism gives the Spirit for human beings to be renewed.[55]

That makes Father, Son, and Spirit all ineliminable. The Son bears a human body, that human bodies may bear the Spirit. The formula makes trinitarian the better-known version, "the Word became human that human beings might become divine."[56] Here it is the body that "humanifies" the Word, while the Spirit deifies the human through the body.[57]

---

52. "It was again Athanasius who saw the connexions and spoke the decisive word in this regard." *CD* I/1, 467.

53. Athanasius, *Discourses Against the Arians* III, 25, 25. Cf. also Athanasius, *Ad Serapion*, translated with an Introduction and Notes by C. R. B. Shapland as *The Letters of Saint Athanasius Concerning the Holy Spirit* (New York: Philosophical Library, 1951).

54. *Contra Arianos* III, 25, 23.

55. Sebastian Brock, *The Holy Spirit in the Syrian Baptismal Tradition*, 2d rev. and enlarged ed. (Poona, India: Anita Printers, 1998), p. 196, citing Jacob of Serugh, *Homiliae selectae Mar-Jacobi Sarugensis*, ed. Paul Bedjan, 5 vols. (Paris and Leipzig: Otto Harrassowitz, 1908-10), vol. I, p. 204.

56. Athanasius, *On the Incarnation of the Word*, ch. 54. For similar Western formulations see Augustine, sermon 128, "In natali Domini," no. 12, *Patrologia Latina* 39:1997, and Aquinas, *Summa Theologiae*, Part III, question 1, article 2, corpus.

57. Christ enacts the work with the bearing of the body, and the Spirit appropriately completes or perfects it when the body bears the Spirit. Or: the Spirit rests on one who has taken on the identity of the Son. The passage also seems to exemplify the rule of Gregory Nazianzen, that

Nor does the human bearing of the Spirit follow automatically or mechanically from the Son's bearing of a body. (To call the Spirit "the power of Christ" is to deploy a mechanical metaphor.) Rather, another intratrinitarian initiative intervenes. The Son *bids* the Father to *grant* human beings the Spirit, as the Son had bid the Father to grant him a body. The body is a gift to the Son; the Spirit is a gift to the body; but each gift is free, not mandated, following in a pattern that reveals character rather than automation. As Basil of Caesarea puts it, "The Holy Spirit is also present *of his own will,* dispensing gifts."[58] The gratuity of a gift in a non-Maussian exchange depends upon an *interval* or a variation rather than a mechanism;[59] it is more nearly musical than mechanical. Athanasius displays a moment or interval of gratitude by the Son for the gift of a human body; an interval of pleasure by the Father at the Son's stewardship of the gift; an interval of prayer by the Son that the Father give the gift of the Spirit even unto others in characteristic or musical response.

Barth lacks the Son's *bidding* of the Father and the Father's non-essential, even superfluous *giving* of the Spirit. If the Spirit is the power of the Son with scarcely any audible remainder, or the essence of the Father-Son relation, then more than one interval *has closed up;* we have one note.

Just if the autonomy of the Spirit is an interval or variation that comes not automatically but musically, then Barth is right to associate the this-worldly activity of the Spirit with history. The interval between the Son and the Spirit in the Trinity is the condition for the possibility of history, of freedom rather than mechanism, in the world. If Barth leaves little or no room for the Spirit to consent with gladness rather than arrive in due course, it becomes harder for him to articulate *human* gladness and diversity over periods of history, stretches of geography, and varieties of experience.

---

the Son is the enactor *(demiourgos)* of the work, and the Spirit the prefecter or perhaps applier of it *(teleopoios),* Gregory Nazianzen, *Oration* 34.8.

56. Basil of Caesarea, *On the Holy Spirit* 16:27, trans. David Anderson (Crestwood, N.Y.: St. Vladimir's Seminary Press, 1980), p. 61.

57. John Milbank, "Can a Gift Be Given? Prolegomenon to a Future Trinitarian Metaphysic," *Modern Theology* 11 (1995): 119-41.

2 Is the Spirit Superfluous?

Or, How the Spirit Does Economics

i. The Plowman suspects the surplus

The upshot of two centuries of trinitarian revivals seems to be this: Anything the Spirit can do, the Son can do better. If the Spirit sanctifies, that is more specifically expressed as following the Son. If the Spirit empowers the subjective human response, that is more concretely expressed as the power of the Son. If the Spirit consummates life together with God, that is more biblically expressed as the wedding of the Lamb. If the Spirit gathers the community, that community is of course better named as the body of Christ. If the Spirit distributes various gifts, then they are better coordinated as gifts that make members of the body of Christ. Anything the Spirit can do, the Son can do: that much is orthodox doctrine; the works of the Trinity toward the outside are indivisible. Anything the Spirit can do, the Son can do *better:* that is the repeated nineteenth- and twentieth-century specification. It is then only a short step to say, The Spirit is, strictly speaking, superfluous. It comforts Christians while Christ is absent; but Christ is not really absent.

That view, expressed or repressed, might be a nineteenth- and twentieth-century aberration. But if Florensky is right, it has deeper roots. If Florensky is right, there must even be something *right,* something theologically correct, about the Spirit's superfluity. We must at least pose the question, What if the Holy Spirit really is superfluous? What if it really is not necessary? What would it be like for Christianity to get along without it? Not without the presence of the Holy Spirit, but without talking about the Holy Spirit?

For purposes of argument, let's say the Holy Spirit *is* superfluous. I propose that there are two kinds of superfluity. One kind is crossing a distance.

The other is gratuitous incorporation.[1] If the Holy Spirit is the last bit of God that finishes crossing a distance, then we can get along without it. There is no further distance that Christ cannot cross. If the Holy Spirit is the gratuity of the divine life, however, then human beings cannot be left out of it, if God is to complete God's purpose.

According to the first model, the Son crosses the infinite distance between God and the world, and the Spirit crosses another distance, which seems quite small by comparison, between exterior history and the interior heart of the individual human being. The second distance, into the human heart, *might* be considered just as great as the first (although usually it is not). It is, after all, the transformation from distance into immanence — a qualitative, perhaps infinitely different change. If, however, Christians leave Christ in charge of distance, and the Spirit in charge of entrance, it looks as if there is something Christ can't do, but which plenty of Christian discourse regards him as doing. Christians are always claiming to have Christ in their hearts: he is portrayed as knocking at the door. In practice, the modalist assignment to the Spirit of crossing that last distance doesn't hold up; it gets assigned to Christ or to the human being who "lets Christ into her heart" with little or no reference to the Spirit. Here too Ockham's razor shaves the Spirit out, even among Christians who have never heard of Ockham. Among theologians, who think about these things, an even greater danger threatens — sometimes acknowledged, sometimes not — than getting along without the Spirit. This greater danger is that of regarding the Spirit with suspicion. So among those who regard Schleiermacher's attention to the Spirit's immanent work as opening the door to anthropocentrism, the Spirit attracts suspicion as a covertly anthropocentric principle. It is dangerous, because it leads straight to Feuerbach, to the claim that God is a self-alienation or projection of human needs and desires and nothing else.[2] Put another way, the Spirit attracts suspicion as an all-too-subjective rival to the objectivity of the Son. Barth both overturns and succumbs to that suspicion. Sometimes he casts the human re-

---

1. Versions of this distinction appear in Rowan Williams, "Word and Spirit," in *On Christian Theology* (Oxford: Blackwell, 2000), pp. 107-27; Sarah Coakley, "Why Three? Some Further Reflections on the Origins of the Doctrine of the Trinity," in Sarah Coakley and David A. Pailin, eds., *The Making and Remaking of Christian Doctrine: Essays in Honour of Maurice Wiles* (Oxford: Oxford University Press, 1993), pp. 29-56; Thomas G. Weinandy, *The Father's Spirit of Sonship: Reconceiving the Trinity* (Edinburgh: T&T Clark, 1995); for application to different Calvinists, see Eugene F. Rogers, Jr., "The Mystery of the Spirit in Three Traditions: Calvin, Rahner, Florensky: Or, You *Keep* Wondering Where the Spirit Went," *Modern Theology* 19 (2003): 243-60.

2. Ludwig Feuerbach, *The Essence of Christianity,* trans. George Eliot, with an introductory essay by Karl Barth and a foreword by Richard Niebuhr (New York: Harper and Row, 1957).

sponse to God as borne by the Spirit incorporating the human being into the intratrinitarian response of God to God — a move that works because it escapes from the distance-crossing model into the incorporative one. And sometimes he promotes the objectivity of the Son at the Spirit's expense. Insofar as theologians succumb to casting Son and Spirit as rivals, the Spirit can look superfluous as danger or as dross, the excess as excrement. In that case, the superfluity of the Spirit is the excess of waste, something of which, with averted eyes, theologians must rid themselves.

Precisely if we favor the second model, the model of divine gratuity, then a second danger threatens. If the Father gives to the Son, and the Spirit is *what* the Father gives, then the Spirit is a different kind of thing from the others, a different kind of hypostasis.[3] That might not be a problem, unless a further reduction threatens. The gift may become a kind of thing, say, grace as a quality. If you have been reading Charles Peirce, as Florensky has,[4] then you might even think this view isn't a threat. It would merely acknowledge the distinctiveness of the third hypostasis. The gift-giving relation is not complete without a third. Even languages have a subjective, an objective, and a dative case. No matter if the Spirit is not a Person like the others: it is a hypostasis, just not "like the others." Indeed, none of the three is like the others among themselves; that's just the point: it is one way theologians distinguish them. The critic could respond: The gift-giving relation is reciprocal between subject and object; but the thing given is different again from the giving-and-receiving dyad: it resembles a thing.

So here's the dilemma. Either the Spirit is a distance-crosser, and strictly dispensable. Or the Spirit is strictly *necessary* to a gift-giving relation, and not personal in the way that the others are. Either superfluous, or reified. No wonder there's a problem.

"Spirit rests on and illuminates the Son" names or better narrates an inner-trinitarian movement that can accommodate or explain all those in-

3. For surveys of this issue, see Ralph del Colle, "The Holy Spirit: Power, Presence, Person," *Theological Studies* 62 (2001): 322-41; André de Halleux, "'Hypostase' et 'Personne' dans la formation du dogme trinitaire," *Revue d'histoire ecclésiastique* 79 (1984): 313-69, and "Personnalisme ou essentialisme trinitaire chez les Pères cappadociens? Une mauvaise controverse" (in two parts), *Revue théologique de Louvain* 17 (1986): 129-55 and 265-92.

4. See Pavel Florensky, *The Pillar and Ground of the Truth,* trans. Boris Jakim (Princeton, N.J.: Princeton University Press, 1997), n. 77, p. 454. For Peirce, properly understood, the third is revealed as a person eschatologically, because thirdness must be realized in behavior, and eschatology involves truth's embodiment. This approaches Florensky's emphasis on eschatology and ascesis. For a modern study of Peirce in a theological context, see Peter Ochs, *Peirce, Pragmatism and the Logic of Scripture* (New York: Cambridge University Press, 1998).

sights. It can explain why the distance-crossers put the Spirit last. It can explain why the Son gets talked about rather than the Spirit. It can accommodate the Peircean/Florenskyan emphasis on matter. It can accommodate Coakley's insight that the *eros* between the Father and the Spirit yields something Christoform.[5] It can explain why Bulgakov wants to yoke Son and Spirit together in a *dvoica.*

You do not need to wait for Derrida to get an analysis of supplementarity as ambivalent between good and bad, or for Milbankian talk about "The Gift." The Christian theological tradition has indigenous discourses — more than one — for thinking about the two superfluities that I have identified as ideal types, one a difficulty and one a gratuity. The two superfluities both appear in fourteenth-century economics, although, like their twentieth- and twenty-first-century cousins, they tend to belong to different discourses and come into conversation with each other hardly at all.

One fourteenth-century discourse about superfluity concerned money. This discourse entertained a number of suspicions, and suspected a number of sins. Fourteenth-century Christian Europe saw anxiety over the rise of mercantile classes, a fomenting of peasant revolts, and the emergence of mendicant orders.[6] In all these cases, thinkers sometimes understood the problem as a form of evil excess. In *Piers Plowman,* "Dame Studie . . . adumbrates an economics that takes surplus as its motivating problem."[7] In the graphic arts, "[m]oney is represented as something to be expelled, as excrement . . . [although n]o one can be rid of it. . . . Apes defecating coins mingle with hybrid beings handling money, in graphic demonstration of the principle that objects situated in the margins have themselves exceeded their natural limits."[8] On the surface, Piers Plowman contrasted "winning" as productive work (such as farming, which wins food from the earth) and "wasting" as the pointless expenditure of suspicious surpluses, or "spill."[9] In this economy fourteenth-century Franciscans constructed an entire Christian economics

5. Sarah Coakley, "Living into the Mystery of the Holy Trinity: Trinity, Prayer, and Sexuality," *Anglican Theological Review* 80 (1998): 223-32.

6. For this paragraph, see D. Vance Smith, "Merchants in the Margin: Gift, Exchange, and the Writing of Grace in Piers Plowman," Chapter 4 in his *Arts of Possession* (2003), pp. 108-54. For editions of Piers Plowman, see A. V. C. Schmidt, ed., *The Vision of Piers Plowman: A Complete Edition of the B-Text* (London: Dent, 1978); Walter W. Skeat, *Langland's Vision of Piers Plowman: The Vernon Text; or Text A.* EETS, 28 (London, 1867); and *The Vision of William concerning Piers the Plowman* (Oxford: Oxford University Press, 1886).

7. Smith, "Merchants," p. 111.

8. Smith, "Merchants," p. 133.

9. Smith, "Merchants," pp. 113, 144.

around a distinction of need and surplus, according to which superfluous material goods constituted spiritual danger, not just wastage. On account of this danger, one had a moral *obligation* to give, an *obbligato di dare*,[10] in order to rid oneself of the dangerous excess, charity rendered compulsory.[11] "[T]he principle of natural sufficiency is troubled not by the possibility that there might not be enough available for everyone, but that there might be too much. For this reason the crucial term in Holy Church's sermon is 'measure,' the regulation of an originary surplus — 'though much were' — that is exemplified as Lot's abuse of drink."[12] Critics of the Spirit have also often compared its excesses to those of drink.

In this fourteenth-century thinking, the superfluous element (money beyond need) incites human self-aggrandizement, and leads to sin, undermining the whole economy of daily life. In some twentieth-century thinking, the superfluous element (pneumatology beyond christology) incites human self-assertion, and leads to Feuerbach, undermining the whole *oikonomia* of redemption. In both cases, a bad superfluity undermines salvation itself. In both cases, superfluity is constructed as an evil that human beings must be saved *from*.

The fourteenth century nursed another suspicion of money that resembles the Spirit. It tended to disappear in being used. In 1344, Edward III introduced a new gold coin called a noble.[13] It bore the legend, "IHC transiens per medium illorum ibat" (Luke 4:20): "But passing through the midst of them [Jesus] went away." The quotation points to the Aristotelian theory, taken up by Aquinas, that the "proper and principal use of money is its consumption or alienation in exchange."[14] Money, according to this theory, "merely marks a passage."[15] Although the legend on the coin names Jesus, it will not escape notice that this is Jesus at his most Spirit-like: quiet, mobile, and prone to disappear. The spirits, like the uses of money, are hard to discern, and subject to abuse. Feuerbach like Aquinas makes alienation the hallmark of a suspect surplus: if for Aquinas it is money, in Feuerbach's case it is Schleiermacher's all-too-spiritual divinity as the self-alienation of humanity.

Still another worry was that money works invidiously.[16] Goods that ought

10. Smith, "Merchants," p. 111.

11. Kelly S. Johnson, *The Fear of Beggars* (Notre Dame, Ind.: University of Notre Dame Press, 2005) interprets begging as one of the last forms of theological resistance against capitalism.

12. Smith, "Merchants," p. 121, spelling regularized.

13. This paragraph follows Smith, "Merchants," p. 123.

14. Smith, "Merchants," p. 123, quoting Thomas Aquinas, *ST* II-II.78.1.

15. Smith, "Merchants," p. 123.

16. Smith, "Merchants," p. 112.

to foster love bring envy; what ought to foster community brings division: so too with charismatic gifts. Worse, mercantile money was no respecter of status; merchants, like enthusiasts might undermine class structure.[17] Here as elsewhere a discourse of excess becomes one of contrariety.

Suspicion of those who now trade in the Spirit resembles the suspicion aroused by those who then traded in money. Trading, according to Thomas Aquinas, "is open to many vices, since 'a merchant is hardly free from sins of the lips.'"[18] According to Pseudo-Chrysostom, negotiations require "one to speak badly of the other," so that "he who buys and sells cannot be without lying or perjury."[19] "Again and again merchants are represented as liars, as abusers of language, and as detractors of the Word itself."[20] Money, like the Spirit, is ambivalent in itself; lying, like Spirit-enthusiasm, represents subjectivity run riot. In both cases the danger is that an egocentric subjectivity should undermine objective value, whether in the mercantile or the christological economy. Detractor of the Word: that is just Barth's complaint against the mystical side of Brunner in his famous answer *"Nein!"*

Suspicions of superfluity were then multiple. Material superfluity was a temptation to excess, like drink; it led to other sins, like lying; it had its own characteristic sin, usury; it caused anxiety because it disappeared; it undermined social stability by exposing status to question; and its enjoyment seemed invidious all the way down. So too suspicions of the Spirit: it tempts to excess and inebriates; it leads to other sins that detract from the Word; it has its own characteristic sin, mysticism or enthusiasm; it tends to disappear, so that it is hard to discern; it undermines social stability by exposing status to question; and its enjoyment seems invidious to authorities and enthusiasts alike. It is easy to see, then, why superfluity might be a bad thing, and why theologians might flee from the anxieties of superfluity to the exigencies of objective value, whether in material goods, or in material christology. William Jennings Bryan's famous "Cross of Gold" speech is about monetary economy, not theological *oikonomia,* but the connection is closer than he knew: christology is theology's gold standard.

One could take this conceit too far. The Spirit is not *only* like money. As I said at the beginning of this chapter, Christianity knows more discourses of superfluity than one. Boethius, for example, saw a way to redeem or transfigure money. "Money is something that only provides enjoyment when it no

17. Smith, "Merchants," p. 140.

18. Smith, "Merchants," p. 147; Thomas cites Ecclesiasticus 26:28.

19. Smith, "Merchants," p. 148, citing Gratian, *Decretum* 1, dist. 88, c. 11, in *Corpus iuris cononici,* vol. 1, ed. Aemilius Friedberg (Graz: Akademische Druck- und Verlagsanstalt, 1955).

20. Smith, "Merchants," p. 147.

longer functions as a measure of wealth or reciprocity, but becomes instead a gift: 'money is more precious when it is generously got rid of.'"[21] The adverb makes all the difference.

Fourteenth-century Christian Europe also continued another and more familiar discourse about superfluity, the tractate on grace. From Paul to Augustine through the fourteenth century and into the present, the counterattack has been the gratuity of grace, the superfluity of riches by which God overturns calculations of human desert. God does not need human beings or their justice, but God grants what God demands; they are God's own gifts that God crowns. God transports, transfers, or transfigures the human being from an economy of scarcity to an economy of abundance — the peaceable kingdom, the new Jerusalem, the heavenly feast. In this fourteenth-century thinking, a second superfluous element (the gratuitous grace of God) elevates human nature, and leads to glory, uplifting the whole economy of daily life. In some twentieth-century thinking, the gratuitous element (pneumatology in excess of christology) excites human humility, and overwhelms Feuerbach, reclaiming the *oikonomia* of deification. If Feuerbach claims that *"Man ist, was er ißt,"*[22] the Eucharist proclaims that this is surpassingly true of the bread of heaven. Then superfluity is a grace that human beings are saved *by*.

Piers Plowman glosses the question of those who "do well" as a question of those who "have well" and "clearly links the conditions of salvation with the conditions of possession."[23] "Most instructive, perhaps, is Wyclif's argument in *De Civili Dominio* that only one kind of 'having' is legitimate: one can only 'have well' if one is in a state of grace."[24] The superfluity that one is saved by can — in theory or in the eschaton — overwhelm and redeem the superfluity that one is saved from.

---

21. Smith, "Merchants," p. 125, quoting Boethius, *Consolatio philosophiae,* ed. James J. O'Donnell, 2d ed. (Bryn Mawr, Pa.: Bryn Mawr College, 1990); *The Consolation of Philosophy,* trans. Richard Green (New York: Macmillan, 1962), book II, prosa 5.

22. "The human being is what he eats." Ludwig Feuerbach, *Die Philosophie der Zukunft,* ed. H. Ehrenberg (Stuttgart: Fromanns, 1922), p. 89.

23. Smith, "Merchants," p. 140, quoting Piers Plowman B VII 113, 116.

24. Smith, "Merchants," p. 141, commenting on this passage: "tercio modo habendi, excellentissimo possibili, quoad genus, habent solum existentes in caritate vel gracia quidquid habent," John Wyclif, *De civili Dominio,* ed. Reginald Lane Poole (London: Wyclif Society, 1885), bk. I, ch. iii, p. 17.

ii. Bulgakov diagnoses the suspicion

Christian theology also knows at least one important theologian academically trained as an economist who writes about just these matters, the relation between agrarian economy and divine economy. Sergei Bulgakov's *Philosophy of Economy: The World as Household* (*Filosofia Kosiastva*, 1912)[25] recalls the Greek etymology of *oikonomia* as household management, including the management by which God oversees the whole world. Already in "The Economic Ideal" (1903) Bulgakov had diagnosed the tendency of which the fourteenth-century discourses were symptoms: "wealth . . . changes from a source of limitation to a source of temptation."[26] Matter is intended at creation for glory; God gives it a share in the human being's destiny of elevation. With the fall, the human being becomes unable to use it well, unable to enjoy and elevate it. Yet with the human being matter too can be redeemed; it can participate in the redemption intended to involve the whole cosmos, and this is the business, in Bulgakov's most general term, of "spiritualizing" matter: not to make it less material, but more meaningful.

According to Bulgakov, nature provides "the raw material for the incarnation of ideas in images accessible to the senses." It is "transformed into an artistic miracle under the sculptor's chisel, and gradually loses its materiality, its mortality, its lack of intelligibility and imperfect permeation by ideal structures." "Nature is capable of being penetrated by the demands of the human spirit."[27] "Nature becomes humanized, she is capable of becoming the peripheral body of the human being."[28]

Metaphors of "penetration," "permeation," and metabolism predominate.[29] They may sound excessively romantic and anthropocentric to contemporary ears — some passages about the human consumption of nature

25. Sergei Bulgakov, *Philosophy of Economy: The World as Household,* trans. and ed. Catherine Evtuhov (New Haven: Yale University Press, 2000); Russian, *Filosofia Khoziastva* (Moscow: Put', 1912; reprinted New York: Chalidze Publications, 1982).

26. Sergei Bulgakov, "The Economic Ideal," in Rowan Williams, ed., *Sergii Bulgakov: Towards a Russian Political Theology* (Edinburgh: T&T Clark, 1999), pp. 23-53; here, p. 47. Russian: "Ob ekonomicheskom ideale," in *Ot marksizma k idealizmu* (St. Petersburg: Tvo "Obschchestvennaia Pol'za," 1903; reprint Frankfurt a. M.: Posev, 1968), pp. 263-87.

27. Bulgakov, "Ideal," pp. 42-43.

28. *Filosofia Khoziastva,* p. 106, quoted in Catherine Evtuhov, *The Cross and the Sickle: Sergei Bulgakov and the Fate of Russian Religious Philosophy, 1890-1920* (Ithaca, N.Y.: Cornell University Press, 1997), p. 168. I have not found exactly those words in Evtuhov's own English translation, but the whole discussion in *Economy,* pp. 100-107 is similar.

29. Cf. Evtuhov, *Cross and Sickle,* p. 168.

sound like a brief for Monsanto. Yet the intent is not most charitably understood as dualistic or titanic.

It is more charitably read as moral rather than metabolic, so that it is "the battle against poverty" that "is a battle for the rights of the human spirit."[30] The abstract transcendental subject of Kant or Schelling becomes concretely the independent peasant, prefigured in Genesis at the gates of Eden, who is primarily a worker in the field rather than a perceiver or a romantic.[31] And Bulgakov's account is more charitably read as eschatological rather than naively progressive. The goal of economy is humanly unreachable without the intervention of God.[32]

So far from dominating nature, the human being participates in Christ's undoing of the fall by *befriending* nature instead of seeking like Adam to rise above it. Adam overreached himself and sought divinity as something to be grasped, and was punished with labor "in the sweat of his brow," Eve with labor in the pain of childbirth.

> God's judgment upon Adam defines the change that took place in the human being's position in the world: from the lord of nature he becomes its prisoner, and from an artist or gardener in God's Paradise he becomes a proprietor and agriculturist. The human being is condemned to *economic activity* [*khoziaistvo*], there arises "labor in the sweat of one's face," everything partakes of economics and labor.[33]

Christ, the Sower in the Field and the Gardener in Gethsemane, redeems the farmer by reversing Adam's overreach. He "humbled himself," and "did not count equality with God a thing to be grasped" (Phil. 2:8, 7). As Catherine Evtuhov puts it,

> Just as a person attending the Orthodox liturgy and partaking of the Eucharist experiences the cosmic drama of Christ's Resurrection (a theme reiterated each year in the festival cycle), so each man relives the Fall and Resur-

---

30. Bulgakov, "The Economic Ideal," pp. 42-43; cf. *Economy,* pp. 19, 220, 245-50, 256, 263, 284.

31. Evtuhov, *Cross and Sickle,* pp. 146, 151, 154, 178.

32. "There is no eschatology *within* the economic process," summarizes Evtuhov, *Cross and Sickle,* p. 181; cf. Bulgakov, *Economy,* p. 147.

33. Bulgakov, *Svet nevechernii* [*The Unfading Light*] (Moscow: Put', 1917; reprint Westmead, England: Gregg International Publishers, 1971), p. 261, quoted in Evtuhov, *Cross and Sickle,* p. 175. A French translation exists, *La lumière sans déclin,* trans. Constantin Andronikof (Lausanne: L'Age d'Homme, 1990). It is one of Evtuhov's contributions to read *The Unfading Light* as not only theology, but also a theological meta-economics undergirding *Economy.* See *Cross and Sickle,* p. 172 and *Economy,* p. 75.

rection as he works in his field. His labor resurrects the soil, redeems it from the inert, lethargic sleep into which Adam plunged it with his original sin.[34]

This is in effect a pneumatology from below. Kant's transcendental subject becomes concretely the human laborer, whose sweat and groanings in travail become the work of the Spirit for "the redemption of our bodies." If the human being spiritualizes and resurrects nature, that is work only of one already being redeemed and participating in the resurrection, one in whose mortal body also the Spirit has dwelled (Rom. 8:11). This conception of Bulgakov's anticipates from below the thesis that occupies the second half of this book: The Spirit rests on the body of the Son. When the Spirit rests on the body of the Son in the human being who imitates the Sower of the parable or the Gardener of Gethsemane, then the world sown and gardened also is transfigured. If the spirit of the human being comes to penetrate and elevate the material world, that is pneumatologically because the Holy Spirit hovers over the waters not only of creation but also of baptism and therefore even of irrigation and childbirth. At Pentecost, Psalm 104:30 is sung antiphonally: "Send forth your Holy Spirit, Lord/Renew the face of the earth."

Bulgakov's pattern consecrates any created gift as sacrament in the epiclesis of the Spirit. Economics extends sacramentology, and thus pneumatology, to the whole material world.[35] The upward journey that Bulgakov portrays is intelligible only as the upward bounce of the Spirit's descent.[36] In Bulgakov as in Christianity generally it characterizes the Spirit to rest upon matter after the pattern of the Son.

We can restate the point in the most graphic terms, those of eating. Bulgakov begins his argument with the divine command to the fallen Adam: "In the sweat of thy face shalt thou eat bread" (Gen. 3:19). That command grounds economics. "In the sweat of thy face" establishes labor, especially the labor of the worker in the field. But, more important, the command "thou shalt eat bread." "Bread" comes to cover all the material goods and culture that human beings pursue and consume.[37] "Food in this sense uncovers our essential metaphysical unity with the world."[38] The human being after the ex-

---

34. Evtuhov, Cross and Sickle, p. 155. Cf. Bulgakov, Economy, pp. 88, 104, 133, 148, 153.

35. Cf. Bulgakov, Economy, pp. 103-5 on eating and the Eucharist.

36. Bulgakov himself portrays the movement in terms of created and uncreated Sophia, but that is an extravagant hypothesis we need not follow. For a sympathetic account, see Evtuhov, Cross and Sickle, p. 152.

37. Bulgakov, Economy, p. 75.

38. Bulgakov, Economy, p. 103.

pulsion from Eden is then defined by Genesis as one who labors and consumes.[39] "I take in the flesh of the world in general in the guise of this bread."[40] Economy is the wresting of food for life from a world headed toward death, and "can ultimately be reduced to a metabolic process."[41] "[L]ife constantly . . . seizes and carries away cold, lifeless matter with its warm tentacles, and transforms it into living material, organizes dead matter into a living body."[42] So far, from below — and so hopeless, since life ends only in death. Life "does not have the strength to maintain this transformation forever; life is not capable of penetrating dead matter with its warmth so thoroughly that it will never cool again. . . . 'Dust thou art, and unto dust shalt thou return' (Gen. 3:19)."[43]

iii. How Feuerbach and Schmemann are what they eat

The great irony is that this command as punishment, "thou shalt eat bread," is also covertly a command as promise. For on account of the incarnation God's own self becomes the bread of human transfiguration. Jesus abbreviates "Thou shalt eat bread" with "Do this": Eat the eucharistic medicine of immortality, the bread of heaven. Then, by the consumption of the Son and the labor of the Spirit, who groans with us in travail, the goal of economy begins to be fulfilled: food becomes life.[44]

Alexander Schmemann makes a similar argument from above — he begins with a divine intention. "In the Bible the food that man eats, the world of which he must partake in order to live, is given to him . . . as *communion with God.*"[45]

> The world as man's food is not something "material" and limited to material functions, thus different from, and opposed to the specifically "spiritual" functions by which man is related to God. All that exists is God's gift to man, and it all exists to make God known to man, to make man's life communion with God. It is divine love made food, made life for man. . . .

39. Bulgakov, *Economy*, p. 75.
40. Bulgakov, *Economy*, p. 103.
41. Bulgakov, *Economy*, p. 95.
42. Bulgakov, *Economy*, p. 97.
43. Bulgakov, *Economy*, p. 97.
44. Bulgakov, *Economy*, p. 104.
45. Alexander Schmemann, *For the Life of the World* (Crestwood, N.Y.: St. Vladimir's Seminary Press, 1998), p. 14; italics in original.

"O taste and see that the Lord is good." . . . The world was created as the "matter," the material of one all-embracing eucharist.[46]

From Schmemann's perspective we can reformulate Bulgakov's thesis from above. Bulgakov says, "Food is *natural communion* — partaking of the flesh of the world."[47] Theologically, this statement is intelligible only as an inference from food as eucharistic communion, not as leading up to it. Food, like nature, is a "remainder concept," one formed (logically, not historically) by subtraction from the context in which God intends it. The bread of the sweat of the brow is left over: it does not so much *supply* the heavenly banquet as *remain* from it by God's gracious permission. In this perspective, breadwinners are like the disciples who take up "what was left over, twelve baskets of broken pieces";[48] the laborer only seeks to go like Ruth "to the field, and glean among the ears of grain after him in whose sight [she] shall find favor."[49] Even the manna of the Israelites falls, like the crumbs of the Syrophoenician woman, from the Lord's table.[50] This too is surplus, the merciful remnant of the Creator's bounty, a sacrament in reserve.

Christian theology has resources even earlier than the fourteenth century for dissolving the ambivalence of excess. The same movement takes place in Paul, who relates two discourses of "excess of nature." But that turns out to be a thesis in Mariology, and a chapter for another Part (pp. 99-104).

46. Schmemann, *For the Life*, pp. 14-15, paragraph boundary elided.
47. Bulgakov, *Economy*, p. 103.
48. Luke 9:17.
49. Ruth 2:2.
50. Mark 7:28.

3 Where the Spirit Rests: Matter and Narrative

Or, How the Spirit Does Material Culture

i. A person seeks to be known

The clarity of those questions begs another. They all ask for something distinctive for the Spirit to *do*. They sit uneasily, therefore, with the concern for God's unity. One guarantee of God's unity is that God's action *ad extra,* or toward what is other than God, is strictly indivisible. The Persons are distinct only among themselves, not toward the world. Thus there is something functional about the demand that the Spirit have something distinctive to do: a distinct *function,* that must be. But precisely if God's activity toward human beings is indivisible, a distinct function is just what the Spirit cannot offer.

Usually theologians solve this difficulty with a doctrine of appropriations. All God's actions toward the outside are indivisible, but Bible, liturgy, and tradition encourage the faithful to "appropriate" them to individual Persons, sometimes as epiphenomena of their intratrinitarian relations. Creator, redeemer, sanctifier refer to the Godhead without further differentiation; but Christians assign them to the Persons "by appropriation." Creator to the Father because the Father is the Father of the Son; Redeemer to the Son because in the Son God was reconciling the world to Godself; Sanctifier to the Spirit, because the Spirit shares its holiness characteristically with others. The doctrine of appropriations sits with the doctrine of God's unity in a dialectical way: here's how you say it, and here's how you take it back. Thus, according to Lewis Ayres, appropriation names a discipline of human poesis responding to the Bible and leading into the mystery of the Trinity.

There is another way of dealing with the Spirit's anonymity. Suppose the anonymity is not the presence or absence of any particular office or function. After all, to exercise or not exercise a particular human office does not confer or detract from the personhood of any human person; how much less in the Godhead. The anonymity of a human person is not a description of function or the lack thereof. The anonymity of a person is a description of a person's own personal activity, of her relations with others. A person is always difficult to know, incapable of being reduced to a function or formula. Among human persons the very attempt is an insult. If even a human person is complex, mysterious, retiring, how much more so a divine one? If even a human person is known not by conceptual analysis, but by narrative — in the portrayal of character in interaction — is it to be expected that we would get to know the Spirit in any other way than by her interactions with other persons? And if the Spirit has identifiable actions over against other persons only *within* the trinitarian life — since toward human persons God acts as One — then how else could Christian believers expect to detect the Spirit's personhood but in her interactions with the Father and the Son? And where else could Christians expect to detect those interactions, except where they get glimpses into the trinitarian life, when Jesus, as narratively portrayed, makes them known, by himself praying to the Father or receiving the Spirit, teaching the disciples or expecting his resurrection? Either that, or Christians must themselves enter into the trinitarian life where those interactions take place, something which they sometimes claim on the basis precisely of the Spirit's work.

In that case the Spirit, so far from hiding herself, would actually be seeking to make herself known, in the only way possible: by incorporating subsidiary persons, human persons, into the trinitarian life, where alone the Spirit's personhood could be experienced, by reading them into the text, narrating them typologically into the stories she shares with Jesus and the Father. There would seem to be no alternative portrayals of a person than narrative; and no alternative ways of access than deification. I would insist that "narrative" and "deification," like "hypostasis" and "Eucharist" might need explication in many and various ways. In particular, you don't need a theory about nineteenth-century centers of consciousness in order to understand character: Aristotle didn't. But strategies other than deification by narrative and narratives about deification would seem designed to fail. Nor does that mean that you have to be deified to follow the narrative. But if a text cannot be read to narrate the interactions of a person with the Spirit, it cannot consistently be read to depict the Spirit as a person; and if trinitarian doctrine claims that only *divine* persons can interact distinctively with the Spirit, then a trinitarian text cannot claim to depict the interactions of the Spirit with other divine persons intelligibly to human beings, without inviting those human beings to join them, to become deified persons. They may follow at a distance, even an infinite distance, as great as that between creator and creature: but that is not a distance that God cannot cross; it is rather a distance that the Persons of the Trinity, in their very distinction from one another, already embrace. Human beings can enter the trinitarian life, only but indeed because the trinitarian life already embraces human beings. It is in a deepening of thought about the portrayal of character, not in flight from it, that the anonymity of the Spirit is best understood: as the complex, storied, audacious reticence of someone who desires and gives herself to be known only and precisely in the community where she is at home *(oikei)* — the better to entice others in.[1] It is an intimate place, the *haram* of the Spirit, the place in which she hovers over the waters of Mary's womb, and thereby over the waters also of the whole world, the intimate and embracing place into which "The Spirit and the Bride say, 'Come!'"

ii. The Spirit deifies: an excursus on Augustine

This book relies on a theory of deification more by coherence and in practice than by explicit, formal argument. But if what the Spirit does is join human beings to the *koinonia* of the trinitarian life, then "deification" is one of the most apt traditional words. Indeed if the Spirit "adds" superfluity to the Father and the Son, one might say that the Spirit adds infinity, and therefore divinity, even to God.[2] Having explained that "the Holy Spirit is specially called by the name of love," Augustine goes on to say that "the deity of God," if I may so translate, "is love,"[3] and "Love, then, which is from God and is God, is properly the Holy Spirit."[4] Still, a few standard qualifications are in order:

1. Deification does not mean the erasure of the boundary of the Creator and the creature; it means the crossing of that boundary.

2. Deification does not mean that human persons become trinitarian persons. They become deified human persons, not persons of deity. They are deified by grace or by adoption, not deity by nature. The relation between participant and participated is no more overcome than that between creature and Creator. The former always exists and participates only on account of the latter.

1. For more on this see Emmanuel-Pataq Siman, *L'expérience de l'Esprit par l'Église d'après la tradition syrienne d'Antioche* (Paris: Beauchesne, 1971), p. 272, and the discussion below in "For and Against Method."

2. This is Colin Gunton's interpretation of a line in Basil's *Hexameron,* Basile de Césarée, *Homélies sur l'Hexaéméron,* 2:6, ed. and trans. Stanislas Giet (Paris: Éditions du Cerf, 1949), p. 168.

3. "Deus ergo ex Deo est dilectio," *De Trinitate* 15.17.31.

4. *De Trinitate* 15.18.32. I adopt the translation of Stephen McKenna in the Fathers of the Church, vol. 45 (Washington, D.C.: Catholic University Press, 1963).

3. Deification does not mean that human beings get to create worlds and redeem their inhabitants and so "play God." It does mean that they get to participate, by grace, in the redemption and recreation of a world they could not make.

4. Deification does mean that human creatures get a share in all sorts of divine characteristics uncontroversial even in Protestantism as features of salvation (better, elevation): immortality, righteousness, full understanding, and so on. In fact, it is odd to call these characteristics "salvation," since they go infinitely beyond the restoration of the Edenic state. Here, for example, is a standard, biblical, and unobjectionable list from Basil's *On the Holy Spirit:*

> Through the Holy Spirit comes our restoration to Paradise, our ascension to the Kingdom of heaven, our adoption as God's sons, our freedom to call God our Father, our becoming partakers of the grace of Christ, being called children of light, sharing in eternal glory, and in a word, our inheritance of the fullness of blessing, both in this world and the world to come.[5]

Another objection is that deification is not the language or conceptuality of the West, or that it is not that of Protestantism. All these misprisions can be easily overcome. Deification is also the language of Augustine, who could also say "God was made human that human beings might be made divine."[6]

That is no mere prooftext; it is also part of the closing conceptuality of *De Trinitate.*[7] The stereotype is that Augustine unifies God along mental lines: but a better reading is that Augustine divinizes the mind along trinitarian lines. But not in an idolatrous way, rather in the way of supernatural elevation or participation. For the mind mirrors God only when all its powers receive unity by having God (not themselves) as their object:[8] when, that is, they participate in the threefold integrity that God enjoys, because God has given God's very self to be the goal of human seeking.[9] Verbs for human participation include exercise, *exercere,* and the whole dialectic of seeking and finding,

---

5. Basil of Caesarea, *On the Holy Spirit* 15:36, trans. David Anderson (Crestwood, N.Y.: St. Vladimir's Seminary Press, 1997), p. 59.

6. Augustine, Sermon 128 "In natali Domini," no. 12, *Patrologia Latina* 39:1997.

7. Rowan Williams, "*Sapientia* and the Trinity: Reflections on the *De Trinitate,*" in B. Bruning et al., eds., *Collectanea Augustiniana: Mélanges T. J. van Bavel* (Leuven: Leuven University Press, 1990), pp. 317-32. In what follows, I owe my attention to *sapientia* in *De Trinitate* to Williams. His article does not go so far as to assert that the *sapientia* of God and humanity is a conceptuality of deification.

8. Williams, "*Sapientia* and the Trinity," p. 319.

9. *De Trinitate* 15.2.2.

quaerere and *invenire* and *pervenire,* God-given activities by which God draws the human being into God.[10]

The noun Augustine prefers for this deifying participation is *sapientia,* wisdom — "let wisdom be the one which we take" — among the names under which God gives Godself to be sought and found.[11] Indeed wisdom is God's essence: "He is Himself His own wisdom, because His Wisdom is not one thing, and His essence another thing."[12] But more than this: *sapientia* recalls both the communal wisdom of Plato's *Republic,* by which the perfect community and the wisest minds are joined in polity, and the practical wisdom of the Bible, in which God and human beings are joined in a new *basileia* by Jesus' practice of sacrificial love. Both the communal and the practical aspects of wisdom make it *unitive: sapientia* is the way in which love is *shared,* and it is the way particularly appropriate to creatures who image God with reason and will, which wisdom humanly perfects. But more: wisdom is also, biblically, both the divine characteristic by which God manifests divinity in creating and governing the world, *and* the way in which human beings share in the gift that God approves in Solomon and treasures in Proverbs.

Theologians of wisdom might say that the reason anthropologists can read meaning off matter is that there is something potentially or already divine about matter: The Spirit pours herself out on all flesh on account of the Incarnation. In the Bible, too, wisdom is high among the words for the way God and creatures commune, how they come by God's grace to have a common task. So Augustine has not only the word "deify"; he has also his own way of explicating the concept, for which he exploits biblical and conceptual resources of wisdom. And he does it in a way that does not derogate the threeness of God, but is well designed to *move* conceptually between threeness and oneness, between community and unity. From Plato's *Republic* wisdom has above all other virtues or powers displayed the good of the community in the souls of the rulers and exemplified the good of harmony in the constitution of the soul — constitution itself a word that displays an analogy between persons and politics. What word, indeed, could Augustine have chosen better to move easily both between the oneness and threeness of God, and between the multitude of human beings and their oneness in God? Love? Yes[13] — but love works better for the communal than the individual. The peculiar advantage of *sapientia* is that it is almost evenhandedly a personal and

---

10. *De Trin.* 15.2 as a whole.
11. *De Trin.* 15.5.
12. *De Trin.* 15.6.9. One wonders if Bulgakov knew this passage.
13. *De Trin.* 15.6.10.

a political virtue like justice. Unlike justice, wisdom can easily suggest development, change, as well as an achieved state: wisdom can work for justice as well as preserve it. Thus wisdom is appropriate for both creatures that grow and the God toward whom they grow: so that Jesus could "grow in wisdom and stature" (Luke 2:52).

It is appropriate, therefore, both that the creature use wisdom to seek God and that the seeking be possible only because God first created in wisdom. Wisdom excels in the human being but is not the human being.[14] Thus wisdom serves as a dynamic principle by which God may join the creature to Godself. Wisdom, like justice, takes in specific political commitments and communities, and thus honors materiality. Wisdom, like justice, is a practical aspect of deification, in that it equips human beings to live in community, in love. This happens because from wisdom proceeds the love of wisdom, which is the Spirit.[15] The Spirit then deifies human beings — and indeed God — in the register of love: "The Holy Spirit, of whom [God] has given us, causes us to remain in God, and God in us. But love does this. [The Spirit] is, therefore, the God who is love."[16] In *De Trinitate* Book 15, Chapter 18, the love by which God is God, and the love by which human beings participate in God, is the same love, the Holy Spirit. "How great a God is the God who gives God?"[17] "To drink of charity the Spirit of God exhorts you: to drink of Himself the Spirit of God exhorts you."[18] "Always, as a human being loves, so that one is. Do you love the earth? Then you are earth. Do you love God? Then — do I dare to say it — you are God. I dare not say it of myself; let us hear the scriptures: 'I have said, Ye are gods.'"[19] Symeon the New Theologian, Orthodoxy's most outspoken defender of theosis begun in this life, could hardly put it more strongly than that. And yet that is so not only because Augustine is not afraid of deification. It is also and more pragmatically so because love of neighbor takes preference over a vertical or abstract love of God, because love of neighbor "is more concrete and leaves less room for self-deception."[20]

---

14. *De Trin.* 15.7.11.

15. *De Trin.* 15.6.10 *in fin.*

16. *De Trin.* 15.17.31, referring to 1 John 4:7-19.

17. *De Trin.* 15.26.46, my translation.

18. *Commentary on the Epistle of Saint John,* in NPNF 7, p. 503, translation modernized.

19. *In Ep. I Joan.* 2:14, *Patrologia Latina* 35:1997. The translation in NPNF 7, p. 475 is more tentative. The psalm is 82:6.

20. Tarsicius J. van Bavel, "The Anthropology of Augustine," *Milltown Studies* 19/20 (1987): 25-39; here, p. 36, with further quotations and references.

There is something you may imagine, if you would see God. "God is love." What sort of face does love have? What form does it have? What stature? What feet? What hands does it have? No one can say. And yet it does have feet, for these carry human beings to church: it has hands, for these reach forth to the poor: it has eyes, for thereby we consider the needy.[21]

I have already suggested that Calvinists approach deification language in Westminster's talk of glorification. They do it in Barth's language of participation, *Teilnahme*.[22] Even Barth's revelation-epistemology is not best understood as a linear conveyance of information, but as a participation in the Way in which God knows God, and not separate, therefore, from the Way in which God loves God, but one of its other-involving consequences.[23] In Barth's doctrine of reconciliation, human beings acknowledge the verdict of the Father, receive the direction of the Son, and enact the witness of the Spirit, a threefold participation in the trinitarian life.[24] They do it also in Calvin's doctrine of the Eucharist and Ascension, by which he insists that human beings can participate in communion with God only by ascending with Christ into heaven when they lift up their hearts: Surely this makes even the Lord's Supper depend on the deification in Christ of human nature.[25] Lutherans, Finnish scholars suggest, approved deification in the language of the presence of Christ, *"in fide Christus vere adest,"* in faith Christ is actually present.[26] Methodists approach deification language in the languages of sanctification and perfection.[27] They do it, too, in the language of hymns:

He deigns in flesh to appear
Widest extremes to join;

21. *Commentary on the Epistle of St. John*, 7:10, in NPNF 7, pp. 504-5, translation modernized.

22. See Joseph Mangina, *"Christus pro nobis* and Participation in God," in his *Karl Barth and the Christian Life: The Practical Knowledge of God* (New York, N.Y.: Peter Lang, 2001), pp. 51-91.

23. I owe this formulation to a line of questioning from Joele Cabrita.

24. Mangina *"Christus pro nobis,"* pp. 51-91.

25. Calvin, *In.* IV.6.10; Davies, *He Ascended into Heaven*, pp. 10, 175, 176n., 177n.; Douglas Farrow, *Ascension and Ecclesia* (Grand Rapids: Eerdmans, 1999).

26. Tuomo Mannermaa, *Der im Glauben gegenwärtige Christus: Rechtfertigung und Vergottung* (Hannover: Arbeiten zur Geschichte und Theologie des Luthertums, 1988); Simo Peura und Antti Raunio, eds., *Luther und Theosis: Vergöttlichung als Thema der abendländischen Theologie* (Helsinki: Luther-Agricola Gesellschaft and Erlangen: Veröffentlichungen der Luther-Akademie Ratzeburg, 1990); Carl Braaten and Robert Jenson, eds., *Union with Christ: The New Finnish Interpretation of Luther* (Grand Rapids: Eerdmans, 1998).

27. See Anthony Baker, "Making Perfection," Ph.D. dissertation, the University of Virginia, 2004.

To bring our vileness near,
And make us all divine
And we the life of God shall know.
For God is manifest below.[28]

They do it even in Wesley's appropriation of Ephrem the Syrian.[29]

iii. The narrative depicts the person

The attempt to reduce the Spirit to a concept or function has had theologians wringing their hands — especially since we tend to denounce one functionality only to replace it with another. But it is precisely the personhood of the Spirit that in classical Christian thinking ought to *explain* the difficulty. A scholar of Antiochian liturgy has put the matter like this:

> At the end of this theological procedure a question presents itself. . . . It has to do with . . . which identity or what personal visage the Syrian Church recognizes in the Spirit across the breadth of their relations. The question is difficult and demands precision. Under the word "identity" or the expression "personal visage" one is not to expect that the Church gives us a definition of the Third Person of the Trinity. A person, all the more so when a divine Person, is a reality inarticulable and indefinable. A person is not some thing. A person is some one, and that one is a singular, indecipherable reality. We can point her out, encounter her, enter into communion with her and unite ourselves with her. But we cannot seize her, define her, sound her most personal and intimate depths, still less make her an object, were it only an object of knowledge. This is why in trying to see what the identity or the personal visage is that the Church, in her experience, recognizes as and gives to the Spirit, we seek to know how the Church names this divine Person who manifests herself to her, enters into communion with her, and communicates to her a new mode of being, life, and destiny.[30]

It is the insistent assertion, if not the invariable explication of the Christian practice of teaching about the Spirit, that the Spirit is a "person" — by no

---

28. Charles Wesley, "Let Earth and Heaven Combine," *Hymns for the Nativity* [*Hymns for the Nativity of our Lord,* facsimile ed. (Madison, N.J.: Charles Wesley Society, 1991)], quoted in Gordon Wakefield, "John Wesley and Ephraem Syrus," *Hugoye: Journal of Syriac Studies* 1 (1998), para. 16, available online at http://syrcom.cua.edu/Hugoye/Vol1No2/HV1N2Wakefield.html.

29. Wakefield, "John Wesley and Ephraem Syrus," esp. paras. 14-19.

30. Siman, *L'expérience de l'Esprit,* p. 272.

means often a nineteenth-century center of consciousness, but still, no matter how abstract the explication or unclear the visage, a character in a story: the one who overshadows Mary, descends over the Jordan, drives into the wilderness, waits to be sent, participates in the resurrection, alights on the disciples. Indeed this Spirit is so much a "person" that to her is appropriated God's personifying work, God's driving human beings to become most fully themselves, thus a Person with a capital P, a person *par excellence*. "Consider," says Cyril of Jerusalem,

> how many of you are now sitting here, how many souls of us are present. [The Spirit] is working suitably for each, and beholds the temper of each, beholds also his reasoning and his conscience. . . . For consider, I pray, with mind enlightened by Him, how many Christians there are in all this diocese, and how many in the whole province of Palestine, and carry forward thy mind from this province, to the whole Roman Empire; and after this, consider the whole world; races of Persians, and nations of Indians, Goths and Sarmatians, Gauls and Spaniards, and Moors, Libyans and Ethiopians, and the rest for whom we have no names. . . . Consider, I pray, of each nation, Bishops, Presbyters, Deacons, Solitaries, Virgins, and laity besides; and then behold their great Protector, and the Dispenser of their gifts; — how throughout the world He gives to one chastity, to another perpetual virginity, to another almsgiving, to another voluntary poverty, to another power of repelling hostile spirits. And as the light, with one touch of its radiance, shines on all things; so also the Holy Ghost. . . .[31]

So too Gregory of Nazianzus:

> [I]f [the Spirit] takes possession of a shepherd, He makes him a Psalmist, subduing evil spirits by his song, and proclaims him King; if He possesses a goatherd and a scraper of sycamore fruit, He makes him a Prophet [Amos 7:14]. . . . If He takes possession of Fishermen, He makes them catch the whole world. . . . If of Publicans, He . . . makes them merchants of souls.[32]

If this Person is also private (not a biblical word), in this sense of one who is and who makes particular *(idios)* and who works most intimately (*interior intimo meo*, as Augustine writes in the *Confessions*, "more interior than I am to myself") — as she does when she enters Mary's womb and makes her the God-bearer — then those are the marks of character and not the lack thereof. The Spirit is inaccessible not because she *lacks* the qualities of a person; the

31. Cyril of Jerusalem, *Cathechetical Orations* XVI, "On the Article, and in One Holy Ghost," 22, in NPNF2 7, p. 121.

32. Gregory Nazianzen, *On Pentecost*, in NPNF2 7, p. 384.

Spirit is inaccessible because she *has* the qualities of a person. She is not inaccessible because *im*personal, but *as* personal.

That is Siman's point. But Siman goes on from there to suggest that the Spirit is *la vie,* life itself. It is an instructive misstep. While it is not false, but even appropriate to associate the Spirit with life, the association does not much distinguish her from the other trinitarian Persons. Did not Jesus say, "*I am the life*"? "Life" is a quality, and as such one shared among the Three. The Spirit is not *the* life, but *a* life, or, better, a Person of the Living One, who gives life to human beings in storied and historical interactions. "Life" is another abstraction, even if it is a biblical one, one that can still reduce the Spirit to the terms of Idealism, however vitalist.

The character of the Spirit, the Giver of Life, is to be sought not in any mysteries of life itself, vitalist or not, but in the particular mysteries of her own particular life, to the extent that human beings can know it, in the life of the One who lives with the Son. While it is true that the Spirit is said to work in or on the heart, it is also true that the *way* she so works, her particular *tropos hyparxeos* (using the patristic phrase in a modern way), is narrated as more nearly physical than psychological. She is not said to be with the Son internally, although undoubtedly the writers would not wish to exclude that, but hovers non-psychologically over his head. The Gospels tell a story of human and divine interaction in which Jesus and John perform a dance of courtesy, where we meet the incarnation of the Son, the voice of the Father, and the Spirit in the form not of an emotion but of a bird. She is said to come upon a human being: but this is expressed externally with the oil of anointing, the water of baptism, the fire of Pentecost, so that she is thought to rest upon or embrace the physical body; she is said to indwell or inhabit a human being: but this is portrayed as physically as the seed in the womb, the priest in the temple, or the householder in her home. You do not need a theory of premotion to see that even as late as Thomas Aquinas (who learned it from Aristotle) to "inhabit" is to habituate, to dwell dispositionally or by training in limbs and muscles physically readied, for love's sake, to act. To inhabit is to habituate, to render love bodily. If Aquinas had had modern medicine but not Descartes to go by, he might have said that the locus of inhabitation was the limbic system. In the New Testament, the Spirit leads, follows, or accompanies the Son into the most intimate places: not, instructively, into his "mind" or "heart," but into much messier places, paradigms of the physical: the womb, the wilderness, the garden, the grave. So the stories depict character without a modern theory of interiority, but with a plotted narrative that enacts intimacy (para)physically. Not to overdraw the contrast, New Testament authors would rather have an advocate in the womb or in the grave than in the mind or heart.

iv. The Spirit befriends matter

In Part II, I will follow several generative procedures in hopes that they will render pneumatology again a site productive of meaning, a womb conceiving words, rather than a dead zone policed round by controversies like the *Filioque*. The first of those procedures is narrative: I intend to read four narratives in which Jesus and the Spirit interact in the presence of the Father. I intend to read them as they have been worked in specific and differing parts of commentarial traditions, and as iconic (although I largely refrain from art historical remarks). But I want to replace merely conceptual accounts of trinitarian relations with some of the narrative pictures that give them rise. So I use the stories as liturgically, exegetically, and iconically worked — as received by a community.

In Part II, I work also quasi-anthropologically.[33] The clue to recovery of a robust Spirit-talk runs through and not around the social sciences, precisely for good theological reasons: Christians believe that Christ has become incarnate in a human being, subjected himself, therefore to the human sciences; after his ascension, Christians say that Christ's body is the church — in which Christ subjects himself to sociological analysis. Any theology that rejects the social sciences is anti-incarnational; any theology that thinks they are evil by privation of good and nothing else forgets that by its own teaching what is assumable is redeemable. So it comes not amiss if Christianity is as Durkheim would describe it; rather, Christians must assert that God can use the social forms for God's own purposes: indeed, at creation God declared them good, and at the incarnation the Spirit befriended them anew.[34] Thus I will follow Barth and Durkheim together in considering that what happens to totemic figures on earth is a reliable guide to their character above. Society recapitulates cosmology in both totemism and analogy.

In each chapter of Part II therefore I consider an iconic encounter of Jesus and the Spirit. I assume that in those cases we get a glimpse not just of economic (this-worldly) interaction but of intratrinitarian relationship. In this I follow von Balthasar and Barth, who is fond of the question after God "ante-

---

33. The idea that theology resembles cultural ethnography became widespread at both Yale and the University of Chicago in the 1980s and 1990s. See George Lindbeck, *The Nature of Doctrine: Religion and Theology in a Postliberal Age* (London: SPCK and Philadelphia: Fortress, 1984); Jonathan Z. Smith, *Map Is Not Territory: Studies in the History of Religions* (Leiden: Brill, 1978); Kathryn Tanner, *Theories of Culture: A New Agenda for Theology* (Minneapolis: Fortress, 1997).

34. Cf. Karl Barth, "The *Aufhebung* of Religion," *Church Dogmatics* I/2, 280-362, performing a similar movement (although deeply supersessionist in considering Judaism the type of human religion in the bad sense, Christianity as God's use of sinful social flesh).

cedently in Himself," or a move on the model of "in that the Father generates
the Son it becomes manifest that God creates the world." The first movement
of each chapter, therefore, is from narratives about Jesus up the analogical hierarchy to claims about trinitarian relations. But the turn to narrative is not
merely a twentieth-century move, however much the twentieth century has
focused on it. Here it is in Gregory of Nazianzus:

> Christ is born; the Spirit is His Forerunner. He is baptized; the Spirit bears
> witness. He is tempted; the Spirit leads Him up. He works miracles; the
> Spirit accompanies them. He ascends; the Spirit takes His place.[35]

The next move however is down the analogical ladder to ways in which
human beings, prayerfully, communally, or morally participate in the trinitarian relations depicted in the life of Jesus and characteristic of the trinitarian life. After that, another move may descend further down the ladder to the
way in which material things are caught up sacramentally as means to the deification of human beings.

But the moves are not deducible from one another or predictably parallel.
Sociologically, you cannot predict the iterated forms that a totemic series will
take: you have to do field work to find them out, and then you can describe
them. Theologically, the analogical series works with interstices of gift, so that
the elements relate with a kind of family resemblance, especially the kind of
family resemblance that interacts with and develops in its environment. The
family resemblance that makes the acts of a community or person intelligible
over time we also call "character," something that is easy to recognize but hard
to predict. In particular, it is the Holy Spirit to whom Christian theology ascribes all these things: sociological reality, since it grants *koinonia;* family resemblance, since it is called the Spirit of sonship; character, since it moves and
writes upon the heart; recognizability, since it manifests and illuminates and
leads into truth; unpredictability, since it blows where it will. Attention to the
Spirit's appropriated activity also directs our attention to the anthropology of
material culture, since it is the Spirit whom Christians call down to sanctify
people and things: deacons, priests, believers, water, wine, oil, incense,
churches, houses, and anything that can be blessed.

Oil, water, bread, wine, the bodies of human beings to be baptized, married, or ordained: in many and various ways the matter of the world becomes
the element of a sacrament. To think about the Spirit it will not do to think
"spiritually": to think about the Spirit you have to think materially. "In the

---

35. *Fifth Theological Oration,* NPNF2 7, p. 327.

last days God poured out God's Spirit on all flesh" (Joel 3:1, Acts 2:17-18). You might object that "all flesh" in that passage means "human flesh": but theological interpreters have taken it both more broadly and more concretely. For breadth consider Charles Péguy:

> Those that are carnal
> are in want of pureness.
> This we know.
> But those that are pure
> are in want of being carnal.[36]

For concrete particularity consider Basil of Caesarea:

> [T]he Lord was anointed with the Holy Spirit, who would henceforth be united with his very flesh.[37]

If the relationship between the Spirit and matter obtained because of some abstract philosophical or anthropological relationship between matter and spirit (which may or may not be), then one would have to proceed from the matter itself, and study the human machine and its behavior or the natural symbology of water and oil. Consider the richness of a passage about oil and the Spirit such as the quotation from Ephrem that opens the volume, or this more recent one from Dumitru Staniloae:

> The chrism symbolizes in the most adequate way possible the fluidity of the Holy Spirit extending into all the parts of the ecclesial organism. He spreads out like an oil, but more especially like a perfume. Whoever receives the Holy Spirit in the Church receives him in the form of a fluid or a fragrance, a breath of life spreading out from him into all the other members of the Church, binding him to them and thereby sustaining the whole organism and its sobornicity. This fluid provides no foundation for rigid structure, but as Spirit in the most precise sense of that word, that is, a wave diffusing outwards, it overcomes every separation and brings things formerly distinct into union among themselves.[38]

36. Charles Péguy, *The Porch of the Mystery of the Second Virtue*, in *Oeuvres poétiques complètes* (Paris: Gallimard, 1975), p. 57, as translated in Cantalamessa, p. 185.

37. Basil of Caesarea, *On the Holy Spirit* 16:39, trans. David Anderson (Crestwood, N.Y.: St. Vladimir's Seminary Press, 1980), p. 65.

38. Dumitru Staniloae, "The Holy Spirit and the Sobornicity of the Church," *Theology and the Church*, trans. Robert Barringer (Crestwood, N.Y.: St. Vladimir's Seminary Press, 1980), pp. 45-71; here, p. 69.

Indeed I considered arranging the next Part in terms of sacramental elements, oil, water, wine, and so on. That arrangement would accrue certain advantages. It could most easily incorporate the cultural anthropology that has some claim to being theology's closest intellectual relative. It would be very concrete and particular, if oil and water define the concrete and the particular. But in terms indigenous to the community under study, it is not some natural symbology of water that controls; any natural symbology of water is Christianly constructed, or pressed willy-nilly into service, according to the community under study, because God so created and deployed it. And in theological terms it is not oil and water that define the appropriate concreteness and particularity — although they do partake in it for contingent historical reasons — but the appropriate concreteness and particularity belong to trinitarian thinking, to Father, Son, and Holy Spirit. So the most famous connection of oil to these matters starts from the meaning of the word "Christ," anointed, and proceeds to think of the Father as the Anointer and the Spirit as the Oil.[39] Oil achieves its significance by being assumed into the intratrinitarian relation. Ephrem gets it right. Oil enjoys its significance because the Spirit has befriended it: it is "the dear friend of the Holy Spirit." It partakes, that is, in the relation between the Spirit and the human being and therefore between the Spirit and the Son. Fail to note these things, and you make of oil no longer something particular, but a general category that eventually loses its significance.

To think about the Spirit, you have to think materially, because, in Christian terms, the Spirit has befriended matter. She has befriended matter for Christ's sake on account of the incarnation. To reduce the Spirit to matter breaks the rule of Christian speech that God is not to be *identified* with the world; to divorce the Spirit from matter breaks the rule of Christian speech that God is not to be identified by simple *contrast* with the world.[40] The Holy

---

39. The translation of this hymn in *Ephrem the Syrian: Hymns,* trans. and introduced by Kathleen E. McVey (New York : Paulist Press, 1989) brings this out. For Latin and Greek usages, see for example Irenaeus of Lyons, *Against Heresies* 3.18.3; cf. 3.6.1; 3.17.1; Basil of Caesarea, *On the Holy Spirit,* 12:28. Biblical texts commonly cited include Acts 10:38, Isa. 61:1, Ps. 45:7. For a comprehensive survey of the Syriac olive imagery, see Robert Murray, *Symbols of Church and Kingdom: A Study in Early Syriac Tradition* (Cambridge: Cambridge University Press, 1975), pp. 112, 115-16, 126-27, 320-24. For the history of liturgical usages, see Gabriele Winkler, "The Original Meaning of the Prebaptismal Anointing and Its Implications," in *Living Water, Sealing Spirit* (Collegeville, Minn.: Liturgical Press, 1995), pp. 58-81. For a modern, historically informed, theological, if somewhat devotional usage of the anointing theme, see Raniero Cantalamessa, *Lo Spirito Santo nella vita di Gesù: Il mistero dell'unzione,* 2d ed. (Milan: Editrice Ancora, 1983). A shorter version is translated as *The Holy Spirit in the Life of Jesus: The Mystery of Christ's Baptism* (Collegeville, Minn.: The Liturgical Press, 1994).

40. Kathryn Tanner, *God and Creation* (Oxford: Blackwell, 1988), pp. 46-48.

Spirit, says John of Damascus, "fills all things with his essence and sustains all things. In His essence He fills the world, but in His power the world does not contain him."[41] God is trapped neither within nor outside the world: so the Son may assume a body, and the Spirit indwell one, not abstractly, but for a purpose: to catch the whole world up into their common life with the Father.

To think about water and matter in Christianity, conversely, you have to think in terms of the Spirit: Because the conception of Jesus in the watery womb of Mary involves the Holy Spirit in the incarnation of the Son, and the Son comes so that "the whole world might be saved through Him," the Spirit pursues the Son into the matter of the whole world. For the sake of the world, the Spirit figures her hovering on the waters of the womb backward to the waters of creation and forward to the waters of the font.

To think about matter you have to think about the Spirit for historical reasons, too. In ancient biology "it was widely held that the *pneuma* ['spirit'] of the father concentrated in the seed and was the active and organizing force that shaped the matter supplied by the mother in the womb."[42] Thus the descendents of an ancestor pre-exist *pneumatikos*, "spiritually," or better *virtually*, where "virtually" does not mean in contrast with the physical, but in the power of the seed. So Hebrews 7 assumes that Levi, existing virtually in the loins of Abraham, paid homage to Melchizedek when Abraham did.[43] If then the *pneuma* of the One who raised Jesus dwells in the mortal bodies of believers, then by the Spirit Jesus and the believer share something that works not like a contrast to matter, but a very powerful stuff. The ancient biology is so mixed that even those adopted can be "worthy of the fame of their [adoptive!] ancestors":[44] Diodorus of Sicily, writing of a Publius adopted by a Scipio, "treats both the biological family and the adopted family as ancestors and has Publius inheriting character traits from both."[45] The Spirit of sonship may be transcendent God, but it is not therefore non-physical. Indeed in Paul's words God's action in adopting the Gentiles is "paraphysical" (Rom. 11:24).

A word about hierarchy. It has gotten a bad name for good reasons. But if Judith Butler is right, we cannot escape but only subvert it, mobilize it for an alternative production. And if canon law is right, abuse does not take away use. The material laying on of hands also invokes the Spirit, so that the Spirit

---

41. John of Damascus, *The Orthodox Faith* 1:13, trans. Frederic Chase (New York, N.Y.: The Fathers of the Church, Inc., 1958), p. 200.

42. Stanley K. Stowers, "A Response to Richard Hays' 'What Is Real Participation in Christ?'" p. 3 of typescript.

43. Stowers, "Real Participation," p. 3.

44. Stowers, "Real Participation," p. 4.

45. Stowers, "Real Participation," p. 4.

not only subverts but mobilizes hierarchy. That is appropriate if the Spirit gives gifts to Christ, who is portrayed as constantly subverting hierarchy and mobilizing it for alternative productions: the last shall be first; who counted divinity not a thing to be grasped, but took the form of a servant; this is my body given for you. Hierarchy may oppress, but it may also serve. By a kind of reversal of hierarchy, the material becomes transfigured, a sacrament, a stepping-stone back up on the way to deification. More important for this essay, matter provides an ineliminable iconic or intertextual clue to the unpredictable way in which a typological series works. Matter, that is, serves as a principle of recognizablity among the family resemblances. So it is no mere conceit to connect the water of the font to the water of the Jordan, the water of creation, and the water of the womb. That is in historical fact the way that traditional exegesis works, and the sort of thing that an anthropologist might describe. It is also a reliable clue to the connections among baptism, incarnation, creation, annunciation, rebirth, and more. Both theologians and sociologists want to pay attention to the lived reality of liturgical practice.

v. What the Spirit can do

Some contemporary students of Christianity want for the Spirit to "have more to do." Although that way of putting the matter crosses the line that because the activity of the Persons toward the world is indivisible, it's not possible for one Person to do (toward the world) any more than the others, it does get across the point that they want Spirit-language to be more robust, and the person-making characteristics of the Person more apparent. These students of Christianity complain that otherwise the Spirit is reduced to a "power," a thing, gets reified.

But other students of Christianity think that the Spirit is indeed not like the others. For Florensky, this is just as it should be. For Peirce, this is indeed as it must be. For Durkheimians who would see Christ as the Christian totem, this is only plausible. The Spirit just *is* a power; "hypostasis" language does not require nineteeth-century personhood, and the scholars in the preceding paragraph need conceptual therapy to understand how the Spirit works.

I propose to synthesize the antitheses, navigate the dilemma, falsify the alternative. I propose that the Spirit is a Person with an affinity for material things. The Spirit characteristically befriends the body.

Those things are true of the Son as well: the Son shows an affinity for material things in the incarnation, and befriends the body from conception to resurrection, ascension and the final judgment.

And they are even true of the Father, if to the Father we appropriate the creation of the material world, and its return to him in the Kingdom.

That the Spirit shows an affinity for material things, and befriends the body, does not itself distinguish the Spirit from the Father and the Son; rather it shows again that the Trinity's activity in the world is of a piece: as Barth puts it, God is the one who loves in freedom also for us, who "so loved the world." But the Spirit does do that triune thing in a particular way; it has its own *tropos hyparxeos,* its own place in the trinitarian taxis. To specify that particular way (so I paraphrase *tropos hyparxeos*) I take language from the sacraments, the ecclesial practices that best imitate with concrete human persons and concrete material things the giving of thanks that the Spirit witnesses, celebrates, enjoys, and keeps faith with in the trinitarian life. The Spirit characteristically incorporates the particular (as in gathering the community, for baptism and Eucharist) and distributes the corporate (as the elements and the gifts).

Those statements as they stand are still inadequate to identify the Spirit, if they speak only to the Spirit's activity in the world (befriending the material). And the statements are inadequate also in a second way, if they make the Spirit's activity some general principle (incorporating the divided). There are thus two potential problems: reduction to the economy and abstraction to a principle. But if the Spirit's activity in the world has a particular shape *(tropos)*, a shape distinguishable from that of the others *(tropos hyparxeos)*, then that shape must arise from and reflect intratrinitarian relations. What God does in the world manifests the way God is, as Barth would put it, "antecedently in Himself." How is it that the Spirit shows an affinity for matter and befriends the body *already in the trinitarian life?* How is it that the Spirit distributes the particular and builds up the corporate *already in the community that God enjoys?*

The tradition — in the person of John of Damascus — suggests an answer to these questions. It is, importantly, not an answer that could be strictly *deduced* from them as if the Spirit's role in the Trinity were a condition for the possibility of its role in the world in the *hard sense,* could be "predicted" from the economy, so that the Trinity became a function of the sacraments. (It is a condition for the possibility in a soft sense; that is, *given* that you know how the Trinity works, then you can see the activity of the Persons in the economy as rationally related to it.) The answer of John of Damascus is: The Spirit rests on the Son.[46] I hasten to add that this is an *active* thing, an alighting.

---

46. John of Damascus, *The Orthodox Faith,* 1:7 ("coming to rest *[anapauein]* in the Word and declaring Him," p. 175); 1:8 ("We likewise believe in the Holy Ghost, the Lord and Giver of

In the world, the Spirit is not Person *or* thing, because the Spirit is Person *on* thing. And the Spirit is Person on thing *because* the Spirit is Person on Person. The Spirit rests on material bodies in the economy, because she rests on the Son in the Trinity. Because (at the undivided act of all three Persons) the Son takes a body, so too (at the undivided act of all three Persons) the Spirit rests on a body. It is the Son's own gift that the Spirit crowns in the economy, because it is God's other Person that the Spirit celebrates in the Trinity. The Spirit's befriending of material bodies is her continual elaboration and crowning and consummation of the Incarnation, which is not the work of the Son only, but of the Father and the Spirit as well. If it is characteristic of the Spirit in the world that what she distributes particularly she also builds up corporately, that is because it is characteristic of the Spirit in the Trinity, that the One she rests on particularly, she also nourishes with gifts. One sign of this relation is the Annunciation, in which the Spirit gives the Son a corporeal body in order that she might alight upon it. Resting upon the corporeal body of the Son is not the end of the Spirit's distribution of gifts, but she rests there that she might rest also on the body of the Son in the Church, and on the body of the Son in the baptized, and on the body of the Son in the bread and the wine, and on the body of the Son in whatever other place she conceives it.

The verb that John chooses, ἀναπαύσεται, originates with the Septuagint of Isaiah 11:2, "And the Spirit of the Lord shall rest upon him." It reappears applied to believers in I Peter 4:14: "If you are reproached for the name of Christ, you are blessed, because the Spirit of Glory and of God rests upon you." Already among the biblical authors, therefore, an analogy operates between the messianic body and the communal body.

In the Orthodox tradition, and lately in Western theologians who have picked it up as a possible solution to the *Filioque* controversy, the verb "rests" tends to sum up, in fairly colorless fashion, many of the other verbs used in Greek to relate the presence or coming of the Spirit "upon" its object: ἐπαναπαύω, "to make to rest upon," as on Eldad and Medad (Num. 11:26) and, of the spirit of Elijah, on Elisha (II Kings [IV Kings in LXX] 2:15); ἐγένετο ἐπί, "come upon" (II Chr. 15:1, 20:14; Luke 1:35; Acts 1:8, 19:16); "be upon" (Num. 24:2; Judg. 11:29; I Sam. 19:20, 23; Luke 2:25); "be in" (Gen. 41:38); "find" (II Kings 2:16); "hover" (Gen. 1:2); "descends" (Matt. 3:16; Mark 1:10;

---

life, who proceeds from the Father and abides *[menein]* in the Son," p. 183), trans. Frederic H. Chase, Jr. (New York, N.Y.: Fathers of the Church, Inc., 1958). Indeed, all of the hypostases "rest and abide" in one another *(Orthodox Faith* 1:14). For historical commentary, see Andrew Louth, *St. John Damascene: Tradition and Originality in Byzantine Theology* (Oxford: Oxford University Press, 2002), pp. 107-10, 115. For theological commentary, see Staniloae, "Holy Spirit and Sobornicity," pp. 21-22.

Luke 3:22; John 1:32); "falls upon" (Acts 10:44, 11:15); "overshadows" (at the Annunciation and Transfiguration: Luke 1:35; Matt. 17:5 = Mark 9:7 = Luke 9:34); "dwells in" (Rom. 8:9, 11; II Tim. 1:14).[47] Verbs of resting, alighting, and abiding also appear in early Greek, Syriac, and Armenian epicleses.[48]

None of its deployers uses the verb of "resting" as passive or inert. As in Aristotle and Aquinas, one assumes that God's rest is unimpeded activity. Bar Hebraeus puts it like this:

> [The Dove] flies without leaving her nest above. . . . She reaches all quarters without stirring from her place. . . . She abides in the East, yet the West is full of her. Her food is fire, and who is crowned by her with wings will breathe forth flames from his mouth. All those who are burning from love and sick from affection reveal their secrets to her and she slakes their thirst.[49]

As Dumitru Staniloae puts it, "'rest' cannot be explained as the opposite of weariness — for the Spirit cannot grow weary, but as an 'end to all further departing', as an 'abiding' in the Son."[50] He continues with an interpretation of the Spirit's procession from the Father:

> This meaning [of coming to end of departing in the Son] is implied also by the word "procession" which does not mean a simple going forth of one person from another, as for example in the case of being born; it means rather a setting forth from somewhere towards a definite goal, a departure from the one person in order to reach another (ἐκπορεύομαι = I set out on the way in order to arrive somewhere). When the Spirit proceeds from the Father he sets out towards the Son; the Son is the goal at which he will stop.[51]

---

47. This list depends on a similar one for the Syriac Bible in Sebastian Brock, *Holy Spirit in the Syrian Baptismal Tradition,* 2d ed., pp. 8-11. Cf. also Exod. 13:27, 19:16, 31:3, 35:31, Micah 3:8, Isa. 11:2, Dan. 13:45-46. See also Gabriele Winkler, "Ein bedeutsamer Zusammenhang zwischen der Bekenntnis und Ruhe in Mt 11,27-29 und dem Ruhen des Geistes auf Jesus am Jordan. Eine Analyse zur Geist-Christologie in syrischen und armenischen Quellen," in *Studies in Early Christian Liturgy and Its Context,* Variorum Collected Studies Series 593 (Aldershot, U.K.: Ashgate, 1997), pp. IV, 66-80, esp. pp. II, 72-78.

48. Gabriele Winkler, "Further Observations in Connection with the Early Form of the Epiklesis," in *Studies in Early Christian Liturgy and Its Context,* Variorum Collected Studies Series 593 (Aldershot, U.K.: Ashgate, 1997), pp. IV, 66-80, esp. pp. 72-78.

49. *Bar Hebraeus's Book of the Dove,* trans. A. J. Wensinck (Leyden: E. J. Brill, 1919), p. 4.

50. Dumitru Staniloae, "Trinitarian Relations and the Life of the Church," in *Theology and the Church,* p. 21.

51. Staniloae, "Trinitarian Relations," pp. 21-22.

In creation, we might add, this goal becomes multifarious and diverse. "[S]ince the faithful, unlike Christ, are not divine hypostases, they have only a partial share in the energy of the Spirit." But "they are united with Christ through the Spirit who never leaves Christ. . . . The Spirit never leaves this position of resting upon Christ, for his rest as a hypostasis is in Christ as the incarnate Son of God. But the Spirit can cease to rest upon the human being for there is no eternal hypostatic relation between human beings and the Spirit."[52]

Staniloae implies an argument according to which the Spirit's work in the economy of gathering the community into the body of Christ, and distributing gifts to the members are the form that its one resting takes, when it enters the realm of finitude. This is not an argument from necessity, an argument that destroys the giftedness of the Spirit's response to Christ's work. The Spirit does not have to rest upon the body of the Son also in particular human beings. That is why the kingdom of the Spirit does not follow immediately or automatically or mechanically upon the coming of Christ, but enjoys the delay, the gratuity, and the variation of a characteristically free donation. Because the Spirit characteristically perfects and diversifies its response, it both gathers finite hypostases and develops their particularity: it builds up, in Paul's metaphor, an organic body, one in which differences are valuable and uniformity would be inappropriate. As we shall see, the celebration in the economy of the life of the Trinity is no necessity but a contingent gift of the Spirit already in its hovering over the deep at creation, for God commands both that the heavens and waters gather, and that the heavens fly, the seas swarm, and the earth crawl with diverse things. From creation to the promise to Abraham to the salvation in Christ, the Spirit characteristically gathers diversity for blessing.

> Inasmuch as through our union with Christ, with the incarnate hypostasis of the Son, we possess the Spirit, two things follow: on the one hand, we form, in a certain sense, one person with Christ;

(and this is the basis for the Spirit's unitive function in the economy)

> on the other hand, because, unlike Christ, we do not possess the Spirit in his hypostatic fullness, but only as much as we can contain and as corresponds to the person of each of us, the Spirit simultaneously accentuates in us what is specific to us as persons[53]

---

52. Staniloae, "Trinitarian Relations," pp. 26-27. For the last claim, cf. Florensky, *The Pillar and Ground of the Truth*, trans. Boris Jakim (Princeton, N.J.: Princeton University Press, 1997), p. 38.

53. Staniloae, "Trinitarian Relations," p. 27.

and this is the basis for the Spirit's distribution to us of particular gifts, ones that accord with our specific vocation. But, Staniloae notes,

> These are not two separate moments as Lossky thinks, but in virtue of the very fact that we are united to Christ through the Spirit, union with Christ also accentuates our growth as persons.[54]

That "accentuation of our growth" honors both our creation as distinctly finite creatures and our destiny as friends of God. It would dishonor our creation to gather us into uniformity, washing out the particularity that the Spirit had first fostered in us, and the command to the heavens, lands, and seas to bring forth multiple kinds and "every living creature that moves" and "everything that God had made." Furthermore it would dishonor God's desire for community with us, if we could not *use* that particularity to participate in our community with God. "It would be inconsistent" for the Spirit to deprive human beings "of that whereby [they] attain to a likeness of God"[55] — or to deprive the triune community of the friendship it desires.

In Aristotle and in Staniloae the purpose of friendship is to grow in virtue.[56] For creatures that is axiomatic. Creatures are made to grow; their createdness is a movement from God to God. God might have made creatures static, but that is a different story — a deist story — from the biblical one. The Spirit therefore wants to foster the virtues, or powers, particular to each of us, so that we may not be left out of our own destiny. For creatures, time-dwellers, it is strictly appropriate to *come* to God over time. That is the flowering that the Spirit presents to the Father and the Son, the harmony of the Trinity also in time. By the Spirit they manifest their friendship to God by growing in virtue; by the Spirit God manifests God's friendship to them by diffusing God's virtue, by giving it to them.

> [T]he shining forth of the Spirit from the faithful is in proportion to their respective stages of growth in virtue, and this could scarcely be the case were the Spirit to shine forth from them in the fullness of [Christ's own] Person. In other words the human persons of the faithful are penetrated only by the *activity* of the Spirit who, as Person, is united with Christ the divine Head of the Body and Head of every believer who is a member of his

---

54. Staniloae, "Trinitarian Relations," p. 27, referring (I suppose) to Vladimir Lossky, "Redemption and Deification," *Sobornost,* Series 3, no. 2 (1947): 55, and reprinted in Lossky, *In the Image and Likeness of God,* ed. John H. Erickson and Thomas E. Bird (Crestwood, N.Y.: St. Vladimir's Seminary Press, 1974), pp. 97-110.

55. Thomas Aquinas, *ST* I.105.4.

56. Aristotle, *Nichomachean Ethics* 9.12, 1172a11-14.

Mystical Body. Hence as human beings the faithful cannot have that integral personal relation with the divine Persons which these Persons have among themselves on the basis of their common essence: they can have only a relation "through grace," that is, through communion or through the activity, the energy of the Spirit.[57]

That means that differences of body and of experience are necessary, not indeed absolutely, but in view of God's contingent and gratuitous *purpose*, necessary in view of some *end*. They are necessary, because otherwise the Spirit would not have the matter to offer in return to the Son. They are necessary, because otherwise the Spirit would have no elements for Eucharist. They are necessary, because otherwise the Spirit would have no object for epiclesis. They have, to put it paradoxically, a necessity of superfluity or gratuity: a strictly *eucharistic* necessity. The Spirit *creates* diversity in matter, in order to offer up the variety of religious experience. If the priest invokes the Spirit at the epiclesis, that can only be because the Spirit has invoked matter at the creation.

Note that the Spirit's gathering of the community and the diversity of her gifts have the same explanation: they converge on the same process by which the Spirit keeps as her own the creatures that the Spirit created as different from one another.[58]

The Spirit keeps seeking and finding the Son, until she has *gathered and united* all into him. And the stopping on multiple material bearers of sonship also counts as *distribution* of the Spirit's gifts, the gifts it gives to the Son. On Staniloae's interpretation, the economic mission of the Son (the gathering of the community and the distribution of gifts) follows characteristically from the eternal procession of the Spirit from the Father to the Son. For even the unity and giving have an intratrinitarian root:

> [B]ecause the Holy Spirit proceeds from the Father and comes to rest in the Son, and therefore is not begotten like the Son, endless multiplication of the divinity is avoided, and a certain internal unity is achieved, for not only is the unity between Son and Spirit made manifest in this way, but that between the Father and the Son is also strengthened. The Spirit proceeding from the Father comes to rest in the Son who is begotten of the Father, and, like an arch, unites Father and Son in one embrace. . . . Thus a

---

57. Staniloae, "Trinitarian Relations," pp. 27-28.

58. This sentence applies to the Spirit a very similar sentence that Kathryn Tanner proposes in a christological context in *Jesus, Humanity and the Trinity*, p. 25, but I do not invoke her authority for its pneumatological application.

unity among the Persons is manifested which is distinct from their unity of essence. The third in the Trinity . . . represents the perfection of the unity of the many.[59]

We might add: The Spirit's *embrace* (a much better metaphor than the impersonal "arch") is not only a principle of unity, but the Spirit's personal *gift* to the Father and the Son, the *crowning, celebration, or rejoicing* ("perfection") of their unity. It is from this pattern that the temporal pattern takes its characteristic shape:

> The "rest" or "abiding" of the Spirit upon the Son or in the Son signifies not only the union of the one with the other in the order of eternity but also their union in the temporal order. The presence of Christ is always marked by the Spirit resting upon him, and the presence of the Spirit means the presence of Christ upon whom he rests.[60]

We see that preeminently in the resurrection, as the next chapter shows, where the Spirit crowns the unity of the Father and the Son by including human beings gratuitously within it.

What is crucial here is that the Father and the Son have not only a unity of their own that belongs to their essence, but that they also have a unity to *receive* as the gift of the Spirit. It is this *received* unity, the *koinonia* or communion of the Holy Spirit, that renders the life of the Trinity dynamic and allows for the inclusion of others within that life without distortion — deified persons. It is this *received* unity, with its characteristic receptivity or openness, that Barth closes up when he makes the bond between the Father and the Son of the Spirit's "essence" rather than of the Spirit's gift.[61] And it has everything to do with the saving effect of the Son's incarnate mission:

> For when the Son becomes human, he receives as human what he has as God.[62]

That paraphrases Athanasius:

> As human is He said to take what, as God, He ever had, that even such a grant of grace might reach to us. The gifts which come from God . . . doth He too Himself receive, that the human being, being united to Him may be

---

59. Staniloae, "Holy Spirit and Sobornicity," p. 23.
60. Staniloae, "Holy Spirit and Sobornicity," p. 24.
61. *CD* I/1, 479-80. For "deified persons," see Florensky, p. 38.
62. Staniloae, "Holy Spirit and Sobornicity," p. 21.

able to partake of them. Hence it is that the Lord says, "All things whatsoever Thou hast given me, I have given them."[63]

He receives this, furthermore, over the *course* of his life — since he receives *as a human being*. The assumption of humanity by the Word is the action of the whole Trinity: we *see* the whole Trinity in the Annunciation, but the assumption of humanity does not end there, it extends over Jesus's whole life as the Word acts in time. "The Word's assuming or bearing of [the effects of sin] in Christ means a fight with it, where success is not immediate but manifests itself only over the course of time." As Tanner says:

> The Incarnation is not, then, to be identified with one moment of Jesus' life, his birth, in contradistinction from his ministry, death and resurrection. . . . what is being assumed and the effects of that assumption vary over time. Jesus does not heal death until the Word assumes death when Jesus dies. . . . The cross saves because in it sin and death have been assumed by the one, the Word, who cannot be conquered by them. . . . Salvation occurs *in* a human life; that life is not incidental to salvation's achievement. Salvation is extended to us, moreover, only as the effects of incarnation come to be realized in Jesus' own life. . . . As the consequences of this identity [of the existence of God with a human being] unroll over the course of Jesus' human life, what humanity and divinity are capable of come to interpenetrate in an active way, through a style of life [*tropos hyparxeos*] that shows human inclinations in the process of being made over, made new, so as to produce a mode of existence that realizes on the human plane the mode of existence that defines the second Person of the Trinity.[64]

But this is not merely a Protestant notion; we find it so in Staniloae as well:

> If it was only at Pentecost that the Apostles fully recognized Christ as God, that was because it was only in the Ascension of Christ that the Spirit which rests upon him and shines forth from him as God was poured out upon him completely as human being.[65]

---

63. Athanasius, *Contra Arianos* 330 (first sentence), 435 (second two sentences). I owe these citations to Tanner, *Jesus, Humanity and the Trinity: A Brief Systematic Theology* (Minneapolis: Augsburg Fortress, 2001) p. 53.

64. Tanner, *Jesus, Humanity and the Trinity*, pp. 28-31. For *tropos hyparxeos*, see Gregory of Nyssa, *To Abblabius: On Not Three Gods* and John of Damascus, *The Orthodox Faith* 1:8 (Chase, p. 186).

65. Staniloae, "Trinitarian Relations," p. 24.

But we human beings receive these things differently from Christ on account of our finitude, and the differences finitude makes are multiple. First, our finite hypostases are divided and diverse, unlike the hypostasis of Christ, which is unified and fit for the purpose — although human diversity and particularity are not in themselves flaws. "Unlike Christ who simply is the Word, we come to Christ from a distance, by way of an external call." "Unlike what happened in Jesus, we are not constituted from the first as subjects by such gifts." Second, after the fall they are already marked by sin, and offer therefore resistance, unlike the relation of the Spirit and the Word, which displays unity of purpose. "Because it occurs after the fact of our existence with an already established character, [our] union with Christ requires tending in a way that humanity's assumption by the Son of God in Christ did not. Our union with Christ must be nurtured through the workings of the Spirit." After sin, the Spirit's gifts "come to us as already constituted persons in opposition to who we already are."[66]

John's formula takes care of both the requirement for particularity or non-abstraction, and the requirement for an intratrinitarian root, or non-reduction. The Spirit rests on the Son antecedently in the Trinity, and therefore the Spirit rests on the Son characteristically in the economy.

It will be noticed that while John of Damascus says "The Spirit rests on the Son," the thesis of this section is that the Spirit rests on the body of the Son. With that modification I mean no disagreement with John's formulation. I mean merely to *apply* it to the Spirit's work in the world. And I mean to apply it to the Spirit's work in the world *in such a way* as to *tie* my statement to one about what happens already in God's triune life. The Spirit rests on the *body* of the Son in the economy, *precisely because* the Spirit rests on the Son in the Trinity. I make this emphasis because it is in the economy that the twentieth-century problem arises, that the undivided work of the Trinity seems to get over-appropriated to the Son at the Spirit's expense. It is in the Spirit's relation to created things that a problem needs to be solved. According to three traditions, this is appropriate. In Eastern Orthodoxy, as is well known, the Spirit so transfigures matter that the whole world becomes a sacramental element, an occasion for offering and thanksgiving, for "the world was created as the 'matter,' the material of one all-embracing Eucharist."[67] In Catholicism, we have the compendious statement of Thomas Aquinas that "In [created] things, the motion which is from God seems to be attributed properly to the Holy Spirit."[68]

---

66. Kathryn Tanner, *Jesus, Humanity and the Trinity*, pp. 55, 57.

67. Alexander Schmemann, *For the Life of the World* (New York, N.Y.: National Student Christian Association, 1963), pp. 4-5.

68. Thomas Aquinas, *Summa contra gentiles* IV.20 (Turin and Rome: Marietti, 1961-67),

And in Protestantism, we have Karl Barth taking up the wording of Romans 8:11 (to which we shall recur at length in the next chapter): "That which the Gospel calls the Spirit dwells in mortal bodies."[69] The application of Gregory's formula in the economy ought to be illuminating rather than controversial.

In that the Spirit rests on the Son, it becomes manifest and worthy of belief that the Spirit befriends the body, turns matter into sacrament, distributes gifts, and incorporates diversity. Because in each one of those cases, the Spirit also rests on the Son. The Spirit rests on the body of the Son when it descends on the elements of baptism or Eucharist. The Spirit descends on the body of the Son when it bestows gifts on believers or gathers the church. Incarnation, church, sacrament, Christian are not *abstracted* from Christ (as Barth accused Schleiermacher of doing) — and they are not *reduced* to Christ (as Barth's critics accused Barth of doing). The work of the Spirit is not reduced to Christ, because the Spirit's gifts and recipients are both unpredictably diverse. The work of the Spirit is not abstracted from Christ, because the Spirit's object becomes multiply and diversely christoform. Ephrem the Syrian has put it incomparably:

> A royal portrait is painted with visible colours,
> and with oil that all can see is the hidden portrait of our
>   hidden King portrayed
> on those who have been signed . . .
> This oil is the dear friend of the Holy Spirit, it serves him,
> following him like a disciple. . . .
> the hidden seal of the Spirit is imprinted by oil on the bodies
> of those who are anointed in baptism: thus they are marked
>   in the baptismal mystery. . . .
> The face that gazes on a vessel filled with oil
> sees its reflection there, and he who gazes hard sets his spiritual
>   gaze thereon
> and sees in its symbols Christ. And as the beauty of Christ is manifold,
> so the olive's symbols are manifold.
> Christ has many facets, and the oil acts as a mirror to them all:
> from whatever angle I look at the oil, Christ looks out at me from it.[70]

#3571. For careful trinitarian commentary on this statement, see Bruce Marshall, *Trinity and Truth* (Cambridge: Cambridge University Press, 2000), pp. 113-14.

69. Barth, *Shorter Commentary on Romans* (London: SCM and Richmond: John Knox, 1959), p. 174.

70. Ephrem the Syrian, *Hymn on Virginity*, no. 7, in Brock, *Harp of the Spirit*, pp. 48-49, 51. The whole poem is relevant.

In Part II, I will consider how the Spirit rests on the Son in the New Testament narratives about Jesus. I consider commentary that works typologically to incorporate other (often earlier) narratives into that pattern, and liturgy that works typologically to incorporate the community and the material world into it.

Typology, of course, is a narrative device. It draws previous stories into later ones and current readers into earlier stories. And if Hans Frei is right about the difference between person and principle, the Spirit, if a person, cannot be reduced to a principle, because character is represented irreducibly in narrative. If the Spirit is a person, we must turn to narrative to identify her. And yet the Spirit is such, that the narratives *of* the Spirit are narratives *about* Jesus. It is to those narratives that we soon turn.

Is there anything the Spirit can do, that the Son can't do better? Yes, rest. The logic of the Spirit is not the logic of productivity, but the logic of superfluity, not the logic of work but the logic of Sabbath. The Spirit like the Sabbath sanctifies.

Just as the Spirit is superfluous in her own characteristic way, in her *tropos hyparxeos*, locating her superfluity, as we shall see, like ointment on the head of the Son or like a seed in the self-sufficient womb of Mary; so too she rests in her characteristic way, according to her own *tropos hyparxeos*, and in no way constrained by the word or the concept. So when the Spirit rests, she is as static as water, as contained as oil, and as passive as fire. The Spirit rests like the wind.

Is there anything the Spirit can do, that the Son can't do better? Yes, rest superfluously on the body of the Son: accompany the One Who has all love, and give gifts to the One who has no need. As Basil of Caesarea puts it:

> The Father's work is in no way imperfect, since He accomplishes all in all, nor is the Son's work deficient if it is not completed by the Spirit. The Father creates through His will alone and does not *need* the Son, yet chooses to work through the Son. Likewise the Son works as the Father's likeness, and needs no other co-operation, but He chooses to have his work completed through the Spirit.[71]

Later he asks: "You hold the Spirit in contempt because he is a gift?"[72] Or because she is superfluous?

71. Basil of Caesarea, *On the Holy Spirit* 16:38, trans. David Anderson (Crestwood, N.Y.: St. Vladimir's Seminary Press, 1980), p. 62; italics in original.
72. *On the Holy Spirit* 24:57, p. 89.

Because my purpose is to be suggestive and not exhaustive — the apparent exhaustion of the Spirit is part of the problem — I will not, could not pursue all the analogical instances that iconic New Testament scenes might generate, but turn now to four: Annunciation, Baptism, Transfiguration, and Resurrection, of which the last shall be first.

II   The Spirit Rests on the Body of the Son

1 Resurrection

"If the Spirit of the one who raised Jesus from the dead dwells in your mortal bodies"; or, the resurrection identifies the Persons, to whom the Spirit joins others

The Spirit rests on the Son in the body of the Crucified. In so doing the Spirit identifies all three Persons by the resurrection and opens their household, gratuitously, also to the Gentiles.

i. The Spirit rests on the Son in the resurrection and so identifies all three Persons by it

This Part depends upon a number of theses. I seek to render them plausible by coherence, or in use. The proof will be in the pudding.

New Testament narratives featuring Father, Son, and Spirit give us a glimpse into the intratrinitarian life and the inclusion of human beings within it. The most important is the resurrection of Jesus in Romans 8. In that passage, all three persons of the Trinity are identified by the resurrection. Not only that, but the participation of the human being in the resurrection is also identified as a participation in the triune life. A richer and more pregnant building up of terms would be difficult to imagine. As Calvin notes, Paul "describes God by a circumlocution, which suited his present purpose better than calling him simply by name."[1] To bring this out, I set it in short lines:

> If the *Spirit*
> of the *One Who raised*
> Christ Jesus from the dead

1. John Calvin on Rom. 8:11, *Commentary on the Epistle to the Romans,* trans. Francis Sibson (Philadelphia: J. Whetham, 1836, repr. LBS Archival Products, 1990), p. 173.

dwells in your mortal bodies,
you too shall rise from the dead (Rom. 8:11).

In the first clause of this complex sentence, the persons of the Trinity are named; in the second clause, a manner of human participation in the life of the Trinity — the resurrection — is specified. The Trinity, then, is the subject of the clause that identifies the precondition and the activator of what comes to pass, while the human being is marked out as the recipient, the one immediately affected, by what is done. This Trinity does not, however, appear as a single individual; for the if-clause refers explicitly to its three members and intimates that the action of the Trinity comes about in and through a complex interrelation that holds among the three. There is then something about their relations with one another that is reflected or manifested in their relation to the human beings that are *"also"* raised from the dead by the Spirit of the One who raised his own eternal Word. Thus the movement from protasis to apodosis does not reflect a simple fiat, but a movement of inclusion that takes the human being and sets it in the place — the relation to the Father or the identity before him — that is Christ's: this is the point made by the "also" of the second clause. Hence the threefold action of the Trinity produces at once an assimilation and an addition: the human person becomes an additional sharer in the life that the Father through the Spirit shares with Christ.[2]

There is something about their *internal* activity that reaches out to involve human beings. The movement from protasis to apodosis is one of causation not by brute efficiency, but by *inclusion*. If God is the One Who loves in freedom, or more specifically raises Jesus from the dead, then God can be and by the superfluity of the Spirit actually is the One who loves the human being *too* in freedom — unnecessarily, graciously, superfluously — the One Who by the Spirit needlessly raises human, mortal bodies *also*. The relation of clauses marks not a mere result, but a result *characteristic* of the Trinity and of the Spirit's role within it, because the Spirit assimilates other human beings to Christ, stamps or seals Christ's character upon them; and a result strictly *superfluous* to the Trinity, because the Spirit includes them within the trinitarian life without need and at some risk and therefore by grace. Resurrection leads to eternal life, according to the theory packed into this verse of Paul's, because resurrection participates in the Trinity's own eternity. Eternal life is not adventitious to the Spirit's saving work; rather, because the Spirit's saving work involves including human beings in the Triune life, it is a good internal rather than external to the event. Calvin adverts all too briefly to the way in which the

---

2. This paragraph has benefited from a paraphrase by Richard Norris of an earlier version.

passage portrays a great inclusion, a great opening out of the Trinity to take human beings in, when he says that the Spirit "absorbs" human mortality.[3]

As far as I can tell, stress on this verse as a trinitarian clue is almost novel in the last quarter of the twentieth century. It may be Robert Jenson's contribution to the history of exegesis to have written,

> The most remarkable trinitarian passage in the New Testament, one amounting to an entire theological system, is the eighth chapter of Paul's letter to Rome. Its conceptual and argumentative heart is verse 11: "If the Spirit of him who raised Jesus from the dead dwells in you, he who raised Christ Jesus from the dead will give life to your mortal bodies also through his Spirit which dwells in you." The subject phrase displays with the uttermost conceptual compression the precise structure we have called "the trinitarian logic": the *Spirit* is *"of* him *who* raised *Jesus."* And from the prepositional structure of this phrase, Paul then develops a rhetoric and argument which sweeps justification and the work of Christ and prayer and eschatology and ethics and predestination into one coherent understanding.[4]

Jenson's student David Yeago has made more of the passage, as, dependent on both of them, have I.[5] Also in the last quarter of the twentieth century, Sarah Coakley has made productive but different trinitarian use of Romans 8, as has Thomas Weinandy.[6] Three reasons present themselves for this new attention. First is the renewed attention to the Spirit that both Jenson's work and this book exemplify. Second, the nineteenth and twentieth centuries have been fascinated with the resurrection. If historical study has separated the historical Jesus, whose story ends with the crucifixion, from the Christ of faith, whose story begins with the faith of the disciples, then such a passage as Romans 8:11 becomes important in distinguishing the biblically narrated character from either of those. And third, Anglo-American analytic philoso-

3. Calvin on Rom. 8:11, p. 172.

4. Robert Jenson, *The Triune Identity* (Philadelphia: Fortress, 1982), p. 44.

5. Cf. David Yeago, "The Doctrine of the Trinity," in *The Faith of the Christian Church* (Columbia, S.C.: Lutheran Southern Theological Seminary, n.d.), pp. 103-31, esp. p. 119; Eugene F. Rogers, Jr., *Sexuality and the Christian Body: Their Way into the Triune God* (Oxford: Blackwell Publishers, 1999), pp. 220, 241, 252.

6. See Sarah Coakley, "The Trinity, Prayer, and Sexuality: A Neglected Nexus in the Fathers and Beyond," *Centro Pro Unione Bulletin* (Rome) 58 (2000): 13-17, and an earlier, more accessible version in the *Anglican Theological Review* 80 (1998): 223-32; both call attention to Origen's *De Oratione* I.3-6, translated in Rowan A. Greer, *Origen* (New York: Paulist Press, 1979). See too Thomas G. Weinandy, *The Father's Spirit of Sonship: Reconceiving the Trinity* (Edinburgh: T&T Clark, 1995), pp. 36-38.

phy — Strawson's *Individuals* — popularized "identity descriptions" of characters in the 1960s.[7] In those historical circumstances, a verse that promised to give identifying descriptions of all three trinitarian Persons by reference to the resurrection could hardly have escaped the notice of well-educated theological readers for long. Mark McIntosh puts it like this:

> St Paul understood the Spirit as the power of God which initiates the vindication of Jesus as Son of God by raising him from the dead (Rom. 8:4). The Holy Spirit is God presenting God's Word to the community and within the community, thus initiating the whole creation's response to this Word spoken in the events concerning Jesus. In this way, the despair and apparent dereliction of Jesus on the Cross are continually unfolding with new meaning in the life of the community. Early Christians connected Jesus' resurrection with the sending of the Spirit who would lead them into the truth of Jesus' words and deeds (John 14.26; 16.12-14); thus the community is initiated into the hidden depths of his relationship with the Father, and from that perspective they begin to think in new ways about Jesus' death. The painful distance that sin seemed to have pried open between the Father and the Beloved Son comes to be seen in a new light, as the outpouring in history of the eternal divine self-giving. The coming of the Spirit within the Christian community makes it possible, even necessary, for the community to participate in the mystery of Jesus' dying and rising, and so to interpret his relationship with the Father *from within* — precisely by becoming, as the Body of Christ, the living sign of God's embrace of all creation within the love of the Father and the Son in their Spirit.[8]

It may be that the pattern, exemplified in Romans 8:11, of identifying all three Persons by the resurrection of the Crucified, has pre-twentieth-century predecessors in art. Eleventh- or twelfth-century Byzantine images could depict the Trinity deliberating on human redemption, as in the Greek *Homilies of the Monk Jacobus,* in which the Trinity sends out and receives back the angel of the annunciation.[9] According to Gertrud Schiller, those become, by the beginning of the thirteenth century in the West, images of the Trinity in which the Father presents the Son on the cross, the two joined by a dove issu-

---

7. P. F. Strawson, *Individuals: An Essay in Descriptive Metaphysics* (London: Methuen, 1964).

8. Mark A. McIntosh, *Mystical Theology: The Integrity of Spirituality and Theology* (Oxford: Blackwell, 1998), p. 156.

9. Gertrud Schiller, *Iconography of Christian Art,* trans. Janet Seligman, 2 vols. (Greenwich, Conn.: New York Graphic Society Ltd., 1971), vol. 1, p. 9 and figs. 10-11. Cf. also pp. 10-12 and figs. 8-9.

ing from the Father's mouth and resting on the head of the Son.[10] Although canonical orthodox iconography would object to portrayals of the Father as a complete human being (rather than symbolized in, say, a hand), the earlier medieval depictions simply bring the Crucified into the Trinity, allowing the Father to remain divine. By the end of the fourteenth century, however, the Father begins to hold the Son in the same position as the Virgin does in a pietà. Although German art historians may call that image *"Not Gottes,"* which seems most often to refer to a patripassian "distress of the Father," it is not clear from the images that they go that far, and even the designation can refer to the passion of the Son.[11] The question is rather this: once an artist shows the Father with a human face, what expression is he to bear? Certainly he does not shed tears. Consider the Trinity of 1577-79 by El Greco in the Prado, or similar images by Dürer, Ribera, or Rubens.[12] The disadvantage of such images is that they call into question the Father's difference from human beings, not only in the anthropomorphism of the image, but also in paralleling him to the Virgin. The Father of the Son and the mother of the Son do not belong on the same level. But the advantage of the image is that the Trinity is depicted as not static but in act. One arresting painting from Germany about 1450 actually shows the Father lifting the Son — one hand under his right armpit, and one supporting his left elbow — out of a stone sarcophagus.[13] In that case the Father does not resemble the Virgin, although one worries that the Spirit merely decorates a transaction between Father and Son. None of the late medieval or early modern images I have examined make the Spirit remotely as prominent as Paul does, nor do they connect the general resurrection clearly to such an image. And yet one might regard the Father in such images as the one who receives or even raises, and the Spirit as the one who hovers over or witnesses to the crucified Son, the occasional bystanders contemplative and future participants in the shared resurrection.

Pre-twentieth-century commentators on Romans 8:11 have usually noted a

10. See, for instance, in an early 13th C. manuscript illustration from Troyes in Schiller, *Iconography,* vol. 1, pp. 9-12 and figure 4. See also vol. 1, figs. 4-16 and vol. 2, figs. 395 (Cross of Lothar), 409 (Christ on the Cross with Trinity, Portable Altar of Maritius), and 413-14.

11. Schiller, *Iconography,* vol. 2, p. 220, esp. n. 53. For examples, see vol. 2, figs. 768-97.

12. Schiller, *Iconography,* vol. 2, figs. 788-91.

13. By an unknown artist, at the Städtisches Museum in Schwäbisch Gmünd, reproduced here, fig. 8, and in Schiller, *Iconography,* fig. 776, and described on p. 221. Cf. also the painting by Hans Baldung Grien in the National Gallery (London), in which the Father lifts the Son out of the tomb — in the presence of Mary and John. Schiller's description of the Father as "mourning" with Mary and John seems unnecessary. The Father's presence raising Jesus arguably breaks in from a plane different from the mourners', while his face arguably expresses purpose. (Schiller, *Iconongraphy,* vol. 2, fig. 778, described pp. 221-22.)

different feature of the verse, and one that will also occupy our attention later: that the Spirit comes to rest upon, or "dwells in" a human body. Barth puts it baldly: "That which the Gospel calls the Spirit dwells in mortal bodies."[14]

Paul seems to have rival notions about the body in the surrounding context. In this verse, the body seems to be something the Spirit can assimilate, assume, catch up into the triune life. The assimilative pattern may be of a piece with the new Adam material from Chapter 5, according to which the Spirit breathes life into the new Adam at the Resurrection, as the Spirit breathed life into the old Adam at creation. The pattern is assimilative because the Spirit brings the new Adam into the trinitarian life.

But another pattern interrupts, one in which the Spirit of life and the body of death are at odds. And it is this pattern, with its simple binarisms, that has mostly fascinated interpreters in the history of exegesis. So Chrysostom passes over the sublime identification of the persons of the Trinity by the resurrection, in order to devote five columns to a tirade against drunkenness. Ambrosiaster reduces verse 11 to verse 10: "Paul repeats here what he has just said," namely "dead in the body, alive in the Spirit." Luther weaves together love of money and fear of death. Barth turns contrast to paradox: "The Spirit is rather the altogether restless death of the body, and as such also its altogether restless life," whatever that means.[15] Certainly these interpreters have the weight of the immediate context on their side. Closely surrounding verses revel in flesh-spirit, death-life, sin-righteousness dualisms.

Yet interpreters could do better. By verse 14 the assimilative pattern, begun in verses 10 and 11 in the contemplation of the Trinity, comes to predominate. Human beings become sons of God; the creation groans in travail; Gentiles await the redemption of their bodies. Some interpreters see a new intervention in verse 11 and pursue it.

Thus interpreters have not missed altogether the implications for the identities of the trinitarian Persons.

Irenaeus of Lyons, writing in the 180s, already anticipates the nineteenth- and twentieth-century problems about the identity of Jesus. In the nineteenth century, the problem about the identity of Jesus was this: that the one who

14. Barth, *Shorter Commentary on Romans* (London: SCM and Richmond: John Knox, 1959), p. 174.

15. John Chrysostom, *The Epistle to the Romans,* trans. J. B. Morris and W. H. Simcox, NPNF 11 (repr. Grand Rapids, Mich.: Eerdmans, 1980), Homily 13, pp. 436-38; Ambrosiaster, *Commentary on Paul's Epistles,* CSEL 81:269, translated in Gerald Bray, ed., *Ancient Christian Commentary on Scripture,* New Testament vol. 6, *Romans* (Downers Grove, Ill.: InterVarsity, 1998), p. 213; Karl Barth, *Epistle to the Romans,* 6th rev. ed., trans. Edwin C. Hoskyns (London and New York: Oxford, 1933), p. 289.

was crucified could be the object of historical research, the "Jesus of history," while the one who was raised could be the object only of belief, the "Christ of faith." New Testament research tended to enforce a change of narrative subject, according to which one character, Jesus, died, to be mysteriously replaced with another set of characters, the disciples, so that Jesus was raised into the faith of the disciples. In the twentieth century, Karl Barth and Hans Frei (with Martin Kähler before them) pointed out that the change of character lost the biblical figure, whose narrative depiction required that the one who was crucified be raised. Thus Frei's book about that narrative logic was called *The Identity of Jesus Christ*.[16] Irenaeus foresees this problem already in the 180s, and adverts to it precisely on the occasion of Romans 8:11, taking as definitive that Jesus is the dead one raised. What Bultmann's idiom treats as something that can be considered only independently, Irenaeus's idiom treats as something that can be considered only integrally. Irenaeus paraphrases the verse: "Do not err . . . : Jesus Christ . . . is one and the same, who did by suffering reconcile us to God, and rose from the dead."[17] Paul, he writes, "knew nothing of the Christ who flew away from Jesus, nor did he of the Saviour above."[18] Although the opponents are different, this is quite similar to the argument that Hans Frei would make almost exactly 1800 years later.

Hilary of Poitiers, writing around 360, uses the verse to argue for the integral identity of the Spirit.[19] The Spirit of God and the Spirit of Christ are the same Spirit, not two, and therefore it is none other than the Spirit of God that dwells in Christians:

> Separate, O heretic, the Spirit of Christ from the Spirit of God, and the Spirit of Christ raised from the dead from the Spirit of God Which raises Christ from the dead![20]

That is a more sophisticated exclamation than may at first appear. It is no mere counting game, but packs in several implications. The Spirit of the Raiser and the Spirit of the Raised are the same Spirit. By sharing a Spirit, the Raiser and the Raised are in communion. The Raiser and the Raised are one God, that is, their relation is internal, not external to one another. The Raiser

16. Hans W. Frei, *The Identity of Jesus Christ* (Philadelphia: Fortress Press, 1974).

17. Irenaeus of Lyons, *Adv. Haereses* 3.16.9, ANF 1, p. 444.

18. *Adv. Haereses* 3.16.9, ANF 1, p. 443.

19. So too Ambrose of Milan in 381, *De Spiritu Sancto* I.4.56, in *Theological and Dogmatic Works*, trans. Roy J. Deferrari, Fathers of the Church 44 (Washington, D.C.: Catholic University of America Press, 1963).

20. Hilary of Poitiers, *De Trinitate* 7.21, in NPNF, 2d series, vol. 9.

and the Raised are shown to be in relation by the resurrection. It is the Spirit that characteristically shows or manifests this.

> Though the Spirit of Christ is in us, yet His Spirit is also in us Who raised Christ from the dead, and He Who raised Christ from the dead shall quicken our mortal bodies also on account of His Spirit that dwelleth in us.[21]

The resurrection of other human beings too, on this account, involves multiple indwellings: the Spirit of Christ is in us; the Spirit of the one who raised Christ is in us; the Spirit who quickens is in us. Hilary puts the matter more cautiously, or paradoxically: "This is no joint indwelling, it is one indwelling: yet an indwelling under the mysterious semblance of a joint indwelling."[22] That is, on account of the Spirit, we take part in the relation between the Raiser and the Raised. By a complex, serial, incremental process of statement and restatement, Hilary reproduces, expands, and to some extent analyzes the double pattern of trinitarian relation and human inclusion. The inclusion of the Spirit of the Raiser and of the Raised within the human becomes the inclusion of the human within God. Nothing makes the resurrection work except the assumption of the human into the trinitarian life: "the Spirit Which is in us cannot but be the Spirit of God,"[23] where "the Spirit is in us" means "we are in God."

Diodorus of Tarsus, who died around 392, uses the verse to resist the reduction of the Spirit to God's "power," and to identify the Father, by implication, as the one whose household the Christian joins. "Having already mentioned the Spirit of Christ," Diodorus notes, "Paul refers to him once more, saying 'the Spirit of him who raised Jesus from the dead dwells in you.' By saying that the Spirit of Christ is also the Spirit of the Father, Paul teaches wisely that from the Son the Spirit is nothing other than divine like the Father and that their power is one, because they share the same essence as the Father." Already here the Spirit becomes an occasion to talk about, first of all, the participation of the Son and the Spirit in the Father's godhead — so that the participation of the human being in their power becomes possible as joining their community. It is not so long before Paul will identify this community as a household: the Spirit becomes the one who makes sons (v. 14), the Spirit of adoption, the one who cries *Abba*, "Father," on our behalf (v. 15), making us "children of God" and "heirs" (v. 17). It is not too soon, therefore, to see

---

21. Hilary of Poitiers, *De Trinitate* 7.21.
22. Hilary of Poitiers, *De Trinitate* 7.27.
23. Hilary of Poitiers, *De Trinitate* 7.21.

household metaphors as underlying Diodorus's ontology already in verse 11: as the Spirit takes up housekeeping (οἰκεῖ) in the human being, so the human being begins to share in the household "goods" or "riches" (οὐσία) of the Father: strictly, the divinity here is not "the Father's" alone (as if Diodorus had written τοῦ πατροῦ), it is "paternal" (πατρικός): it belongs, as Jesus put it, to his Father's *house*. So too a little later Gennadius of Constantinople (d. 471) would explicate the passage in terms of the *koinonia* that Christ has with the dead.[24]

By the time of Aquinas, the Western commentarial tradition has accumulated intertextual biblical references at this point, references far removed from Paul's context. They identify God as one whose hallmark is to be involved so deeply in human mortality and sin as to raise human beings from the dead. Immediately Aquinas quotes Psalm 40:11, "You, Lord, have mercy on me, and raise me up," and Acts 3:15, "this one God raised up." But this power is again not the power of just any god, because it is not the Father's *unshared*. Christ and the Father share "the same power," and Christ himself rose by his own power *(propria virtute)*. Nevertheless something is to be gained by Christ's reception of the resurrection from the Father: The *exercise* of raw power is not joinable, because unlike Christ human beings do not have that power as their *proprium:* but the *reception* of power is joinable, "because what God the Father did in Christ, he does also in us."[25] Because Christ can also receive the Spirit, Aquinas implies, we can become the Spirit's receptacles, "according to the dignity that our bodies possess such that they become receptacles of the Holy Spirit." It is the pattern, the narrative pattern, or *taxis*, that is shareable.

That is not mere trinitarian theory, high, remote, and abstract. Commentators associate the passage with the practice and water of baptism. So Chrysostom, after he first introduces the verse, declares: "But this has been done in the Font. It [the body] has therefore had first its crucifixion and burial, and then been raised. This has also happened with the Lord's body."[26] Irenaeus too treats baptism, in the passage we considered earlier: Jesus must be the same one who died and was raised, for a liturgical reason: believers are baptized into his death, in order to be raised into his life.[27] In a possibly related metaphor, Irenaeus insists against simple dualisms that "the flesh is not

24. Both passages appear in Karl Staab, *Pauluskommentare aus der griechischen Kirche aus Katenenhandschriften gesammelt* (Münster: Aschendorff, 1933), pp. 92, 377.

25. Thomas Aquinas, *In Romanos* 6:11, in *Super epistolas S. Pauli lectura*, 8th rev. ed., ed. Raphael Cai (Turin: Marietti, 1953), #630.

26. Chrysostom, *Epistle to the Romans*, Homily 13, in NPNF 11, p. 436.

27. Irenaeus of Lyons, *Adv. Haereses* 3.16.9, ANF 1, p. 444.

destitute . . . but their whole body partakes of life," as a sponge partakes of water. "And therefore, since the Lord has power to infuse life into what He has fashioned, and since the flesh is capable of being quickened, what remains to prevent its participating in incorruption, which is a blissful and never-ending life granted by God."[28] In one of the more extended discussions in the history of exegesis, Irenaeus returns to the verse six times over eight chapters in *Adversus Haereses,* all to the point that it is the mortal body that the Spirit does not finally contrast with but assimilates or grafts into the trinitarian life.[29] The Spirit, you might say, *befriends* the body in baptism. Augustine has the most compact and profound statement combining resurrection, baptism, moral change, and the morning of the new creation. Augustine (in a formulation he might have improved from his mentor Ambrose) puts even the resurrection in terms of the Spirit on water:

> In the morning I shall stand and shall see my God, . . . who also will quicken our mortal bodies by the Spirit that dwells in us, because in mercy he was moving over our lightless and restless inner deep.[30]

Rowan Williams (commenting on von Balthasar) describes the role of the Spirit in the resurrection as one of overcoming the distance death causes between creature and Creator by her intratrinitarian overcoming of the distance between the dead Jesus and the Father:

> Our distance from God is itself taken into God, finds place in God; by the Spirit of adoption we enter the relation between Father and Son, the relation of exchange and mutuality. In the Incarnation, God distances himself from himself: the divine, intra-trinitarian love is enacted and realized in the world by the descent of Christ into Hell. And the separation between Father and Son is bridged by the Spirit. . . . The inconceivable self-emptying of God in the events of Good Friday and Holy Saturday is no arbitrary expression of the nature of God: this is what the life of the Trinity is, translated into the world. "God causes God to go into abandonment by God while accompanying him on the way with his Spirit. The Son can go into the estrangement from God of hell, because he understands his way as an expres-

---

28. Irenaeus, *Adv. haereses* 5.3.3, ANF 1:5329-30.

29. Irenaeus, *Adv. haereses* 5.3-10.

30. Augustine, *Confessions* 13.14.15, in Library of Christian Classics, ed. and trans. Albert C. Outler (Philadelphia: Westminster, 1955), p. 308. Compare Ambrose, *De Spiritu Sancto* 2.31-32, who follows his quotation of Rom. 8:11 with the question, "Who indeed can doubt that the Holy Spirit quickens all things, since he, too, . . . is the Creator of all things, . . . for even in the beginning of creation the Spirit moved over the waters?"

sion of love for the Father and he can give to his love the character of obedience to such a degree that in it he experiences the complete godlessness of lost man."[31]

In Barth too the crucifixion is "to be salvaged only by God's freedom to be Spirit, to resurrect Jesus. . . . The Resurrection, indeed, is not simply the verdict of the Father, but the verdict of the *Spirit*," because the Spirit presents the relation of Father and Son "precisely as a relation which is not closed or fixed, but one into which the human world may be brought."[32]

In that the Holy Spirit witnesses and celebrates the love within the Trinity between Father and Son, it can take human beings up also into that office in the created world, so that their chief end becomes "to glorify God and enjoy God forever." The intratrinitarian witness of the Holy Spirit to the love between the Father and the Son enables the victory of love over death in the resurrection.[33] When the Father "gives life to our mortal bodies also through the Spirit that dwells in us," we partake of the Spirit's proper office of celebrating the love of the Father for the Son and become guests at the wedding of the Lamb, for "the kingdom of heaven is like a Father who gave a wedding feast for his son."[34]

ii. The Spirit gives to Gentiles in the Son what Jews keep in the Messiah (against supersessionism)

Recent exegesis of Romans is not much interested in the trinitarian relations of the Son and the Spirit as in the social and eschatological relations of Jews and Gentiles. But the two topics are related, because according to Paul the mission of the Son was to the Jews, while the result of his forbearance was the coming in of the Gentiles: and that surprising reversal was the work of the Spirit.

Interpreters after Stendahl have stressed that Paul does not in fact write about human beings in the abstract, but about Jews and Gentiles. It is crucial

---

31. Rowan Williams, "Barth on the Triune God," in *Karl Barth: Studies of His Theological Method,* ed. Stephen W. Sykes (Oxford: Clarendon, 1979), pp. 145-93; here, p. 177, commenting on Hans von Balthasar, *Herrlichkeit,* 3 vols. in 7 (Einsiedeln, Switzerland: Johannes-Verlag, 1961-69), vol. III.2.2, pp. 367-69 and 196-200, and citing von Balthasar, *Elucidations,* trans. John Riches (San Francisco: Ignatius Press, 1998), p. 51.

32. Williams, "Barth on the Triune God," pp. 182-83, citing Barth, *Church Dogmatics* IV/1, 306-9 and 919ff.

33. Cf. Yeago, "The Doctrine of the Trinity," pp. 103-31, esp. p. 119; also Robert Jenson, "The Trinitarian Logic and Experience," pp. 21-55.

34. Matt. 22:2. Cf. Rogers, *Sexuality and the Christian Body,* pp. 196-204, 249-56, 265-68.

to ask at every stage of Paul's argument which group he is talking about. That procedure has proved immensely fruitful in chapters of Romans that mention Jews and Gentiles together, most of all in Romans 9–11. Its fruitfulness elsewhere depends on its application also to other chapters, like Romans 8, which *seem*, to interpreters unversed in Paul's distinctions, most congenial to the traditional distinctions of human and Christian instead of Jew and Gentile. But what difference does it make if we apply the Jew/Gentile distinction to Romans 8? What would it say about the identification of the Persons by the resurrection, and about the role of the Spirit?

The question once posed is easy to answer. Romans 8 is talking about Gentiles.[35] Even if, more modestly, Romans 8 is talking about all human beings, it is not talking about an abstraction, but about the Gentile majority of humanity taken for humanity as a whole, because the human beings described in Romans are constructed not with Jewish characteristics, but with Gentile characteristics. This interpretation will seem strange to many readers, including those who are used to seeing the Jew/Gentile distinction at work in other places in Paul's letter. But the strangeness itself need come as no surprise. "One alarming aspect of the business of interpretation," observes Frank Kermode, "is that by introducing new sense into part of the text you affect the interpretation of the whole."[36] In order to argue that Romans 8 is not a part of the whole, one would have to argue that Paul has changed his audience and his topic at once and without saying so. In the larger context, Paul is trying to answer what we might call the Gentile question: Why are the Gentiles coming now, and without circumcision, to worship the God of Israel? In the narrower context, critics must answer what we might call the anthropological question. If Paul is talking about human beings as a whole and in the abstract, why do they have Gentile characteristics? At best, Paul is talking about a *differentiated unity* of Jews and Gentiles when he talks about human beings; at least, Paul is allowing his views of a Gentile majority of humanity to construct his view of a human nature out of relation to the God of Israel. The second construction may be conscious and deliberate — especially if Paul gives Adam some Gentile characteristics — or it may be unconscious and implicit.[37] Even Enlight-

---

35. See most recently Runar M. Thorsteinsson, *Paul's Interlocutor in Romans 2: Function and Identity in the Context of Ancient Epistolography* (Stockholm: Almqvist & Wiksell International, 2003).

36. Frank Kermode, *The Sense of an Ending: Studies in the Theory of Fiction: With a New Epilogue* (Oxford: Oxford University Press, 2000), p. 63.

37. Adam is not circumcised and does not have Torah; but he is in relation with God and the ancestor of the Jews (and the Gentiles). So he is a protean figure who gets used in different ways for different rhetorical purposes. If for Paul Abraham is the first Jew, then it would seem to fol-

enment anthropology constructs human nature on a model, whether the model is Rousseau's ideal savage or Kant's rational Aryan. Interpretations of Romans that attend to the Jew/Gentile distinction raise the question, what is Paul's conscious or unconscious model for the human beings in Chapter 8?

In several places, we can see more than one tendency in Paul's thinking. There is both a tendency to construct an "all" as a differentiated unity of Jews and Gentiles, and a tendency to turn Jews' ethnic stereotypes of Gentiles against Jews themselves — to say that Jews do what Gentiles do. The two tendencies co-incide to render Paul's construction of humanity doubly "gentilified." First, he tends, perhaps unconsciously, to construct the *anthropos* as a narrated character, rather than a philosophical abstraction, and to characterize that one with Gentile features. Second, even in the differentiated unity he tends, this time quite insistently, to extend Gentile characteristics also to Jews. It is the direction that is fascinating. Although Paul insists that (as a matter of theological priority and divine intention) Christ comes, and Paul preaches, "to the Jew first and also to the Greek," Paul nevertheless reverses that movement in describing both the contingent *need* for the Gospel and its concrete working out. So in Romans 1, Paul describes Gentile sinfulness and then assimilates an *anthropos* to it: "you, O *anthrope*, whoever you are, . . . are doing the very same things" (2:1), with the extreme rhetorical force of the listener caught in a trap.[38]

Paul's speech in character at Romans 7:13-25 is also made with Gentile characterization:[39] either he is speaking as a Gentile in solidarity with his audience, or he is speaking as a Jew who is "also" afflicted with Gentile-like weakness of will. This "also" is the "also" of Gentile assimilation. It is the same pattern — the same surprising and mysterious pattern — as that of 9:30, "that the Gentiles who did not pursue righteousness have attained it, . . . but that Israel who pursued righteousness . . . did not succeed." If "there is no distinction between Jew and Greek," that is because of the assimilation of the Jew to the Greek in respect of Gentile sin, and the assimilation of the Greek to the

---

low that Adam counts as a Gentile; but these things do not always follow. In halakhic cases, for example, the construction of Adam is more a literary or legal than a logical matter. See Raphael Loewe, "Potentialities and Limitations of Universalism in Halakah," in *Studies in Rationalism, Judaism, and Universalism in Memory of Leon Roth*, ed. Raphael Loewe (London: Routledge & Kegan Paul and New York: The Humanities Press, 1966), pp. 115-50, esp. 126-32.

38. This is true no matter how you identify the target in 2:1, whether Jew or judaizing prose-lyte, and whether you think the figure in 2:17 ("you call yourself a Jew") is the same or different. Stowers thinks the figure in 2:1 is a judaizing proselyte under the influence of a Jewish teacher in 2:17; Thorsteinsson thinks the figures in 2:1 and 2:17 and into Ch. 7 are the same, a judaizing proselyte.

39. See Thorsteinsson, *Paul's Interlocutor*, on Rom. 7 and 8 as to and about Gentiles.

Jew in respect of God's mercy. "For God has consigned all human beings to disobedience, that he might have mercy upon all" (11:32). That is, the differentiated unity of Jews and Gentiles is assimilated to Gentiles in their disobedience, and to Jews in their reception of mercy.

If this narrative pattern were a philosophical anthropology it would be predictable; but it shows the reversals and surprises of a story, so that the writer of Ephesians persistently calls it a "mystery." "When you read this you can perceive my insight into the mystery of Christ . . . that is, how the Gentiles are fellow heirs, members of the same body, and partakers of the promise in Christ Jesus through the gospel" (Eph. 3:4, 6). The author of Ephesians both distinguishes a "we" group from "the Gentiles," and assimilates the two. He portrays the letter's "we" group with such Gentile characteristics that the "we" group becomes also "by nature children of wrath, *like the rest of humankind*," i.e., like Gentiles (2:4). Like Paul, he distinguishes in order to unite. Afterwards, "real" Gentiles have to be singled out as "you Gentiles in the flesh," to distinguish them from human beings assimilated to Gentiles by a retrospective humility, a sinfulness revealed by the Gospel, and a solidarity with sinners formed on Christ's own. The writer of Ephesians models that solidarity when he identifies himself as "I, Paul, a prisoner for Jesus Christ on behalf of you Gentiles" (3:1). Indeed, "on behalf of you Gentiles" says it all. The pronoun "you" marks the penultimate separation; the preposition "on behalf of" marks the solidarity. A human unity is constructed backward from the "new human being," Christ, "in place of the two" (2:15). The two are Jews and Gentiles. In sharp contrast with Christian supersessionism, the community constructed out of the "new human being" has Gentile characteristics (such as wrath) in its past and life with the God of Israel *(koinonia)* in its future.[40] The writers of both Romans and Ephesians tend to appropriate the life with the God of Israel to the Spirit of life, who founds *koinonia*: "you also are built into it for a dwelling place of God in the Spirit" (2:22).

In the narrower context, the Gentiles are the ones who have been condemned (Romans 8:1 answering the wrath of 1:18) and who are subject to "the law of sin and death" (8:2, answering the decree of 1:32). Paul, in describing himself as subject to sin and death in Chapter 7, is speaking in character. Gentiles are by God's decree those who "deserve to die" (1:32), and God has in fact given Gentiles up to non-procreative desires so that they will die out

---

40. This is significantly different in its use of terms, and reversed in direction, from Barth's doctrine of Israel in *Church Dogmatics* II/2, where despite qualifications and disclaimers Barth identifies "the Synagogue" with wrath and the almost entirely Gentile church with the future. For Paul, Israel never ceases to be the future. For more on this complex topic, see Eugene F. Rogers, Jr., *Sexuality and the Christian Body* (Oxford: Blackwell Publishers, 1999), pp. 140-92.

(1:27). The writer of Ephesians has understood the peculiar mortality that Pauline thinking ascribes to Gentiles when he calls them "by nature children of wrath" (Eph. 2:3, cf. Rom. 1:18). This mortality of the Gentiles is *strictly appropriate* to their defining sin of idol worship, in which they "exchanged the glory of the immortal God for images resembling a mortal human being" (Rom. 1:23). Those who worship the mortal *become* mortal "in their own persons" (1:27). It is Gentiles who exemplify what Paul means by "flesh" in the negative: those are the sins compendiously described in Romans 1:18-32. It is the Gentiles whom Paul describes as constitutionally incapable of observing Torah: "the mind that is set on the flesh . . . does not submit to God's law, indeed it cannot; and those who are in the flesh cannot please God" (8:7-8). It is Gentiles who in their inability to observe Torah resemble slaves (8:15),[41] because they receive their punishment in their bodies (1:27, 8:23).

This is not universal metaphysics. *This* mortality is a Gentile characteristic. It is mortality born of *corruptibility;* the idol a Gentile worships is φθαρτός, mortal in the specific sense of being corruptible, from the verb φθείρω, which can mean to ruin, seduce.[42] Since the chief characteristic of Gentiles is that they are labile, seducible, overly sexual, this fits in exactly with the portrait of sexual behavior in excess of nature (παρὰ φύσιν) described in Romans 1:24-27. This is Gentile stereotype, exaggerated, perhaps, for the purpose of showing God's mercy. It is the Gentiles who are "ungodly" (ἀσέβειαν, 1:18) in the precise sense of being out of relation to the God of Israel, in having no true God of their own, but only false ones. It is Gentiles whose "bodies are dead because of sin" (8:10), according to the description and decree of Chapter 1. It is therefore the Gentiles who need to receive the Spirit of life who is the Spirit of God. It is the Gentiles who need to receive the Spirit of adoption (8:23), as ones not already in relation to the God of Israel, as not those "to whom belong the sonship" (9:4 — υἱοθεσία in both cases). Gentiles are the ones who do not yet possess, but must take on, the identity of sons (children with rights of inheritance, 8:16-17), and they are the ones who must learn to call God "Abba" (Gal. 4:6), which the Spirit teaches them in killing off their prior identity (Rom. 8:13). It is Gentiles who need the Spirit to come to dwell in their mortal bodies, so that they might dwell in the household of God,

41. When Paul in Galatians 4 speaks of Jews as enslaved to the law, that is not a contrast case. Paul is not distinguishing enslavement as a Jewish characteristic, but painting Jews for complex rhetorical purposes as Gentiles, assimilating children to slaves.

42. So too in I Thess. 4:3-5 Paul parallels lability and lack of relation to the true God as Gentile characteristics. See recently Kathy L. Gaca, *The Making of Fornication: Eros, Ethics, and Political Reform in Greek Philosophy and Early Christianity* (Berkeley: University of California Press, 2003).

where Jews already belong. The Gentile worshipper of a mortal human being (φθαρτοῦ ἀνθρώπου) of 1:23 has one of the mortal bodies (θνήτα σώματα) of 8:11; but the one who has the Spirit of Christ (the immortal human being) belongs to him (8:9), and it is thus Gentiles who await "adoption as sons, the redemption of our bodies" (8:23).

You might object that Chapter 8 takes up themes not only from Chapter 1, where the Jew/Gentile distinction is clear, but also from Chapter 5, which introduces the Adam/Christ typology, and displays Paul's closest approximation to a genuinely universal anthropology. The fact remains, however, that Paul is talking to Gentiles about what will happen to them. The primary characterizations of the human beings in Chapter 8 are Gentile characterizations, and nothing suggests that they are Jews. Even in Chapter 5, Paul suggests that death reigned "from Adam to Moses," a historical rather than universal designation — a designation in terms not of universal history, but of the history of Israel. "Paul emphasizes that the one/all analogy works, but works only for the period between Adam and the giving of the law (5:13-14)."[43] By Chapter 8, furthermore, Paul has relegated Chapter 5 to background: what is in the foreground here is the Spirit of adoption teaching Gentiles to say *Abba* — something that Jews, who already call the God of Israel "father," do not need to learn.[44] The use of that background here is this: The God of Israel's Messiah, who is to continue the trajectory of God's salvation — God's seminal *pneuma* — that ran from Adam through Abraham to Moses, has done something surprising. The reversal of Adam's sin involves *not* grasping divinity. Not grasping divinity means obedience unto death. Obedience unto death means *not* bringing the eschaton to completion too soon with the immediate salvation of the Jews. Not yet bringing the eschaton to completion for the Jews involves the planned or adventitious salvation of the Gentiles. In short: The reversal of Adam leads, by a number of switchbacks, not to a universal salvation, but to a differentiated salvation, a salvation of Gentiles and Jews.

That many Gentiles follow Christ before all Israel does is not the only thing about God's timing that Paul struggles to understand. Death before Christ's return is another. Both phenomena seem premature; both indicate delay in what Paul expects; both are called a "mystery"; and in both cases he reaches for a similar solution. He attributes the delay to a surprising gift of the Spirit. His exclamations might almost be translated, *O felix dilatio!*

43. Stanley Stowers, *A Rereading of Romans: Justice, Jews, and Gentiles* (New Haven and London: Yale University Press, 1994), pp. 38-39.

44. Also in Galatians 4 the Spirit of adoption enables inheriting sons to cry "Abba" (v. 6). If Galatians 4 seems to undermine Jewish claims to inheritance, that is again not to characterize Jews as disinherited, but a rhetoric of solidarity with Gentiles.

Just as Paul's whole vocation and theology have been transformed by his perception of the "mystery," that the Spirit of life in Christ Jesus is being poured out on the Gentiles, so his views of Adam and of death are being transformed, too. Adam can be read in two ways: as the first genealogical father of Israel, the one to whom Israel is traced back, and therefore proto-Jewish; and as the first sinner, the one who not only disobeyed the God of Israel, but tried to achieve divinity for himself, and therefore the first idolater, a proto-Gentile.[45] Without ascribing to Paul the later Western Christian doctrine of original sin, we can see Paul plying a *number* of decline narratives derived from Genesis, of which Adam's disobedience is merely or signally the first instance. Adam, Cain, the builders of Babel, those who ignore Noah, the inhabitants of Sodom all stand in the background. Romans 1 does not mention Adam, and seems to have more in common with a decline narrative centered on the contrast between Abraham's hospitality to the three visitors and the Sodomites' hostility to them. But echoes of Genesis 1 assimilate the earlier decline narrative with the later one, and tend to paint Adam with the characteristics of a proto-Gentile rather than those of a proto-Jew, in conformity with Adam's appearance in Romans 5. After all, Adam is not circumcised and does not observe Torah. Paul is reading backwards from his experience. Because Christ's work both so surprisingly reverses Gentile idolatry, while it necessarily reverses Adam's disobedience, Paul allows his new experience with Gentiles to illuminate his portrayal of Adam.

Something similar happens with the death that came by Adam. Paul does not tell us about his views on the resurrection of the Jews, except to say that "All Israel will be saved," because he is not concerned with that; given his audience and his theme, he expresses his great amazement that resurrection will come to Gentiles, too, since they so surprisingly enjoy the Spirit of life in their mortal bodies. One might assume that Jews are already resurrectible, if there is to be a resurrection: but what's at stake in Romans is the participation of the Gentiles in the eschaton, that is, the resurrection of Gentiles, which is to say, of the dead, the really dead.

Thus "some will ask, 'how are the dead raised? With what kind of body do they come?'" (I Cor. 15:35). Now, if Paul knows two kinds of bodies, circumcised and uncircumcised, this is a reasonable question. Will Gentiles come

---

45. See Loewe, "Potentialities and Limitations." You might object that Adam's sin is unlike Gentile sin in that Adam transgresses a specific commandment known to him. But Paul argues extensively in Romans 1 that the ignorance of the Gentiles is not exculpatory but culpable, because in their idolatry they have "detained" a truth known to them. We are in a realm of degrees and kinds of knowledge. Be that as it may, Adam's sin resembles Gentile idolatry in that both carry the punishment of death.

into final fellowship with the God of Israel as identifiably Gentiles, or do they have to be circumcised? Paul rejects the question about which kind of body, exclaiming "You foolish man!" and disambiguates the implicit contrast between circumcised and uncircumcised bodies with one about flesh and spirit. The fleshly body is perishable, dishonorable, weak, physical, and of dust; the spiritual body is imperishable, glorious, powerful, spiritual, and of heaven. "Lo, I tell you a mystery," he says. "Mystery" always echoes the mystery of Gentile inclusion for Paul. And so the people who have all been assimilated to Gentiles are now all assimilated to Jews. "We shall *all* be changed" (I Cor. 15:51) — again a differentiated unity of those who "sleep" and those who do not, and a unity elsewhere tending to be resolved as those who are circumcised and those who are not. In that change, Paul responds to the original question: then the difference between circumcised and uncircumcised — "with what kind of body do they come" — will be "swallowed up in victory" (15:54).

The circumcised and the uncircumcised will all be resurrected, and whether that involves more change for the Gentiles and less change for the Jews will not matter, because there will be no law to make the distinction, and therefore no power of sin, and therefore no sting of death (15:56).[46] Both the Jews' "spirit of stupor" in Romans 11:7 and the "falling asleep" of those who die early in I Corinthians 15:20 defeat Paul's expectation about God's plan. They cause him the same kind of conceptual difficulty, so that it should come as no surprise if he reaches for the same kind of solution. Both the reawakening of those who have died, and recognition of Jesus as Messiah by the Jews await a trinitarian resolution: both lie in the hands of the Father whose will is certain; both await the delayed completion of Christ's mission; and both occur by the Spirit of filial inheritance.

The bizarre detour of the plot described in Romans 11 as stumbling without falling, the delay of the pacesetter, the grafting of the wild branches onto the domestic olive tree — a detour so strange that Paul can call it "contrary to nature" — is also here at work. In John, "salvation is *from* the Jews," and Paul

---

46. I have not been able to find a clear answer to the question whether Paul could have considered a differentiated resurrection among Jews and Gentiles, but cf. Jon Levenson, "Resurrection in the Torah," *Reflections* 6 (2003): 2-29. George Foot Moore, *Judaism*, 3 vols. (Cambridge, MA: Harvard University Press, 1927), vol. 2, pp. 304-6, 315, 385-86 still gives a clear overview of the variety of rabbinic and pre-rabbinic ideas about Gentile resurrection; more recently see George W. E. Nickelsburg, Jr., *Resurrection, Immortality, and Eternal Life in Intertestamental Judaism* (Cambridge, Mass.: Harvard University Press, 1972); and Christine E. Hays, *Gentile Impurities and Jewish Identities: Intermarriage and Conversion from the Bible to the Talmud* (Oxford: Oxford University Press, 2002).

would not disagree. But he beholds a mystery: somehow it also runs *through* the Gentiles, even, finally, for Israel. In Romans 8, that is true even of the resurrection of the dead. Not that Paul expects Jews not to be resurrected: by no means! But the wonder is that he has come to expect the resurrection of the Gentiles, those whose function it is to represent sin and death. They are the exception that proves the rule. They are the pledge, the *proof that* death is really defeated. If Christ is the firstfruits of those who have died, the Gentiles are the firstfruits of the Spirit of life. If even the Gentiles, the worshippers of dead idols, the corruptible, labile, fleshly ones can be changed, then we shall all be changed. Which is the greater mystery, the resurrection of the dead, or the coming in of the Gentiles? False alternative! Both are works of the Spirit of life in Christ Jesus, and the latter serves now as proof of the former.

This does not mean that Gentiles come to possess what Jews lack, but that Gentiles come to share what Jews keep. *This pattern causes Jews and Gentiles together to represent the Son's relation to the Spirit.* If the Son receives from the Spirit as human, what he already possesses as God, then it is deeply parallel if Gentiles receive from the Spirit as aliens, what Jews already possess as householders. This analogy has no necessity about it, but it follows the pattern that the Spirit makes matter diversely christoform in surprising ways, as an unexpected gift to the Son. This pattern is not on the surface of Paul's text. In order to expose its roots there, we have to look at the Pauline account of Christ's vulnerability, and the response of the Spirit.

Perhaps because of his own apparent failure as a missionary to the Jews, Paul is deeply attuned to the apparent failure (or more mildly, forbearance)[47] of Christ — and the chances of unexpected success elsewhere, in the mystery of God's design. That there is apparent failure is confirmed by Paul's denial: "But it is not as though the word of God had failed" (Rom. 9:6). Talk of Christ's "failure" sounds shocking to Christian ears. In the most obvious case, however, it need not be; it is merely a straightforward description of the crucifixion. No one would deny that the *ordinary, human* course of Christ's life ended in defeat. No one would deny that its continuation at the resurrection counts as the deepest mystery and greatest surprise. That defeat should be followed by surprise is in some ways the most familiar pattern of action of the God of Israel. That God does not cease to surprise should come as no surprise — except that the conclusion of that paradox denies its premise. But Paul is

---

47. "Forbearance" is Stanley Stowers's characterization of such Pauline terms as *epiekeia* and *praütēs*, which imply "power over others that one does not exercise," as in II Cor. 10:1. Stowers, *A Rereading of Romans*, p. 218.

certainly entitled to apply the pattern of failure and surprise to his own mission, and, another level, to the mission of Jesus.

Paul assumes that Jesus' primary mission, like his own, is "to the Jew first." Paul assumes further that God has allowed Jesus' mission to the Jews to fail for some larger mysterious purpose involving the eschatological bringing in of all peoples to worship the God of Israel. Stanley Stowers describes this narrative as one of "the Messiah who delayed."[48] According to Stowers's reading of Paul, "Jesus did not exercise the powers given to him because if he had, much of Israel and most of the Gentiles would have been lost. Jesus died and postponed the world's judgment out of love for the ungodly." Stowers does not say so, but this characteristic forbearance of Jesus might have much to do with the Spirit, because it is most explicitly displayed in the temptation narratives: After his baptism, the Spirit drives Jesus into the wilderness, where he practices forbearance in refusing the unfaithful exercise of divine power. In Paul, "Jesus refused to use his divine powers to the point even of not escaping capture and execution by the Romans." It is the Spirit who, according to the Synoptics, drives Jesus into the practice of forbearance: and it is the Spirit, according to Romans 8, who reunites Father and Son after the crucifixion, and rewards and expands upon the forbearance of the Son with the gift of the Gentiles.

This is why Paul opens Romans with a reference to the Spirit's role in making good on Jesus' apparent failure, and real forbearance, in allowing himself to be crucified: Romans is about "the good news concerning his Son who was born from the seed of David with regard to the flesh and who was designated Son of God in power according to the Spirit of holiness by the resurrection from the dead" (Rom. 1:3-4). The piling up of prepositional phrases is vague and hard to understand. The clue, I think, is in the verbal noun: The gospel is τοῦ ὁρισθέντος, of the one picked out, designated, defined, bounded, characterized. But Paul does not mean the fairly colorless election by the Father, so he adds not one but two prepositional phrases to specify the manner of this picking out, and both of them have to do with the peculiar relation of Jesus and the Spirit. No doubt this verse of Paul's could be taken in an adoptionist direction. But that's not required by the kinds of specifications Paul adds, and it's not the *kind* of specification Paul adds here. Here Paul specifies rather the kind of power Jesus exercises, and how his story finishes. What defines Jesus is first of all power "according to the Spirit of holiness," power exercised with forbearance, power in accord with faithfulness to the purpose of the Father, the kind of power the Spirit teaches in the wilderness.

48. Stowers, *A Rereading of Romans*, pp. 213-26.

And what defines Jesus is secondly power after or on the occasion of his resurrection from the dead, which Romans 8:11 will further specify as the Spirit's
vindication of forbearance by the bringing in of the Gentiles. Later theologians would insist that not just any exercise of power would mark the particular, concrete character of the Word become human: killing people to resurrect
them for sport, for example, would not count. Stowers puts it this way:
"Paul's Christ does not give up inherited messianic roles as warrior, judge,
protector of the righteous, restorer of Israel's life, and agent of God's promises, but these roles are projected into the future and reoriented around the
theme of God's love and Christ's willingness to die for the ungodly."[49] The enacting of divinity-in-humanity particular to *this* character came to bear the
technical name τρόπος ὑπάρξεως, one's concrete way of being in the world.
This is what Paul is giving an initial sense of at the beginning of the letter. To
paraphrase: Paul tells the good news of the one bound to exercise power according to the Spirit, and vindicated by that Spirit since the resurrection.

In particular, the forbearance taught and vindicated by the Spirit makes
space for Gentile repentance, the Spirit's unexpected gift to the Son. That has
everything to do with Paul's eschatological expectations:

> According to a basic assumption for Paul, God's people, the Jews, will expe-
> rience God's judgment and salvation first at the final reckoning (for exam-
> ple, Rom. 2:10, 1:16). Only then will God turn to the other peoples.[50]

That means that Gentiles who come to worship the God of Israel before
the final salvation of the Jews can get into the kingdom of heaven. Paul explains this with the metaphor of a race. In Romans 11 Paul describes a stumbling that is not a fall (11:11), a race in which it is not about competition between Jews and Gentiles but about keeping abreast of a pacesetter. Gentiles
who enter the kingdom before the Jews do succeed in the race, but Jews who
enter after Gentiles do not lose. "The race ends when Israel crosses the finish
line. In the logic of this race, all who finish before the pacesetter win; all who
finish after that runner lose. God had to trip the Jews in order to provide opportunity for the Gentiles and show that he is a just God,"[51] for unlike Athena
who fixes the race at the funeral of Patroclus in favor of Odysseus, the God of
Israel does not play favorites (2:6, 3:23, 4:16, 10:11, 11:32, et al.).[52] The failures of
Jesus and of Paul have their divinely ordained purpose, and it is specifically

---

49. Stowers, *A Rereading of Romans*, p. 217.
50. Stowers, *A Rereading of Romans*, p. 217.
51. Stowers, *A Rereading of Romans*, p. 316.
52. Stowers, *A Rereading of Romans*, pp. 314-15.

the Spirit who makes good on them. The Spirit never makes good on failure by a return to *status quo ante*. The Spirit always makes good by a greater inclusion, by a movement of excess.

Of course the clearest expression of Christ's forbearance in Paul is the Philippians hymn (2:5-11), which in the theologically interested translation describes Christ Jesus, who, though he was in the form of God,

> did not count equality with God a thing to be grasped,
> but emptied himself,
> taking the form of a servant,
> being born in the likeness of human beings.
> And being found in human form
> he humbled himself
> and became obedient unto death, even death on a cross.
> Therefore God has highly exalted him
> and bestowed on him the name which is above every name,
> that at the name of Jesus every knee should bow. . . . (RSV)

Later (under the rubric of baptism) we shall consider how this hymn reverses the grasping of divinity at the Fall. But now we need to note how the pattern of forbearance marks Jesus' character, because it is on that account that God has "given him a name," recalling the picking out or designation of Romans 1:3. The Philippians account, too, does not explicate the form of Christ without the participation of the Spirit. The hymn opens with Paul's command that they should "have it in mind" (Phil. 2:5). Having the form of Christ in mind is instrumental to the community's "being of the same mind" (v. 3). And the community has the mind of Christ by "participation *(koinonia)* in the Spirit" (v. 1). It is in the community of the Spirit that both Christ and community learn to receive the forbearance the Spirit teaches and the excess with which the Spirit vindicates.

It is not the Jews who fail, as Christian supersessionism would have it. In the crucifixion it is Jesus who fails. And it is the Spirit who gives Jesus the freedom to fail. In the Spirit, Jesus can choose to receive from another rather than to keep for himself. The advantage of that for human beings is that we who do not have for ourselves can receive from the Spirit in and with him. He can lose his life rather than save it, because he can receive it again from the Spirit. Because he can receive from the Spirit what he has given up, human beings can receive with him from the Spirit what they have never had. Jesus has the freedom to fail in his mission, because he can rely on another to guarantee its success. Because he can receive from the Spirit the success he deferred, Gentiles can receive from the Spirit what he preached to the Jews. In both cases failure leads to an unpredictable expansion and inclusion. The Son's resurrection leads — because the Spirit dwells also in other human bodies — to the general resurrection. The failure of the Son before Israel leads — because the Spirit pours out also on the nations — to the coming of the goyim to worship the God of Israel. This does not mean the replacement of Israel. As the Son receives from the Spirit what he possesses as God, so the Gentiles receive from the Spirit what she guarantees to Israel.

No theologian has spoken more movingly about the power of God in weakness, in what he does not hesitate to call the "defeat" of Jesus, than Donald Mackinnon, who trained a generation of British theologians after the Holocaust. But since Mackinnon's version of Stowers's insight depends on a reading of how the Spirit, on Jesus' baptism, drives him into the wilderness to be tempted, I defer it until that chapter (pp. 164-68).

So the Spirit makes good on the resurrection by being *not merely* the Spirit of the one Who raised Jesus from the dead, but by being *also*, gratuitously, the one who indwells the mortal bodies of *other* human beings — Gentiles, as it happens — to include them too in the household of the God of Israel. The resurrection of Christ's body comes to include, by the surprising excesses of the Spirit, even those bodies that are by nature mortal — that is, mortal by their Gentile nature.

The Spirit not only makes good on the crucifixion in the resurrection; the Spirit also makes good on the failure of the mission to the Jews in a mission to the Gentiles, which does not finally come at the Jews' expense. This is not doing evil that good may come, but taking evil and bringing good miraculously out of it. Ephrem the Syrian (at least in one place) gets both the parallel and the paradox:

> From the rock water gushed forth for the Jewish people who drank
>   and were strengthened,
> From the wood on Golgotha the Fountain of Life gushed forth
>   for the Gentiles.[53]

Thus the Spirit rests on the body of the Son in the resurrection, identifying all three Persons by it and celebrating it by adding the resurrection of the really dead, the Gentiles.

---

53. Ephrem the Syrian, Armenian Hymn no. 49, *Patrologia orientalis* 30:229, quoted in Sebastian Brock, "The Mysteries Hidden in the Side of Christ," *Sobornost* 7 (1978): 462-72; here, p. 471.

2 Annunciation

*"The Spirit of God will come to you, and the power
of the Most High will overshadow you"*

In the Annunciation the Spirit rests on the Son in the waters of the womb of
Mary. Her womb becomes the locus of excess, a happy opening, where consummation and contingency coincide. In the Annunciation it becomes manifest
that the Spirit does this also elsewhere, both in the Trinity and therefore in the
world. Paraphysically she accompanies, befriends, and exceeds the physical.
The Spirit dilates: she opens, she takes time. At the Annunciation the Spirit
seals her resting on the Son antecedently in the womb of the Father and anticipates her resting on the Son in the womb of his side. In these she keeps faith
with her hovering over the waters already at creation.

i. The Spirit rests on the Son in the womb of Mary

> Mary's eyes   beholding Eve
>   and looking down on Adam,   were impelled to tears;
> but she stays them   and hastens
>   to conquer nature   she who *para phusin* gave birth to Christ
>   her son.
> Yet her entrails were stirred   in suffering with her parents
>   — a compassionate mother   accorded with the Merciful one
> So she tells them   — Cease your lamentations,
>   and I will be your ambassador   to him born from me.[1]

---

1. Romanos the Melodist, Hymn XI (Nativity II), strophe 4, in *Hymns II,* ed. José Grosdidier
de Matons, Sources Chrétiennes 110 (Paris: Cerf, 1965). Translation by Margaret Alexiou in *After*

So Romanos the Melodist, the greatest liturgical poet of the Greek Church, speaks of something *para phusin* in only one defining instance. The defining instance of God's acting in excess of nature is, in his corpus, the virgin birth. Here too it is something like sexuality that, in Greek as in English, attracts the use of *phusis*, the natural or the physical. In Romans, Paul uses the phrase *para phusin* in two significant ways, which may turn out to be the same: in Romans 1:26, to describe the sexual consequences of Gentile idolatry, and in Romans 11:24, to describe the procedure by which God saves the Gentiles. Romanos clearly takes Paul's second usage as controlling, in which God's action transfiguring nature works for the economy of salvation in grafting the Gentiles *para phusin* onto a domesticated Jewish olive tree.

In Part I we saw that in both the fourteenth century and the twentieth, in *Piers Plowman* and Sergei Bulgakov, Christian thought enjoyed deep resources for thinking about superfluity, even the superfluity of the Spirit. But Christianity possessed resources much earlier even than the fourteenth century for dissolving the ambivalence of excess. In Romanos the Melodist, God's excess has one paradigmatic location: the womb of Mary.[2] In the Epistle to the Romans, God's excess has one paradigmatic location: the salvation of the Gentiles. Both instances show the *Spirit* consummating God's saving work in a surprising, even shocking way.

The same movement as in *Piers Plowman* takes place first, perhaps, in Paul, who relates two discourses of "excess of nature." The social location here is not the merchant economy but the economy of salvation of the Gentiles. The Greek preposition *para* is well suited to contain the ambiguities of excess. Its root meaning is spatial: beside, alongside, as in the word "parallel." If the lexicon lists the meaning "against," that is best understood as "*compared* against," as in "paragon," "paradigm," "parable," which indicate no opposition. It would be misleading to indicate contrariety rather than comparison. No one supposes contrast in such words as "paraenesis" or "Paraclete." Even "parasite" is one that "feeds beside," while "paradox" and "paranormal" connote what is beside or in addition to the normal, rather than against it. A "paraphrase" is supposed to say the same thing, not something opposed. Modern coinages such as "paramedic" and "paralegal" continue the correct understanding of those who work with or alongside, not against others.

A neutral translation of Paul's usage would be "paraphysical." In one case

Antiquity: Greek Language, Myth, and Metaphor (Ithaca, N.Y.: Cornell University Press, 2002), pp. 422-23.

2. For Western accounts, see E. Ann Matter, "The Woman Who Is the All: The Virgin Mary and the Song of Songs," in *The Voice of My Beloved: The Song of Songs in Western Medieval Christianity* (Philadelphia: University of Pennsylvania Press, 1990), pp. 151-77.

it refers to Gentile sexuality; in another case to Gentile salvation. In both cases English translations are accustomed to say "contrary to nature." But that strains against the nuance of the Greek. *Para* never indicates contrariety. It is not the same as *anti*. Even though the Vulgate helps to cause the problem by translating *"contra naturam,"* some Latin theologians nevertheless clearly understand the sense of the Greek as excess. So Thomas Aquinas classifies "the vice against nature" *not* as a vice of contrariety but as a vice of excess: it belongs in the genus of *luxus*, "which is a certain superfluity."[3] This is seen also by modern New Testament critics such as Dale Martin.[4] Paul's complaint about Gentile sexuality is that it is excessive, or as we might now say, kinky. Paul is stereotyping the Gentiles for a purpose — to turn the tables in 2:1 — and the stereotype is not that Gentiles have an opposite sexuality from Jews, it is that they have a more appetitive sexuality than Jews.

That "excess" must be the correct translation appears when we consider Paul's second usage, in which he says that God saves the very same Gentiles by an excess of God's own. What would be natural for God is to save the Jews; what is excessive is that God would save the Gentiles as well. In so doing, God shows solidarity with the Gentiles' own characteristic of excess; there is more than a hint here that God's saving the Gentiles is something like sleeping with someone else. The agricultural metaphor is that God grafts the wild olive onto the domestic root. *Para* signals a shocking comparison to usual agricultural practice: as if wild lemons (which are bad to eat but have vigorous rootstock) were grafted onto navel orange stems (which are good to eat but do not reproduce)[5] — instead of grafting the edible olive onto the more vigorous wild rootstock. The implication exceeds that of reversing a typical agricultural practice to make a point about households, God's *oikonomia*, God's practice of farming the land, in a very Bulgakovian metaphor. The domestic olive indicates the house of Israel, and the wild olive the wild or undomesticated nature of Gentiles, those not yet integrated into the household of God. The metaphor, that is, is one of integration or grafting not reversal, of *addition*, of adding alongside the great trunk, roofing over a great house.

The usage in Romans 1 is taken to be excess of the bad sort (wastage), the usage in Romans 11 of the good sort (winning). But winning overwhelms wasting. That is the whole point of Romans. God's economy so runs on excess

---

3. Thomas Aquinas, *Summa Theologiae* II-II.53.1 *ad* 1, 154.12. For commentary see Mark D. Jordan, *The Invention of Sodomy in Christian Theology* (Chicago: University of Chicago Press, 1997), pp. 145-47.

4. Dale B. Martin, "Heterosexism and the Interpretation of Romans 1:18-32," *Biblical Interpretation* 3 (1995): 332-55.

5. John McPhee, *Oranges* (New York: Farrar, Straus & Giroux, 1967).

that the attempt to take excess as evil finally fails, opening to the inclusion of precisely the one who sins excessively, the Gentile, or, in fourteenth-century terms, the merchant. Who are prostitutes and tax collectors but those whose relations with sexuality and money are excessive, and whose excess is overwhelmed by the great abandon of the kingdom of God? And yet those are also the ones Jesus notoriously chooses as friends, rather than those who exercise parsimony, probity, or control. The Pharisees and the rich young ruler who kept all the laws are painted — with some injustice toward actual Pharisees — as those who turn away. But God recognizes some analogy between human excess and divine excess, something salvageable in human passion. Indeed, for Aquinas, passion comes to provide the animal energy that it is the point of grace to channel or habituate into virtue, the energy without which the human being could do nothing at all.

But all this still verges on the abstract: nature and excess hardly resist dialectic better than nature and contrariety. Even the friends of Jesus can reduce to illustrations of an abstract principle. Where does the excess of God's grace become concrete, root itself in the trinitarian life, so that it shows definite rather than ever-malleable characteristics?

Liturgical poetry, another discipline that honors the concrete, offers an example. In his hymn "On the Nativity" (II), Romanos writes the lines that opened this chapter. The proper context of *para phusin* is there nothing more, less, or other than God's economy of salvation and graciousness in elevating human beings to involvement in it: She who exceeding nature gave birth to Christ her son. The translators tend to use "contrary to nature," which the language of victory *(nikan)* might suggest. But nothing else about the passage entails contrariety; nothing else opposes nature to grace. Rather the stanza opens and closes with Mary's compassion for Eve, whom her eyes behold and her embassy befriends; she does not oppose but intercedes for her; Mary does not defeat but vindicates her. Indeed, in absolute senses *nikaō* also means "to prevail," "to succeed in," even, most suggestively, "to be superior," "to win one's cause."[6] These senses color the transitive sense, even if "conquer" seems the most obvious translation. Here Romanos invokes not the language of contrariety but a verb of excess similar to *Piers Plowman*'s winning. God will succeed in God's purpose with nature; God will prevail in God's intention; God is superior and will win God's cause. God's initial cause and intention is not nature's defeat, but nature's elevation. In the womb of Mary, the Spirit takes the lost cause of human flesh to be her own cause, her own resting place;

6. Henry George Liddell, Robert Scott, and Henry Stuart Jones, *A Greek Lexicon* (Oxford: Clarendon, 1996), *s.v. nikaō.*

the place of wastage to be the site of winning, the flesh unseated to become the throne of grace.

So in an exactly parallel strophe in the next Nativity hymn, Romanos varies the preposition from *para*, "beyond," to *hyper*, "above." The context is once again the virgin birth.

> At your conceiving without seed, O Mother of God,
> Joseph was struck with wonder as he contemplated
> > what was *hyper phusin*,
> and he brought to mind the rain on the fleece,
> the bush unburned by fire,
> Aaron's rod which blossomed.
> And your betrothed and guardian bore witness and cried to the priests,
> > "*A Virgin gives birth, and after childbirth remains still a virgin.*"[7]

In a third instance, *para phusin* reappears, with a usage that gives sense to the conventional translation of "contrary to nature." The speaker is the leper whom Jesus heals.

> A doctor cannot complete the nature that comes to him incomplete,
> as Christ did for the one born blind from his mother's womb.
> And from this, it is clear that he is the creator
> of the first-formed man, whom he made from the earth.
> For recently too he brought forward from the earth the one I spoke of,
> and he is fashioner and Master of nature [*phuseos esti plastes*
> > *kai depostes*] and eternal God.
> For me the strength of the flesh rebels, *para phusin*,
> but he above all nature [*hyper phusin pasan*] was willingly born
> from a virgin womb, the Lover of mankind,
> > *Saviour and alone without sin.*[8]

On closer reading, this exception proves the rule. Romanos allows *para phusin* to mean in the most immediate context the rebellion of the leper's flesh. But the larger context is again God's saving intention, the miraculous consummation of the flesh by its creator, the carrying out of God's creatorly purpose. Romanos again explicitly and repeatedly describes God as the maker, master,

---

7. Romanos the Melodist, Hymn XII (Nativity III), proemium 1-7, in *Hymns II*, pp. 118-19. Translated as "On the Mother of God," in *On the Life of Christ: Kontakia*, trans. Ephrem Lash (San Francisco: HarperCollins Publishers, 1995), p. 17.

8. Romanos the Melodist, Hymn XX (The Leper), strophe 8, in *Hymns II*, pp. 368-69. Translated in Lash, *On the Life of Christ*, p. 54.

and lover of precisely that nature. Even where the virgin birth seems not to belong — in a treatment of healing the leper — Romanos associates what is *para phusin* explicitly and almost immediately with Mary's womb. Even where the first meaning of *para phusin* does express contrariety and rebellion, he confronts that sense with an immediate challenge. In the very next line he glosses it with *hyper phusin*. This is, to be sure, a gloss by contrast. And yet paradox does not appear here for its own sake. It appears to shock. It appears to highlight God's salvific purpose. It has the force of "even": even the leper can show God's consummating glory. This is just the point of Paul's initial use of *para phusin,* too: even the Gentile can receive God's mercy. Romanos like Paul intends to keep God's salvation firmly in the most unsavory company, whether lepers or Gentiles. That is how excessive it is.

This is not just any excess, but an excess governed by God's *philanthropia;* and not just any philanthropy, but a philanthropy lived out in a particular form of life or *tropos hyparxeos,* philanthropy incarnate, God become human. The Spirit conceives and keeps faith with *this* excess. Romanos can hardly help himself in moving from the story of the leper to that of the virgin birth, because for him the virgin birth is where the language of excess of nature *belongs.* The virgin birth marks the site of this language — its physical location, the place where it takes up space in the world. The virgin birth, like the salvation of the Gentiles, is neither merely physical nor anti-physical: it is strictly paraphysical; it accompanies and exceeds nature. Romans 11:24 marks one of the places in which Paul implicitly moves beyond the notion that *pneuma* is a physical force or energy to one that has divine effects; as the Spirit of adoption it is paraphysical.[9] In Romanos as in Paul, the paraphysical is physical, in that it proceeds alongside, in solidarity with nature, and *para,* in excess of nature: a companion to nature, befriending, restoring, consummating, and exceeding it. The womb is where the Spirit conceives this excess, that God should become human, who has no need to do so, who has no need of flesh, but takes it as if to God's detriment, except that God has made our cause God's own, takes flesh for our sake, for excess of love, for *philanthropia.*

Indeed, the excessiveness of the virgin birth is what some Protestants don't like about it. The virgin birth seems not only excessive but exorbitant, out of control — and even physically excessive. Especially when (as in the hymn on the leper) one speaks of *virginitas in partu.* Why this excess?

It can only be that God chooses this way because God likes it; chooses because God desires and loves and befriends human bodies. God the Spirit does

---

9. For references relating the Spirit of adoption to Roman adoptive practice, see Stanley K. Stowers, "What Is Real Participation in Christ?" unpublished typescript.

not have disgust at the physical: she has *philia* for it; she takes up a place alongside *(para)* and in solidarity with it; she loves and befriends it; at creation she hovered over and at the resurrection will consummate it. The resurrection is above all things paraphysical.

In what follows, I consider that excess in two ways: First as a gratuitous consummation of human beings, in excess of creation and redemption, that God did not have to grant; and then as a pattern of reception, exposed to view in the womb of Mary, that marks the life of God with scandal. One might call this the paraphysicality of the Spirit.

ii. *Felix dilatio:* The Spirit favors the order of consummation over the order of redemption

> In the delay of the Parousia, *as in the opening of Mary's womb, the Spirit dilates time and space for additional gifts. O* felix dilatio: *O happy delay, O blessed opening.*

The opening of Mary's womb brings the advent of God's realm, a realm traditionally called God's kingdom, but also the heaven of which Catholic tradition calls her queen and Catholic devotion calls her the *ianua coeli,* the gate.[10] As a woman of low estate, she opens up a time for justice; as a willing recipient of the Spirit, she opens up a site of joy. In preparing the justice of God's realm, she plays the role of the prophet. In preparing the joy of God's realm, she plays the role of patriarch. Mary as prophet belongs to the order of redemption, that which saves human beings from something bad, such as injustice suffered or committed. Mary as patriarch belongs to the order of consummation, that which brings human beings to the gratuitous, superfluous end for which God did not need to create them, but for which the Spirit leads them anyway, in celebration of God's love. The Spirit holds open two orders or plots by the spatial opening of Mary's womb and the temporal opening for the Gentiles: the order of redemption spoken by the prophets and the order of consummation promised to the patriarchs. Because the intratrinitarian office of the Spirit is to celebrate, while her office to keep faith in times of difficulty belongs to this world, redemption is for consummation's sake. The logic of consummation has priority over that of redemption.

10. See, for example, Raniero Cantalamessa, *Mary: Mirror of the Church,* trans. Frances Lonergan Villa (Collegeville, Minn.: The Liturgical Press, 1992), p. 198.

The call of Mary resembles the call of a prophet, indeed of the prophet *par excellence,* since she is the one who delivers the Word of God. A prophet "eats" the scroll of God's Word and "fills his stomach with it"; Mary's stomach was more literally filled with the Word.[11] Prophets announce the advent of God's justice; Mary brings the one who justifies. Prophets do not announce the future as such, but rather announce that God's rule is at hand, and that sinners may therefore repent; Mary delivers the kingdom of God and the cause for repentance. Because it is primarily justice that prophets announce, the tradition has never felt much embarrassment about *ex eventu* prophecy, or the proclamation of justice after the fact. Prophets do, however, mostly share their people's fear of justice, at least at first. Justice, after the Fall, always involves redemption from sin and a change of life, for both the individual and society. Therefore it is typical of prophets to resist their call. Justice is typically not in their immediate interest. Moses, Jonah, Isaiah, Paul characteristically require coercion into working for justice; the Spirit drives them. Mary is uniquely portrayed as saying without demur, "Let it be with me according to your will" — a disanalogy with other prophets so great as to explain, in part, why she appears among them prominently, as far as I know, only in Irenaeus.[12]

The other reasons why Mary appears so rarely among the prophets are also of interest. She is a woman, and she has little to say. These features liken her to Miriam (Exod. 15:20-21) and Anna (Luke 2:36-38), two other prophets little mentioned.[13] But all of the unusual features — her alacrity, her gender, her reticence — have to do with the way the order of redemption becomes a *subplot* to the order of consummation. In Mary, a lowly estate causes her to desire rather than resist the call of justice. In Mary, the men's narratives of prophecy coincide with women's narratives of the erotic tricksters named in Matthew's genealogy — Tamar, Rahab, Ruth, and Bathsheba, described as "the wife of Uriah." In Mary, the word is not proclaimed, because the word becomes flesh. In Mary, justice is not announced, but accomplished, because God is present. Bernard of Clairvaux puts it to Mary directly, "Only say the word and receive the Word: give yours and conceive God's."[14]

---

11. I owe this comparison to Cantalamessa, *Mary,* p. 176, citing Jer. 15:16, Ezek. 3:1-2, Rev. 10:8-9.

12. Irenaeus of Lyon, *Against Heresies* III.10.2, in Robert M. Grant, *Irenaeus of Lyon,* Early Church Fathers series (London: Routledge, 1990); *Adversus Haereses,* in *Irénée de Lyon: Contre les Hérésies,* ed. A. Rousseau, *Sources Chrétiennes,* vol. 100 (Paris: Éditions du Cerf, 1965).

13. That Miriam and Anna are called prophets and have little to say was pointed out to me by Aaron Riches.

14. Bernard of Clairvaux, *Homilia in laudibus Virginis Matris* IV.8, in Jean Leclercq and H. Rochais, eds., *Sancti Bernardi Opera* IV (Rome: Editiones cistercienses, 1966), 13-58; here,

Let "redemption" name a plot defined by its starting point: it begins in slavery, in *that from which* one is redeemed. Let "consummation" name a plot defined by its endpoint: it ends in joy, in *that to whom* one is united.[15] Redemption and consummation pick out compatible but distinguishable aspects of the complex relations that the Spirit plots with her people.

Gentiles tend to stress redemption-stories about the God of Israel, because the Bible constructs Gentiles as idol-worshippers, those who have no God, who then undergo a drastic change of life, and come to worship the God of Israel and be saved. The plot of Gentile worship of the God of Israel involves a reversal. Gentile psychology, "soul-logic," arises from *metanoia*. They find it hard to feel secure in their relationship with the God of Israel. They are anxious (like Luther) that God hates them and will cut them off. Paul goes so far as to tell them this. How much easier will it be for God to lop them off! (Rom. 11:21). In the typical Gentile relationship with the God of Israel, redemption is a source of amazing grace, as if the God of Israel had raised up followers from the stones, as if they were brands snatched from the burning. Index of this wonder is that their salvation is not restoration to the status quo only, but involves elevation, too. That Gentiles have escaped non-relationship and meaninglessness is one thing; that they are destined for heaven is denouement. We can see that in Anselm's *Cur Deus homo:* Glorification is a surprising, excessive, unexpected *reward* for Jesus' good service.[16] It is part of the denouement of the story, not integral to the plot. It has a certain graciousness to it. In *such* a plot, redemption is the main plot; consummation, then, denouement or grace note.

For Jews, on the other hand, the relationship with the God of Israel, their God, their covenanted one, is secure. Sin and redemption take place as a subplot, like the obstacles in a marriage that the security of the relationship can be relied upon to overcome. The plot involves twists and turns, no doubt. It can be episodic, a pilgrimage. But the reversals are minor. They do not settle what kind of plot it is.

So both Jews and Gentiles have redemption in their master plots, and both Jews and Gentiles have consummation in their master narratives. But the emphasis is reversed. For Israel, consummation is the main plot, redemp-

---

"Homily IV in Praise of the Virgin Mother," in *Homilies in Praise of the Blessed Virgin Mary*, trans. Marie-Bernard Saïd (Kalamazoo, Mich.: Cistercian Publications, 1993), p. 54.

15. I first learned to distinguish the order of redemption from the order of consummation from David Kelsey. But the most exciting use of this distinction belongs to R. Kendall Soulen, in his book *Christian Theology and the God of Israel* (Minneapolis: Fortress Press, 1996).

16. Anselm of Canterbury, *Why God Became Human*, in *A Scholastic Miscellany: Anselm to Ockham*, ed. and trans. Eugene R. Fairweather, Library of Christian Classics, vol. 10 (Philadelphia: Westminster Press, 1956), Book II, Ch. 19.

tion a subplot. Their standing with God is secure, and reversals leave it largely unthreatened. Jews generally do not worry about damnation. For the almost entirely Gentile church, however, redemption is the main plot. Their standing with God is beset by anxiety because they come to it by reversal. Either they worry about damnation, or protest their salvation too loudly.

If Gentiles misread the history of Israel as *primarily* (rather than incidentally) a redemption narrative, they are likely to lay stress on Israel's sins, suppose that Israel's relation to her God is like their own, and worry about the salvation of the Jews. They will misconstrue their doctrine of Israel on the model of their doctrine of justification (as in Barth).[17] If Jews misread the history of the nations as *primarily* (rather than incidentally) a consummation narrative, they are likely to lay stress on the Gentiles' supersessionistic claims, suppose that the Gentiles' relation to their God is like their own, and worry about God's adultery. But both of these worries are misplaced, if I am right about tendencies to misread another's story as one's own.

You might take redemption as the condition for consummation, or you might take consummation as the anticipation of redemption. These tendencies appear in Christian doctrine as the conflict between sanctification and election. The most profound Christian theologians have favored the latter: God redeems human beings, because God first loved them. While they were yet sinners, Christ died for them. Repentance and belief are first possible because the kingdom of heaven — the good consummation — is at hand, so that they may leave their chains to sin behind, put down their litters and walk. Thus the most anxious of Christian theologians (and therefore too one of the most likely to misapply the redemption plot to the disadvantage of the Jews) is the one most emphatic in his discovery that the consummation plot must predominate for Gentile Christians to leave their anxiety behind: I mean Martin Luther. He had a correspondingly high Mariology, one that compared the virginity and childbirth of Mary to the divinity and humanity of her Son.

In Mary the consummation and redemption plots coincide; in the annunciation the consummation plot predominates. It is a story of union, not a story of reversal; a story of arriving at a goal, not one of turning around on the road. It is no accident that she makes the flesh of Jesus Jewish. And to overcome the Israel-forgetfulness of most Christian narratives,[18] it is important to get that part of her story right.

17. A main thesis of Katherine Sonderegger, *That Jesus Christ Was Born a Jew: Karl Barth's "Doctrine of Israel"* (University Park, Pa.: Pennsylvania State University Press, 1992).

18. For the argument and the phrase "Israel-forgetfulness," see Soulen, *Christian Theology and the God of Israel.*

Both prophet and trickster narratives seem to have reversals embedded in them.[19] Both prophets and tricksters act out of a sense of what the world would be like if just. They are portrayed as acting out of the just future, as unconstrained by the injustice of others or of the past. They are a breaking in of a justice that does not so much react as change the prevailing conditions. So they do the Spirit's work.

Prophecy and fulfillment make a dangerous trope for Christian theology, because they almost always show up in a supersessionist, anti-Judaic way. The pattern usually is that Israel has the prophecy while Christianity has the fulfillment.[20] In Luke, too — in the Gospel that presents Mary as receiving a prophetic call — Jesus is presented as the last in a long line of prophets killed in Israel. It may be, however, that attention to the consummation trope can help to solve this problem. The order of consummation has logical priority, in God, over the order of redemption. That is, redemption requires no change in God's intention to consummate God's relationship with human beings, to bring human beings into fellowship with God. A reversal is visible only from the human side. God, as Anselm puts it in a chapter title, would merely "complete what God began."[21] God remains true to God's purpose, and does not take no for an answer. Consummation is a denouement external to the integrity of the plot, if redemption is the main plot, a gracious superfluity, from the reigning Gentile point of view. But from the point of view of the God of Israel, redemption is an episode internal to the plot of consummation, the carrying through in the face of an obstacle of God's creatorly intention. In accord with such a theological insight, prophecy-fulfillment schemes ought to be read in light of the *final* rather than the penultimate fulfillment, in the light of the fulfillment that *both* Christianity and Judaism await.[22] This is what Paul does, after all, in Romans 11.

The second point is exegetical and typological. The very thing that distinguishes Mary from most prophets — that she accepts her call with alacrity — puts her into correspondence with a figure usually regarded as less a prophet and more a *patriarch*. As Mary says, *fiat mihi*, let it be to me, so the prophet

19. On trickster narratives, see Susan Niditch, *Prelude to Biblical Folklore: Underdogs and Tricksters* (Urbana, Ill.: University of Illinois Press, 2000).

20. Karl Barth famously intoned this pattern to Michael Wyschogrod, who replied that the promises of God are like money in the bank, so that the gap between promise and fulfilment dissolves. "You know," Barth replied, "I never thought of it that way." Michael Wyschogrod, "A Jewish Perspective on Karl Barth," in *How Karl Barth Changed My Mind*, ed. Donald McKim (Grand Rapids: Eerdmans, 1986), pp. 156-61; here, p. 161.

21. Anselm of Canterbury, *Why God Became Human*, book II, ch. 4.

22. George Lindbeck, "The Church," in *Keeping the Faith: Essays to Mark the Centenary of "Lux Mundi,"* ed. Geoffrey Wainwright (London: SPCK, 1989), pp. 179-208.

Samuel says *hineni,* here I am (I Sam. 3:4); and so, too, before both of them does the patriarch Abraham, *hineni,* here I am, at the beginning of the story of the binding of Isaac (Gen. 22:1). Mary represents both the prophets of redemption and justice — and she represents the Abraham of erotic consummation. Mary like Abraham follows God without complaint and offers senseless erotic sacrifice. According to Cleo Kearns,

> [Mary's] parallel with Abraham is, . . . though hitherto obscured by an excessive focus on gender, in many ways more revealing. For in undergoing the ritual purification required by the cult, in presenting her child in the Temple, taking him to Jerusalem for his coming of age and arguably even in accompanying him to the cross, Mary is always, no more and no less, an Abrahamic figure, the faithful, prudent, and circumspect daughter of the *akedah,* the binding of Isaac.[23]

Kearns has predecessors not only in Bernard of Clairvaux, but more elaborately in Amadeus of Lausanne.[24] The Holy Spirit "filled Abraham with faith and an obedience that should profit his descendants, but saved by [Mary's] faith and obedience, the whole world gives thanks."[25] Amadeus makes Mary heir to the burning bush of Moses and the seed of Abraham — perhaps even its source:

> You were on fire like the bush which once was shown to Moses and you were not burnt up. . . . The fire revealed a shining dew, the shining dew produced an anointing, the anointing furnished the holy seed by which Abraham was promised that in it all nations should be blessed.[26]

Later Amadeus recalls the binding of Isaac *to Mary at the foot of the cross:*

> In spirit Abraham suffered when, being bidden to sacrifice his only son Isaac whom he loved, he was deeply moved by his fatherly love and was stirred to the depth of his heart by his affection for his son. Nevertheless as a

23. Cleo McNelly Kearns, "The Scandals of the Sign: The Virgin Mary as Supplement in the Religions of the Book," in *Questioning God,* ed. John Caputo et al. (Bloomington, Ind.: Indiana University Press, 2001), pp. 318-40; here, p. 331.

24. Cf. Amadeus of Lausanne, *Homiliae octo felicis memoriae Amadei episcopi Lausannensis de laudibus beatae Mariae,* ed. G. Bavaud, Sources chrétiennes 72 (Paris: Éditions du Cerf, 1960); here, "On the Praises of the Virgin Mary," Homily 1 in *Magnificat: Homilies in Praise of the Blessed Virgin Mary by Bernard of Clairvaux and Amadeus of Lyon,* Cistercian Fathers Series 18, trans. Marie-Bernard Saïd and Grace Perigo (Kalamazoo, Mich.: Cicstercian Publications, 1979), p. 64.

25. Amadeus of Lausanne, Homily III, p. 85.

26. Amadeus of Lausanne, Homily III *in fin.,* p. 86, paralleling Gen. 22:17-18 with Luke 1:42; paragraph boundary elided. Cf. also Homily IV *in init.,* p. 87.

diligent workman he performed the task laid upon him and, hastening to obey the divine command, he reached in a three days' journey Mount Horeb. There, as commanded, he put together a heap of wood, bound Isaac and laid him upon it. He seized his knife and would have slain his son had he not been checked by a voice from heaven and heard "Stretch not your hand against the lad. Now I know you fear God." . . .

Therefore the glorious lady, triumphing in this kind of suffering, the more glorious as she was nearer them all, clung to the revered cross of the Lord's passion, drained the cup, drank the passion and, having quaffed the torment of grief, was able to endure a grief unlike any other. She hastens after Jesus not only for the scent of his perfumes, but in the abundance of his sorrows. . . .[27]

Indeed in this case it is hard to see who *else* the human antitype to Abraham might be, if not Mary. *Joseph* is not depicted as standing at the foot of the cross. *If* a human parent offers this son, it can only be Mary, as part of her "let it be to me according to your will" and her standing at the foot of the cross. It is not Joseph who makes such a promise. It is not Joseph who offers such a witness. When both Joseph and Mary present Jesus in the Temple, it is explicitly and only to Mary that Simeon is said to deliver his prophecy of Jesus' fate; it is to Mary alone that the tradition ascribes the purity to which a priest may merely aspire. Given the question whom *Joseph* most resembles, Abraham or Sarah, the answer might well be Sarah — the supporting character, the silent one, the one who needs divine reassurance about intensity developing between God and the spouse. It is primarily to Abraham and to Mary that a son is promised; it is primarily from Abraham and from Mary that a son is demanded. It is Sarah who laughs and Joseph who resolves on a quiet divorce. If the gender of the types is reversed, that does not mean that this interpretation overlooks gender. Rather, this reversal of gender recalls those other reversals of gender, according to which a man alone gave rise to a woman in Genesis, while a woman alone gave rise to a son in the Gospels,[28] and the male-gendered sacrifice of meat and blood is presented in a female-gendered sacrifice of bread and grape.[29] Of course, the usual interpretation is that God the Father copies Abraham — a typology not without its trinitarian problems. But nothing excludes a human offerer. The very vehemence with which the

27. Amadeus of Lausanne, Homily V, pp. 99-101.

28. Anselm of Canterbury, *Why God Became Human*, book II, ch. 8.

29. Stanley K. Stowers, "Does Pauline Christianity Resemble a Hellenistic Philosophy," in *Paul Beyond the Judaism/Hellenism Divide*, ed. Troels Engberg-Pedersen (Louisville, Ky.: Westminster/John Knox, 2001), pp. 98-99.

Catholic Church refuses Mary the role of the priest suggests its plausibility. If anything, Abraham is *less* the priest, since by divine command he is expressly *forbidden* to sacrifice: "Stretch *not* your hand."

Mary overwhelms the distinction of Hebrews that the Spirit has spoken in many and various ways by the prophets, and now by the Son. In Mary the Spirit speaks both by the prophets *and* through the Son.

iii. The Spirit rests on the Son in the womb of the Father

The very rubrics of this chapter have made the author anxious. In the first place, I was raised Presbyterian. While Presbyterians do not deny that Jesus is God already in the womb, they have little or no use for Mariology, and therefore the phrase "Mother of God" does not function for them, and rings all too Catholic in their ears. I have come to write this chapter because my theological commitments require me to. If I want to consider the places in the New Testament where the Persons of the Trinity seem to interact, then I have to consider the Annunciation.

But leftover Presbyterian narrowness is not the only problem. I also want to consider ways in which the interaction among the Persons in the New Testament narratives manifests something "up" the analogical ladder about the Persons' interactions among themselves in the Trinity, and "down" the analogical ladder about the Persons' concrete integration of human communities and human hearts into their own life. Various bits of various traditions have in fact made those moves up and down. If the Spirit rests on the Son in the womb of Mary, that ought to say something both about the Spirit's resting on the Son in the Trinity and about the Spirit's resting on the Son in the human community. The bits of the tradition that made such moves have made them precisely by extending the language of womb above and below.

While it is well known that Christian God-language works in such a way as to transcend gender, and necessarily so, it may still shock to learn that in Augustine and in the Eleventh Council of Toledo the Father has a womb, or that in Syriac poetry and in twelfth-century Cistercian thought there is a womb, or a womblike receptacle, in the wound in Christ's side. Readers may think I am seeking to make the Spirit interesting by making it outré. That reaction may arise from internalized and insufficiently criticized Presbyterianism, or internalized and insufficiently repented gynophobia. The way forward insists that womb symbolism is powerful just because it involves bodies and boundaries and the hint of sex. Without getting into Freud we can acknowledge that boundary-crossing and penetration into forbidden spaces — according to anthropologists — is always loaded. But there are more important reasons for overcoming this discomfort than the limitations of Presbyterianism and misogyny, more important reasons than Mary Douglas or Sigmund Freud can diagnose for us.

The theological issue is this: Distaste before the womb is not just pathology, it is heresy. It lies on the borders of Nestorianism. If God did not avoid the womb, neither may Christian thought and liturgy. Regard what follows, therefore, not as psychotherapy for squeamishness, nor as the sociology of a prohibition, but as ecclesial therapy against a heresy. If bits of this chapter make you uncomfortable, you have exposed your inner Nestorius.

If your inner Nestorius is very powerful, you will even find yourself nourishing objections already at this point. Nestorius, you will say, was not concerned about wombs as such or even Mary as such; Nestorius was concerned with the technical language for expressing the union of the divine and human in Christ. And that is true. Perhaps it is even the case historically that "Mother of God" language was more dear to Cyril than ugly to Nestorius. But consider the logical consequences.

The nub of the problem, as of so many, was about the language of public prayer. What should Christians say in church? Shall they call Mary "Mother of God"? Nestorius thought that phrase was a mistake. He preferred to call Mary "Mother of Christ." According to his critics, "Mother of Christ" was a failure of nerve, because it made "Christ" the name of a third thing, neither fully divine nor fully human, neither one among human beings nor God to save them. Nestorius's Christ, according to its critics, failed on both counts to measure up to "God with us." For this third thing could neither (as human) exhibit real solidarity with human beings, nor (as God) save them from their plight.

Why did Nestorius feel that the language of "Mother of God" would be not just mistaken, but wrong? So many theological arguments proceed out of a conviction that one's opponents *should not talk that way.* So many theological anathemas amount to teaching believers, "Don't say that!" or, "Wash your mouth out with soap." Philosophical accounts tend to overlook the fact that it was precisely mother-language that set him off. It was not philosophical language that excited controversy, although that's the language in which the controversy was conducted. It was concrete, gendered, bodily language that set him off. It was the kind of concrete, gendered, bodily language that this chapter considers.

It is difficult, to be sure, to lay misogyny at the feet of the historical Nestorius, just as it is difficult to lay many versions of semi- and crypto-Pelagianism at the door of the historical Pelagius. Here, then, I am offering, for heuristic purposes, a theologico-mysogynistic objection to the phrase "Mother of God," which may be unrelated to that of the historical Nestorius, but would share his desire to keep the divine apart from the human through the mediation of a third term. So, if you like, you can give it scare quotes and call it "Nestorianism," or you can give it a distancing prefix, and call it neo- or quasi- or pseudo-Nestorianism.

I think Nestorius (or "Nestorius") and many low-church Protestants today are against the language of "Mother of God" because they find it unseemly, indecent. They find it so because they cannot imagine that very God would inhabit such a place. They find it unthinkable that God would enter the world through a vagina. Urine and menses pass through the same opening. The reader can supply less savory words. How can God be there? They find the image self-evidently disgusting. Similar concerns underlay controversies over whether Jesus really ate — and shat.

Unable to resist the force of the narrative, neo-Nestorians cannot deny the birth of Christ. They can only make distancing distinctions. This Christ must not have had the divine nature, the same nature as the impassible Father. A human being enters the world passing headfirst through a vagina. Even a hero-savior may do that on our behalf. But God? Is nothing holy? Must everything be made impure and unnatural as the Gentiles and their sexual practices? Do not dirty the face of God with female orifices! Something indeed must be kept clean. "Christ" is the name Nestorius used and neo-Nestorians might use to name the emissary that God sent to do his dirty work. Mary, according to such theologians, could not be "Mother of God," because that would not be pious. Some theologians, like pornographers, want to pry into places they should leave decently alone; sometimes words have to be interposed to protect community standards.

The orthodox, Cyrillian winners of the debate with Nestorius did not settle for upholding the view that Christ was fully God and fully human. They insisted on the "communication of the attributes," on a theory of predication such that what happened to Jesus happened to God (or God took it on). The important theological claims concerned the crucifixion: God took on a human nature in order to undergo suffering on behalf of human beings. "One of the Trinity died for us." "Impassibly he suffered," that is, by free choice and in pursuit of his own saving purpose.[30] The one who died and the one who was resurrected and the one who saves are the same one.

---

30. Cyril of Alexandria, "3rd Letter to Nestorius," in *Select Letters of Cyril of Alexandria,* ed. and trans. Lionel Wickam (Oxford: Oxford University Press, 1983); Second Council of Constantinople, "Anathema 10," in *Documents of the Christian Church,* 3rd ed., ed. Henry Bettenson and Chris Maunder (Oxford: Oxford University Press, 1999), p. 101.

But the important *liturgical* result concerns the Annunciation. Cyril and others do not compromise on the claim that moves others to disgust. They insist on it. In their opponents' faces they require the phrase, "the Mother of God." Here the issue is not the crucifixion, in all its bloodiness, but the birth, with the orifice and fluids that pertain thereto. If this is scandalous — as indeed it is — it is but the beginning of the scandal of the Incarnation.

It is important not only for Nestorius or "Nestorius," but also for twentieth-century forgetfulness of the Spirit. If the twentieth century tends, with Barth, to announce the Spirit and talk about the Son, then that is a problem precisely in the Annunciation. In the twentieth century, all the work of conceiving takes place by means of christology, so that even the Spirit is conceived by the Son. That is, to be sure, a taking seriously of the Incarnation. But not in the right way, since it reverses the biblical pattern. In the Annunciation, the angel announces the Son, who is conceived by the Spirit. The angel does not announce a spirit, who is conceived by the Son. To take the Annunciation seriously is to conceive the Son by the Spirit, not the other way around.

The rest of this chapter takes the Annunciation seriously, not in order to shock (unless shock is part of the therapy), but precisely where older Christian traditions, East and West, have done so. For the womb is not only the bodily origin of Jesus, but for that reason also a place in which the Spirit delights to rest. We must therefore linger too.

Sometime between 510 and 580 St. Benedict published his *Rule*, by far the most important document of monasticism in the Christian West. It set the *Magnificat* as the canticle for Vespers[31] and directed the reading of Psalm 110 (109 in the Vulgate) as the first psalm on Sundays.[32] The monks, therefore, would have said the *Magnificat* and Psalm 110 in close proximity every single week. They would always have read Psalm 110, that is, with the Annunciation in mind.[33]

Psalm 110 begins, "The Lord says to my lord, 'Sit at my right hand,'" which already the New Testament took in a christological sense (cf. Matt. 22:44, Acts 2:34, I Cor. 15:25, Eph. 1:20, Heb. 1:3, 13). The commentarial tradition, too, identifies the speaker as God the Father, and the character addressed, the second lord, the you-character, as the Son. However difficult that reading might be

---

31. *The Rule of St. Benedict in English*, ed. Timothy Fry (New York: Vintage Books, 1998), Ch. 17.

32. *Rule of St. Benedict*, Ch. 18.

33. I am grateful to Brian Daley and Derek Krueger for conversations about this material.

consistently to carry through, it applied also through verses 2 and 3, which read in the Vulgate, *"ex utero ante luciferam genui te,"* "out of my womb before the morning star I bore you."[34] The antecedent for the I-character, in the Vulgate, is still the Lord, and the you-character is still the Son. Since the psalm was, furthermore, taken to assert the preexistence of the Son with the Father before creation, the womb in question was not the earthly womb of Mary, but the preexistent origin of the Son in the substance of the Father. The constant, daily association in Benedictine prayer of the metaphorical womb of the Son's origin in the Trinity with the physical womb of the Son's gestation in his human mother Mary was a liturgical practice that increased both the felt naturalness of that association, and theological attention to it.

Already long before Benedict, Augustine had authored his *Explanations of the Psalms,* and posed this question about the line "out of my womb I bore you":

> If God hath a Son, hath He also a womb? Like fleshly bodies, He hath not; for He hath not a bosom either; yet it is said, "He who is in the bosom of the Father *(in sinu Patris),* hath declared Him" [John 1:18]. But that which is the womb, is the bosom also: both bosom and womb are put for a secret place. What meaneth, "from the womb"? From what is secret, from what is hidden; from Myself, from My substance; this is the meaning of "from the womb;" for, "who shall declare His generation?" [Isa. 53:8]. Let us then understand the Father saying unto the Son, "From My womb before the morning star I have brought Thee forth." . . . This expression, "before the morning star," is used both figuratively [i.e., indicating the "time" before creation] and literally, and was thus fulfilled. For the Lord was born at night from the womb of the Virgin Mary.[35]

If the Benedictine liturgy renders familiar the association of the womb of the Father with that of Mary by bringing them together every Sunday at Vespers, Augustine renders the association theological by a twofold interpretation of "before the morning star." If the confluence of Augustine and the liturgy is not powerful enough, we have in addition the perceived echo of Isaiah 49. Just as Augustine has interpreted the psalm so that the womb of the Father parallels the womb of the virgin instead of coinciding with it, so too Isaiah 49:1 is interpreted differentially, so that the two clauses name two parallel events instead of the same one:

34. A modern translation from the Hebrew has "From the womb of the morning like dew your youth will come to you" (RSV) and notes that the meaning cannot be accurately recovered.

35. Augustine, *Enarrationes in Psalmos* 109.10, in NPNF 8, p. 543.

The Lord called me from the womb, from the body of my mother he named
my name.

Again, the Lord is the father, and the I-character is the Son; the first womb is
the Father's, even if the body of the mother is Mary's. The Lord is compared
to a woman with a womb more clearly at verses 14-15:

But Zion said, "The Lord has forsaken me,
    my Lord has forgotten me."
Can a woman forget her sucking child,
    that she should have no compassion on the son of her womb?

Even if the son in question here is more clearly Israel, still it is undeniable to
early medieval Christian interpreters that figuratively at least the Father has a
womb. It is not that one may say so in an excess of zeal; the scriptures and the
liturgy seem to require it.

It is the less surprising, therefore, that after over a hundred years of weekly
practice of Benedictine devotions the Eleventh Council of Toledo, in 675,
would give the Augustinian exegesis Western conciliar force: "One must believe that the Son is begotten *and born* not from nothing, nor from some
other substance, but *from the womb of the Father* [*de Patris utero*], that is,
from his substance."[36]

In the East, the great liturgical poet Romanos the Melodist plays with the
same paradox on the occasion of the same psalm, relating the dawn of the
psalm to the star of the Nativity, in opening a *kontakion* addressed to Mary:

He who was born before dawn   from father without mother
    today without father   has been made flesh from you;
whence the star   brings glad tidings to the magi.[37]

Thus such a phrase as "womb of the Father" arises neither from contemporary feminism nor from the queer theory of Judith Butler. Rather it is gender bending from an earlier period and context, something that arises from
the interaction of the christological interpretation of the Psalms with the
birth narrative of Luke. In medieval Eastern art, the head of the Son appears
in a circle over Mary's abdomen (see fig. 2); so in the early twelfth-century
West we get the Father displaying the Son in the same womblike circle. The

36. Heinrich Denzinger and Peter Hünermann, *Enchiridion Symbolorum*, 37th ed. (Freiburg
im Breisgau: Herder, 1991), n. 526.
37. Romanos the Melodist, "On the Nativity II," in *After Antiquity*, pp. 417-29, with facing
Greek; here, p. 417.

1. Baptism, Monastery Church, Hosios Loukas, Greece. Mosaic, 11th C.

Baptism is a trinitarian event in which the Spirit rests upon and manifests the Son in the presence of the Father. This image navigates between representing too little of the Trinity and too much, showing all three Persons — the Father as a hand, the Spirit as a dove — without giving a human face to either. The placement of John's hand takes human agency into an intratrinitarian event. No doubt unintentionally, the water mounds and ripples over the human body of Jesus like the robe of glory that Syriac sources credit him with leaving for other baptizands in the water. (The small figure at the bottom personifies the river, as in Roman art.) The blue of the water echoes the blue of the circle from which the hand of the Father emerges and recalls the blue that often robes or surrounds Jesus in Eastern Orthodox depictions of the transfiguration. Erich Lessing / Art Resource, NY

2. Mary *platytera* with the Trinity, from the Byzantine Khludov Psalter, marginal manuscript illumination, second half of the 9th C.

The conception of Jesus too is a trinitarian event in which the Spirit rests upon and manifests the Son in the presence of the Father. Here too the Trinity embraces and empowers human agency, this time that of Mary. Here too blue is the color of epiphany, surrounding and including the human being. Moscow, State Historical Museum, Cod. Gr. 129, fo. 44, detail

**3. Annunciation, Bamberg Cathedral, Georgenchorschranke, detail.
Stone relief, c. 1230-40**

Here the Spirit rests on the Son implied in the Annunciation to Mary.
Unlike many annunciations, this one makes the Spirit prominent in an
almost pregnant dove. The heavy clouds would usually also represent the
Spirit "overshadowing" Mary, although here they may represent the Father. The relief makes the Spirit the source of the word also in delivering
the scroll to the angel. Bildarchiv, Marburg, Germany

4. Allegory of the Transfiguration, S. Apollinare in Classe, Ravenna, Italy. Apse mosaic, c. 549
Only the half-figures of Moses and Elijah identify this image as a Transfiguration. It represents all three Persons of the Trinity in a rebus: the Father in the hand, the Spirit in the thin clouds that follow the line of the circle, and the Son in the cross. The Spirit might be said to rest — however lightly and at a distance — on the body of Christ not only in the Cross but also in the figure of St. Apollinarus at the bottom and in the sheep. The epiphanic blue usually reserved in Orthodox art for the robe of the transfiguration here surrounds the cross. The indirect and mysterious character of this image makes it unusually apophatic, so that it points to the unrepresentability ascribed to the Trinity and often appropriated to the Spirit. For discussion, see Henry Maguire, "The Language of Symbols," in *Earth and Ocean: The Terrestrial World in Early Byzantine Art* (University Park and London: Pennsylvania State University Press, 1987), pp. 1-15. Scala / Art Resource

5. Transfiguration by Andrea Previtali (c. 1480-1528), Pinacoteca di Brera, Milan
As opposed to the previous Transfiguration, this one is unmysterious to the point of vulgarity —
and appears here for contrast. All three Persons show up, but hardly in the way that the biblical texts
imply them. The Spirit, here represented as a dove, appears more subtly in Luke as overshadowing
clouds. The Father, who seems here to have appropriated the clouds, speaks rather bluntly by means
of a cartoonist's scroll. Jesus, in orans posture, is praying, as in Luke, but appears oddly
untransfigured and alone. Here too the Spirit rests on the Son in the presence of the Father, but all
too demystified. Erich Lessing / Art Resource, NY

6-7. Ascension and Pentecost, Book of Hours, France, 1st half 16th C.
Ascension and Pentecost often show up as a matched pair in Eastern Orthodox
church programs, and here in a Western Book of Hours. The footprints make it
look as if Christ has pushed off with his feet, giving his ascent a strong sense of
vertical movement, which links the image by contrast with the more spreading

descent of the Spirit on this page. Indeed, it is the tongues of fire that seem to gentle the Spirit's descent, since their natural movement is upward. Here the Spirit rests upon and manifests the Son in the persons of his followers, if the dove can be said to rest upon fire. Fol. 47 verso–48 recto. Musée de la Renaissance, Écouen, France. Réunion des Musées Nationaux / Art Resource, NY

8. Resurrection (*Not Gottes* with Trinity), painting, c. 1450, Schwäbisch-Gmünd, Germany
The resurrection as a trinitarian event: the Father raises the Son from the grave at the instigation of the Spirit. Whispering in his ear, the Spirit of fidelity seems to inspire or speak the word to the Father. The image risks modeling the Father after Mary, both in composing Father and Son as a pietà and in positioning the dove at the Father's ear (as in some Western scenes of Mary's conception of the Word). And yet it is hard to know how else to represent the trinitarian character of Romans 8:11, especially since the image seems to grant the initiative to the Spirit. Das Museum im Prediger. Schwäbisch-Gmünd

miniature decorates the initial "I" of John 1:1: "In the beginning was the Word, and the Word was with God."[38] So too Thomas Aquinas: "In the generation of the Word Holy Scripture attributes to the Father all those things which in fleshly generation belong separately to the father and to the mother: thus the Father is said both 'to give life to the Son' and 'to conceive and give birth [*concipere et parturire*]' to the Son."[39] "Conceive and give birth" is no mere metaphor. It is the quotation from Isaiah 7:14 that Matthew uses to describe the birth of Jesus from Mary: "Behold, a virgin shall *conceive and bear* a son, and his name shall be called Emmanuel" (Matt. 1:23). In good, orthodox fashion, the Father is not male, but the source of human characteristics, male and female in God's image. Theologically, it is this image that the Son begins to restore by causing his mother to pattern his father's womb.

This means that, once again, what the Trinity does in the economy has its character from what the Trinity does in its own life. The theological precondition implied in the acceptance of this usage is one we have seen repeatedly: what the New Testament narrates as happening among the Persons in the economy may provide glimpses into their relations in the Trinity, and their revealed relations among one another in the Trinity are taken reliably to provide a pattern for their actions in the economy. In these particular cases, both the Council of Toledo and Thomas Aquinas preserve what the East would call the *monarchia*, the sole source, of the Father. They also preserve the rule that the Father transcends gender, or, better, that both earthly genders reflect the Father, whom neither can capture. Meanwhile, these statements do not prevent our appropriating to the Spirit in the economy a role that goes unmentioned in those accounts of what happens in the Trinity, a role that the text of Luke requires, that of overshadowing or coming upon Mary, bearing her response. Rather, what happens in the economy, Mary's reception of the Son by the Spirit, happens that way because it does so already in the Trinity: it is by the Spirit that God in Trinity chooses and desires to *receive*. And as it is by the Spirit that the Trinity receives, so too it is by the Spirit that also the economy receives.

Phrases like "the womb of the Father" suggest that there is some sense in traditional conceptualities in which even the Father receives. Assertions like

---

38. The Bible of Saint-Bénigne in the Bibliothèque Municipale of Dijon, reproduced in Gertrud Schiller, *Iconography of Christian Art,* trans. Janet Seligman, 2 vols. (Greenwich, Conn.: New York Graphic Society Ltd., 1971), vol. 1, figs. 1-2, described on pp. 6-7.

39. Thomas Aquinas, *Summa contra gentiles* IV, 11. I owe this and the citation from Denzinger to Bruce Marshall, *Trinity and Truth* (Cambridge and New York: Cambridge University Press, 2001), p. 16, n. 16.

"the Father conceives the Son" suggest the same. And yet the traditions have been cautious in the extreme about such implications. The same authors who wrote those phrases also believed in the Father's impassibility, that the ability to undergo pain, and even "experience," of a human kind, *pathos* in Greek, is no part of divinity, but of humanity, so that the Trinity can suffer only *in the Person of the Son,* and in the Son only because of the flesh. While it is orthodox, and even necessary, to say "God suffered" because Christ did, it is the patripassian heresy to say that the Father suffered. The reason for this, it is felt, is that if the Father suffers then there is nothing in God for us but solidarity. Solidarity is one of God's greatest gifts to human beings, to be God with us, but if that is *all* God offers, then there is no salvation: we are all suffering together in the same sinking boat. The roadblock against all sinking together is the impassibility of the Father. So if we say that the Spirit is the one by whom the Trinity receives, we must avoid denigrating either the Father's impassibility, or the Son's suffering.

Rather both are received at the hands of the Spirit. The Father chooses not to have his impassibility from himself alone, but to receive it as a gift from the Spirit. The Father does not desire out of neediness; but the Father may choose to desire.

The Son also chooses not to have divinity as a thing to be grasped, but to receive it from the Spirit. Token of this double reception is the resurrection. At the resurrection the Father chooses to receive the Son in victory not only because the Son rises in the Word's conquest over death (although he does), and not only because the Father raises the Son in love and vindication (although he does): but also because the Spirit dwells in his mortal body superfluously and gratuitously, in order to make Father and Son a gift of additional, undeserving — Gentile — human beings. At this the Father not only acts out of his impassibility, but also receives his Son from another, from the Spirit, and *thus* exercises the salvation of the human race beyond solidarity. In this way the Father not only exercises his impassibility, but also receives it from the Spirit, because it is from the Spirit that the Father receives those he also loves in face of death.

This new life is conceived in the Father by the Spirit in election. Predestination is implied at the Eleventh Council of Toledo to take place in the womb of the Father, and yet predestination is enacted in the world by the Spirit moving in external circumstances and internal loves. If none comes but whom the Father shall draw, then the Father may draw. But the Father draws by the Spirit. Newness of life is conceived by the Spirit, "the Lord, the Giver of Life," who pours out on all flesh; new life is conceived in the Father by the Spirit resting, or mediating, on the Father's Word; it is conceived in Mary by the Spirit resting on the Son; it is conceived in the font by the Spirit resting on those who will be baptized.

iv. The Spirit rests on the Son in the womb in Christ's side

The idea that the Father, in the exercise of his impassiblity, and that the Son, in the undergoing of his suffering, choose to receive those roles from the Spirit, shows up also in other places in the traditions, in metaphors describing human entry into God. The Spirit comes to rest on human beings as it rests on the body of the Son because they are said to enter into the Trinity through the womb of his side. In this the Son resembles his mother. At Ravenna we see Mary in the womb of her Son; Dante's *Paradiso* famously calls her *figlia del tuo figlio,* the daughter of her Son; Ephrem proclaims, "O Christ, you have given birth to your own mother in the the second birth that comes from water."[40] We turn to visions of human beings going up into the figurative body of God the Father and the wounded body of God the Son.

Gregory of Nyssa, in his *Life of Moses,* makes contemplative practice of going up into the bowels of God, on the occasion of Moses's seeing God's back side. The Father is entered through his back side in a way that at least one recent scholar has found anal-erotic.[41] But Gregory has been by no means the only one to portray the "male" members of the Trinity as penetrable. William of St.-Thierry moves from the side of the Son to the side of the Father, praying, "Open to us your body's side, that those who long to see the secrets of your Son may enter in," as if the Son is hidden in the Father's side as in a womb.[42] Here too one might speak of a *felix dilatio.* The twelfth-century Cistercian Guerric of Igny does it too. As Caroline Walker Bynum describes him, "Guerric is fascinated by images of pregnancy and of the womb. He not only speaks at length of the soul hiding in the wounds and heart of Christ, he

---

40. Ephrem the Syrian, "Hymns on the Nativity" 16.9, quoted in Sebastian Brock, *The Holy Spirit in the Syrian Baptismal Tradition,* 2d ed. (Poona, India: Anita Printers, 1998), p. 195. The original can be found in *Corpus scriptorum christianorum orientalium,* vol. 175.

41. Virginia Burrus, "Queer Father," in *Queer Theology,* ed. Gerard Loughlin (London: Routledge, forthcoming). See also the chapter on Gregory in her *Begotten, Not Made: Conceiving Manhood in Late Antiquity* (Stanford, Calif.: Stanford University Press, 2000), pp. 80-133 and Verna E. F. Harrison, "Receptacle Imagery in St Gregory of Nyssa's Anthropology," *Studia Patristica* 22 (1989): 23-27. For a modern use of womb symbolism, see Catherine Keller, "Adam's Womb," in *Face of the Deep: A Theology of Becoming* (London: Routledge, 2003), pp. 36-37.

42. *Meditative Orations,* Chap. 10, PL 180, cols. 225D-226A; trans. Sister Penelope, *The Works of William of St.-Thierry* 1: *On Contemplating God,* Cistercian Fathers Series 3 (Spencer, Mass.: Cistercian Publications, 1971), p. 131.

also explicitly associates heart and womb and produces a bizarre description of the soul as child incorporated into the bowels of God the Father."[43] The child in question is the prodigal son — not, therefore, a young child but a full-grown man, and God is identified as Father because the parable refers to the father of the prodigal. Bynum provides the following quotation:

> He draws [the wretched] into his very bowels and makes them his members. He could not bind us to himself more closely, could not make us more intimate to himself than by incorporating us into himself.

The Latin is even more suggestive than the published translation: *suisque inserit membris*. This is either a womb metaphor, or it is a sexual metaphor; like all of Guerric's writing, it is carefully, deliberately, and effectively phrased: why not therefore both? Some readers, impressed by the sense of *viscera*, have wondered whether the sexual suggestion could be implicitly anal-erotic. Homosexually oriented hearers or readers, to speak anachronistically, might not find such an image "bizarre." If *"inserit membris"* recalls a further, independent sense and usage where God the Father is subject of the verb "insert," this time to graft, then Guerric is also playing on Romans 11:17, 23, 24, in which God the Father grafts the Gentiles into the Jewish olive tree, acting explicitly, in the Vulgate, *"contra naturam"* (Rom. 11:24). Either way, the theological import of the image is the same; it is to bring home the divine compassion of Luke 15:20, the standard Greek expression for which refers to the bowels (ἐσπλαγχνίσθη). It is to render God actively receptive by ringing the changes on the receptivity of Mary, not as some independent human contribution apart from God, but as a human imitation of God borne and elicited by God — indeed, as this passage shows, a pattern that can only originate if God opens himself (I use the masculine pronoun advisedly), draws human beings up into himself, however inadequate are human bodies, female or male, to image the interior of God.

Christ is entered through a wound in a Latin in which *vulnera* and *vulva* are not that far apart, whether in imagery or in language. Long before the twentieth century, the tradition was busily engaged in masculinizing the feminine and feminizing the masculine, in the service of denial that God has gender at all. But these moves also serve the insistence that God can receive: God welcomes human beings into the divine life, and God welcomes them by the Holy Spirit, and none of the Persons are left out of this hospitality, but when

43. Bynum, "Jesus as Mother and Abbot as Mother: Some Themes in Twelfth-Century Cistercian Writing," in *Jesus as Mother: Studies in the Spirituality of the High Middle Ages* (Berkeley, Calif.: University of California Press, 1982), pp. 110-69; here, p. 121.

they exercise it toward the world, they do so indivisibly. When this hospitality takes bodily form, whether in the body of Jesus or of Mary, of disciple or believer, and even in the figurative body of the Father, the sight of whose backside is affirmed only to deny the sight of his face, it is a happy opening that one might appropriate to the Spirit. For as the priest invokes the Spirit over the matter of the Great Thanksgiving, so the Spirit invokes the body of Mary for the thanksgiving of the Magnificat.

Most often, the womb of the Father is tied up with the womb in Christ's side, which often stands alone. Bynum finds "references (perhaps with womb overtones) to the soul entering the side of Christ" in William of St.-Thierry.[44] Bernard of Clairvaux associates his own side with Marian motherhood: "As a mother loves her only son, so I have loved you, when you clung to my side, pleasing my heart [*haerentem lateri meo, placentem cordi meo*]." It is but a small step to associate motherhood with the side of Christ. Using *viscera,* a word applied often to Christ, Guerric of Igny speaks alliteratively of little ones being torn from his bowels *(avulsa . . . a me viscera mea parvuli . . .),* as though he himself were giving them birth.[45] It is Guerric who best exemplifies a rich piety of entering into Jesus' body through the wound in his side. It displays deep metaphors of the openness, receptivity, and vulnerability that, I have argued, the Son allows himself to receive from the Spirit. Whether or not uterine language is used, Guerric portrays the Son as receiving human beings through an opening in his body, where they in turn receive a safe haven from sin and experience comfort and gifts of the Spirit. To describe this condition of the Son, he goes so far as to use the word *pregnans.* His piety provides another example of the pattern that what happens with Mary reflects relations already enacted among the Persons of the Trinity and in which other human beings come subsequently to be included. It is not too much to say that the wound reveals a womb.

We begin, appropriately enough, with a sermon for the Annunciation.[46] Guerric follows Isaiah to apply the verb "to open" *(aperire)* to both the sprouting of the earth and the conception of Mary, as the prophet puts it: "Let the earth open, that salvation may sprout forth, and let it cause righteousness to spring up also" (Isa. 45:8). The ground brings forth a rock *(petrus),* which is Christ, the cornerstone. The next thing commanded to open, following Mary's

44. Bynum, "Jesus as Mother," pp. 119-20.

45. Bynum, "Jesus as Mother," p. 116, quoting Bernard of Clairvaux, Letter 201, at PL 182, cols. 369B-C and Letter 144, col. 301A.

46. Guerric d'Igny, "2d Sermon for Annunciation," §1, in *Sermons,* Latin and French on facing pages, *Sources chrétiennes,* vol. 166, Série des Textes Monastiques d'Occident vol. 31, p. 124.

example, is the breast *(pectus)* and mouth *(os)* of the believer: "This is to say, thus she offers her devotion; this is clearly to open the breast to the Lord, this is also to open the mouth and attract the Spirit"— playing on Psalm 119:131 (Vulgate 118), "with my open mouth I pant."[47] In what is indeed an entire sermon on expansion, dilation, aperture, conception, opening, ears and doors also open, until we get to the peroration:

> O faithful soul, billow your bosom *[expande sinus]*, spread out your good will *[dilata affectum]*, do not narrow yourself in your bowels *[visceribus]*, conceive what the creature cannot capture. Open *[aperi]* to the Word of God the hearing ear. This is the way of the conceiving Spirit to the womb of the heart *[ad uterum cordis via spiritus concipiendi]*, for this reason were knit together the bones of Christ, that is, the virtues, in the belly of the pregnant one [*in ventre pregnantis,* playing on "the bones in the womb" of Eccl. 11:5]. Thanks to you, Spirit, who blow where you will.[48]

Here Guerric sets up a series of parallel openings: *uterus* (womb), *venter* (womb, belly), *viscera* (bowels), to which in other sermons he will add a fourth, *vulnus* (wound).[49] Of these Christ and Mary can share the central two (belly and bowels), and for that reason identify the first and last (womb and wound). We have already seen that Augustine can explicitly equate *sinus* (bosom) with *uterus* (womb) — both words used also by Guerric — in the case of God the Father. The Annunciation sermon is not, however, devoted to the blessed noun, the womb, or any of its multiple associations. The Annunciation sermon is devoted rather to a blessed verb, to open. The blessed earth, the blessed virgin — door, ear, mouth, breast, heart — and the listener who would be blessed all perform the same receptive action: they *open* or dilate. The question of *what* opens, in *this* sermon, is extremely diverse. What the openings have in common, is the activation of the Spirit who blesses and gives new life, the diversely opening Spirit whom Guerric invokes toward the end of the sermon with *"Gratias tibi, Spiritus,* who blows where you will" — in context one might almost say, "who opens."

Thus it comes as no surprise that Christ also opens. Like his Mother, Christ opens to the Spirit, this time as a dove nesting in a cleft in the rock, in such a way that other believers, too, can take refuge there, so that the Spirit, in resting on Christ, rests also on them. The dove that flies into a cleft or hides in

---

47. Guerric, "2d Sermon for Annunciation," §3.

48. Guerric, "2d Sermon for Annunciation," §4.

49. As Bynum notes, "the same Hebrew word that is translated *viscera* is also translated *venter* and *uterus* (Gen. 25:23, Isa. 48:19)," "Jesus as Mother," p. 122, n. 34.

an opening is the dove of the Song of Songs 2:14: "O my dove, in the clefts of the rock, in the covert of the cliff" — and always also the Spirit resting on Christ the Rock.

> [The wounded Christ] is the cleft rock . . . do not fly only to him but into him. . . . For in his loving kindness and his compassion he opened *[aperuit]* his side in order that the blood of the wound might give you life, the warmth of his body revive you, the breath of his heart flow into you. . . . There you will lie hidden in safety. . . . There you will certainly not freeze, for in the bowels of Christ charity does not grow cold. . . .[50]

> Therefore the dove of Christ, the beautiful dove of Christ whose own wound furnishes an opening *[foramen]* so secure and so welcome for the building of a nest rightly sings joyful praises everywhere this day, and the sweet voice resounds in the ears of the bridegroom with the memory or the imitation of the passion, with the meditation on the wound as with the opening *[foramen]* of the rock.[51]

> Blessed is the one who, in order that I might nest in the clefts *[foramen]* of the rock, brought himself to be pierced *[perforare]*, hands, feet and side, and that he might open his whole self to me *[se mihi totum aperuit]*, that I might enter *[ingrediar]* into the wonderful tabernacle and be protected in the hiding-place of his tabernacle, . . . even the gracious habitation of doves, whose clefts offer so many openings and favor in the wounds over almost his whole body *[tot vulneribus toto fere corpore patentia]*.[52]

Here Christ's body becomes a tissue of openings, an aperture to the Trinity, a way in. Guerric insists that this entering into Christ is not merely a clinging "to" him. It is important to him that Christ has an accessible *interior:*

> Why not indeed flee not only to him but into him *[non ad ipsum tantum sed in ipsum fugere]*, enter *[ingredere]* into the clefts of the rock, hide yourself in the channels of the rock, the very perforations of his hands, in the trench in his side? For the wound in the side of Christ, what is it if not an entrance *[ostium]* into the ark of salvation in the face of the flood? (*Sermons* 2:212)

---

50. Guerric, "Fourth Sermon for Palm Sunday," *Sermons* 2:212-14, trans. in the monks of St. Bernard Abbey, *Liturgical Sermons* 2:77-78. I owe my attention to this passage to Bynum's quotation of it, "Jesus as Mother," pp. 121-22.

51. *Sermons* 2:214, my translation.

52. *Sermons* 2:210.

Christ opens his side, or allows soldiers to open it not only in Guerric but also in Aelred of Rievaulx (d. 1167):

> Then one of the soldiers opened his side with a lance and there came forth blood and water. Hasten, linger not, eat the honeycomb with your honey, drink your wine with your milk. The blood is changed into wine to gladden you, the water into milk to nourish you. From the rock streams have flowed for you, wounds have been made in his limbs, holes in the wall of his body, in which, like a dove, you may hide while you kiss them one by one. Your lips, stained with blood, will become like a scarlet ribbon and your word sweet.[53]

This is not just an oddity of Cistercian devotion, or a mere association of ideas. Rather, it shows up also elsewhere, and it has roots in concrete practices in other Christian groups. Not only does the devotion to the side of Jesus move twelfth-century Cistercian meditation and prayer practice — as far away as twenty-first-century Egypt the wound is adduced as a reason for the particular door that Coptic Christians use to enter a church. Facing east, a Coptic church represents the body of Christ, with his head at the altar and his feet at the west door. But since Coptic iconography depicts the wound as occurring on Jesus' right side (left as one faces him), they enter by the door to the left as one faces the altar, always by the north door.[54] So they enter the church concretely through the wound in the side of Christ.

Such bodily practices correspond with other meditative and commentarial practices among still other Eastern Christians worshipping in Syriac, for whom the wound in the side of Christ reopens the door to paradise, found inside his body (which is also the membership of the church). Not only is the womb of Mary a *felix dilatio,* but the body of Christ is a tissue of openings, a way into the triune God, itself held open by the Spirit for the accommodation of others into its communion.

---

53. Bynum, "Jesus as Mother," p. 123, quoting Aelred, *De institutione inclusarum,* Ch. 31, *Opera Omnia* 1:671, ed. A. Hoste and C. H. Talbot, CCCM 1 (Turnhout, 1971), trans. M. P. McPherson, *Works of Aelred of Rievaulx* 1: *Treatises and Pastoral Prayer,* Cistercian Fathers Series 2 (Spencer, Mass.: Cistercian Publications, 1971), 1:90-91.

54. So I was told by a monk of St. Anthony's Monastery in Egypt. I have not found a written source to shore up this piety.

v. The Spirit rests on the Son in the womb of the wine

Insofar as Mary resembles Abraham in seeing the sacrifice of her Son, other human beings participate in that sacrifice as often as they celebrate the Eucharist. As the Spirit rests on the historical body of Christ in the waters of the womb, so she comes to rest also on the churchly body of Christ in the wine of the sacrament. Sebastian Brock points out a deep "connection . . . between the Annunciation and the epiclesis," or the priest's invocation of the Holy Spirit over the elements of the Eucharist.[55]

> Just as the Holy Spirit descended to the womb of Mary . . . and made the body of God the Word from the flesh of the Virgin, so too the Spirit descends on the bread and wine on the altar and makes them into the Body and Blood of God the Word which originated from the Virgin.[56]

Ephrem the Syrian brackets the whole career of the Spirit and Christ with Annunciation and Eucharist:

> In the womb that bore you are Fire and Spirit,
> Fire and Spirit are in the river where you were baptized,
> Fire and Spirit are in our baptism too,
> And in the Bread and Cup are Fire and Spirit.[57]

It is unremarkable to explain the Eastern epiclesis like this: "For bread and wine, representatives of the material world, to take on their new vivifying and sanctifying role as the Body and Blood of Christ, the priest as representative of the faithful has to invoke the Holy Spirit, who effects this." But according to Brock, Annunciation and epiclesis are not just associated, but form as it were two sides of one relationship between Spirit and matter:

> There is thus a striking complementarity between the Annunciation and the epiclesis in the Eucharist. To bring out the point, one could put the matter in somewhat bizarre fashion and say that for God to become part of the material world and to take on flesh and blood, the Holy Spirit has to invite — one could almost say 'invoke' — Mary for her cooperation.[58]

55. Sebastian Brock, "Mary and the Eucharist: An Oriental Perspective," *Sobornost* 1 (1979): 50-59.

56. Moshe bar Kopha (d. 903), "Commentary on the Liturgy," in *Two Commentaries on the Jacobite Liturgy*, ed. R. H. Connolly and H. W. Codrington (London: Williams and Norgate, 1913), p. 60, cited in Brock, "Mary," p. 51.

57. Ephrem the Syrian, "Hymns on Faith" 10, 17, in Brock, "Mary," p. 51.

58. Brock, "Mary," p. 55.

To see the depth of this, recall some high christology. What the Word assumes is a human nature, not a human person. There is no self-subsisting human being in there, but the Word. That distinction is crucial, so that sophomores cannot evade the seriousness of Jesus' suffering and death by saying, "but only the human part suffered [by which they mean a self-subsisting other human person in a schizoid Jesus], so it wasn't real for God." The doctrine of the hypostatic union replies, "Ain't nobody in there but the Word."

On the other hand, that does not mean that in the assumption of human nature God changed. Rather the human nature was elevated to be with God. So not only did God become human that human beings might become divine, but the Word elevated human nature in order to become human. Even better, the Spirit gave the Word a body so that those with bodies might receive the Spirit, and not only that, but the Spirit needed a body to conceive the Word. Here the conception of Jesus reverses the epiclesis of the Mass. Brock has found a Marian/eucharistic version of the Athanasian dictum that God became human, that human beings might become divine.[59] Here the Spirit invokes a human being, that a human being might invoke the Spirit. But this time the Blessed Exchange is less abstract and conceptual. Its terms are no longer "the human" and "the divine," but quite concretely the blood of childbirth and the blood of the cup. Thus Ephrem can even say "Mary has given us the Bread of rest."[60]

Because the Eucharist both recalls the crucifixion of Jesus that Mary observed and serves as healing medicine for human beings, Romanos the Melodist obligates Jesus to explain to her why he has to go to death to heal humanity:

Be patient a little longer, Mother, and you will see
how, like a physician, I undress and reach the place where they lie
and I treat their wounds,
cutting with the lance their calluses and their scabs.
And I take vinegar, I apply it as astringent to the wound,
when with the probe of the nails I have investigated the cut,
    I shall plug it with the cloak.
And, with my cross as a splint,
I shall make use of it, Mother, so that you may chant
    with understanding,

59. Cf. Brock, "Mary," p. 52.
60. Ephrem, "Hymns on Unleavened Bread" 6.7, quoted in Brock, "Mary," p. 57; text in *Corpus scriptorum christianorum orientalium*, vol. 248.

"By suffering he has abolished suffering,
    my Son and my God."[61]

In *Sexuality and the Christian Body* I wrote that the Trinity breaks not apart but open with the breaking of the bread; the Eucharist also makes a blessed opening and a waybread for the delay. With that I meant to claim that the *opening up* of the Trinity goes all the way down, while the form that its opening takes ("breaking") is contingent. A metaphysics of rupture, therefore, can only be a contingent, postlapsarian metaphysics, even if it is also, *felix culpa*, a metaphysics of healing, the rupture of exploration, exposure, and surgery. God comes close to us in nuptial mystery and exposes the worst we can do, so that we can be healed. *Felix dilatio* becomes *felix culpa* under conditions of sin, as God transforms the place of welcoming into a place of healing.

Rupture and surgery do not go all the way down, but respond to sin. All three Abrahamic traditions tell a story in which God seeks to transform sinful human nature with an offering (promise and feasting) that becomes sacrifice by interruption, by God's attempt to take up, assume, and redeem human sin, before being revealed as essentially thanksgiving. One imagines that apart from sin gift would turn to gratitude without interruption, as in the trinitarian life. Only after the Fall does the offering of thanks become sacrifice for sin. I Corinthians 10:17 glosses the fraction of the bread as distribution for unity's sake: "we who are many are one body, for we all partake of the one bread," and that conception predominates into the second century (as in Ignatius of Antioch).[62] Gradually the fraction came to carry a more complicated symbology, that of the opening or breaking of Christ's body, so that in some rites the priest pierces the bread with a lance.[63] The complexities of thanksgiving's persistence and restoration are clearer in narrative than in conceptual analysis. Consider the complex of stories in Genesis 18, appropriate here because Mary is like Abraham, and because the Spirit hovers over the wine of the Eucharist as she hovers over the waters of the womb.

Between the promise of a son and the ransom of Isaac another episode intervenes: the hospitality of Abraham.[64] In Genesis 18, three visitors appear to

---

61. "On the Lament of the Mother of God" 13, in St. Romanos the Melodist, *Kontakia on the Life of Christ*, p. 148. I owe the insight that Christ is both physician and patient to Stephania Gianulis.

62. Rowan Williams, *Eucharistic Sacrifice: The Roots of a Metaphor* (Bramcote, Nottinghamshire: Grove Books, 1982), p. 14.

63. See George Galavaris, *Bread and the Liturgy* (Madison, Wis. and London: University of Wisconsin Press, 1970), pp. 86, 91-92, 168-69.

64. The next five paragraphs were composed in slightly different form for the Children of

Abraham and Sarah at the oaks of Mamre, and Abraham makes them a great feast of cakes of meal, a calf, curds, and milk. The three visitors repeat the promise of the covenant. In Genesis 18 some passages refer to three men and some passages refer to two angels and the Lord. That shifting back and forth between the three and the Lord has caused some traditional Christian interpreters to see the Trinity here. Furthermore, since the members of the Trinity, Father, Son, and Spirit, one God, are here feasting with human beings, those interpreters see a foretaste of the feasting or celebrating or dancing that God intends human beings to share when they come to participate in God's own trinitarian life. Jesus says, "The kingdom may be compared to a father who gave a feast for his son."[65] This is the feast that God has prepared for his people from before the foundation of the world, and to which they look forward at the end — the feast that Abraham shares with God under the oaks of Mamre and at the reception of the promise.

Abraham receives a promise that by him all the nations of the earth shall be a blessing one for another. Abraham celebrates with three visitors at a festive meal. Abraham exposes his son to the knife. Abraham receives a ram to restore the son. Christian interpreters have often read the sequence meal-sacrifice-restoration in the context of another meal, sacrifice, and restoration: namely the Last Supper, crucifixion, and resurrection of Jesus. Christians celebrate that sequence as often as they take bread and wine in memory of him. Thus too they enact the hospitality of Abraham, the binding and ransom of Isaac as often as they do it.

But the story does not end with a festive meal. The meal precedes a sinister episode in which the feasting exchange of gift and gratitude is exposed to traditions of first-born sons sacrificed to Molech.[66] The critics of religion are right: religion, like love, is highly ambiguous; the highest form of human activity becomes, under conditions of sin, precisely the most dangerous. Can God deal with this feature of human beings, or does holiness tie God's hands? The text does not portray God as stopped or thwarted or pulled up short by the ambiguities of human loves and loyalties, or even by human religious tendencies to violence. God exposes the worst that human beings can do, so that it can be healed. God risks *telling* Abraham to sacrifice his son in order to

---

Abraham Institute at the instigation of Peter Ochs and appear independently as "The Ransom of Isaac," *Journal for Scriptural Reasoning* 1:2 (2001/02). Available online at http://etext.lib.virginia.edu/journals/ssr/.

65. Matt. 9:15, 22:1-14; Luke 14:16-24, Matt. 8:11, Luke 13:29, 5:34, Mark 2:18-22, Isa. 62:5, Rev. 19:9; Prodigal Son, Luke 15:22-23.

66. See Jon D. Levenson, *The Death and Resurrection of the Beloved Son: The Transformation of Child Sacrifice in Judaism and Christianity* (New Haven: Yale University Press, 1993).

show Abraham what to offer instead. God provides a ram — a ram that according to rabbinic interpretation God had prepared for the covenant since before the creation of the world. The initial command is chilling, as if to say "Okay, go ahead." But the story as a whole enacts a dramatic irony and relief. God transforms the Molechite impulse to violent sacrifice into the peaceful offering of praise and thanksgiving. This *transformed* offering becomes the Jewish Tamid and the Christian Eucharist.[67]

The New Testament does not soften but intensifies that pattern. God imitates Abraham: "For God so loved the world that he gave his only Son" (Jn. 3:16). Jesus cries out from the cross as if in the voice of Isaac, "My God, my God, why have you forsaken me?" (Mk. 15:34).

And yet Jesus and the Father, like Isaac and Abraham, are oddly not at odds. Jesus like Isaac is willing. Abraham and Isaac, Jesus and the Father are at one in pursuing the promise. That feature of the stories is odd enough to become one reason why Christians say that both Jesus and the Father are God, so that God's sacrifice is first of all a sacrifice of himself. Thus we return to the feast. "This is my body," Jesus says, "given for you." God would renew the feast even on the night in which he was betrayed. A vain attempt, perhaps; a deathbed wedding. But God risks the worst that human beings can do — crucifixion, child sacrifice — and transforms it into yet another invitation to the feast, another occasion of gift. God gives back for love the son that Molech would kill; God gives back for feasting the body the Romans would break. When Christians break the bread of communion, it is the breaking of God's own body that they enact. By God's dramatic irony it does not so much break apart, as break open: the Trinity takes this occasion to lay itself open — *O felix dilatio* — and human beings, with Abraham and Sarah under the oaks of Mamre, join Father, Son, and Spirit in feasting. Surely the feast of Abraham will turn hostility into hospitality, as in the Twenty-third Psalm, "Thou preparest a table before me in the presence of mine enemies." It is part and parcel of this pattern that the community formed by the Eucharist provides a means to resist both evil and victimage: Turning the other cheek, walking the extra mile, loving one's enemies, and praying for those who persecute one both expose evil and preserve agency.[68] Then the promise will be fulfilled that by the name of Abraham all the nations of the earth shall be — not curses — but blessings to one another.[69]

67. Cf. Rowan Williams, *Eucharistic Sacrifice*, pp. 14-17.

68. This sentence paraphrases David Matzko McCarthy, *Sex and Love in the Home* (London: SCM, 2001), p. 236, n. 26.

69. Cf. Kendall Soulen, "YHWH the Triune God," *Modern Theology* 15 (1999): 25-54.

In a subversive engagement with sacrificial bodies, Jesus redeploys the diversifying creativity of the Spirit, using it to deconstruct a structure of violence.[70] Apply the following passage to the Eucharist:

> To deconstruct the concept of matter of that of bodies is not to negate or refuse either term. To deconstruct these terms means, rather, to continue to use them, to repeat them, to repeat them subversively, and to displace them from contexts in which they have been deployed as instruments of oppressive power. Here it is of course necessary to state quite plainly that the options for theory are not exhausted by *presuming* materiality, on the one hand, and *negating* it, on the other. It is my purpose to do precisely neither of these. . . . it does not freeze, banish, render useless, or deplete of meaning the usage of the term; on the contrary, it provides the conditions to *mobilize* the signifier in the service of an alternative production.[71]

At the Last Supper, the Spirit allows Jesus to mobilize or open up the body for the production of grace, neither presuming nor negating nature. As Williams suggests, Cavanaugh's *Torture and Eucharist* is a spellbinding account of how the Eucharist might yet preserve that power of mobilization here on earth.[72]

James Alison uses the term "beyond resentment" to signal the power of the Eucharist to get beyond violence and create fraternity. And yet there is more, something beyond not only resentment, but beyond even its absence. The eucharistic sequence of feasting — sacrifice — and feasting, whether in Genesis or in Jesus is somehow also non-reactive. "I am talking about beginning," he writes — a creatorly beginning — "beginning to sense a creative project of love which is not really beyond resentment at all. It is so much prior to resentment that it has to hide a vast, playful laugh at bringing us into being, lest we misinterpret such playfulness and such joy from within our resentment and shrink back, refusing to believe that all that tenderly suppressed mirth is not 'at' us but 'for' us."[73] For after all, "Isaac" means laughter.

---

70. Since *Sexuality and the Christian Body* I have learned from theologians like Gerard Loughlin and Sarah Coakley how to read Judith Butler theologically. See Coakley's reading of Butler as revealing an eschatology of yearning in "The Eschatological Body: Gender, Transformation and God," in *Powers and Submissions* (Oxford: Blackwell, 2001), 153-67.

71. Judith Butler, "Contingent Foundations," in Seyla Benhabib et al., *Feminist Contentions: A Philosophical Exchange* (London and New York: Routledge, 1995), pp. 35-57; here, pp. 51-52, paragraph boundary elided.

72. William Cavanaugh, *Torture and Eucharist* (Oxford: Blackwell, 1998) makes a marvelous, magisterial application of this theme.

73. James Alison, *Faith beyond Resentment: Fragments Catholic and Gay* (New York, N.Y.: Crossroad, 2001), p. 124.

The subversive redeployment of sacrifice does not end with Jesus' gift or Sarah's laughter, but gains sociological continuity in the church every time that Christians give thanks in an unselfish and self-sacrificing way. Protestants may be worried about the language of sacrifice and offering, but the worry would be misplaced. In the first place, "this offering (as Irenaeus has made clear . . .) is primarily our gratuitous love for the poor and deprived — free love as gratitude, of which the ritual offering is the articulation."[74] In the second place, the offering depends entirely on its trinitarian counterpart of gift received and thanks returned, so that "[i]n the presentation [of the Christ child to the Lord at the hands of Symeon in the Temple], in the Eucharist [at the hands of the bishop], and in the Crucifixion [at the hands of sinners], the agency appears to be [univocally] human; but in fact all that human beings are doing in each of these instances is involving themselves in the divine action which presents them to the Father."[75] Or better, *God* involves human beings in the divine action. "The way in which our eucharistic worship is united with Christ's offering is, characteristically, through the agency of the Holy Spirit."[76] According to Ephrem, the fire of the Spirit can kindle the human offering only because the human heart has already caught fire by the same Spirit. The human heart, likewise, can hope to stay alight by consuming the fire the Spirit rekindles in the bread.[77]

Under conditions of sin, the sacrifice of praise offered by one constituted liturgically is not without cost. The theology of glory does not oppose but enfolds the theology of the cross. For

> [e]very act of praise itself involves a costly giving — not simply the giving up of time, but the reorientation of hope and imagination outwards. Praise, celebration, adoration, is a direction away from self-preoccupation, anxiety, defensiveness: like any entry into a wider participation, it demands the yielding of certain protective mechanisms (the loss of all we do and all we possess to defend ourselves against God and others and death). It is a letting-go of the constant anxious defense of one's own solidity and worth in order to affirm the worth of something other. . . . And if the reality we confront is self-sufficient, endless and unchangingly "worth-while," then to open ourselves to it in praise is to embark on a project with no imaginable ending, something beyond our power to limit. To be able to praise and adore God worthily is not something instantly and easily accessible: our

---

74. Williams, *Eucharistic Sacrifice*, p. 11. Cf. Irenaeus, *Adv. Haer.* 18.5.

75. Williams, *Eucharistic Sacrifice*, p. 22.

76. Williams, *Eucharistic Sacrifice*, p. 22.

77. Williams, *Eucharistic Sacrifice*, pp. 22-23, in commenting on Ephrem, Hymn X *On Faith*.

praise is tied in with the sacrifice, the giving up, of our own sinful and self-protective definition of what we are — and so with the whole act of accepting Christ as the form of the new humanity.[78]

This self-sacrifice is at once wonderful for human beings, in that it is almost too good to be true that they might let go of anxiety and participate in God's own exchange of gift and gratitude (and therefore a mystery) — and hard for human beings, in that they find themselves in bondage to sin so that they cannot free themselves (and therefore a problem). Self-sacrifice is possible only because God has gone to it first, to show human beings the way, and has returned from it, by the constancy of the Holy Spirit keeping faith with love. If "true giving is participating,"[79] so that "sacrifice and offering . . . have to do with the maintenance of fellowship, at the simplest level,"[80] then self-sacrifice is self-defeating if it destroys the fellowship. The Holy Spirit is, already within the divine fellowship, and therefore also by grace in ours, the guaranty and witness to fellowship, even in the case of death: it is the giver of life, the keeper of faith. "We cannot effect anything new through our offering" — which is to say that we can only effect our offering — "because God has acted first, acted according to his nature: he has determined to be the ground of our beseeching."[81]

At the Annunciation, God's love is turned into a human being. At the Eucharist, a human being is turned into God's love. St. Isaac the Syrian puts it like this:

> When we have found love, we eat the heavenly bread and we are sustained without labor and without weariness. Heavenly bread is that which has descended from heaven and which gives the world life; this is the food of angels. He who has found love eats Christ at all times and becomes immortal from then onwards. Blessed is he that has eaten from the bread of love which is Jesus. Whoever is fed with love is fed with Christ, who is the all-governing God. John witnesses to this when he says: "God is love." Thus he who lives with love in this creation smells life from God; he breathes here the air of the resurrection. Love is the kingdom of which our Lord spoke, when symbolically he promised the disciples that they would eat in his

78. Williams, *Eucharistic Sacrifice*, pp. 29-30. In the parenthesis I interpolate a phrase appearing earlier on the page.

79. Williams, *Eucharistic Sacrifice*, p. 28, quoting J. van Baal, "Offering, Sacrifice and Gift," *Numen* 23 (1976): 161-78; here, p. 177.

80. Williams, *Eucharistic Sacrifice*, p. 28.

81. Williams, *Eucharistic Sacrifice*, pp. 16-17.

kingdom: "you shall eat and drink at the table of my kingdom." What should they eat, if not love? . . . This is the wine that gladdens the heart of the human being. . . . This is the wine which the debauched have drunk and they became chaste, the sinners have drunk and they forgot the paths of stumbling, the drunk and they became fasters, the rich and they became desirous of poverty, the poor and they became rich in hope, the sick and they regained strength, the fools and they became wise.[82]

The womb of the Mother, the womb of the Father, the womb of the side, the womb of the wine: there are other wombs I have not mentioned: the womb of Jesus' death, from which springs the life of the resurrection; and its type, the womb of baptism. The Maronite and Syrian Orthodox churches both pray: "He, the Lord, by his own will and by [the will of the Father] dwelt in the world for our sake in three different abodes, in the womb made of flesh, in the womb of baptism, and in the gloomy abode of Sheol."[83] Didymus of Alexandria writes that the font "becomes the mother of all believers by the power of the Holy Spirit."[84] Philoxenus of Mabbug places the following prayer on the lips of Jesus in the Jordan:

Do you, Father, open the heavens at my prayer and send your Holy Spirit upon this baptismal womb, and as the Spirit descended upon the womb of the Virgin and formed me from her, so may he likewise descend into the womb of the baptismal water to fashion human beings and give birth from it to new children, making them your sons and my brothers and fellow heirs of the kingdom.[85]

Jacob of Serugh sums the pattern up, as we saw in Part I:

Mary gave a body for the Word to become incarnate,
while Baptism gives the Spirit for human beings to be renewed.[86]

---

82. Isaac of Nineveh, *Mystical Treatises,* trans. A. J. Wensinck (Amsterdam: Koninklijke akademie van wetenschappen, 1923), pp. 211-12, quoted in Brock, "Mary," p. 55.

83. Sebastian Brock, *The Holy Spirit in the Syrian Baptismal Tradition,* 1998 ed., p. 194, citing Add. 14518 §31. Although it is not my concern here, the tropes seem to display a historical development from womb to tomb; see Gabriele Winkler, "The Original Meaning of the Prebaptismal Anointing and Its Implications," *Worship* 52 (1978): 24-45.

84. Didymus of Alexandria, *On the Trinity* II.13, PG 39:692.

85. Brock, *Holy Spirit,* p. 195, citing *Philoxeni Mabbugensis tractatus tres de trinitate et incarnatione,* ed. Arthur Adolphe Vaschalde, Corpus Christianorum, Scriptores Syri, 9-10, 2 vols. (Louvain: L. Durbecq, 1955), vol. II (2), p. 304.

86. Brock, *Holy Spirit,* p. 196, citing Paul Bedjan, ed., *Homiliae selectae Mar-Jacobi Sarugensis,* 5 vols. (Paris and Leipzig: Otto Harrassowitz, 1908-10), vol. I, p. 204.

Or as Brock restates it,

> Through Mary the divine becomes human
> Through Baptism the human becomes divine.[87]

But baptism is such an iconic interaction of Jesus and the Spirit, such a happy opening of the womb of the Trinity to receive those who would be reborn, that it deserves a chapter of its own.

87. Brock, *Holy Spirit*, p. 196.

3 Baptism

"And when Jesus was baptized, . . . he saw the Spirit of God descending like a dove, and alighting on him; and lo, a voice from heaven, saying, "This is my Son, my beloved, with whom I am well pleased" (Matt. 3:16-17 and pars.)

The Spirit rests on the Son in the waters of the Jordan and therefore on the disciples at the waters of the Galilee and on other human beings in the waters of the Font. This first makes manifest that the Holy Spirit rests on the elect of the Father, and for that reason witnesses and celebrates this election not only in God but also in the baptism of Jesus and finally in others, electing further witnesses to the good pleasure of the Father in the Son. At the Baptism the Spirit continues to befriend the body, allowing the Son to receive as human what he has as God, so that he might count equality with God not a thing to be grasped, and reverse the grasping of the Fall.

This chapter concerns water in its multiple meanings — creation, baptism, interior person, and much more — because water gives an important material clue about the relation of the Spirit to creation as a whole. Other materials taken up into the liturgical life of the community also give clues — bread, wine, oil, incense, and more — but water may be the most elemental. "Nature" is not a common biblical word outside Paul, but "water" is. Let "water" stand for nature, and consider its relation to the Holy Spirit in traditional typology. The Spirit hovers on the face of the waters at creation. The Spirit overshadows the waters of Mary's womb. The Spirit alights upon Jesus in the waters of the Jordan. The Spirit overshadows the Transfiguration with clouds of water. The Spirit so far rules over nature as to kindle fire in water: the Spirit is fire in the water of the womb, and of the Jordan; fire in the wine and fire like water on the head.[1]

---

1. See Sebastian P. Brock, *The Holy Spirit in the Syrian Baptismal Tradition*, The Syrian Churches Series, vol. 9 (Poona, India: Anita Printers, 1979; 2d ed., 1998). Predecessor studies in-

Artists have deployed the numinous and polyvalent possibilities of over-shadowing clouds, associated with the Father and the Son as well as the Spirit, in depictions of the Annunciation, Baptism, and Transfiguration, among other scenes. So by a manuscript illustration of Psalm 72:6, "He shall come down like rain upon the mown grass," we find the marginal gloss, "This psalm speaks of the birth of the Lord. He descends like rain in little clouds, that is God in the womb of Saint Mary."[2] A heavy relief on the Bamberg Cathedral shows a dove emerging organically from stony clouds to overshadow Mary[3] (fig. 3). The right hand of the Father emerges from overshadowing clouds to release a dove in many depictions of Christ's baptism; an ivory relief from Lorraine in the tenth century uses clouds in three registers: clouds hide all but the hand of the Father; clouds frame the dove of the Spirit; and clouds overshadow the baptism of the Son.[4] Typically, the baptismal water mounds up like clouds and the overshadowing clouds recall the water. Clouds form a nimbus around Jesus in numerous Transfigurations, including Raphael's, while in an unsubtle Transfiguration by Andrea Previtali in the Pinoteca in Milan both a dove and a pretty little cloud speak by means of unfurled scrolls (fig. 5).[5]

i. The Spirit rests on the Son in the waters of the Jordan

Why is Jesus baptized? According to orthodox doctrine, Jesus is like other human beings in every respect except sin: "he made him to be sin who knew no sin" (2 Cor. 5:21). According to the Nicene Creed, Christians "acknowledge one baptism for the remission of sins." Is Jesus a sinner after all, so that he needs baptism? Or is he enacting a charade? Or is that a false alternative, as the performance theorists also tell us?

The conundrum of Jesus' baptism makes sense, if we assume a sup-pressed premise. The baptism of Jesus is primarily to be understood as an intratrinitarian event, in which other human beings participate by their own baptism. It is an event in which the Spirit bears witness to the love be-

clude Edmund Beck, "Le baptême chez S. Ephrem," *L'Orient Syrien* 2 (1956): 111-36 and Georges P. Saber, *La théologie baptismale de Saint Ephrem* (Kaslik, Lebanon: Université de Saint-Esprit de Kaslik, 1974).

2. Gertrud Schiller, *Iconography of Christian Art*, 2 vols., trans. Janet Seligman (Greenwich, Conn.: New York Graphic Society Ltd., 1971), vol. 1, p. 43 and fig. 90.

3. Schiller, *Iconography*, vol. 1, p. 44 and fig. 89.

4. Schiller, *Iconography*, vol. 1, p. 138 and fig. 367.

5. Milan, Pinacoteca.

tween the Father and the Son. In the baptismal interaction, the Father expresses his love ("this is my Son, my beloved, with whom I am well pleased"); the Spirit hovers over the waters of the Jordan as she hovered over the waters of creation and the waters of the womb; and Jesus receives the love and witness in a way that other human beings can participate in — he comes to the Jordan "to perfect baptism," i.e., to accomplish its potential for initiating human beings into the triune life. The baptism of Jesus does not make sense without the presence of the Spirit. For what the Spirit adds to the expression and reception of love is this: that she witnesses it in such a way that she can also celebrate it, by electing further witnesses to the love between the Father and the Son among the disciples and among other human beings.[6] At the baptism of Jesus, the Spirit, with her presence, indicates, marks, points out — bears witness to — the love between the Father and the Son *in such a way* (tropos hyparxeos) *that it can be shared.* It is characteristic of the Spirit to take up and render holy concrete, physical, sociological structures — like the ritual bathing practiced in Judaism and by John. It is so that she renders the life of the Trinity in matter, in history, in community, in all their human contingency. Redemption is the form that consummation takes, when the wedding of the Lamb is lived out among sinful human beings. What baptism accomplishes is a participation in the life of the God of Israel; what baptism washes away is a lack of participation in the life of the God of Israel (Kendall Soulen). Thus the adopted daughters of Jews are bathed in the mikvah; Paul was particularly impressed that baptism could also wash away the lack of relation to the God of Israel attributed to the Gentiles, and join them as children to the One True God; and as a corollary of its uniting other human beings to the life of God, baptism also washes away that lack of participation in God's life that is sin.

The Syriac tradition does not portray baptism as a grim moment in which sinners grit their teeth and try to wrest their redemption from the cold and unforgiving water. The tone is entirely different: one of praise, thanksgiving, and wonder, as befits a glimpse into the trinitarian relations and a share in the feasting at the wedding of the Lamb:

> How fearful and full of awe is this moment when the supernal beings stand in silence upon this baptismal water — thousands upon thousands of angels, ten thousands of Seraphim hover over this new mother, holy baptism, the spiritual mother who gives birth to spiritual sons who enter into the

---

6. See Robert W. Jenson, "The Holy Spirit," in *Christian Dogmatics,* ed. Robert W. Jenson and Carl Braaten, 2 vols. (Philadelphia: Fortress, 1984), vol. 2, pp. 101-78, esp. pp. 134-39.

bridal chamber of life that is full of joys. . . . They stand by the river Jordan to receive the Son of God who has come to perfect baptism. The Holy Spirit descends upon him from the uppermost heights, not to sanctify him, but to bear witness to him.[7]

The Syriac tradition can see the entire history of salvation and the entire Christian life in terms of the wedding parable of Matthew 22, in which putting on the wedding garment is putting on the Spirit. In both cases the wedding feast is the eschatological banquet at the end of time for which God has been preparing the human race since the beginning. Baptism washes human beings not primarily because of sin, but *for the feast*. Baptism is the great washing before meals. Bathing is already part of the joy of preparation even for the clean; so much the more so for those who are dirty. Consummation is logically prior to redemption, as the goal specifies the species of an act.

Furthermore, the wedding feast is the consummation for which all human beings were created. The Spirit who hovered over the waters at creation is bringing up her creation over time, when she hovers also over the waters of the font. The wedding garments are prepared already. The guest who was cast into the outer darkness for the lack of a wedding garment was not one who had never had one, but one who had been given one and lost it.

Christ came to baptism, he went down and placed in the baptismal water the robe of glory, to be there for Adam, who had lost it.[8]

That applies to all the children of Adam:

7. Brock, *Holy Spirit*, 2d ed., pp. 200-201, italics added, citing Jacob of Serugh, *Homiliae selectae Mar-Jacobi Sarugensis*, 5 vols., ed. Paul Bedjan (Paris and Leipzig: Otto Harrassowitz, 1908-10), vol. 2, pp. 332-34; with liturgical parallels in Giuseppe Luigi Assemani, *Codex liturgicus ecclesiae universae . . . occidentis & orientis*, 4 vols. in 13 (reprint ed. Westmead, Hampshire, 1968-69), vol. 2, pp. 291-92.

8. Sebastian P. Brock, *Spirituality in the Syriac Tradition*, Moran Etho Series No. 2 (Kerala, India: St. Ephrem Ecumenical Research Institute, 1989), p. 64, citing Jacob of Serugh, *Homiliae*, vol. 3, p. 593. Cf. Brock, "Baptismal Themes in the Writings of Joseph of Serugh," in *Symposium Syriacum 1976*, ed. Arthur Vööbus (Rome: Pontificium Institutum Orientalium Studiorum, 1978), pp. 325-47. Note that since in Syriac the word for Spirit is grammatically feminine, and the overshadowing is considered a feminine activity, one writer found lesbian connotations of the conception of Jesus vivid enough to deny: "Some have said that Mary conceived of the Holy Spirit. They are wrong, and they do not realize what they are saying, for when did a woman ever conceive of a woman?" (Coptic Gospel of Philip, §17, in Brock, *Holy Spirit*, 2d ed., p. 7.) Cf. "The Gospel according to Philip," in *Gnostic Scriptures*, ed. Bentley Layton (New York: Doubleday, 1995), pp. 325-58.

You [Christ] who were without need were baptized in the river Jordan and left in it the garment of divinity for those who were naked that they might be clothed with it.[9]

The children of Adam become children of the Father by being clothed again in the Spirit:

You have clothed us in the robe of glory of the gifts of your Holy Spirit, and you have granted that we should become spiritual children to the Father in the second birth of baptism.[10]

This baptism is taken to begin to fulfill the prophecy of Psalm 132:16, which reads in Syriac, "I will clothe her priests in salvation and her just in glory."[11] Then the baptized may "recline with confidence at the royal feast, as [they] eat this spiritual banquet, and so [they] will not have to hear those gloomy words, 'Friend, how did you enter here without a wedding garment?'" (Mt. 22:12).[12] Jesus often receives a robe in pictorial baptisms, and although I have not found a robe in the water, the water often also robes Jesus — whether from prudery or theology — in shapes and folds that only clothes could hold. So in the mosaic of the baptism at Hosios Loukos the water clings to Jesus against gravity up to his neck, while in other cases it flows down from him as if he is its source or it is his garment (fig. 1).[13]

The Syriac tradition associates the Spirit with weddings also for an etymological reason. One of the most characteristic technical terms in Syriac translations of the Bible for the activity of the Spirit is *agen*, to overshadow or hover (Exod. 33:22, Ps. 138:8, Luke 1:35, Acts 5:15, 10:44, 11:15; cf. Gen. 1:2). This the Syriac translators associate with the related word *gnuna*, "bridal chamber." The Spirit overshadows, covers, protects, shelters, tabernacles, or canopies the eschatological feast and the earthly wedding of Christ and the church

9. Francis Acharya, ed., *Prayer with the Harp of the Spirit: The Prayer of the Asian Churches,* 4 vols. (Vagamon, India: Kurisumala Ashram, 1982-86), vol. III, p. 496; cited in Brock, *Spirituality,* p. 64.

10. West Syriac rite of baptism attributed to Severus in Brock, *Spirituality,* p. 64. Texts in Giuseppe Luigi Assemani, *Codex Liturgicus* I-III, and in Latin translation in H. Denzinger, *Ritus Orientalium* (Würzburg, 1863), vol. 1. Cf. also Syriac with facing English in Mar Athanasius Yeshue Samuel, *The Sacrament of Holy Baptism according to the Ancient Rite of the Syrian Orthodox Church of Antioch* (Hackensack, N.J.: A. Y. Samuel, 1974) and Brock, "Studies in the Early History of the Syrian Orthodox Baptismal Liturgy," *Journal of Theological Studies,* n.s., 23 (1972): 16-64.

11. Brock, *Holy Spirit,* 2d ed., p. 85.

12. Severus, "Homily 43 on John 1:16," *Patrologia Orientalia* 84-86, translated in Brock, *Holy Spirit,* 2d ed., p. 87.

13. See Schiller, *Iconography,* figs. 362, 367-68, 370-72, 374-76, 379, 384.

or the soul.[14] The hands of the priest similarly tabernacle and canopy those particular individuals about to be baptized by the laying on or "shadow" of his hands.[15] If the wedding garment also shelters and protects, that is another way in which consummation is logically prior to redemption.

At the baptism of Jesus the Spirit (a) bears witness to the love between the Father and the Son. She (b) attracts further witnesses to this love in the economy by initiating analogical or totemic structures in human society. She can do so (c) because she makes intervals for a love of receptivity and freedom already antecedently in the trinitarian life.

(a)   Some of the most prominent references to the Spirit in the New Testament give her the personal identity and work of a witness:

> When they deliver you up, do not be anxious how you are to speak or what you are to say; for what you are to say will be given to you in that hour; for it is not you who speak, but the Spirit of your Father speaking through you (Matt. 10:19-20).

> And when they bring you to trial and deliver you up, do not be anxious beforehand what you are to say; but say whatever is given to you in that hour, for it is not you who speak, but the Holy Spirit (Mark 13:11).

> But when the Counselor comes, whom I shall send to you from the Father, even the Spirit of truth, who proceeds from the Father, he will bear witness to me; and you are also witnesses, because you have been with me from the beginning (John 15:26-27).

> When the Spirit of truth comes, he will guide you into all the truth; for he will not speak on his own authority *(aph' heautou),* but whatever he hears he will speak, and he will declare to you the things that are to come. He will glorify *(doxasei)* me, for he will take what is mine and declare it to you. All that the Father has is mine; therefore I said that he will take what is mine and declare it to you (John 16:13-15).

> But you shall receive power when the Holy Spirit has come upon you; and you shall be my witnesses *(martures)* in Jerusalem and in all Judea and Samaria and to the end of the earth (Acts 1:8).

---

14. Brock, *Holy Spirit,* 2d ed., pp. 5-6.
15. West Syrian liturgy attributed to Severus in Brock, *Holy Spirit,* 2d ed., p. 73.

And we are witnesses to these things, and so is the Holy Spirit whom God has given to those who obey him (Acts 5:32).

By this we know that we abide in [God] and he in us, because he has given us of his own Spirit. And we have seen and testify that the Father has sent his Son as the Savior of the World (I John 4:13-14).

The Spirit is the witness (I John 5:6).

The East tends to fault the West for failing to think of the Holy Spirit sufficiently as a trinitarian Person. The West tends to think of the Spirit as (famously) the "bond of love," the *vinculum caritatis* between the Father and the Son, or the Gift itself of grace, or the "power of Jesus Christ" (Barth). It is a wind that blows where it wills. None of those designations is wrong in itself, unless, as usually happens, they go no farther. They tend to become reductive, because they tend to portray the Holy Spirit as a bond or power of one or more other Persons — rather than as a Person in her own right.

The Spirit is not just any witness, either. The Spirit is witness to a particular love, the love between the Father and the Son. And in the New Testament she is witness to that love in particular circumstances — those of the solidarity of the Son with human beings, even unto death. She is the witness to a marriage feast, that of God and humanity, which turns out, with the death of Jesus, to be a deathbed wedding. In those circumstances she keeps faith with the office of a witness to a wedding: she plays its guarantor; she works to hold it together.[16] The Spirit witnesses to the love between the Father and the Son, and it is therefore her characteristic but unexacted gift to the Son that she creates witnesses to that love also among human beings. Thus the Spirit elects the waters of creation to become also the waters of the Jordan, and the waters of the Jordan to become also the waters of the Font.

Part of the usefulness of the Bible's language of the Holy Spirit as "witness" is that it can help repair that reductive tendency. A witness is irreducibly a third, tied to the two, but giving its own testimony. A witness can be the bond of love between the Father and the Son *in Person* and not as an inanimate chain. A witness can give herself in testimony or martyrdom *as a friend does* and not as a thing. A witness can be the power of Christ *in relation to* and not in abstraction from him. A witness can blow where it will *with the agency* of one with a will, and not with the passivity of mere weather. It can even blow in a trinitarian pattern:

---

16. For more along these lines, see Eugene F. Rogers, Jr., *Sexuality and the Christian Body: Their Way into the Triune God* (Oxford: Blackwell, 1999), pp. 195-96, 250-56.

Within the Trinity the Spirit blows where he wills. He remains a movement in the direction from Father to Son, from the Father through the Son. He surrounds the human being, but because he is movement, he does not cease to blow but returns with the human being to the Father.[17]

(b)   In the baptism of Jesus, God does a human thing — submit to a human ritual with a consummating result — divinely, and a divine thing — begin to divinize human beings with watery matter — humanly. That practice initiates human beings into a whole series of human practices that God can turn to God's own purposes. In the life of Jesus, God becomes human; in the life of the baptized, human beings become God. Because by the Holy Spirit God was conceived in the womb of Mary and became human, Christianity can be a human religion, divinization can have a history that runs through baptism, and analogy can practice a conceptuality that looks like totemism. Because the Holy Spirit conceived Christ in a body that human beings might become divine, religion can be salvific, baptism can initiate deification, and totemism can yield anagogy.

Here's another reason why the Spirit may pale beside the Son: The Spirit is not the Christian totem, but Christ is.[18] Is there a deep sociological reason that anything the Spirit can do, the Son can do better?

Durkheim's analysis goes like this. Australian aboriginal groups define themselves and their world with an ordered series of religious terms.[19] A (socially constructed) kinship group names itself after, say, the kangaroo.[20] But consider cavaliers.

My students are "Cavaliers"; they distinguish a historical Cavalier in the English Civil War; a mascot Cavalier at football games; football-player Cavaliers, in a more exalted sense; Cavalier images appear on T-shirts, bumper stickers, notebooks, and backpacks, while a Cavalier spirit transcends worldly instances and bids them admire Thomas Jefferson and honor the Code. "Reunions" (Durkheim's word) produce "moral effervescence"[21] (at football games and post-commencement bashes) and renew the society (through the

---

17. Adrienne von Speyr, *The Word Becomes Flesh: Meditations on John 1–5*, trans. Lucia Wiedenhöver and Alexander Dru (San Francisco: Ignatius, 1994), p. 191, on John 3:8, translation modified.

18. Emile Durkheim, *The Elementary Forms of the Religious Life* (New York: Free Press, 1965), pp. 13, 107, 115, 121, 123.

19. As is well known, Durkheim relied on the fieldwork of others. But it is possible to find his analysis heuristically useful without trusting his data.

20. Durkheim, *Elementary Forms*, p. 157.

21. Durkheim, *Elementary Forms*, pp. 240-42.

sale of Cavalier *Tracht* and the success of Annual Giving). Borrowing a term from Algonquin religion, and following the usage of his predecessors,[22] Durkheim calls the tendency to create such an ordered series "totemism."[23]

Durkheim does not unpack the analysis for Christianity. Coyly he notes that higher religions complicate the elementary forms. But the application is clear. Christ centers a series in which Jesus is the body of Christ and the believer is the body of Christ, the church is the body of Christ and the bread is the body of Christ, on until the body of Christ is the body of God.

Christian theology has not only insisted on the body of Christ as focusing an ordered series of its most important usages. It has also worked out an indigenous *theory* structurally isomorphic with totemism, called the doctrine of analogy. Analogy and totemism even share some technical vocabulary: the totem, like the prime analogate, is "the very *type* of sacred thing,"[24] and the totemic like the analogical system works by "participation,"[25] Durkheim's word — and Aquinas's. Christian thinkers have insisted on the analogous or totemic identity of Christ's body with the community, so that if you were looking for precursors of sociology you could do worse than Maximus the Confessor on *The Church's Mystagogy.*[26] The sociological argument tends to raise the stock of pre-Nominalist theologians.[27]

For those reasons you might regard Christ as the Christian totem and prime analogate, and that would not be wrong. You might regard the Christ-series as inhibiting Spirit-language, and you might be right. But Gregory Nazianzen offers an alternative analogical series based on the Spirit.

Gregory's treatise on baptism offers a complex and serially ordered definition of the baptized and their world. He explicitly invokes analogy with the technical term "names." And he explicitly compares the Spirit-series with the Christ-series, using the name of the Spirit that is Gift. Here Gregory recasts Christianity as a Religion of the Gift. In accord with analogical thinking,

22. Durkheim, *Elementary Forms*, pp. 107, 123, 134.

23. Durkheim, *Elementary Forms*, p. 107.

24. Durkheim, *Elementary Forms*, p. 140.

25. Durkheim, *Elementary Forms*, p. 217.

26. Maximus the Confessor, "How and in What Manner Holy Church Is an Image and Figure of God," in *Maximus Confessor: Selected Writings* (Mahwah, N.J.: Paulist, 1985), pp. 186-87.

27. Against revisionists like Sallie McFague who writes, after an explanation of the doctrine of analogy, as if moderns can't do that anymore: "Now, try as we might, many if not most of us cannot work ourselves back into this mentality. . . . the classic Catholic mentality — is not viable today. . . ." But according to Durkheim, there is no alternative: it is the elementary form of religious life. Sallie McFague, *Metaphorical Theology: Models of God in Religious Language* (Philadelphia: Fortress, 1982), pp. 12-13. For the counter-argument, see Janet Martin Soskice, *Metaphor and Religious Language* (Oxford: Clarendon, 1985), especially the last chapter.

"Gift" is both the gift that is the Spirit and the gift that is Baptism — and much else besides:

> As Christ the Giver of it is called by many various names, so too is this Gift. . . . We call it the Gift, the Grace, Baptism, Unction, Illumination, the Clothing of Immortality, the Laver of Regeneration, the Seal, and everything that is honorable. We call it the Gift, because it is given to us in return for nothing on our part; Grace, because it is conferred even on debtors; Baptism, because sin is buried with it in the water; Unction, as Priestly and royal . . . ; Illumination, because of its splendour; Clothing, because it hides our shame; the Laver, because it washes us; the Seal, because it preserves us. . . .[28]

Now, just as Christ centers a series in which Jesus is the body of Christ and the believer is the body of Christ, until the body of Christ is the body of God, so too the Gift centers a series in which baptism is the Gift and the Holy Spirit is the Gift, the community is the Gift and the neighbor is the Gift, until by the Gift the believer becomes God. The analogical or totemic relation can stretch just as far for the Spirit as for the Son.

(c)   But what is it in which the Spirit invites other human beings to participate at the baptism of Jesus? At the baptism of Jesus, the Spirit hovers over the Son. This does not sanctify the Son; the Second Person of the Trinity is already holy. This does not deify the Son; the Second Person of the Trinity is already God. This does not adopt the Son; the Second Person of the Trinity is already Son. But because the Spirit wishes to celebrate the holiness, deity, and sonship of the Son, the Spirit makes those qualities new by granting them also to human beings. Because the Spirit wishes to manifest the holiness, deity, and sonship of the Son, the Spirit causes those qualities to show up also in human beings. Because the Spirit wishes to bear witness to the holiness, deity, and sonship of the Son, the Spirit takes that occasion to distribute those qualities also to human beings. The newness conferred by the Spirit is a surprise, a celebration, so new as to count almost as a reversal: The Son does not receive sanctity, deity, or sonship originally from the Spirit: he receives them *anew,* as the Spirit guarantees or confirms or seals them; as the Son allows the Spirit to guarantee or confirm or seal them in him, so the Spirit gathers human beings together to guarantee or confirm or seal gifts also, *ab origine,* on human beings in him. The Spirit gathers human beings in him, and distributes gifts to human beings, as a gift upon the gift that Spirit returns to the Son. This pro-

28. Gregory Nazianzen, Oration XI "On Holy Baptism," ch. IV, in NPNF2, vol. 7, p. 360.

cess incorporates or in-members human beings into a *community* constituted by the exchange of gift and gratitude, in which the Persons delight to receive what they have. In learning from them to receive what they have, human beings begin to participate already here below in the trinitarian life. What human beings have is not really their own, until they receive it as gift from another.

This is true not only of goods — "material goods" — as in Luther's view of the commandment against stealing. By the goodness of the Spirit this potential for giftedness is built right into human bodies. So our bodies are not our own, until we give them away in fidelity and receive them again at the hands of another. Sexuality shows that the economy of gift, and our creation for joy, does not leave out human bodies but assumes them. And this is why the transfiguration of sexuality does seem to have something religious in it. Not that sexuality is divine (except by the grace of adoption) but that if God created human beings for the manifestation of the faithful exchanges of gift and gratitude of the trinitarian life, and created human beings with bodies, it would be odd if those bodies were built with no echo in their structure of that exchange.

The Son is pleased to receive baptism under the shadow of the Spirit; the Son is pleased to exercise holiness at the Spirit's driving him into the wilderness; the Son is pleased to count equality with God not a thing to be grasped. That the Son enjoys a divine attribute by right is no barrier to his receiving it also from another in humility. This ability to receive from the Spirit becomes an ability to receive even from human beings. At the annunciation the Spirit announces Jesus adopted *by Joseph*. At the baptism the Spirit overshadows Jesus baptized *by John*. In the wilderness the Spirit drives Jesus to be tempted *by material things*. At the transfiguration the Spirit reveals Jesus to be glorious *to the disciples*. At the Last Supper the Spirit transforms the blood of murder into the blood of redemption *for the whole world*.

In each case the Spirit takes something that *Christ does not need* and *presents it to him as gift*. Similarly, in each case Christ *does not hold on to what is his* but *receives it from another as gift*. So it is a heresy that Christ is a human being adopted by God, but the truth in that heresy is that the Spirit implies Christ to be a divine-human being, in that he is adopted by Joseph. And because the divine human being is adopted by Joseph, other human beings may be adopted by the Father in him. But this is not just a word game, according to which the Father adopts, and the Son enacts an adoption, and the Spirit illuminates the play. Rather it is an incorporation by which the exchange is humanified, so that the human being may be deified. The Spirit so manifests the action of the whole Trinity in the economy, *by giving human beings a part in it*. The Spirit so manifests the action of the Trinity in the economy, *that human beings partici-pate in the Trinity's own life.* The illumination of the Spirit, and the reception of the Son, are not a mere show, but a means to involve and transform human beings. Human beings could not perceive the illumination, and we could not receive with the Son, did not the Spirit enlighten not only the scene but also human minds, did not the Spirit bind them with him.

So too Christians do not say that Christ needed to be sanctified by bap-tism, but the Spirit overshadowed Christ's baptism, and Christ received what he did not need as gift, in that he is baptized by John. And because Christ is baptized by John, other human beings may be sanctified by God in baptism.

So Christ did not need to be glorified on Mount Tabor, but the Spirit ex-panded his prayer, and Christ received what he did not need as gift, so that the faces of the disciples also might shine.

Note how Christ could not do this alone. It is not enough that Christ should submit to baptism, that we should be baptized. For Christ does *not* submit, as a mere reversal of power relations. (That is the kind of atonement theory that leads Christians to accept abuse without protest.) Rather Christ *receives.* Furthermore, what Christ receives he could not receive from John alone. For John, as mere human being, cannot sanctify. Rather, part of the gift is that John is allowed to give. *Because the Son receives the gift of the Spirit that he does not need, John can give the gift of the Spirit that he does not have.* Be-cause the Spirit can give, we can give, and this too is part of our deification, that we are allowed to participate not only in thanksgiving but also in giving.

The Son receives what he has from the Father. Thus the Son receives what he *already* has from the Spirit. Receiving what you already have is not the same as receiving what you have. Receiving what you have can inspire grati-tude. But receiving what you already have can inspire graciousness. It is the graciousness of courtesy, of celebration, of playfulness, of tossing a ball more than once, of the sexual in and out that is more than a thrust and hold. What the second gift adds is a kind of play, a kind of circulation, something the tra-dition has called a dance. To receive what one already has changes what one has into something new. Thus it is characteristic of the Son already in the Trinity that "he counted equality with God not a thing to be grasped, taking the form of a servant" — that is, one who receives.

But he does not receive only from the one from whom he first received; he receives also anew from someone else. Because he can receive from someone else already in the Trinity, it is characteristic of him to receive from someone else also among human beings. So he receives nourishment from the waters of Mary's womb. He receives learned wisdom from his human teachers. He receives baptism from the waters of John's Jordan. He receives sanctity from the resistance of material temptation. He receives glory from in the clouds of Mount Tabor. He who is himself the Life receives resurrection from the Lord, the Giver of Life.

And because he can receive the gift of what is already his, he can also defer or put aside what is his to receive. He can wait. And in waiting he can also welcome the delay or absence of gift. He can even receive what is not yet gift. So he can receive finitude and ignorance, suffering and death, guilt and punishment, burial and hell, which are not his, and which are not yet gift, for the Spirit's sake, so that the Spirit may *transform* them into gift, may make them his for humanity's sake. Thus the Spirit gives to the Son human beings made immortal, because he received finitude. The Spirit gives him human beings rendered wise, because he received ignorance. The Spirit gives him human beings made joyful, because he accepted suffering; the Spirit gives him human beings returned to life, because he accepted death; human beings justified, because he carried guilt, and human beings redeemed, because he accepted punishment; human beings resurrected, because he accepted burial, and human beings freed, because he went down to hell.

And *this* is the movement by which God is the God of Abraham, Isaac, and Jacob, the God of covenant and blessing, and not just any god; so *this* is the movement by which God is "deified," or is the God that God is by nature. Earlier theology sometimes suggests that the Holy Spirit — always without need — makes God God, or at least the God that God is, because the Spirit searches even the depths of God (I Cor. 2:10); Basil remarks in passing that the Holy Spirit "completes" or "fills out" even the Trinity itself.[29] Thus we read that God "is Spirit" (John 4:24), because it is by the Spirit that God is characteristically open rather than enclosed, a God who not only gives and receives what God has, but *keeps* giving and receiving, not only gives and receives once and for all, but gives and receives as an everlasting life, not only gives to one and receives to one, but can give also to another and receive also from another. That is, the other ontological claim about God in the New Testament — that "God is love" (I John 4:16) — follows from the first, that God is the Holy Spirit. Thus it is characteristic — not necessary, but deeply characteristic — for God to give also to human beings, for God to receive also from human beings. It is characteristic of the love of the Father and the Son that their love is not static but can incorporate others into that life without distortion — can incorporate others into that life as a manifestation, as an application, of what they do with the

---

29. I owe the reference to Colin Gunton, who takes it in a strong sense. The verb is *symplerō*, in Basile de Césarée, *Homélies sur l'Hexaéméron*, ed. and trans. Stanislas Giet (Paris: Éditions du Cerf, 1949), p. 168.

Spirit. The whole incorporation of the human being into the trinitarian life is therefore appropriated to the Spirit. Even though the trinitarian action is indivisible toward human beings, it would not have the character that it has without the Spirit. It would not be so roomy or accommodating.[30] It would not be built in that the Trinity reaches out to embrace.

Because the Holy Spirit stretches the Trinity to extremes of reception and gift, even the death of Christ is included within her ambit. And because even the death of Christ lies within her ambit, even the sins and deaths of other human beings can be accommodated, can be enveloped by the Trinity without distortion. As we have seen, "Our distance from God is itself taken into God, finds place in God; by the Spirit of adoption we enter . . . the divine, intra-Trinitarian love . . . realized in the world by the descent of Christ into Hell . . . bridged by the Spirit."[31]

If there were no re-exchange — if there were no interval there would be no possibility of "room" for us. God does not need to make room for us — the doctrine of the Spirit means that God does not lack even for reciprocity, interval, musical space, celebration, or beauty. But because God has all riches already within God, the sort of "space" that human beings would occupy in the divine life is not foreign or alien to God. Because of the Holy Spirit, the dyad is not stuck together. The intimacy of two is not closed off.[32] The contract of two is not completed and over. Only because the life of the Trinity accommodates the Spirit, or the Spirit proceeds from the Father, is there room "between" the two, is there air, breath. Only because of the Spirit's expansive force does love not become the gravity that slams things together into a black hole. Only because of the play of the Spirit can the Father take or make time for human beings. In this way everything that is, depends on the Spirit — as it does not cease to depend also on the Father and the Son.

ii. The Spirit rests on the Son in the waters of creation

The Spirit rests on the Son in the waters of creation: as the Spirit hovers over the waters of creation to elaborate the intratrinitarian intervals with a diver-

---

30. For roominess as a technical term applied to God, see Robert W. Jenson, *Systematic Theology*, 2 vols. (New York: Oxford University Press, 1997), vol. 1, last chapter.

31. Rowan Williams, "Barth on the Triune God," in *Karl Barth: Studies of His Theological Method*, ed. Stephen W. Sykes (Oxford: Clarendon, 1979), pp. 145-93; here, p. 177.

32. For a Peircean argument in favor of that thesis, see Pavel Florensky, *The Pillar and Ground of the Truth*, trans. Boris Jakim (Princeton, N.J.: Princeton University Press, 1997), pp. 36-38.

sity of creatures destined to fill the earth, so at baptism she hovers over the waters of the font to initiate a diversity of persons witnessing to the love between the Father and the Son. As the Spirit dwells in the world she celebrates the trinitarian life by directing the development of a full and interlocking habitat on the earth, in the heavens above the earth, and in the waters under the earth: as the Spirit dwells among the people of God she celebrates the trinitarian life by directing the development of a full and interlocking company of witnesses to inhabit the trinitarian community.

"Nature" introduces multiple ambiguities into discursive and bodily Christian practices. Nature can be unfallen, fallen, or redeemed; essential or constructed; individual or corporate. I propose that nature plays a narrative or dramatic role in various Christian practices of sacrament and storytelling; the Spirit becomes the author or playwright to which Christians ascribe their natural or unnatural, fallen or redeemed performances. The Spirit directs them to enact those performances liturgically in worship, baptism, Eucharist, marriage. The Spirit plots nature's changing circumstances in traditions Syriac, Latin, Greek, German, and Russian. Mobile as water, nature is not static, but dynamic. A creature of the Spirit, it is to grow. Ontologies of nature depend on the narrative for which they seek conditions. Christian nature-narratives require a dynamic and differentiated account.

Paul differentiates natures according to theological considerations we might call narrative. Stories about God's relations with Israel set a context in which Paul's use of nature makes sense.[33] For Paul, "nature" works differently for free Jewish men (Torah-observers) and others (slaves, Gentiles, women). It is surprising to read Paul's usages together: *Every case but one is about the distinct natures of Jews and Gentiles.*[34] The other case (I Cor. 11:14) is about the heads of women. As de Certeau suggests "this surface, articulated but not unified, obeys . . . a different type of coherence than philosophical discourse."[35]

33. The instances of *phusis* in authentic Pauline letters seem to be Rom. 1:26, 2:27, 11:21-24; I Cor. 11:14; Gal. 2:15 and 4:8. I have worked out this paragraph in conversation with Stanley Stowers. Readers should not assume that he agrees with conclusions not found in his published work, and should assume that mistakes are mine.

34. Cf. Stanley K. Stowers, *A Rereading of Romans: Jews, Gentiles, and Justice* (New Haven and London: Yale University Press), pp. 108-9.

35. Fritz Bauerschmidt, "Michel de Certeau and Theology," *Modern Theology* 12 (1996): 1-26; here, p. 12, quoting Certeau, "La Rupture instauratrice," in *La Faiblesse de croire*, ed. Luce Giard (Paris: Seuil, 1987), pp. 215-16. If I had wanted to increase my philosophical commitments, I might have put the project of *Sexuality and the Christian Body* in Certeau's terms: *Sexuality and the Christian Body* seeks to see whether marriage yet retains derivative reservoirs of mean-

In all cases but one, the natures in question have explicitly or implicitly to do with a *story*, a decline narrative, in which God chose one ethnic group, Jews, to be a witness to others, Gentiles, whom God gave up to their desires so that they would die out (1:32).[36] This pattern is if anything confirmed by the writer of Ephesians, referring to Gentiles as "by nature [what a phrase] children of wrath."[37] The odd example — that of covered women — is also part of a decline narrative: women should cover their heads, because they had sinned with the Watchers who looked down and saw their heads in Genesis 6. In every case, therefore, natures are given and given up by God according to God's plotted initiative in stories that God shares with differentiated human groups.

In the widest variety of Christian traditions, nature is no sheer rival to God,[38] but creature of God for consummation in God. Ephrem makes "nature" a hoard of types unlocked by Christ, a harp played by the Spirit, an olive planted by the Father.[39] Aquinas glosses "nature" appearing without further qualification as "nature reformed by grace."[40] Even Barth can call "nature" a sign that no one is "living in some forgotten corner of the world, where God

---

ing. One might regard Certeau as providing a pneumatology for that. Marriage is "no longer what animates discourses," for it has become a site that "no longer functions as an institution which founds a sense, capable of organizing a representation," but "has ceased to be a site of production" (Michel de Certeau, "The Weakness of Believing: From the Body to Writing, a Christian Transit," *The Certeau Reader*, ed. Graham Ward [Oxford: Blackwell, 2000], p. 218). Its recovery involves what de Certeau calls "the work of an excess" (p. 224), the kind of excess that God works when he grafts wild-olive Gentiles *para phusin* onto the domesticated, Jewish stock, or when the Church grafts "prodigal" same-sex marriages onto "domestic" cross-sex ones. "It is a risky proliferation, but controlled by procedures proper to this or that textual practice" (p. 232). Cf. Stowers, *A Rereading of Romans*, pp. 111-18.

36. A possibility pointed out to me by Wayne Meeks. Cf. Stowers, *A Rereading of Romans*, pp. 90-91, who does not quite draw that conclusion.

37. As Stowers pointed out to me. Cf. Eph. 2:3; Rom. 1:26 and 2:27.

38. For systematic accounts of nature and grace directly rather than inversely related, see Kathryn Tanner, *God and Creation: Tyranny or Empowerment?* (Oxford: Blackwell, 1988), esp. pp. 46-48, and more recently Tanner, *Jesus, the Trinity, and Humanity* (Edinburgh: T&T Clark and Minneapolis: Fortress, 2002).

39. Ephrem the Syrian, "Hymns on Virginity and the Symbols of Our Lord," Hymn 4, in *Ephrem the Syrian: Hymns*, trans. Kathleen McVey (Mahwah, N.J.: Paulist, 1989), pp. 275-80.

40. "Unde exponendum est 'naturaliter,' id est per naturam gratia reformatam," Thomas Aquinas, *In Romanos* 2:14 (*lect.* 3), #216, in *Super epistolas S. Pauli lectura*, 8th rev. ed., ed. Raphael Cai (Turin: Marietti, 1953). Cf. also terminological distinctions at Thomas Aquinas, *In Johannem* 6:44 (*lect.* 4) in *Super Evangelium S. Ioannis lectura*, 5th ed. (Turin: Marietti, 1952). For commentary, see Eugene F. Rogers, Jr., *Sexuality and the Christian Body* (Oxford: Blackwell, 1999), pp. 105-6 and Rogers, *Thomas Aquinas and Karl Barth* (Notre Dame, Ind.: University of Notre Dame Press, 1995), p. 170.

is not God or cannot be known as God."[41] Romanos the Melodist compares "nature" to water, on which the Spirit hovers to collect the seas or wash in the river, the substrate of miracle.[42]

Nature *might*, if Christians depicted a deist world, have an integrity apart from the Spirit. But it doesn't. Multiple traditions can treat nature also as a creature of the Spirit. Nature, in short, is what Spirit does with it.

That sounds as if nature can mean anything at all. One wants to know the controls. The controls, I've suggested, are narrative. Even natural-law reasoning, in Aquinas, reflects God's providential — storied — interaction with creation.[43] "Nature" is a character in a story, a story liturgically enacted by the community in baptism and Eucharist. The ontologies of nature that the Church and its theologians have from time to time produced are, like all ontologies, reflections upon stories. Reflection upon nature is about what must be the case for the biblical stories to work. The interaction of plot and circumstance identifies nature as a character. Nature is created with an end in view; it is to grow. It falls not into stasis, but into a counter-movement, into decay. Nature is redeemed not to status quo but more growth. These are the changes of an almost human character. Consider a passage by the Marxist economist turned theologian Sergei Bulgakov:

> The "physical" world [the world of *phusis*, nature] . . . is not closed off from or alien to the Spirit. Created out of nothing, the world receives its reality, matter, and elements from the Holy Spirit, so that its most material elements are, at the same time, its most spiritual ones by virtue of their [Spirit-grantedness]. Further, the diversity of the world . . . in the sense of the presence of all its aspects . . . , becomes real by the Holy Spirit, who is the reality

---

41. So that Barth can "gladly concede that *nature* does objectively offer a proof of God, though the human being overlooks or misunderstands it." *A Late Friendship: The Letters of Karl Barth and Carl Zuckmayer*, trans. Geoffrey Bromiley (Grand Rapids: Eerdmans, 1982); *Gesammtausgabe: Briefe* 5, §286. For commentary on these passages, with answers to the obvious objections, see Rogers, *Thomas Aquinas and Karl Barth*, pp. 3-9 and 183-202. See also Karl Barth, *Shorter Commentary on Romans* (Richmond: John Knox, 1959), pp. 28-29. Not a version of the manifesto of the twenties, the *Kurze Erzählung des Römerbriefes* (Munich, 1956) is an independent work.

42. As we saw above, in the chapter on the Annunciation, where Romanos compares the water of the womb with the rain on the fleece. Cf. Ps. 72:6, taken in a christological sense.

43. See Eugene F. Rogers, Jr., "Narrative of Natural Law in Thomas's Commentary on Romans 1," *Theological Studies* 59 (1998): 254-76; John R. Bowlin, *Contingency and Fortune in Aquinas's Ethics* (Cambridge and New York: Cambridge University Press, 1999); and, with a different interpretation of "narrative," Pamela Hall, *Narrative and the Natural Law: An Interpretation of Thomistic Ethics* (Notre Dame, Ind.: University of Notre Dame Press, 1994).

of the "cosmos." . . . [T]he world participates in the Spirit by the fact that it is real. . . . It is open to the Spirit; it is materially spiritual.[44]

That leaves room for more diversity than one often associates with Christian views of nature. Suppose "be fruitful and multiply" belongs with "let the earth put forth vegetation" and "Let the waters bring forth swarms" and "let the earth bring forth everything that creeps upon the ground": In all these cases, the earth and the waters bring forth things different from themselves, not just more dirt and more water; and in all these cases, they bring forth different kinds of things: one might almost translate, "Be fruitful and diversify."[45] Multiplication is always in God's hand, so that the multiplication of the loaves and the fishes, the fruit of the virgin's womb, the diversity of the natural world, and God's husbandry alongside (para) nature in grafting the wild olive onto the domestic does not overturn nature but parallels, diversifies, and celebrates it.

On Bulgakov's view, the Spirit can also redeploy or mobilize nature. Christian discourse calls the variety of productions "nature," and the mobilizer of alternatives it calls Spirit.

How does the Spirit mobilize alternatives? By applying the Image — with a "repetition" that varies, redeploys, mobilizes, subverts, creates — to the members, and in so doing to deify matter, or return it to God. In what follows I want to elaborate two interlocking theses: (1) It is appropriate to the Spirit to apply the Image to the members. (2) That application explains the deification of matter. For matter outside of God's own humanity in Christ cannot participate in deification without change. Indeed, "we all . . . are being changed into the likeness of the Lord from one degree of glory to another; for this comes from the Lord who is the Spirit."[46]

It is the office of a witness to relay a message to one who has not yet heard, to perfect — extend — particularize — its publication. It is the office of the witness of a wedding to protect against particular, unforeseen threats. It is the office of the Holy Spirit to give particular gifts to the community in its community-building activity, including gifts of distinct tongues that the mes-

44. Sergius Bulgakov, The Bride of the Lamb, trans. Boris Jakim (Edinburgh: T&T Clark and Grand Rapids: Eerdmans, 2002), p. 401. For a compatible neopatristic account, see Dumitru Staniloae, "The World as Gift and Word," in Orthodox Dogmatic Theology, vol. II, trans. Ioan Ionita and Robert Barringer (Brookline, Mass.: Holy Cross Orthodox Press, 2000), pp. 21-63.

45. Cf. Bulgakov, Bride of the Lamb, pp. 65-66; the exegesis can stand even without the conceptual context.

46. II Cor. 3:18.

sage may come to particular people. According to II Corinthians, God establishes the people "into Christ," or "has put his seal upon us and given us his Spirit as a guarantee."[47]

The language of the seal rings with the implication of a particular impression or application of the image. Such language offers a way to distinguish appropriations: The Son restores the image; the Spirit applies it. A seal is a sign of personal authority or ownership. And if the Son is the "hand" of God, the Spirit is, according to Didymus the Blind in the East and Ambrose in the West, God's "finger," since Jesus casts out demons alternatively "by the Spirit" (Matt. 12:28) and "by the finger of God" (Luke 11:20) — a finger that points out a particular person and "stamps the Divine image on the human soul."[48] A finger and a stamp: are these not impersonal images again, the recurrence of a mere tool, instrument, or power? No: they mark again characteristic acts of a witness: to point out or to set a seal to the particular ones whom the Spirit gathers into community. The seal "comes to mean that which closes or seals up, and so can be equivalent to 'completion' or 'perfection', in the sense of that which completes and sums up a process or series."[49]

A similar particularization of human persons, and appropriation of that work to the Spirit, appears when the Spirit is associated with the oil used to anoint the baptized in Syriac traditions. It paints the image of Christ onto the baptized and reflects the image of Christ in individual refractions, as in the poem of Ephrem that serves as epigraph to this book, and deserves re-reading here:

> A royal portrait is painted with visible colours,
>> and with oil that all can see is the hidden portrait of our
>>> hidden King portrayed
> on those who have been signed . . .
> This oil is the dear friend of the Holy Spirit, it serves him,
> following him like a disciple. . . .
> the hidden seal of the Spirit is imprinted by oil on the bodies
> of those who are anointed in baptism: thus they are marked
>> in the baptismal mystery. . . .

47. II Cor. 1:21-22; Eph. 1:13-14, 4:30. See G. W. H. Lampe, *The Seal of the Spirit: A Study of the Doctrine of Baptism and Confirmation in the New Testament and the Fathers,* 2d ed. (London: SPCK, 1967), p. 3.

48. Didymus, *De Spiritu Sancto* 34-37, in the Latin of Jerome, and translated at length in Henry Barclay Swete, *The Holy Spirit in the Ancient Church* (London: Macmillan, 1912; repr. Grand Rapids: Baker, 1966), pp. 224-534; Ambrose, *De Spiritu Sancto* iii.3-5.

49. Lampe, *Seal of the Spirit,* p. 8, citing PG 89, 113D.

The face that gazes on a vessel filled with oil
sees its reflection there, and he who gazes hard sets his
    spiritual gaze thereon
and sees in its symbols Christ. And as the beauty of Christ is manifold,
so the olive's symbols are manifold.
Christ has many facets, and the oil acts as a mirror to them all:
from whatever angle I look at the oil, Christ looks out at me from it.[50]

Ephrem involves both Christ and Spirit in restoring the image of the Father. Similarly, according to Gregory Nazianzen's Fifth Theological Oration, it is the appropriated work of the Father to be the source (*aitios*) of the image. It is the appropriated work of the Son (*demiourgos*) to work or restore the image. And it is the appropriated work of the Spirit (*teleopoios*) to perfect or *apply* the image, in authors as diverse as Gregory and Ephrem. "What Christ has accomplished universally, the Spirit perfects particularly."[51]

The Spirit's peculiar bearing witness to the Image, or resting on the Son, may owe its articulation to a problem in neo-Platonic thought: in what way, indeed, individual human beings could bear the image or icon of the divine.[52] Did the Son's restoration of the image indeed finally reach human beings individuated by bodies? The doctrine of the Spirit both asserted that it did, and explained how. It solved a problem in soteriology — how the work of soteriology applied to me without ceasing to be God's work — and took up a position in neo-Platonist thought: yes, a human being could bear and instantiate the image, by the constant pressure of God the Spirit forming her from within and from without.

The usual phrase, in Athanasius and others, is that the human being is deified "by the Son in the Spirit" (*di huiou en pneumati*).[53] What does "in the Spirit" mean or add to the agency of the Son? It means at least a double negative: the Son does not work *without* the Spirit — the Son does not work *without* changing, sealing, anointing his members. In that case, "in the Spirit" means "not without transformation" or "not without *koinonia*," communion. That is, the Son does not redeem human beings without the Spirit's integrat-

---

50. Ephrem the Syrian, "Hymns on Virginity," Hymn 7, in Sebastian P. Brock, trans., *The Harp of the Spirit: Eighteen Poems of Saint Ephrem*, 2nd enlarged ed. (San Bernardino, Calif.: Borgo, 1984). The whole poem is relevant.

51. Donald F. Winslow, *The Dynamics of Salvation: A Study in Gregory of Nazianzus*, p. 129.

52. For the Plotinian background of doctrines of deification, see Jules Gross, *La divinisation du chrétien d'après les pères grecs* (Paris: J. Gabalda et Cie., 1938), pp. 59-67.

53. Cf. Thomas G. Weinandy, *The Father's Spirit of Sonship: Reconceiving the Trinity* (Edinburgh: T&T Clark, 1995), *passim*.

ing them into the triune life. That is what "in the Spirit" adds.[54] "By" is a preposition of agency; "in" is a preposition of place. What is this place? The *koinonia* that the Spirit creates in and with the Trinity. "*In* the Spirit" means *in community,* and then in form of life, in history, in circumstances, in witness, in a person like a mother or a saint: the preposition indicates a mode or form. Thus in Basil it becomes explicit, though not, to be sure, exhaustive or reductive:

> The more I meditate on this short and simple syllable "in," the more I discover its multiple and varied senses, of which each finds its application to the Holy Spirit. One says that the form *(eidos)* is in the matter *(hyle)*, the power in the one that receives it, the disposition in the one who is affected, and so on. Therefore, in perfecting the reasonable creature . . . the Holy Spirit plays the role of form. For whomever . . . is conformed to the image of the Son of God is called spiritual.[55]

Athanasius had explained that because those sealed bear the image of God from the inside out, they are thereby partakers of the divine nature.[56] As Cyril puts it, "We are transformed into the divine image, into Christ Jesus, not by undergoing a bodily refashioning, but . . . by partaking of the Holy Spirit"[57] — that is, by a refashioning from the inside out. It is as if Christ's work changes the human nature or form, while the Spirit reconfigures or re-forms recalcitrant matter into the new shape.[58] The Spirit thus seals, imprints, forms, trans*figures* — these are the characteristic verbs — conforming the human being to the restored image.[59] Clement describes the indwelling Spirit as a "shining character," and Athanasius makes the Spirit the seal applied by the Logos.[60] Alternately, the Spirit seals and identifies individuals with the

---

54. This way of putting the matter occurred to me while reading the interpretation of Athanasius given in Gross, *La divinisation,* pp. 210-16.

55. Basil, *On the Holy Spirit* 9.22-23. For commentary see Gross, *La divinisation,* pp. 239-44.

56. Athanasius, *The Letters of Saint Athanasius concerning the Holy Spirit,* trans. C. R. B. Shapland (New York: Philosophical Library, 1951), 1.23. This text is also known by its recipient as *Ad Serapion.*

57. Cyril of Alexandria, *De recta fide ad Theodosius* 36 as translated in Lampe, *Seal of the Spirit,* p. 257. See Edvardus Schwartz, *Acta Conciliorum Oecumenicorum* (Berlin: de Gruyter, 1935).

58. Cf. Gross, *La divinisation,* p. 290.

59. Cf. J. Mahé, "La sanctification d'après saint Cyrille d'Alexandrie," *Revue d'histoire ecclésiastique* 10 (1909): 475-80.

60. Lampe, *Seal of the Spirit,* p. 258, citing Clement, *Stromateis* 4.18 (PG 9, 1325A) and Athanasius, *Letters to Serapion on the Holy Spirit* 1.23 (PG 26, 584-85).

soldier's tattoo, the Prodigal's ring (both Ambrose), or the sheep's brand (Macarius).[61] And yet this formal analogy is never merely mechanical, but remains joined to the sense of community: in the Spirit always continues to mean "in the *koinonia* of the Spirit," in the triune community that the Spirit creates, celebrates, and enlarges.

Or as Vladimir Lossky has put it, the work of the Son deifies human nature, and the work of the Spirit deifies the human person.[62] For "the idea of our ultimate deification cannot be expressed on a christological basis alone, but demands a pneumatological development of doctrine."[63] As the letter to the Hebrews puts it, God speaks uniformly through the Son but through the Spirit "in many and various ways."[64] A baroque metaphor of Ignatius of Lyon confirms the impression that it is the work of the Spirit to honor diversity in applying the work of Christ. The faithful members of the church are "stones of the Temple, prepared beforehand for a building of God the Father, hoisted aloft by that engine of Jesus Christ, His Cross: using the Holy Spirit for a rope, while your faith is your windlass, and your love the way that leads up to God." Swete comments: "Apart from the Spirit, the Cross stands inert, a vast machine at rest, and about it lie the stones of the building unmoved. Not till the rope has been attached can the work proceed of lifting" — reconfiguring, vivifying, deifying — "the individual life through faith and love to the place prepared for it in the Church of God."[65]

Cyril of Jerusalem says, "not that the Spirit was divided, but that His grace was distributed in proportion to the vessels, and the capacity of the recipients."[66] The Church is familiar, from its sacramental life, with something that is distributable but not divisible: the eucharistic body of Christ. Like the Eucharist, the Spirit is a gift and a thanksgiving, indeed the Gift par excellence. But the Eucharist, as a material gift, is a better guide for material creatures in how to understand the Spirit. The Spirit's application of the Image works

61. Lampe, p. 258, citing Ambrose, *De obitu Valentiniani*, 58, in *Corpus scriptorum ecclesiasticorum latinorum* 73, 329-67; *In Lucam* 7, in *Corpus scriptorum ecclesiasticorum latinorum* 32/4; Macarius, *Spiritual Homilies*, 5.12 and 12.13; cf. *Pseudo-Macarius: The Fifty Spiritual Homilies and the Great Letter*, ed. George F. Maloney (Mahwah, N.J.: Paulist, 1992).

62. Vladimir Lossky, "Redemption and Deification," *Sobornost*, Series 3, no. 2 (1947), p. 55. Cf. also Florensky, *The Pillar*, p. 38.

63. Lossky, "Redemption and Deification," p. 51.

64. Heb. 1:1.

65. Ignatius quoted from his letter to the Ephesians in Swete, *The Holy Spirit in the Ancient Church*, p. 15; for text, see Ignatius, "Letter to the Ephesians," in *Early Christian Fathers*, ed. Cyril Richardson (New York: Touchstone Books, 1995), pp. 87-92, here, p. 90.

66. Cyril of Jerusalem, *Cathechetical Orations* XVI, "On the Article, and in One Holy Ghost," 25, in NPNF2, vol. 7, p. 122.

through baptism and the Eucharist, the distribution of the fire in the water and the bread. So the Eucharist provides a continual means of perfection in time even as it anticipates the completion of the end. As one epiclesis prays,

> May the Holy Spirit come, . . . who proceeds uninterruptedly, who perfects, unhampered by time, who brings to completion in a divine fashion. . . .[67]

In summary, we may improve upon Winslow's thesis, by rendering it in a eucharistic key: The Spirit distributes the corporate and incorporates the divided. A sacrament, like the Spirit, takes place both "in" a concrete form (the body of Christ) and "in" a community (the body of Christ). This is not to reify the Spirit. If the Eucharist manifests the logic of the Spirit, that must be because, theologically speaking, the sacrament participates in the Spirit's work.

If the Spirit distributes the corporate and incorporates the divided, then the very matter that divides human beings in their finitude, and renders them recalcitrant in their fallenness is incorporated by the Spirit into the matter that saves. The Spirit renders the body liturgical, a site from which, by the Spirit's gift, God gives Godself to be perceived, and a site in which, by the Spirit's gift on gift, God gives Godself to be met. "God created the body to be a means of knowing God and of being in God's presence."[68] Because the Spirit witnesses — indicates — points out, the finger of God applies to human beings a seal, it incorporates each one into a body, a community, not only of the Church, but of God's own life, into the virtuous circle in which God is known by God and partaken by God, so that human reception of God is not passive but participant. In the phrase "participants in the divine nature," neither the word "participant" nor "nature" is abstract, but both are as concrete as sacramental language. "Nature" is related to form language, *phusis,* and "participant" is the very center of community language, *koinonos.*[69]

If we have seen the Spirit distribute the corporate in the self-offering of Christ, in the crucifixion as mobilized by the Eucharist, we have also seen how the Spirit incorporates the divided at the beginning and the renewal of the life of Christ. At the annunciation, the Spirit overshadows Mary and bridges the

---

67. Anaphora of Dioscorus of Gazarta (late 13th C.), in Brock, *Holy Spirit,* 2d. ed., pp. 181-82, without a reference; presumably from *Anaphorae Syriacae,* 6 vols. in 2 (Rome: Institutum Pontificium Studiorum Orientalium, 1939-), vol. I/3.

68. Susan Harvey, "Embodiment in Time and Eternity: A Syriac Perspective," *St. Vladimir's Seminary Quarterly* 43 (1999): 105-30; here, p. 106. See also Susan Harvey, "The Sense of a Stylite: Perspectives on Symeon the Elder," *Vigiliae Christianae* 42 (1988): 376-94.

69. II Pet. 1:4.

division between divine and human. It bridges that division, furthermore, in, with, and under a body, that is, corporately, in the Incarnation, divine and human at one in the human body of God. The Spirit incorporates — reconciles — God and humanity in the flesh of Jesus. And as we have also seen, the Spirit does the same thing at the other end of Jesus' earthly life, at the resurrection. The Spirit is characteristically re-incorporating the divided, body and soul, Father and Son, human and divine. It is the Spirit, the Breath and Giver of Life, who re-incorporates Jesus, body and soul. It is the Spirit, the bond and guardian[70] of love, who reunites the Father and the Son when their bond had been stretched to the breaking point by death. It is the Spirit who restores breath to the Son, and who "frees" or "renews" the Father for raising him from the dead. And it is the Spirit who incorporates us other human beings for the first time into this opening in the body of God and in the trinitarian communion, taking advantage of death to expand the body of God, to incorporate the Gentiles divided from Israel and the humans divided from God, into the general dance. In taking up dwelling in our mortal bodies also, the Spirit at once enlarges the body of Christ, and distributes the life of God.

The Spirit incorporates human beings into the body of Christ and distributes the life of God not only in the resurrection of Jesus and the celebration of the Eucharist, but paradigmatically in baptism. The Spirit alights upon Christ at his baptism in the Jordan at the beginning of Christ's ministry to accompany the restoration of the image of God in the human being, the re-forming of the corporate human nature, drowned in the water and anointed for deification in the chrism. It is this corporate baptism of the human race as a whole that the Spirit distributes in the baptism of the members, in-corporating us into the corpus, making a liturgical body.

According to Ephrem's meditations upon the chrism or oil of baptism above, the oil painted upon the forehead in the sign of the cross not only incorporates human members into the anointed Christ, but it distributes the image in distinct reflections. Christ appears now reflected, each time a little differently, in the face of each of his members. So the incorporation is not a melting together, but requires a diversity of members sharing the one restored corporate person. In Paul's famous metaphor the body of Christ needs the differences among its members. "Consider," writes Cyril of Jerusalem,

> how many of you are now sitting here, how many souls of us are present. He is working suitably for each, and beholds the temper of each, beholds also

---

70. Cyril of Jerusalem, *Cathechetical Orations* XVII, "Continuation of the Discourse on the Holy Ghost," 13 *in fin.*, in NPNF2, vol. 7, p. 127.

his reasoning and his conscience. . . . For consider, I pray, with mind enlightened by Him, how many Christians there are in all this diocese, and how many in the whole province of Palestine, and carry forward thy mind from this province, to the whole Roman Empire; and after this, consider the whole world; races of Persians, and nations of Indians, Goths and Sarmatians, Gauls and Spaniards, and Moors, Libyans and Ethiopians, and the rest for whom we have no names. . . . Consider, I pray, of each nation, Bishops, Presbyters, Deacons, Solitaries, Virgins, and laity besides; and then behold their great Protector, and the Dispenser of their gifts; — how throughout the world He gives to one chastity, to another perpetual virginity, to another almsgiving, to another voluntary poverty, to another power of repelling hostile spirits. And as the light, with one touch of its radiance, shines on all things; so also the Holy Ghost. . . .[71]

But for that very reason they are not "individuals," defined by their apartness from each other; they are defined by their place in the whole world being made one, in their service to the whole human nature being made new. They refract the image diversely, they inflect, they sing, they celebrate the glory of God in Christ. In this they do the Spirit's work. The glory, the beauty of Christ, as Ephrem says, is manifold; he has many facets, and the oil of baptism "acts as a mirror to them all," so that "from whatever angle I look at the oil, Christ looks out at me." So these are not "individual" refractions; rather precisely in their diversity they reflect the corporate one.

Since it is characteristic of the Spirit's work to distribute the corporate and incorporate the divided even between the Father and the Son during the life of Jesus, and since it is characteristic of the Spirit's work also within God's triune life to witness and celebrate the love of the Father for the Son and the gratitude of the Son to the Father, we may assume that the distributing that the Spirit does in the economy is somehow the temporal analogue of a distributing that the Spirit does in the Trinity, a making manifold, a making full and rich and overflowing the glory of the divine love. At least when human beings come to participate in the Triune life, that participation will be because the Spirit has already flowed through their mortal bodies, beginning to incorporate them into the general dance. But dare we say, that if the Spirit in the economy also incorporates the divided into one, that even incorporation, even embodiment, must be somehow a temporal analogue of something the Spirit does already in God's triune life?

Robert Jenson has suggested that a "body" is a place where a person is

71. Cyril of Jerusalem, *Cathechetical Orations* XVI, "On the Article, and in One Holy Ghost," 22, in NPNF2, vol. 7, p. 121.

available.[72] Clearly the divine Persons are all available to one another in an unimaginably pre-eminent way. But in God there seems to be no "place." And yet as Jenson also suggests, that way of putting the matter gets it exactly backwards. For God is not so much "no place" as infinite place, unending room, one whose life is so roomy as to accommodate an infinity of others into that life without distorting it.[73] So the body of God on earth is the temporal analogue of that infinite availability and roominess of God by which an infinite number of created persons can be incorporated into the Person (or if you like the body) of the Son. And the incorporating work of the Spirit on earth is the temporal analogue of that infinite enlarging and refracting work of the Spirit by which the love of the Father and the Son is endlessly magnified, not made vague, but endlessly inflected, specified, and made concrete, the work of a witness.

The characteristic way or *tropos* in which the Person of the Spirit incorporates human members into the Triune life also helps explain why human members do not distort the Trinity into a Quaternity, Quinity, Infinity. The reason is twofold. First, the Spirit's way is to include diversity within herself, so that human beings come to share, not to individuate, the divine life. Second, the Spirit rests upon the one person of the Son, and on his human members precisely in him.

The Trinity is complete, rich, full in itself. In the Triune life, God has no need of us. Yet "there could exist more than three by the reception of certain new subjects into the bosom of the trinitarian life."[74] These would not be necessary to that life. They would not share the necessary existence that God enjoys. They would be unnecessary, contingent, conditioned — extra. They would be "extra" also in that word's Latin sense of being beyond or outside God. They would be creatures. They would have their existence not from themselves, but from God, not by nature, but by grace. Should they come to share in existence, that would be by leaning upon the Three. They would owe their existence to the Father, the one source of the Three and therefore also of anything extra to them. They would owe their creation to the begetting of the Son, in whom it is characteristic of the Father not to exist for himself alone, but to love another. And should they receive a share not only in creation, but also in the life of the Three, they would owe it to that Spirit who establishes the love of the Father and the Son in a Third that not only guarantees and es-

72. Robert W. Jenson, *Visible Words: The Interpretation and Practice of Christian Sacraments* (Philadelphia: Fortress, 1978).

73. Robert W. Jenson, *Systematic Theology,* 2 vols. (New York: Oxford University Press, 1997), vol. 1.

74. Staniloae, pp. 92-95, quoting Florensky, pp. 37-38.

tablishes it but diversifies and celebrates it. "[T]hey would not appear as internally necessary for [God's] absoluteness. They would be *conditioned* hypostases which, as far as [God] were concerned, might or might not be. Hence they cannot be called hypostases in the proper sense of the term" — i.e., they cannot be the same as trinitarian Persons, necessary Persons, divine Persons — "and might better be named *deified* persons."[75]

Human nature, like the divine nature, is meant to be distributable over multiple persons, but not divisible into so many monads. From Eve on, human nature *is* human nature in its filling out. Not in procreation, necessarily — it is not a necessary infinity, a compulsory fertility — but as an anticipation of the eucharistic sharing and inclusion. If human beings have human personhood, it's not because of procreation, it's because of the Eucharist. There thanksgiving gets diversified as part of the Spirit's freedom and innovation. So although the nature is the nature in its filling out, nature is not the ground of the filling out, but the person is, as the Father is the source, the Son the other, the Spirit the incorporator into one, and the diversifier of the corporate.

This happens by involving human beings in a circle. It is a virtuous circle, indeed the virtuous circle *par excellence*. It happens, that is, by involving them in the Trinity's own perichoresis, which Gregory of Nyssa calls "the revolving circle of the glory moving from Like to Like." This is deification, glorification, for God the Spirit to involve human beings too in that circle, as Gregory notes at the end:

> You see the revolving circle of the glory moving from Like to Like. The Son is glorified by the Spirit; the Father is glorified by the Son; again the Son has his glory from the Father; and the Only-begotten thus becomes the glory of the Spirit. For with what shall the Father be glorified, but with the true glory of the Son: and with what again shall the Son be glorified, but with the majesty of the Spirit? In like manner, again, Faith completes the circle, and glorifies the Son by means of the Spirit, and the Father by means of the Son.[76]

The circle takes in human beings first in Christ, and then in them as in him. Cyril of Alexandria puts it this way:

> But when the Word of God became human, He received the Spirit from the Father as one of us, (not receiving ought for Himself individually, for He was the Giver of the Spirit); but that He Who knew no sin, might, by receiv-

---

75. Florensky, *The Pillar*, p. 38; my italics.
76. Gregory of Nyssa, *On the Holy Spirit*, NPNF2, vol. 5, p. 324.

ing It as a human being, preserve It to our nature, and might again inroot in us the grace which had left us. For this reason, I deem, it was that the holy Baptist profitably added, "I saw the Spirit descending from Heaven, and It abode upon Him." For It had fled from us by reason of sin, but He Who knew no sin, became as one of us, that the Spirit might be accustomed to abide in us, having no occasion of departure or withdrawal in Him. . . . so does He also receive the Spirit for our sakes, that He may sanctify our whole nature. For He came not to profit Himself, but to be to all of us the Door and Beginning and Way of the Heavenly Goods.[77]

The Spirit's perfecting also takes place, appropriately for human persons, over time, as Irenaeus observes in general — "we have not been made gods from the beginning, but at first merely human beings, then at length gods"[78] — as Gregory observes, typologically, again, in the disciples:

[The Spirit] gradually came to dwell in the disciples, measuring Himself out to them according to their capacity to receive Him, at the beginning of the Gospel, after the Passion, after the Ascension, making perfect their powers, being breathed upon them, and appearing in fiery tongues.[79]

Gregory Nazianzen works out the Spirit's "personification" of the human being, or perhaps better the Spirit's perfecting (teleiopoiesis) of the human person in a typological way. In each case a person becomes a more particular servant of the corporate body, more herself as the Spirit intends and moves her to be:

[I]f [the Spirit] takes possession of a shepherd, He makes him a Psalmist, subduing evil spirits by his song, and proclaims him King; if He possesses a goatherd and a scraper of sycamore fruit, He makes him a Prophet [Amos 7:14]. . . . If He takes possession of Fishermen, He makes them catch the whole world. . . . If of Publicans, He . . . makes them merchants of souls.[80]

That is what it means for the Spirit to perfect or glorify a human being. As Irenaeus had put it, "For the glory of God is a living human being; and the life of the human being consists in beholding God."[81] That is what it means that,

---

77. Cyril of Alexandria, Commentary on the Gospel According to Saint John, trans. P. E. Pusey and T. Randell, 2 vols. (London: Rivingtons, 1874-85), vol. 1, pp. 142-43.

78. Irenaeus, Adv. Haer. 5.38.4, in ANF, vol. 1, p. 522.

79. Fifth Theological Oration, in NPNF2, vol. 7, p. 326.

80. Gregory Nazianzen, On Pentecost, in NPNF2, vol. 7, p. 384.

81. Irenaeus, Adv. Haer. 5.20.7, in ANF, vol. 1, p. 490.

again as Irenaeus had put it, "the Spirit [is] truly preparing the human being in the Son."[82] God's work is the elevation of God's image, the human being, to fellowship with God, grace on grace, the claiming of the human being as God's own. Under conditions of sin, the elevation of the human being to fellowship with God also involves redemption from sin.

iii. The Spirit rests on the Son in the Wilderness

In the Hebrew Bible there is another portrait of the Spirit which is not "still" and "small"; it is the Spirit that hounds prophets and drives human beings mad. It is this Spirit that drives Jesus into the wilderness to be tempted.

Isaac of Nineveh connects the witness of the martyrs directly with the Spirit's breath at creation:

> If a person of humility comes near dangerous wild animals, then the moment these catch sight of him, their ferocity is calmed; they come up to him and attach themselves to him as though he were their master, wagging their tails and licking his hands and feet. This is because they smell that fragrance that emanated from Adam when he named the animals in Paradise before the Fall: this fragrance was taken away from us at the Fall, but Christ gave it back to us at his coming.[83]

"Fragrance" is perhaps apt as the fragrance of *food to the hungry,* a prominent theme in the Gospel of Luke. If Jesus returns human beings to paradise after the Fall, it is not least in the Temptation that he does this. The first temptation, in Luke's account (and Matthew's), is that of food:

> And Jesus, full of the Holy Spirit, returned from the Jordan, and was led [Mark: driven] by the Spirit for forty days in the wilderness, tempted by the devil [Mathew: the tempter]. And he ate nothing in those days; and when they were ended, he was hungry. The devil said to him, "If you are the Son of God, command this stone to become bread." And Jesus answered him, "It is written, 'The human being shall not live by bread alone'" [Lk. 4:1-4].

Filled with the fragrance of the Spirit, someone like Isaac might say, Jesus is able to resist, when appropriate, even the tempter's evocation of the smell of

---

82. Irenaeus, *Adv. Haer.* 5.20.5, in ANF, vol. 1, p. 489.
83. Isaac of Nineveh, Discourse 82, in Brock, *Spirituality,* p. 88.

bread. But the fragrance of the Spirit is not here a gentle wafting thing, but something heady, driving, almost cruel.

Matthew orders the next two temptations so that the devil prompts Jesus second to throw himself down from the pinnacle of the Temple — as if perhaps in parody of his coming down from heaven — and last to receive human kingdoms and their glory. But Luke reverses the order of those two, so that the temptation to descend from the Temple comes last.

We are now in a position to take up the promise of the resurrection chapter, to consider Donald Mackinnon's account of Jesus' temptations. They are temptations to certain kinds of grasping, temptations to grasp certain kinds of success, even the real success of the Messiah. The proposed descent from the pinnacle of the temple is indeed a parody, a counterfeit of the descent *de coelis,* because it would come to amount to a descent, according to Mackinnon, from the cross.

According to Mackinnon, "it is very important that in his account of Jesus' temptations Luke finds the climactic temptation not in the offer of the Kingdoms of this world . . . but in the suggestion Jesus test his status *vis-à-vis* the Father by a descent from the pinnacle of the Temple" (Luke 4:9-12).[84] The devil departs until "an opportune time" (4:13), "to return in the hour of the power of darkness [22:53], to enter into Judas, to sift Peter as wheat, and above all to renew his challenge to Jesus to prove himself." It is Luke who specifies that "Then Satan entered into Judas Isacariot" (22:3) and retains Jesus' fruitless instruction to the disciples to "Rise and pray that you may not enter into temptation" (22:46). The reappearance of the devil does not serve to introduce a dualistic element into Luke's account, so much as to make explicit the connection between the temptation of the wilderness and the temptation of the Passion. Jesus' reply to the wilderness temptation that Luke puts last is messianic: "It is said, you shall not tempt the Lord your God" (4:12). It is a temptation to be the Lord in a different way, a way that grasps success for a Messiah, and does not receive suffering from the Spirit. The true Messiah receives anointing from another, the oil of the Spirit, by trusting the Spirit of fidelity to turn suffering into something humanly unforeseen. The Spirit rests on him like oil in the womb, alights on him like oil at the baptism, anoints his feet (rather than his head) at the hands of a sinner (7:46), and renews her fidelity at his death among the women who would

---

84. These paragraphs follow Donald Mackinnon, "Incarnation and Trinity," in *Themes in Theology: The Three-Fold Cord: Essays in Philosophy, Politics and Theology* (Edinburgh: T&T Clark, 1987), pp. 145-67; here, pp. 152-53, n. 13. See also Mackinnon, "The Evangelical Imagination," in *Religious Imagination,* ed. James P. Mackey (Edinburgh University Press, 1986), pp. 175-85, esp. p. 179.

"prepare spices and ointments" (23:56). The temptation to claim the Messiahship for himself contrasts with the *Spirit's* giving of words to say (12:12),[85] so that the refusal to answer juridical questions becomes a renewed refusal of temptation and a renewed reliance on the Spirit:

> Then they seized him. . . . Now the men who were holding Jesus mocked him and beat him; they also blindfolded him and asked him, "Prophesy! Who is it that struck you?" And they spoke many other words against him, reviling him (22:63).

Here Luke portrays Jesus as "held" and "blind" and subject to "words." In so doing he reverses the stories of the healings. The Gerasene demoniac had been "seized," was "under guard, and bound with chains and fetters." But unlike Jesus "he broke the bonds." And unlike Jesus "he was driven into the desert" not by the Spirit but "by a demon" (Luke 8:29b). In a telling point, the demoniac "lived not in a house but among tombs" (8:27). Similarly, the blind man asks to "receive his sight"; Jesus commands him, "Receive your sight," and using the verb a third time, Luke concludes, "immediately he received his sight." Sight is something even Jesus does not give himself, but waits to receive; like prophecy, it comes by the Spirit. The words that Jesus receives from his tormenters, "reviling him," differ from the words that he awaits from the Spirit (12:12).

Luke continues: "When day came, the assembly of the elders people gathered together, . . . and they said, 'If you are the Christ, tell us'" (22:66-67). The words that Jesus then says, or perhaps receives from the Spirit to say, do not deliver him from the final temptation, as he has prayed. If the Spirit is giving him the next words to say in this hour, they are ones not well designed to mollify his hearers. They are all too clever, words his hearers will take as sarcasm, words that will drive him, as the Spirit drove him before, into a further, crueler temptation. In an ironic designation, the hearers use the word "testimony," a hallmark of the Spirit.

> But he said to them, "If I tell you, you will not believe; and if I ask you, you will not answer. But from now on the Son of man shall be seated at the right hand of the power of God. And they all said, "Are you the Son of God, then?" And he said to them, "You say that I am." And they said, "What further testimony do we need? We have heard it ourselves from his own lips" (Luke 22:66-71).

85. But cf. the Son's giving his followers "a mouth and wisdom," Luke 21:15, echoing Ps. 37:30 and Prov. 31:26.

The challenge to descend from the cross appears in Matthew, close by a reference to the temple, from which the devil had called upon Jesus to leap in the earlier temptations:

> And those who passed by derided him, wagging their heads and saying, "You who would destroy the Temple and build it in three days, save yourself! If you are the Son of God, come down from the cross." So also the chief priests, with the scribes and elders, mocked him, saying "He saved others; he cannot save himself. He is the King of Israel; let him come down now from the cross, and we will believe in him" (Matt. 27:39-43).

Mackinnon sees the same temptation in Luke's retention of repeated commands from onlookers that Jesus should "save himself" (Luke 23:35, 36), so that "Luke's narrative of the Passion" — like his narrative of the wilderness — "is one of a final overwhelming temptation, and that temptation reaches its climax in the challenge to descend from the Cross, the axis of Luke's treatment of the crucifixion. Such a descent, if executed, would have vindicated Jesus' claim, but at a cost totally destructive of his mission."[86] Only in refusing such a descent can Jesus so remain in the Spirit as to offer his spirit back to the Father in the words Luke makes his last, "Father, into thy hands I commend my spirit" (23:46); and only after refusing such a descent can Jesus, now dead, receive from another the testimony that "Certainly this man was innocent" (*dikaios,* righteous, 23:47).[87]

Mackinnon sums up Jesus' defeat in two ways. First, his immediate defeat as a human being:

> What it was for him to be human was to be subject to the sort of fragmentation of effort, curtailment of design, interruption of purpose, distraction of resolve that belongs to temporal experience. To leave one place for another is to leave work undone; to give attention to one suppliant is to ignore another; to expend energy today is to leave less for tomorrow. We have to ask ourselves how far this very conformity to the complex discipline of temporality, this acceptance of the often tragic consequences of its obstinate, ineluctable truncation of human effort, belongs to the very substance of Jesus' defeat. Jesus' acceptance of this part of his burden can arguably be interpreted as a painfully realized transcription into the conditions of our existence, of the receptivity, the defined, even if frontierless, receptivity that constitutes his person . . . a receptivity that in the manner of the Incarnate

---

86. Mackinnon, "Incarnation and Trinity," p. 153, n. 13.
87. Mackinnon, "Incarnation and Trinity," p. 153, n. 13.

life is expressed . . . in the role of the Spirit Who within his history is presented as effective in the order of his coming and going. . . .[88]

But Mackinnon characterizes Jesus' failure also in a second, more chilling
way, one that renews Mackinnon's attention to the Temple.

> At the heart of that ministry we find realized a final, a haunting receptivity.
> Yet that receptivity never rots away into a passive acceptance. It is not only
> that, for instance, the temple is cleansed; it is rather that tragic failure in the
> circumstances of Jesus' mission is characterized for what it is, 'O Jerusalem,
> Jesursalem'. 'Daughters of Jerusalem, weep not for me, but for yourselves.'
> The situation is not mastered, nor is it accepted; it is lived through and met
> by agony. . . . 'And the Spirit drove him into the wilderness.' The Spirit's role
> in the mission of the Incarnate needs much further treatment, if this pic-
> ture is to be, I will not say, complete but tolerably adequate.[89]

An anonymous author from much earlier in the tradition sees the trouble
that the death of Jesus causes, and the hope that the Spirit can somehow
make good on it:

> The whole universe was on the point of chaos and being scattered in con-
> sternation because of the passion, if the wonderful Jesus had not given up
> his divine Spirit exclaiming: "Father into thy hands I commit my Spirit"
> (Luke 23:46). And at the moment that everything shook and was rent with
> fear, the divine Spirit was given up and the universe became stable again as
> if reanimated, vivified, and consolidated.[90]

Despite the stirring cosmic expansion of a passage like that, it is nevertheless,
from a point of view like Mackinnon's, a domestication. The trouble caused
by the death of Jesus cannot be ("merely") cosmic at the expense of the historical. The "further treatment" of which Mackinnon speaks cannot be a cosmic "consolidation," but must have everything to do with the agony that Paul
undergoes as Jesus' apostle when he wonders why the Spirit is pouring so
contrarily or excessively onto the Gentiles, and must have everything to do
with the situation in which the Spirit works historically, according to Paul, as

---

88. Mackinnon, "Incarnation and Trinity," pp. 162-63. I have transposed the last phrase
about receptivity from earlier on p. 162.

89. Mackinnon, "Incarnation and Trinity," p. 154.

90. Anonymous, "Ancient Paschal Homily," 53, in *Sources Chrétiennes* 27, p. 181, as translated
in Raniero Cantalamessa, *The Holy Spirit in the Life of Jesus* (Collegeville, Minn.: The Liturgical
Press, 1994), p. 191.

we saw, at the resurrection. For Mackinnon, like Paul, sees that the "curtailment," "interruption," and "obstinate, ineluctable truncation" of Jesus' design and mission have not only individual but profound *social* consequences for Jerusalem.

Elsewhere he continues this theme.

> [D]octrine inevitably fails if it encourages the believer to avert his attention from the element of sheer waste, the reality of Christ's failure. To speak of Christ's readiness to embrace failure and defeat is familiar [. . . but] we have only to recall historical actualities and . . . the element of abdication of responsibility for his people's welfare involved in the way that Jesus took. It is admittedly speculation to ask whether by other methods he could have helped to avert the catastrophe that was to overtake the Jewish people less than forty years from the crucifixion. It is at least arguable that he had enough influence to achieve at least a little; but he seems to have preferred a road which, if it led to the unmasking of human motives, also involved many of his contemporaries in a terrible guilt and provided inevitably an excuse for his followers in later years to fasten responsibility for the crucifixion upon the Jewish people and their descendants. . . . [P]art of the price paid for the accomplishment of these things in human history was the unmentionable horror of an anti-Semitism whose beginnings can perhaps be traced in the New Testament itself, and whose last manifestation in our own time was Christian acquiescence in the "final solution." To say this may seem wilful exaggeration; but . . . doctrine is blunted by refusal to recall the concrete detail of the events with which it deals. So the mystery of God's presence in human existence is diminished through induced forgetfulness of the depth to which he descended.[91]

iv. The Spirit rests on the Son in reversing the Fall

Because the Spirit gives consummation in the economy, it also therefore gives redemption to human beings. Consummation is the intention of the Spirit's befriending human beings — friendship without limit of extent or degree — and redemption follows from consummation in the case of sin. Consummation is not earned by good behavior, but consummation prepares itself by making our behavior good. Repent and believe, for the kingdom of heaven is at hand.

91. Mackinnon, "Atonement and Tragedy," in *Borderlands of Theology and Other Essays* (Philadelphia and New York: J. B. Lippincott, 1968), pp. 97-104; here, 103-04.

In a collection of Syriac biblical texts edited by Sebastian Brock, the Spirit "hedges in, protects, canopies" the body in a nuptial way.[92] The Spirit, in short, befriends the body — not what we would expect on those readings of the fall in which the body bears the blame. From another tradition, Sebastian Moore, a Benedictine monk, explains (like Benedict) how the Spirit carries out God's intention to consummate human beings, to befriend them through their bodies, even in the case of sin. Moore does this by contrasting his reading of the story of the Fall with a more familiar one offered recently by John Paul II. But he does this by following up on John Paul's own insights.

John Paul II argues that the creation story offers a very deep insight into why God created human beings sexual, and that the story of the Fall goes a long way toward explaining why human beings are so screwed up about sex.[93] Because of the Fall, that is, a glimpse of God's intended meaning for sexuality ought to surprise us. We are created, argues John Paul, yearning for another. We are created with desire for consummation with God. It would be odd if our bodies did not reflect this, if there were no bodily correlate to our intended union with another, if we were created with bodies, only to have those bodies left out of our growth toward God. Thus John Paul connects Adam's cry on seeing the woman, "Bone of my bone, flesh of my flesh," with the mystical recognition and completeness of the Song of Songs, and its traditional interpretation as being about the union of God with God's people, or with the soul. It is no accident that the theological tradition has turned to erotic poetry, in the Song of Songs, to speak of the relation of God and God's people, or God and the soul; it is no accident that the theological tradition has borrowed a sexual metaphor, consummation, to talk about the final union of the human being with God. At least as sex was created.

But what about the Fall?

John Paul argues that what happens in the Fall is a loss of harmony between higher and lower. First this happens because the human being is out of harmony with God. That lack of harmony is then reflected in the body, where

92. The Spirit protects in 2 Kings 19:34, Isa. 31:5, Wisd. 5.16, Ex. 33:22, Ps. 138:8; it protects in the liturgy; it protects in the Resurrection; comforts (Acts 9:31); cf. Advocate language; Syr. *ruhhafa* = *rahhef*, "hover," which translates "have pity, compassion," Isa. 27:11, 30:18; Jer. 13:14; Prov. 3:22; Isa. 63:9; Zech. 12:10. This list comes from Brock, *Holy Spirit*, 2d ed., p. 10, where there is much more.

93. For what follows, see Sebastian Moore, "The Crisis of an Ethic without Desire," in *Jesus the Liberator of Desire* (New York: Crossroad, 1989), esp. pp. 100-104; and John Paul II, *The Original Unity of Man and Woman: Catechesis on the Book of Genesis*, now reprinted in Eugene F. Rogers, Jr., ed., *Theology and Sexuality: Classic and Contemporary Readings* (Oxford: Blackwell, 2002), pp. 157-69 and 170-78 respectively.

"lower" desires like sex fall out of harmony with the "higher" part of the human being, or reason. Moore agrees about the lack of harmony, and that the two lacks of harmony (between the human being and God, and between body and spirit) correspond. But what exactly is the mechanism of the fall out of harmony?

Here Moore thinks John Paul has proved his own prediction true, that the Fall can lead theologians astray. "What happens on the pope's account is that they eat the fruit, that is, disobey God, and as a result experience the lustful *rebellion of their lower nature,* as the result of which experience they are filled with shame and cover their sexual organs."[94] On John Paul's account, therefore, it is the lower part that rebels. Adam rebels against God, and, as a result, the sexual organs rebel against Adam. Adam covers himself, Adam is ashamed, on this account, because the lower organs have rebelled.

According to Moore, however, that's too fast, because the Genesis account doesn't quite work that way.

Adam does not disobey by lowering himself. Adam disobeys by overreaching — by wanting too soon and too independently to elevate himself. It is the higher part of Adam that disobeys, wanting to be God. *After* the higher part has disobeyed, it is ashamed of the sexual organs because they prove to Adam that he is not God. The lower organs continue faithfully to act in a creaturely fashion. They have not rebelled. But Adam covers them because they make him ashamed of himself. That is, they make him ashamed of the overreaching of his reason. It is the upper part that has rebelled, and the upper part that is ashamed.

Here is, then, the disharmony between God and the human being as a result of the Fall. With God, the higher befriends the lower: God befriends the human being. We see this in creation, redemption, and consummation. In creation, the higher part of the human being befriends the lower part — or better, in creation Adam remains integral, and does not suffer division into parts — but, to put it into Thomistic language, Adam's body tells him reliably what is good for him in terms of food and companionship, while Adam's reason seeks those goods for himself. At the Fall, reason seeks an apple which is not good for food. Reason has abandoned the body. After the Fall, reason is ashamed of the body. It has contempt for it as a sign of the continuing creaturely state. Adam's sin, as regards God, is presumption; Adam's corresponding sin, as regards the body, is contempt. Finally reason hates the body. This hatred is the reversal that affects sex. Instead of befriending the body as God does, reason abandons it, shames itself, and hates it. God befriends the

94. Italics changed.

body; reason scorns the body. The body continues, at least initially, to bear true witness to Adam: that he is a creature.

So Adam is not initially ashamed of the body because of *lust,* but ashamed because of its true witness. Adam, as one who counted divinity a thing to be grasped, is ashamed of his true creatureliness. Adam's sin is not one of lowering himself, but one of overreaching himself.[95] Adam's sin is attempting to take by force what God would give in time. It is the sin of the Sodomites and the crucifiers, who would take God's body instead of receiving it as gift. It is a failure of reception — a rejection of the Spirit of reception. It is a failure that Christ specifically reverses when he counts divinity *not* a thing to be grasped. And it is a failure that Christ reverses in the Farewell Discourse in John, and in numerous communion prayers: "On the night that he was betrayed, he took bread, and broke it, and said, 'This is my body, given for you.'" You can't take it: my giving anticipates you, even on the night that you would betray me. The gift at the Eucharist is in one important respect a renewal of the gift at creation: in both cases it is the gift of a body. In both cases contempt for the body is the refusal — not the successful grasping — of the gift. In both cases the body in question tells us the truth about ourselves. In both cases the right attitude is one of reception — which (as in the case of Mary) is the work of the Spirit.

Lust comes afterward, when the body is left abandoned and unbefriended. Shame does not come because of *lust;* shame comes because of pretensions to divinity. Rather, lust comes because of *shame:* it is despair of the unbefriended, the anger of vulnerability scorned.

"'Man is ashamed of his body because of lust' is repeated twice in the text [of John Paul II]. But what the story is saying is that man is ashamed of his body because *it* remains faithful to God in being what it is, while man tries to be God."[96] The Second Adam, on the other hand, befriends the thief and does not descend the cross, does not try to be God.[97] He can put that aside, and maintain solidarity with us embodied thieves, because he is full of the Spirit, can wait and rely on the Spirit.

---

95. Not only Moore, but Ephrem, according to Brock, takes a similar view. See Sebastian Brock, *Holy Spirit,* p. 64, citing Ephrem, *Commentary on Genesis* 3.26.

96. Moore, pp. 163-64.

97. Mackinnon, "Evangelical Imagination," p. 179.

4 Transfiguration

"And as he was praying . . . a cloud came and overshadowed them" (Luke 9:29-35 and pars.); or, the Holy Spirit is the transfiguring and praying God

The Holy Spirit incorporates human prayer into the prayer of the Son to the Father.

i. The Spirit rests on the Son in prayer on Mount Tabor

Only one of the Synoptic accounts, Luke's, indicates that Jesus was praying at his Transfiguration. As in the baptismal accounts, the Father makes himself known in the sound of a voice declaring, "This is my Son, my beloved, with whom I am well pleased." Unlike at the Annunciation, Baptism, and Paul's account of the resurrection, the Spirit is not named as present. Nevertheless, various traditions of both exegesis and painting are eager to read the Spirit into the cloud that "overshadows" Jesus. Furthermore, it is common to associate the Spirit with prayer, as we saw in the case of Romans 8. This is also a feature of Luke's portrayal of Jesus and the Spirit; for example, when Jesus is being baptized, Luke alone adds the tag, "and was praying." Glorification, such as Jesus undergoes on Mount Tabor, is also properly the Spirit's appropriated work. The Eastern tradition of hesychastic prayer has always held as uncontroversial that the Holy Spirit rests on the one praying, and bestows a Taboric or transfiguring light. Here, too, readers and icon-painters have always understood, we have a scene in which Father, Son, and Spirit are all present.

It is well known that the Gospel of Luke lays special emphasis on Jesus' prayer, while Acts lays special emphasis on the Spirit. The Lukan version of the Lord's Prayer calls, in some manuscripts, for the coming of the Spirit rather than the kingdom.[1] Already in the 1930s it was possible to sum up evidence relating prayer and Spirit in the two, often treated as one work in two parts.

> Praying, Jesus submits himself to baptism, undergoes election, and receives the Spirit (Luke 3:21; cf. Acts 8:15, 6:6, 13:3, 14:23 on the establishment of offices and the reception of the Spirit). Praying alone, he gathers the strength for his daily work, whereby even his healings appear as the indirect fruit of his prayer (Luke 5:16; cf. Acts 9:40, 28:8). Praying, he brings the night to a close before the decisive choice of apostles (Luke 6:12; cf. Acts 1:24). After individual prayer he places the disciples before the decision of faith (Luke 9:18; cf. Acts 9:11). At individual prayer he experiences above himself the revelation of the glory of God (the transfiguration, Luke 9:28f; cf. Luke 1:10, Acts 10:9, 30, 11:5, 22:17). Praying, he prepares himself against the Tempter and triumphs over him (Luke 22:40ff; cf. Acts 12:12, 16:25). He prays at the judgment for his own (22:31f; cf. Acts 20:36, 21:5), indeed even for his enemies (Luke 23:34; cf. 6:28, Acts 7:60), and praying he gives his soul over to God (Luke 23:46, cf. Acts 7:59).[2]

The Gospel of John does not have a transfiguration scene. But the scene at Gethsemane, which corresponds in interesting particulars, tends to reinforce the impression, when compared with Luke, that prayer and the trinitarian life have something to do with each other. This comparison of Luke and the Fourth Gospel helps to point up Luke's emphasis on prayer:

> Luke emphasizes (9:29) that Jesus was at prayer on the Mount of the Transfiguration (contrast Mark and Matthew in parallel). This may be simply a way of explaining Mark ("this type cannot be cast out except by prayer") but equally it could form a link with the greatest moment of Jesus praying, Gethsemane. The disciples are said to have been tired (9:32) yet stayed awake — the sleeping of the disciples in Gethsemane is emphasized and explained by Luke as exhaustion caused by sorrow (22:45). The ministering angel is a Lukan special feature (22:43) functioning in a way similar to the heavenly voice and the overshadowing cloud at the Transfiguration. Although [John] has neither of the two scenes, motifs of each seem to be combined: in John 12:27-28a clear echoes in wording and structure of the prayer in Gethsemane; v. 28b the voice from heaven, v. 29 misunderstood by the

---

1. For one lengthy discussion, see Wilhelm Ott, *Gebet und Heil: Die Bedeutung der Gebetsparänese in der lukanischen Theologie* (Munich: Kösel-Verlag, 1965), pp. 92-123.

2. Friedrich Hauk, *Das Evangelium des Lukas* (Leipzig: Scholl, 1934), p. 153.

bystanders, echoing the voice at the Transfiguration and the misunder-standing of the three disciples. If the parallels are close enough to require a connection between John and Luke (the plausibility of which is based on many much closer parallels elsewhere in these gospels) then it could be that John is symbolically combining and explicating the two Lukan accounts, or that Lukan redaction is influenced by the [Fourth Gospel].[3]

ii. The Spirit rests on the Son in prayer in the Trinity

If Jesus is praying to the Father at Gethsemane, then one Person of the Trinity is praying to another. One might qualify any interest out of that claim by pos-iting that it is "only the human" in Jesus who prays. But that qualification breaks a rule of the Incarnation, that whatever Jesus does is an action of the Person who assumed the humanity. There is no other "person" in Jesus than the Word; the Word assumed a human nature, not an independently existing human being. The human nature of Jesus is the human nature of the Word, and no one else's. So it is undeniable that the Son is praying to the Father, even if we do not know what that means.

You might also try to undo the offense of talking about prayer in God by claiming that Jesus's prayer is still, if not on account of some non-divine human being, nevertheless on account of the Incarnation. That may be, but I find it shallow. That would disallow the presence of bidding and granting and courteous structures in the divine love. Rather, the testimony of Romans 8 and Luke's account of the Transfiguration reverse the order of implication. They do not imply that only humans can pray to God. They imply that only God can pray to God, so that when human beings pray, they are caught up into the triune activity of the Persons praying one to another. That is why the Spirit has to "pray for us," as Romans so clearly puts it. On this account, prayer is *what the Trinity does,* and that is the explanation for why prayer "works," if it works. Prayer does not "change God's mind": prayer is a transfiguration of human beings who do *not* know how to pray as they ought.

Adrienne von Speyr takes the account of trinitarian prayer with the ut-most seriousness:

3. John Muddiman, personal correspondence. Cf. also Ott, *Gebet und Heil,* and Louis Monloubou, *La prière selon saint Luc: recherche d'une structure* (Paris: Cerf, 1976). For the latter minority view see M. E. Boismard, *Comment Luc a remanié l'évangile de Jean* (Paris: J. Gabalda, 2001) and Barbara Shellard, *New Light on Luke: Its Purpose, Sources and Literary Context* (London: Sheffield, 2002).

[T]he functions exercised by each Person in the work of creation are ultimately determined in the context of the divine petitionary prayer . . . they only become concrete when Son and Spirit offer themselves for the sake of the Father's work, when they ask to be allowed to cooperate in it and when the Father asks for their collaboration. They want to explore and experience in eternity what humankind will do and experience later in petitionary prayer. The Lord's word, "All that you ask the Father in my name will be done for you," is to have its basis in God himself. And just as all three Persons petition each other together, they also grant fulfillment to one another. The whole work of creation lies in this divine granting.[4]

iii. The Spirit rests on the Son not only in the Transfiguration on Mount Tabor, but graciously allows human beings also to participate in her work of glorifying the Son when they pray, that is, in human liturgy

This book has been a theology of glory. Luther famously contrasted a theology of glory with a theology of the cross. We need not do that. Rather, as the Westminster Shorter Catechism famously puts it, "man's chief end is to glorify God, and to enjoy him forever." Gathered in "assembly where the Spirit abounds,"[5] primitive eucharistic communities such as that of Addai and Mari quickly came to identify themselves as "those who 'glory' in the name of Jesus,"[6] and to this day all Christians might see themselves as proceeding from glory to glory, from God "Who from the foundation of the world hast been pleased to be glorified in them whom Thou hast chosen"[7] to the heavenly liturgy of the seraphim which they anticipate here below in the Sanctus, "the 'glory' that the inhabitants of the heavenly world continually offer to God."[8] The East Syrian mystic Abdisho describes the "fifth sign of the Spirit" as "joy, jubilation, exultation, praise, glorification, songs, hymns and odes of

---

4. Adrienne von Speyr, *The World of Prayer*, trans. Graham Harrison (San Francisco: Ignatius Press, 1985), pp. 69-70, translation slightly modified.

5. Hippolytus, *Apostolic Tradition* xxxi, 2, in *The Treatise on the Apostolic Traditions of St Hippolytus of Rome*, ed. Gregory Dix and rev. Henry Chadwick (London: SPCK, 1968), p. 58.

6. *Addai and Mari — the Anaphora of the Apostles: A Text for Students*, with Introduction, Translation, and Commentary by Bryan D. Spinks (Bramcote, Nottinghamshire: Grove Books, 1980), p. 25, commenting on the text of the priestly prayer found on p. 14; cf. Robert J. Ledogar, *Acknowledgment: Praise Verbs in the Early Greek Anaphoras* (Rome: Herder, 1968), p. 153. Spinks continues: "Its form recalls the *Qaddis* of the Synagogue liturgy which blesses the divine name."

7. Hippolytus, iii, 2, p. 4.

8. *Addai and Mari*, p. 26.

magnification."[9] A theology of glory need not oppose a theology of the cross if its goal is to glorify not the human being but God. In particular, this book explores what it would mean to glorify God the Spirit and enjoy the Spirit forever.

The Spirit is peculiarly appropriate to a theology of glory. It is the Spirit's own proper role within the trinitarian life to glorify the love between the Father and the Son. In glorifying God, human beings participate in the Spirit's own proper work. They do that in the liturgy of the Church and in the liturgy that their lives perform in fulfillment of their chief end. In the same liturgies in which the people already glory in Jesus, they also pray for the Holy Spirit to come down in the epiclesis, since what they enjoy they do not possess. The Nicene Creed defines the Spirit liturgically, as the One "Who with the Father and the Son is worshipped and glorified."[10] It is in terms of the Church's trinitarian worship and Christians' trinitarian glorification of God that the Creed identifies the Spirit. That liturgical definition is fitting because it is the Spirit's appropriated office among the triune Persons to witness and to manifest the glory of the exchange of love and gratitude in which God's triune life consists. The Spirit models in the Trinity the glorification of God that it enables here below. That empowerment of human beings to share in the divine celebration is mystagogical; that is, it leads human beings into a mystery. Theologically speaking, a mystery is not that which human beings do not understand, although they don't; it is that which overwhelms their understanding on account of its goodness. (Evil is not intelligible, and is for that reason not a mystery.) To be led into a mystery is to be led into ever more wonderful goodness. The liturgical mystery into which the Spirit leads human beings is that heavenly feast to which "The Spirit and the Bride say, 'Come.' And let him who hears say, 'Come.' And let the one who is thirsty come, let the one who desires take the water of life without price."[11]

The Westminster Confession identifies this glorification in its very first question as nothing less than "the chief end of man." "To glorify God and enjoy him forever" is indeed not two but one work of the Spirit, because to glorify and to give life are the same work. From an entirely distinct tradition, Saint Ephrem the Syrian puts it like this:

9. Sebastian P. Brock, *The Holy Spirit in the Syrian Baptismal Tradition*, The Syrian Churches Series, vol. 9 (Poona, India: Anita Printers, 1979; 2d ed., 1998), p. 138, citing Abdisho bar Brika (d. 1318) in *Woodbrooke Studies: Christian Documents in Syriac, Arabic, and Garshuni*, ed. and trans. Alphonse Mingana and intro. Rendel Harris, 7 vols. (Cambridge: W. Heffer & Sons, 1927-34), vol. 7, p. 167.

10. Paul Evdokimov, *L'Esprit Saint dans la tradition Orthodoxe* (Paris: Cerf, 1970), p. 10.

11. Rev. 22:17. Cf. Evodokimov, *L'Esprit Saint*, p. 10.

While I live will I give praise, and not be as if I had no existence;
I will give praise during my lifetime, and will not be a dead man
      among the living.
  . . .

Though the limit of our life is short, praise can lengthen it,
for, corresponding to the extent of our love,
we shall acquire, through praise, life that has no measure.
For the Spirit of praise is also the life-giving scent wafted from [the
      bones of Elisha as a type of Christ] and entered the dead corpse
— a symbol of Him who gives life to all.[12]

Indeed in the Syriac tradition the Christian emerges from baptism wearing a "'robe of praise' [Isa. 61:3] with which Adam and Eve had, according to Jewish legend, been clothed in Paradise."[13]

The robe of glory that was stolen away [by Satan] among the trees of Paradise have I put on in the waters of baptism.[14]

Instead of fig leaves, God has clothed human beings with glory in the baptismal water:

I have invited you, Lord, to a wedding feast of song
but the wine — the utterance of praise — at our feast has failed.
You are the one who filled the jars with good wine,
fill my mouth with your praise.

The wine that was in the jars was akin and related to
this eloquent wine that gives birth to praise,
seeing that wine gave birth to praise
from those who drank it and beheld the wonder.

You who are so just, if at a wedding feast not your own
you filled six jars with good wine,
do you, at this wedding feast, fill not the jars
but the ten thousand ears with its sweetness.[15]

12. St. Ephrem the Syrian, *Nisibene Hymns*, no. 50, in Sebastian P. Brock, trans., *The Harp of the Spirit: Eighteen Poems of St. Ephrem*, Studies Supplementary to *Sobornost* (Society of St. Alban and St. Sergius, 1983), pp. 57, 58; and Brock, *Studies in Syriac Spirituality*, The Syrian Churches Series, vol. 13 (Poona, India: Anita Printers, 1988), p. 5. For the last verse read II Kings 13:21 together with Rom. 8:11.

13. Brock, *Studies*, p. 5.

14. Jacob of Serugh (Bedjan I, 209) in Brock, *Studies*, p. 5.

15. Ephrem, *Hymns on Epiphany* XII, 4, in Brock, *Studies*, p. 5.

The Spirit is liturgically defined because it is the condition within the Trinity of the possibility of human being becoming what *it* is: liturgical being. What does it mean that the chief end of the human being is to glorify God and enjoy God forever? Alone among creatures, the human being can glorify God intentionally, that is, in prayer, in offerings of praise. That humans' chief end is to glorify God means that the human being is a liturgical being, a glorifying being, a blessing being, a thanks-giving being, a being that not only receives, but receives also the permission to give back and again.[16] As Alexander Schmemann puts it, the human being is properly *homo adorans:*

> [T]he unique position of man in the universe is that he alone is to *bless* God for the food and the life he receives from Him. He alone is to respond to God's blessing with his blessing. The significant fact about the life in the Garden is that man is to *name* things. . . . [I]n the Bible a name . . . reveals the very essence of a thing . . . as God's gift. . . .
>
> To name a thing, in other terms, is to bless God for it and in it. And in the Bible to bless God is not a "religious" or a "cultic" act, but the very *way of life.* God blessed the world, blessed the man, blessed the seventh day (that is, time), and this means that He filled all that exists with His love and goodness, made all this "very good." So the only *natural* (and not "supernatural") reaction of man, to whom God gave this blessed and sanctified world, is to bless God in return, to thank him, to *see* the world as God sees it — and in this act of gratitude and adoration — to know, name, and possess the world. . . . [The human being is] first of all *"homo adorans."* . . . He stands in the center of the world and unifies it in his act of blessing God, of both receiving the world from God and offering it to God — and by filling the world with this eucharist, he transforms his life, the one that he receives from the world, into life in God, into communion.
>
> The world was created as the "matter," the material of one all-embracing eucharist. . . .[17]

This Eucharist is primarily a participation in the giving and thanksgiving prepared for human beings already in God's own trinitarian life.

We glorify the name of God by glorifying the name of Jesus in our liturgy (thus once more fulfilling Malachi's prophecy about incense being offered

16. For a Jewish account, see Max Kadushin, *Worship and Ethics: A Study in Rabbinic Judaism* (Evanston, Ill.: Northwestern University Press, 1963; repr. Westport, Conn.: Greenwood, 1978), pp. 63-96.

17. Alexander Schmemann, *For the Life of the World* (New York: National Student Christian Association, 1963), pp. 4-5.

to the *name* of God) — a notion which refers us back to Irenaeus' starting point, that God and his Son eternally give glory to each other, sharing with one another the abundance of life and joy which is their nature. Our privilege is to reflect what Father and Son do: in the gratuity, the overflow of a thanksgiving which God does not need, we experience in ourselves something of God's own gratuity which is the giving of glory.[18]

That is the "link between the earthly offering of praise and the eternal 'liturgy' of the Trinity."[19] For "To grow in the Christian life is to activate the priestly role given at baptism and to learn how to see the created world as a sacrament."[20]

iv. The Spirit rests on the Son in the transfiguration of creation

The condition for the possibility of creating is the Father. The condition for the possibility of creation is the Son. The condition for the possibility of creation's having time and space to be created — to be material and enduring — is the Spirit. That is why what the Spirit adds is beauty, reality, perceptibility to creation.

One may ask: What does it mean to say, "The Spirit adds reality"? Why does creation need to be perceptible, experienceable? What is the necessity of beauty? All those things — reality, perceptibility, experience, beauty — seem to add a subjective element, an element that need not be there. They raise again the deeper question: What is the necessity of the Spirit? Or, more exactly, why can't Christianity — or God, for that matter — do without her? If what the Spirit adds is mere beauty or perceptibility, then perhaps the observers are right who see that in much nineteenth- and twentieth-century high theology Christianity seems to be able to get by without the Spirit. If the surplus that the Spirit offers is mere perceptibility, then perhaps nineteenth- and twentieth-century theology's binitarian practice is in fact better justified than its trinitarian professions. The surplus of the Spirit, in that case, is strictly superfluous, and therefore it is as it should be if for longer or shorter periods from the Apologists to the present Christian thinkers have tended to give her short shrift.

---

18. Rowan Williams, *Eucharistic Sacrifice: The Roots of a Metaphor,* Grove Liturgical Studies 32 (Bramcote, Nottinghamshire: Grove Books, 1982), p. 10, interpreting Irenaeus, *Adversus Haereses* 17.6 in light of Louis Bouyer, *Eucharist* (Notre Dame, Ind.: University of Notre Dame Press, 1968), pp. 55-56, 97, and Jean Daniélou, *The Theology of Jewish Christianity,* trans. John A. Baker (London: Darton, Longman, & Todd, 1964), pp. 147-63.

19. Williams, *Eucharistic Sacrifice,* p. 11.

20. Brock, *Studies,* p. 19.

To put it paradoxically, the non-necessity of the Spirit may be her very *advantage*. Her non-necessity may make her distinctive *contribution* both to the trinitarian life and to our participation in it. Deity, consummation, beauty, form (in the sense of what is *formosa*, beautiful) are indeed *not* strictly necessary. They are non-functional. They are, in a word, gratuitous. The whole point of grace, after all, is its gratuity, its non-necessity.

Now we would not want to turn grace into arbitrariness in the abstract, or caprice. The gratuity of grace has a character, a goodness, a beauty of its own — it has the gratuity that not just anybody would exercise, such as the gratuitous violence of a Machiavelli — but it has the gratuity that someone specific would exercise: the Comforter, the Spirit of Jesus Christ.

Deity, consummation, beauty, form are indeed not necessary, except in view of some end[21] — that God desires and chooses to be a God who (already *in se*) is beautiful, glorious, and gracious. They are not necessary to human beings, either, unless God should desire to share that beauty, glory, and grace, which God has chosen for God's own character, also — grace on grace — with human beings.

Consider Karl Barth's comments on the beauty of God, famous for Hans Urs von Balthasar's prominent quotation of them:

> The concept which lies ready to our hand here, and which may serve legitimately to describe the element in the idea of glory that we still lack, is that of beauty. If we can and must say that God is beautiful, to say this is to say how He enlightens and convinces and persuades us. It is to describe not merely the naked fact of His revelation or its power, but the shape and form in which it is a fact and is power. It is to say that God has this superior force, this power of attraction, which speaks for itself, which wins and conquers, in the fact that He is beautiful, divinely beautiful, beautiful in His own way, in a way that is His alone, beautiful as the unattainable primal beauty, yet really beautiful. He does not have it, therefore, merely as a fact or a power. Or rather, He has it as a fact and a power in such a way that He acts as the One who gives pleasure, creates desire, and rewards with enjoyment. And He does it because He is pleasant, desirable, full of enjoyment, because He is the One who is pleasant, desirable, full of enjoyment, because first and last He alone is that which is pleasant, desirable and full of enjoyment. God loves us as the One who is worthy of love as God. That is what we mean when we say that God is beautiful.[22]

21. For "necessity in view of an end," see Thomas Aquinas, *ST* I.82.1 and commentary in Michel Corbin, *Le Chemin de la théologie chez Thomas d'Aquin* (Paris: Beauchesne, 1974), p. 695.
22. Barth, *CD* II/1, 650-51.

That passage of Barth's avoids a number of pitfalls and trips into one. It avoids making God's beauty an external compulsion, imposed by some outside force or prior conception. It avoids making God's beauty an internal compulsion, driven by some divine counterpart to the human hunger for approval. It avoids making God's beauty mere caprice, unconnected with God's other characteristics. And it avoids making God's beauty subjective, dependent on the observation of a creaturely beholder. But it defines God's beauty as an impersonal thing, "this superior force, this power of attraction." This impersonality is not unrelieved. It can be the subject of verbs: "it wins and conquers." It even "speaks for itself." God has this beauty, furthermore, "in His own way, in a way that is His alone." Barth goes on to *take back* the claim that God's beauty is an impersonal thing. "He does not have it, therefore, merely as a fact or a power." In qualifying the claim, he returns to this business of the "way" in which God has beauty: "Or rather, He has it as a fact and a power in such a way that He acts as the One who gives pleasure, creates desire, and rewards with enjoyment." Practiced readers of Barth will remember that he has previously made much of that word "way," *Weise*.[23] Barth follows the Greek in defining trinitarian persons as *tropoi hyparxeos*, which he translates into German as *Seinsweisen*, ways of being. Suppose he had followed his own lead here. Then beauty would be not only a characteristic of the whole Godhead, but also the *personal* contribution of one of the persons, perhaps the Holy Spirit. Indeed Barth makes one more nod in that direction. The beauty of God belongs to the more biblical category, for Barth, of God's glory. And almost grudgingly he concedes:

> It is as well to realize at this point that the glory of God is not only the glory of the Father and the Son but the glory of the whole divine Trinity, and therefore the glory of the Holy Spirit as well. But the Holy Spirit is not only the unity [*das Verbindende*] of the Father and the Son in the eternal life of the Godhead. He is also, in God's activity in the world, the divine *reality* [*Gotteswirklichkeit*] by which the creature has its heart opened to God and is made able and willing to receive Him. He is, then, the unity [*Einheit*] between the creature and God, the bond [*das Verbindende*] between eternity and time. . . . It is in this way that [the creature] participates [*nimmt Teil*] in His glory and therefore in the glory of God.[24]

23. This impression may be even stronger among readers of Barth in English, because the next section will in turn make a great deal of Jesus Christ as "the beginning of all God's *ways* and works": but those ways are *Wege* not *Weisen*.

24. Barth, *CD* II/1, 669-70, italics added. The final "His" is ambiguous between the Holy Spirit and Jesus Christ.

"What is the chief end of man? To glorify God and enjoy him forever." To glorify and enjoy God forever is certainly *not* what we would call "necessary." Neither is the human being or any part of God's creation. The Spirit bears witness not only among us but also in God to this glorious non-necessity and its specific character, to "the causeless loving delight of God," and to the supposition that "we are created that we may be caught up in this," the life of the Trinity, in "non-functional joy."[25]

The "necessity" of the Spirit is "only" so that God should not be without beauty, without celebration, creation, and (grace upon grace) even human beings. The Spirit has the non-necessity of things that take and delight in time, like music and liturgy and sex. Freud thought that repetition (liturgical or sexual) was usually obsessive: artists and liturgists, on the other hand, think that repetition makes certain forms of life possible and good. What would dance, music, sex be without repetition? Their repetition may appear excessive in some sense, but in another sense it is its own end. They make room for life. Constant novelty is exhausting; return allows the taking of time. The Holy Spirit allows God to take time for human beings. Or if "allows" sounds too strong, the Holy Spirit is the divine Person *in whom* God takes time for human beings.

The *tropos hyparxeos* of the Holy Spirit allows God to participate in those features of human life that outstrip the particularity of a single life, the *tropos hyparxeos* of the Son. Or, the Holy Spirit is the one *in whom* God takes on, not the particularity of a single human life in Jesus of Nazareth, but gathers and distributes multiple particularities; in which God *diversifies* Godself both *in se* and in human beings. Thus it is in the person of the Spirit that God participates in community, gender, culture, period, history, generational change, all kinds of circumstance. If plot is the interaction of character and circumstance, then God does not lack for plot already in the trinitarian life, for the Spirit is the master of circumstance.

We human beings — like the Trinity — do things over and over. We do not do them over and over because something has not "gotten done" or to fill any lack but to create and enact community. Common meals are not (just) for food; sexual intercourse not (just) for satisfaction; chamber music or community theater or sports teams are not (just) for the performance: they are "for" the activity that they *are*. Their end is in themselves, in the enjoyment not added but integral to the activity, in what Augustine called *fruitio*.

25. Rowan Williams, "The Body's Grace," in *Theology and Sexuality: Classic and Contemporary Readings,* edited by Eugene F. Rogers, Jr. (Oxford: Blackwell Publishers, 2002), pp. 309-21; here, pp. 312, 318.

With consummation, with fruit, it is not a question of "when does it stop" but a matter of "it never ends." It's not a question of "how much is enough" but a matter of *"semper major."* It is an economy of excess and an ethic of always. This is why the Holy Spirit is not a finite thing but a person: because the language of ending and enoughness is one of competitive economy, whereas the Trinity and, by grace, the creation bound for it are an everlasting community.

v. The Spirit rests on the Son in the transfiguration of society, in ascetic practices sanctified by liturgy: marriage, *adelphopoiesis,* the Stylite's liturgy

The distinctive contribution of Irenaeus of Lyons to Christian theology stresses that the conformation of the human being to the triune identity takes *time.* If God's work in the world did not take time, it would bypass something essential to creatures. It would bypass, indeed, the very creation God undertook to save, because creatures would be left out, in their creatureliness, of their own salvation. The Spirit works, therefore, in concrete structures that nourish human change over time. Part of the Spirit's work of fidelity is that she can take time over human beings. Part of the Spirit's work of celebration is that she can shower human beings with time. Because the Son can wait for the Spirit, so can human beings: because the Son finds that time is not too short, even as crucifixion approaches, humans too can find that the Spirit has time enough and more.

> For this reason, the one who was the perfect bread of the Father offered himself to us as milk for children: he came in human form. His purpose was to feed us at the breast of his flesh, by nursing us to make us accustomed to eat and drink the Word of God, so that we would be able to hold in ourselves the one who is the bread of immortality, the Spirit of the Father. . . . Anyone upon whom the apostles imposed hands received the Holy Spirit, who is the food of life. They could not hold him, however, because their capacity for dealing with God was still weak and undeveloped. . . . The Father decided and commanded; the Son molded and shaped; the Spirit nourished and developed. Humanity slowly progresses. . . . People who do not wait for the period of growth, who attribute the weakness of their nature to God, are completely unreasonable. . . . they are more unreasonable than the dumb animals. The beasts do not blame God for not making them human.[26]

26. Irenaeus of Lyons, *Adversus Haereses* bk. IV, ch. 38, 1, 2, 3, 4, in J. Patout Burns, *Theological Anthropology* (Philadelphia: Fortress, 1981), pp. 23, 24, 25.

How does the Spirit *concretely* nourish and develop a human being? How does the human being grow in the Spirit over time? To ask these questions is to ask about the *external* fostering of the Spirit's habituation of the human being, the external correlate to the Spirit's internal habitation. The Spirit's indwelling the heart, and socializing the body, are two sides to the same process. The second takes place visibly in space and time: it takes place in particular communities, at particular times, in particular locations, among particular people. We may sum up that it takes place *liturgically,* if that word is taken in the widest possible sense, to denote social formation that reaches a certain paradigm in the society of the church at prayer. It takes place therefore also *in the Spirit,* whom the liturgy expressly or tacitly calls down, or who (in the words of the Creed) "with the Father and the Son is worshiped and glorified." I take three examples: the liturgy of the Stylite, the formation of marriage, and the formation of other friendships in the church.

The work of Susan Harvey has shown how the ascetic prodigies of the elder Simeon the Stylite — who spent decades atop a narrow pillar exposed to wind and sun — received liturgical formation. We meet the saint, of course, not as he was, but as the authors of his life have formed him for the instruction of others, and sometimes for being read out in church. They show us not only how the saint himself may or may not have been liturgically formed, but how others after him might be liturgically formed on his authorially worked example.

The liturgy grants form in two ways. It provides categories through which the body can display social meaning: theologically speaking, the body becomes a medium, mirror, or icon in which others can perceive God, the Spirit can perform her appropriated office of illumination and transfiguration. And it provides patterns through which society can govern the body: theologically speaking, the body becomes a channel through which God can reveal Godself, the Spirit can perform her appropriated office of divine manifestation. Of course, these are two sides of the same coin; the Spirit incorporates the diverse and diversifies the corporate. We take first the way in which the liturgy comes to govern Simeon's body — which is to say moderates it and first renders it capable of bearing meaning — then the sorts of meanings it grants.

Simeon continually proposed and undertook disciplines that his superiors found too severe. His disciplines were undisciplined, his asceticism untrained. His bodily practice — gesture, stance, eating, timing, location — lacked formation.

> In these early years, Simeon is portrayed [in all three *Vitae,* two Greek and one Syriac] as every monk's nightmare: a rebellious individual in the midst of community life. As such, he was always and profoundly out of order. He did

not participate in the collective worship rituals; he did not follow the calendar of the community. Instead, he pursued his own routines of fasting, chanting, and ascetic practice. He did not obey his abbots. The idiosyncratic and idiorhythmic extremes of his discipline clashed with the carefully dictated order followed by the rest of the brethren, upon which their harmony as a community depended. The results were chaos for everyone. Not only did Simeon himself stick out as a wild extremist, but further, the monks fell into disastrous bickering among themselves, disturbed by jealousy, competitiveness, envy, strife. . . . The monastery could not contain Simeon; his expulsion was necessary for everyone's well-being: his own as he continued to court death by his practices, and that of the monks as their community life unravelled.[27]

What finally gave Simeon's austerities meaningful shape was an application of the liturgy and the church calendar. The imposition of order first succeeds at the hands of an itinerant local priest in a diocesan structure. It is the normal, hierarchical order of the diocesan church, not the extraordinary, charismatic community of the monastery, that works for Simeon. In that setting and under that authority, the inspiring circumstance is not that the presence of other ascetics inspires competition, but that the presence of an itinerant priest and a mixed laity of men, women, rich, and poor demands example and advice. The social body of the diocese — so much more various than the monastery both in its makeup and in its needs — *requires* a diversity that permits and even sees a *use* for the sort of embodied difference that Simeon represents. "Symeon's devotional activity is set aright by the local church. . . . Discipline, form, and order are laid upon his ascetic labors by Mar Bas, the local *periodeutes* (itinerant priest), who sets immediate constraints on Simeon's practices with respect to extent and duration."[28]

Mar Bas finds a way to *give* to an ascetic, or he finds a way for an ascetic to *receive*. Mar Bas offers a setting, land owned by the priest on a mountain outside the village of Telneshe; he offers a laity — one might almost say an audience — of surrounding parishioners; he offers the services (food and clothing) that a stylite on a pillar cannot provide himself. Simeon offers obedience in return. If ascetic practice is performance of certain bodily exercises for the good of the community, then Mar Bas is, in both senses of the word, his spiritual *director*. The texts present Simeon as needing a spiritual director as a performer (if I may say so) needs an impresario. He needs a public, both for his own good and theirs. The Spirit, who builds in public as in secret, works on

27. Susan Ashbrook Harvey, "The Stylite's Liturgy," *Journal of Early Christian Studies* 6 (1998): 523-39; here, p. 527.

28. Harvey, "Stylite's Liturgy," pp. 527-28.

both sides, disciplining the performer, inspiring the director, and bringing the two together. The gift of the Spirit is entirely mutual. Mar Bas donates place, structure, and service as placeholders for signification: Simeon donates his body as a communicative sign.

> In sharp contrast to his monastic experience, here Simeon bows to authority, obedient to every order these clergy set upon him. Slowly and steadily the periodeutes Mar Bas subsumed Simeon's vocation into the life of the church, forcing Simeon to undertake his great feats of mortification within a clearly defined ritual context. The eucharistic liturgy was celebrated at the commencement and conclusion of these exceptional efforts, administered by Mar Bas directly to Simeon. In due course, Mar Bas brought Simeon's practice into accord with the ecclesiastical calendar, so that his most severe practices were undertaken during Lent.[29]

Structure comes to inform Simeon's daily life as well. He spends night and day in prayer until the ninth hour (the hour of Christ's death). Then he preaches, heals, and resolves quarrels. The laity must receive instruction; the sick must be healed; disputants reconciled. Pilgrims must receive communion on feast days. The severest austerities must be saved for Lent. This means that Simeon may not be as alone as he might like. He must eat more at festivals. Otherwise his disciplines cannot mean as much as they might.

They come to mean a great deal. So in the Syriac *Vita*, according to Harvey, we find someone formed in the image of fire and incense:

> But what did the action [of pillar-standing] mean [in the Syriac *Vita*]? Simeon took the place of incense on the altar of stone, as he would later takes its place on higher altars when the pillars of successive height were built. We have been told that the pillar is also a crucible that purifies gold through fire, as storax through fire is purified from resin to incense: a fire which burns but does not consume, a fire that reveals. On the pillar — on the altar — Simeon is . . . transfigured, as Christ himself was once transfigured on top of the high mountain. . . .[30]

---

29. Harvey, "Stylite's Liturgy," p. 529.

30. Susan Ashbook Harvey, "The Sense of a Stylite: Perspectives on Simeon the Elder," *Vigiliae Christianae* 48 (1988): 376-94; here, pp. 385-86. The Syriac *Life* appears in P. Peeters, *Bibliographica Hagiographica Orientalis* 10 (Brussels, 1910, repr. 1954), pp. 1121-26. For references see Harvey's essay. All three *Lives* are translated in Robert Doran, *The Lives of Simeon Stylites* (Kalamazoo: Cistercian Publications, 1992). Since, as Harvey documents, it is perfectly possible to read the original texts without seeing their liturgical implications (and thus their implications for accounts of the Spirit), I take the unusual course of citing her in preference to the originals.

Simeon began his pillar-standing as an attempt to escape people: but was transformed into the very center of liturgical life. He found himself giving advice on topics from statecraft to cucumbers.[31] When he went on strike, angels told him to continue serving those who came to him.[32] When he died, his body became the object of processions; within a generation, his people built the largest church in Christendom to surround his pillar. Thus was the body changed not only of the Stylite but also of the church.[33] The body of the witness — site of the Spirit — changes too, "if one can stand near to a gangrenous stylite and smell not rot but the sweet aroma of paradise."[34]

> The sweet savor increased in intensity until Simeon finally died. Having become the fulfillment of prayer ascending, Simeon's presence filtered throughout the world that knew him. Roads and towns and city filled with the processions in honor of his death, the crowds carrying light candles and burning sweet-smelling incense in homage to their saint.[35]

Although (or since) Harvey notes the christoformity of pillar-standing, we may find it pneumatoform, too. Simeon's body becomes spiritual, anticipating the spiritual bodies of heaven, in taking on characteristics or metaphors associated with the Holy Spirit: fire, light, incense, presence on the altar, formation of the seeker, production of the witness, gathering of the community.

Similarly, the texts stress the christoform nature of the Stylite's calendar, whereas — or better, so that — we may see it too as Spirit-bearing. Lenten austerities recall Christ's trials in the wilderness, where "the combat with Satan is fought in and with Christ's humanity," and "Christ's victory is wrought and manifested by means of his body."[36] It is the Spirit, according to the same story, that alights on Jesus' head at baptism, drives him into the wilderness, fills his body for ministry and transfigures it on Tabor. In both cases we see not so much that the Spirit deifies (although it does), as that the Spirit renders distinctively human: so that the very peculiar humanity of someone like Simeon is rendered less reckless and out of order, and more integrated and serviceable; no less embodied because now socially embodied; rather, more embodied because more meaningful, more donative; no less human because more inspired, but more recognizably so. Under his own authority, Simeon is

---

31. Harvey, "Sense of a Stylite," p. 376.
32. Harvey, "Sense of a Stylite," p. 383.
33. Harvey, "Stylite's Liturgy," p. 538.
34. Harvey, "Stylite's Liturgy," p. 534.
35. Harvey, "Sense of a Stylite," p. 386.
36. Harvey, "Stylite's Liturgy," p. 529.

simply crazy, pathological, an extreme example of an amorphous group: under the liturgical formation of the Spirit, he is unique and original not as an individual but to and for his fellows, the subject of *Lives* and continuing scholarship: he is the Stylite.

Paul Evdokimov has argued that marriage, too, ought to be understood as an ascetic practice — so much so that marriage and monasticism are but two forms of the same discipline,[37] in which human beings are formed by the perceptions of others to whom they are so committed that they cannot easily escape. Marriage like monasticism exposes the worst in human beings, so that it can be healed. These are concrete, liturgically celebrated forms, by which the spouses or monks give their bodies over to a larger community to manifest theological meaning, to participate in the Spirit's work of witnessing to love. It is precisely their bodies that do this. The sexual fidelity of the married, the bodily poverty of the monk, the commitments of both to granting time and staying in place for an embodied other make the Spirit's transformation of the human being a communal thing inseparable from concrete times and spaces. Marriage, like monasticism, is primarily a structure for the transformation of the human being by the grace of God, which is to say the Holy Spirit: the difference is whether specific human members of the body of Christ reach the appropriate vulnerability for transformation through the mediation of a single human focus, or whether they can find their bodily transformation in the sight of God as the one to whom they devote the time and place for its long working out.

In earlier work I have pointed out how the wedding ceremony itself involves even, or especially, the congregation in the work of the Spirit.[38] The witnesses at a wedding celebrate, glorify, testify, and pledge fidelity to the love of two, as the Spirit celebrates, glorifies, testifies, and pledges fidelity to the love of the Father and the Son. Weddings catch all the participants, and not just the spouses, up into a parable of the trinitarian life. But that is not to deny — rather to affirm — that the Spirit is at work in the sanctification of the couple. Indeed the learning of holiness is a goal the spouses and their

37. Paul Evdokimov, *The Sacrament of Love: The Nuptial Mystery in the Light of the Orthodox Tradition,* trans. Anthony P. Gythiel and Victoria Steadman (Crestwood, N.Y.: St. Vladimir's Seminary Press, 1994). For selections, see Eugene F. Rogers, Jr., *Theology and Sexuality: Classic and Contemporary Readings* (Oxford: Blackwell, 2002), pp. 179-93.

38. Eugene F. Rogers, Jr., *Sexuality and the Christian Body: Their Way Into the Triune God* (Oxford: Blackwell, 1999), pp. 195-96; Dumitru Staniloae, "The Holy Trinity: Structure of Supreme Love," in *Theology and the Church,* trans. Robert Barringer (Crestwood, N.Y.: St. Vladimir's Seminary Press, 1980), pp. 92-96; Richard of St. Victory, *De Trinitate* III.15.

friends all must seek together. Holiness is never an individual achievement or possession. Since the point of marriage is training in holiness, there is no reason why same-sex couples should not also participate in it. No conservative has yet seriously argued that same-sex couples need sanctification any less than cross-sex couples. The more so if the Spirit so arranges the body of Christ that our limitations are intended for our benefit, so that different kinds of people need one another.[39] This principle is not overturned but redoubled if to some is given the capacity to find their appropriate otherness — the otherness that makes vulnerable and can therefore sanctify — in someone of the same sex. The Spirit diversifies the body of Christ, so that Christians are not all procreative members, but calls some to imitate God's own work of adoption, including the Spirit's adoption of Gentiles alongside nature.

Children are themselves gifts of the Spirit — and not requirements — that further celebrate, glorify, and bear witness to love. (To think of children as required by marriage risks dishonoring the resurrection, which alone guarantees, on Christian grounds, the continuation of embodied human life.) It is for this reason, too, that Paul calls the Spirit the Spirit of *adoption*. Adoption is a practice specifically developed in non-procreative forms of Christian community — in the oblation of unwanted infants at the doors of monasteries — and one in which all Christian couples can participate.[40] Adoption bears witness to the Spirit that works by grace alongside nature, to baptism, of which it is a type, and to the resurrection, in which human adoption to be children of God by the Spirit is made complete.

Sergei Bulgakov has proposed that the Spirit constructs the Christian community of the church *concretely* from actual friendships apart from those founded on the difference of the sexes, and even apart from "father and mother, brothers and sisters, etc."[41] It would be an extraordinary reduction to

39. Maximus the Confessor, *Ambiguum 7: On the Beginning and End of Rational Creatures*, in *On the Cosmic Mystery of Jesus Christ: Selected Writings from St Maximus the Confessor*, trans. Paul Blowers and Robert Louis Wilken (Crestwood, N.Y.: St. Vladimir's Seminary Press, 2003), pp. 45-74; here, pp. 59-60. Greek, PG 91:1068D-1101C. For commentary see Polycarp Sherwood, *The Earlier Ambigua of Saint Maximus the Confessor and His Refutation of Origenism*, Studia Anselmiana 36 (Rome: Herder, 1955), pp. 155-80. For a use of this passage in the context of marriage, see Rogers in Mark Jordan, *Authorizing Marriage* (Princeton, N.J.: Princeton University Press, 2005).

40. Rogers, *Sexuality and the Christian Body*, pp. 260-65. For a history of oblation, see John Boswell, *The Kindness of Strangers: The Abandonment of Children in Western Europe from Late Antiquity to the Renaissance* (New York: Vintage Books, 1990).

41. Sergius Bulgakov, *The Comforter*, trans. Boris Jakim (Grand Rapids and Cambridge: Eerdmans, 2004), pp. 320-23; here, p. 321.

suppose that the church is composed of marriages alone, and a great abstraction to suppose that actual friendships among church members do not compose a great deal of its connective tissue. "In general," writes Bulgakov, "the concept of friendship as personal love and spiritual eros that accompanies it ought to be extended to *different* forms of this love; and the difference between the sexes does not by any means play the central role here, although its existence obviously qualifies or conditions love itself."

> In general, personal love is diverse and does not admit any single definition. What is important is to establish that these forms of natural love can also become forms of churchly love precisely by receiving the gracious gift of this love by the action of the Holy Spirit, even though there is no special sacrament that establishes and sanctifies these forms of love.[42]

Here it occurs to Bulgakov in a note that "There once existed the ancient rite of *adelphopoiesis* ('brother-making'), which sanctified personal friendship."[43] He means the rite of *adelphopoiesis* that Boswell would later study.

The ecclesial charism of personal friendship, if one may so interpret Bulgakov, arises from the resting of the Spirit on the Son in two ways. First, it is "a *personal* relationship in love, rooted in the life of the Church. One loses one's life for Christ's sake with reference to a particular person to whom one is linked by friendship."[44] Second, this foundation is itself the "foundation of churchly friendship in Christ's Friendship with us. He tells His disciples, 'Ye are my friends [*philoi*]. . . . I have called you my friends; for all that I have heard from my Father I have made known unto you'" — that is, Christ includes his friends indirectly in his own relationship with his Father.[45] This friendship, in Jesus' narrative interactions with his disciples, is not general, like that of *agape;* rather, it is "qualified, individualized, personal love, love as friendship."[46]

This friendship may even have an erotic or (relatively) exclusive aspect, insofar as it is a "spiritual syzygy." "Friendship, as a certain spiritual pair-syzygy, also includes traits of erotic love in this sense, for it is accompanied by or even consists of a particular *mutual* inspiration, an overcoming of personal self-enclosedness through the life together of two persons, but 'with one soul'" (I Sam. 17:1; 19:1; 20:17). Here too the Spirit does not act on individuals. Rather,

---

42. Bulgakov, *Comforter,* pp. 321-22.
43. Bulgakov, *Comforter,* p. 322, n. 58.
44. Bulgakov, *Comforter,* p. 320.
45. Bulgakov, *Comforter,* p. 320, quoting John 15:14-15.
46. Bulgakov, *Comforter,* p. 321.

Bulgakov interprets *eros* itself as "inspiration, the transcendence of oneself."[47] On his account, the erotic aspect of human friendship could not properly be left out of ecclesial formation. Here it occurs to him, again in a footnote, to cite the story of David and Jonathan as "an Old Testament rite" of *adelphopoiesis*.[48]

Two other treatments of *adelphopoiesis* are better known. I have already mentioned Boswell's. Bulgakov himself mentions Pavel Florensky's, which he calls "a true theological revolution, because for the first time friendship as an ecclesial relation has been incorporated in the theological doctrine of the Church, and is seen as having a legitimate place in the life of the Church."[49] In Boswell, *adelphopoiesis* is presented as a rite of individuals analogous to marriage.[50] In Florensky, it is presented as a gift of the Spirit in romantic, mystical terms.[51] What is noteworthy here after Boswell is no longer the sublimation or spiritualization of same-sex eros. Rather it is the ecclesial aspect. Whatever this rite meant, or may mean again, Bulgakov proposes something neither merely mystical, nor merely for couples, but something *structural*, something that by the gift of the Spirit upbuilds and constitutes the church. The very nerves and sinews of the church, its connective tissue, are formed by a network of personal friendships graced by the Spirit with an ecclesial charism of love, regardless of whether they might be solemnized with the old rite, and even if Bulgakov does not seem to consider the possibility of unmarried cross-sex friendship. Here too the Spirit does not float free from concrete human bodies, but rests upon, inspires, and takes embodied life from them.

vi. The Spirit rests on the Son transfiguring the human being at prayer: hesychastic aspect

Symeon the New Theologian (949-1022) — "new" because he wrote in the eleventh century — is also called "theologian" because of greater insistence upon the deity of the Holy Spirit than his fellows, including another illustri-

---

47. Bulgakov, *Comforter*, p. 321.

48. This long and substantive note — on the occasion of the "one soul" of I Samuel — has unfortunately disappeared from the English translation, leaving the impression that the "one soul" is a piece of romanticism rather than a piece of exegesis. The French translation, prepared in consulation with the author, retains the note. See Serge Bulgakov, *Le Paraclet*, trans. Constantin Andronikov (Paris: Aubier, 1944), pp. 308-9, n. 4.

49. Bulgakov, *Comforter*, p. 320, n. 54.

50. John Boswell, *Same-Sex Unions in Premodern Europe* (New York: Villard Press, 1994).

51. Pavel Florensky, *The Pillar and Ground of the Truth*, trans. Boris Jakim (Princeton: Princeton University Press, 1997).

ous Symeon, Symeon the Studite. Blasphemy against the Holy Spirit is famously the unforgivable sin,[52] since to reject the Spirit of Christ is to reject
the Spirit of forgiveness. Symeon wonders what this sin might be, and includes the following description:

> [T]o deny that at this present time there are some who love God, that they
> have been granted the Holy Spirit and to be baptized by Him as sons of
> God, that they have become gods by knowledge and experience and con-
> templation, that wholly subverts the Incarnation of our God and Savior Je-
> sus Christ (Tit. 2:13)! It clearly denies the renewal of the image that had been
> corrupted and put to death, and its return to incorruption and immortality.

Blasphemy against the Holy Spirit, according to Symeon, includes the denial
of God dwelling in human beings. Symeon has identified God again in a new
way — in us. How can this be?

The Eastern Orthodox tradition reserves the title "theologian" for only
three. They count John the Theologian, the Evangelist; and Gregory the Theologian, of Nazianzus; and Symeon the New Theologian. There is some argument about the principle that explains what historically distinct designations
may have in common.[53] But it seems that to be a theologian in the strict sense
is to identify God by the Spirit. That means to participate in the Spirit's work
of witness, of interpreting, or, in the face of sin, re-interpreting the relation of
Jesus and the Father in celebration of the divine self-giving. John participates
in the Spirit's witness in the field of narrative by telling God's earthly story

---

52. Luke 12:10, Matt. 12:32, Mark 3:28-30; Luke 12:10; cf. 1 John 16.

53. The title seems to have been first applied to Gregory already at the Council of Chalcedon
in 451. The context is the attribution to "the holy (makarios) Gregory the Theologian" of a quotation about the two natures of Christ from a letter to Cledonius (Ep. 101). See Acta Conciliorum
Oecumenicorum, ed. Edvardus Schwartz (Berlin: De Gruyter, 1935), tomus 2, volumen 1, pars 3,
p. 114, l. 14, and Frederick W. Norris' Introduction to Faith Gives Fullness to Reasoning: The Five
Theological Orations of Gregory Nazianzen (New York: E. J. Brill, 1991), p. 12, n. 56. According to
Athanasius and Theodoret, "theology" refers to the immanent Trinity, as opposed to
"oikonomia" (Athanasius, PG 26:49A; Theodoret of Cyrrhus, Eranistes II, ed. G. H. Ettlinger, 40:
20-21). For a short, useful account, see Karl-Heinz Uthermann, "Theologian," in Alexander
Kazhdan, et al., Oxford Dictionary of Byzantium, 6 vols. (New York: Oxford, 1991). For a survey
of citations with unhelpful analysis, see Ferdinand Kattenbusch, Die Entstehung einer
christlichen Theologie: Zur Geschichte der Ausdrücke theologia, theologein, theologos, Libelli 69
(Darmstadt: Wissenschaftliche Buchgesellschaft, 1962), pp. 38-45. Irénée Hausherr has investigated the manuscript evidence for the attribution of the title "New Theologian" to Symeon and
concludes that it is applied because Symeon approaches John the Evangelist as an equal. "'New
Theologian' means 'New St. John.'" La Méthode d'oraison hésychaste, Orientalia Christiana fasci-
cle series no. 36, or Orientalia Christiana 9 (1927): 98-210; here, p. 102, n. 1.

from the beginning to the coming of the Counselor. Gregory participates in the field of formal argument by throwing off the caution of Basil. And Symeon does it in the field of the human soul by identifying the Spirit's dwelling. To identify God by the Spirit is already a work of the Spirit in the human being, because in so doing the human being participates in the Spirit's own proper work of bearing witness to — or identifying — God. To participate in the Spirit's own proper work is to identify God *from within*, to participate in God's own self-identification, to participate, in short, in God. Regardless of whether the theologian knows it, doing theology properly involves God's bringing the theologian into God's own triune life. "By this we know that we abide in him [God] and he in us, because he has given us of his own Spirit."[54]

vii. The Spirit rests on the Son in the habits of the law

When the Father sends the Son, he does not send the Son alone, but with the Spirit. That pattern obtains also among those whom the Father will draw to himself in the Son. The Father does not abandon them, and the Son sends them a Comforter. Human beings are apparently never left alone when they are initiated into the trinitarian communion. To imagine that the Son begins something that the Spirit abandons is to deny the trinitarian pattern that the Spirit abides with, rests upon, witnesses to the Son, and those who belong to him. The sort of worry that plagues Protestant readings of Aquinas is not really one based in anthropology. It is at best one that misunderstands the depth of his trinitarian thinking — at worst one that mistrusts the reliability of God's trinitarian acting.

So the trinitarian God does not leave human beings alone with the work of Christ, but initiates them into the trinitarian community, the love stronger than death. It is characteristic of the triune God not only to come down to them, but also to bring them up to Godself. Thomas describes this movement in terms of grace. But grace just is the effect of the Holy Spirit dwelling in their hearts and writing a new law upon them. When they bless God, they are doing what the Spirit does in the life of the Trinity. When the Spirit writes a new law on their hearts, it comes out in human acts, and therefore habits, which are as new, and as reliable, as the Spirit. The movement from the human creature up to God is no independent human movement, but belongs within the movement from God to God by which the Spirit adds a new song to the love between the Father and the Son.

54. I John 4:13.

Thomas takes up a Pauline expression when he defines grace as "the law of the Spirit." Consider the glorious piling up of characterizations in Romans 8:1-2. We read first of "the law." As if to confute those who would divorce the spirit from the letter, it becomes "the law *of the Spirit*." In case anyone would think that another spirit, or suppose that law had gotten the upper hand over liberty, Paul goes on to specify it as "the law of the Spirit *of life*." And lest that be just any spirit of life, any biological vitality with its Darwinian laws, Paul characterizes it finally as "the law of the Spirit of life in *Christ Jesus*." That is then the passage that Thomas Aquinas chooses as rubric for his tractate on grace. He wants to affirm, I think, that grace is a *structure that liberates*. It is no *nomos*, which gives rise to an antinomian rebellion. Rather, it completes, it consummates *the life in Christ Jesus*. As Anselm wrote so beautifully in *Cur Deus homo*, "God would complete what he began."[55] As a structure that liberates, it is the consummation of Torah, the law of the Psalms that is "a delight to walk in," of the songs of the Spirit, what completes human beings not measurelessly, but humanly, from measure to measure.[56] It is, as James puts it, "the perfect law, the law of liberty" (1:25), which it is the office of the Spirit to perfect.

As the giver not of legalisms but of newness of life, the Spirit appropriates two features of human nature that Protestants hate to see deified. They are reason and habit — the structure of knowing and the reliability of love. In appropriating these, the Spirit takes hold of human beings all the way down, and redeems them in a bodily way. For both reason (composing and dividing) and habit (a settled disposition to act) depend upon sense impressions and temporal sequence — that is, upon bodies.

Protestants may say, But wait! Reason and habit are the very places where the human rebellion against God takes place. Reason, in Luther's famous phrase, is the devil's whore. Habit is where sin persists even in the justified. Is it not a perverse denial of what Niebuhr called the only *empirical* feature of Christian doctrine — namely sin — to speak of the work of the Spirit in reason and habit, of all places?

Thomas's reply, I think, would in this case be consistent with the famous line of Bernard in speaking of good works. "The entire work is *in the will*," Bernard wrote, "just because the entire work is *from grace*."[57] Will and grace,

---

55. Anselm of Canterbury, *Why God Became Human*, in *A Scholastic Miscellany: Anselm to Ockham*, ed. and trans. Eugene R. Fairweather, Library of Christian Classics, vol. 10 (Philadelphia: Westminster, 1956), book II, ch. 4.

56. Cf. John 3:34, Eph. 4:7.

57. Bernard of Clairvaux, *De gratia et libero arbitrio, in finem*, as translated in Hans Küng, *Justification: The Doctrine of Karl Barth and a Catholic Reflection*, 2d ed. (Philadelphia: Westminster, 1981), p. 266, italics modified. (Standard translations are not quite as pointed as the one in Küng.)

reason and faith, habit and spirit are not rival agents.[58] While Thomas would not want to deny that human beings are agents, he would want to deny that they are agents of such a kind as to rival grace. Bernard's language of agent and *place* locates God's agency in a human field — under conditions of sin, in a human battlefield. Reason and habit *must* be the places where grace works, *just because* they are the places where sin reigns. This is a matter of what Thomas would call *convenientia,* or fittingness, the suitedness of the story to the case, indeed evidence that God has a sense of dramatic irony. Catholics tend to express God's dramatic irony with the words of the Easter vigil, *Felix culpa, quae tantum ac talem meruit Redemptorem:* "O happy fault, that merited such and so great a Redeemer." Protestants can express God's dramatic irony in the observation of Luther that God insists on working *sub contrario.* It suits God's sense of dramatic irony to take the worst that human beings can do (with their wills, their reason, their settled dispositions to sin), finally their crucifixion of the Son, and use precisely *that* as the means of salvation. That the sacrifice of the cross, and the great thanksgiving, should come together in the Eucharist represents the Church's participation in and celebration of God's work, that God makes the worst that humans can do the occasion of their benefit. As it is in salvation history, so it is in the cure of souls. The Father elects reason and habit — the very places where humans rebel — to be the places where the Spirit redeems. How indeed could it be otherwise?

We can easily see why the contrast between law and Spirit is false if we look to Christians' own talk of participation in the life of the Spirit, their own inspired liberty. The liberty that the Spirit inspires in human beings is neither antinomian nor empty. It has a spontaneity, but not in a vacuum. Rather, the spontaneity of inspired liberty retains the personal character that it receives from the Spirit. It is the spontaneity not of just anybody, not of what any abstract, nondescript, imaginable person might do, but the spontaneity of a particular person with a history and a character — an innovative history and a surprising character, but a history and a character nevertheless. The spontaneity that the Spirit grants to human beings not only remains characteristic of a particular Spirit, but it comes as appropriate to a human being. It is spontaneity in the service of something, a freedom for something; it enjoys intentionality and participates in personal agency. Thus the law can be the object of love and delight, just when it is indwelt by a Person, for it is the law "of the Lord," the Spirit, the giver of life. See how deeply the psalmist intertwines with the languages of law the languages with which Christians praise

---

58. For the best treatment of the noncompetitive relation between nature and grace, see Kathryn Tanner, *God and Creation: Tyranny or Empowerment?* (Oxford: Blackwell, 1988), esp. p. 48.

the Spirit: the law gives delight; it offers testimony; it is a counselor; it comes by grace; it works in the heart; it testifies before kings; it keeps faith steadfastly; it is the object of love; it is the giver of life:

> Blessed is the one
> [whose] delight is in the law of the Lord,
>   and on his law he meditates day and night.[59]
>
> Put false ways far from me,
>   and graciously teach me thy law!
> I have chosen the way of faithfulness,
>   I set thy ordinances before me.
> I cleave to thy testimonies, O Lord;
>   let me not be put to shame!
> I will run in the way of thy commandments
>   when thou enlargest my understanding!
>
> Teach me, O Lord, the way of thy statutes;
>   and I will keep it to the end.
> Give me understanding, that I may keep the law
>   and observe it with my whole heart.
> Lead me in the path of thy commandments,
>   for I delight in it.
> Incline my heart to thy testimonies,
>   and not to gain!
> Turn my eyes from looking at vanities;
>   and give me life in thy ways.
>
> Behold I long for thy precepts;
>   in thy righteousness give me life!
>
> I will keep thy law continually,
>   for ever and ever;
> and I shall walk at liberty,
>   for I have sought thy precepts.
> I will also speak of thy testimonies before kings,
>   and shall not be put to shame.
>
> Thy statutes have been my songs,
>   in the house of my pilgrimage.

59. Ps. 1:1-2.

When I think of thy ways,
    I turn my feet to thy testimonies;
I hasten and do not delay
    to keep thy commandments.

The earth, O Lord, is full of thy steadfast love;
    teach me thy statutes!

Oh, how I love thy law!
    It is my meditation all the day.
Thy commandment makes me wiser than my enemies,
    for it is ever with me.
I have more understanding than all my teachers,
    for thy testimonies are my meditation.

How sweet are thy words to my taste,
    sweeter than honey to my mouth!

If thy law had not been my delight,
    I should have perished in my affliction.
I will never forget thy precepts;
    for by them thou hast given me life.[60]

The languages of law and of the Spirit are not just intertwined. They are the same. How could they ever have come apart?

They both have a structure, a structure that liberates, a structure that gives beauty to liberty. As a Person the Spirit does not oppose the letter. Indeed it writes — it writes upon the heart.[61] Even Augustine could ask, "What are the laws of God, written by very God upon hearts, if not the presence itself of the Holy Spirit?"[62] As a Person the Spirit does not oppose rules; she is the Person that writes them — makes them. "As the law of works was written upon tablets of stone, so the law of faith has been written upon the hearts of the faithful."[63] The Spirit does not oppose rules: The Spirit rules.

But does the Spirit rule eventfully, like the wind, or habitually? Karl Barth, and more recently his defender George Hunsinger, have strenuously argued the former. But it is a false contrast. A habit, after all, is not a static thing, but dy-

---

60. Ps. 119:29-37, 40, 44-46, 54, 59-60, 64, 97-99, 103, 92-93, RSV.

61. Heb. 8:8, 10, quoting Jer. 31:33.

62. Augustine, *On the Letter and the Spirit*, ch. 21, in NPNF2, vol. 5; cf. Aquinas's use of this passage at *ST* I-II.106.1.

63. Augustine, *On the Letter and the Spirit*, ch. 24.

namic all the way down. It abbreviates a series of events. Either a series of events lays down a habit, or a habit retrospectively names the beginning of a series of events. The Spirit not only blows like a hurricane but like a *prevailing* wind.

Protestants worry that habits give too much continuity to the creature. Before turning to a defense of that continuity, I want to point out two ways in which Aquinas's habits are just as eventful as human action in Barth. In Thomas, virtuous habits depend upon God's constant intervention for both their origin and their every working out. Good habits are nothing other than the gently condescending courtesy of grace, or the robust, insistent humanity of God.

Luther famously imagined virtuous habits, informed by theological virtues, as disciplines that Thomists falsely believed could be built up by our own natural powers. That is a supposition that the language of *infused* virtues is supposed to block. If all human action, to be human, is habitual, then it is habitual in two ways. One, all human acting *arises* out of structures or pathways previously laid down; two, all human action *builds or blazes* such structures or pathways. An infused virtue is a grace not previously worked out by a human being, from which real human acting arises. If a human being does a good deed, therefore, the habit from which it arises must be a divinely laid down one. The infusion of virtues insists upon and protects the absolute prevenience of grace in the transformation of the human agent. Any human building up of true virtue must have a divine intervention behind it. Infused virtues are settled dispositions to act, not because we have so disposed ourselves, but because God has so disposed us. In Irenaean fashion, God respects our time- and body-boundedness by working within them, habitually. Indeed, every divine intervention, if it leaves any trace at all in the human being, must leave a trace in the form of an incipient habit. If God transforms the human agent without violating the creature, then God dramatically or gently changes human habits. For Thomas it is not controversial, just analytic. If God redeems us, God habituates us.

Is God's work then just the first intervention, leaving us to work out our salvation on our own? By no means! God's intervention is constant, unceasing, and eventful. Thomas signals it with a much controverted word, *auxilium*. Non-Latinist Protestants see it translated as God's "help" and imagine that *auxilium* is a matter of God and the human being engaged in Pelagian or semi-Pelagian collaboration, God and the human being pulling on the same rope. Catholics see the same word and think of sixteenth-century controversies about the mechanics, physical or otherwise, of God's intervention. Neither the Protestant reduction nor the sixteenth-century inventions are helpful.

I believe that Thomas does use *auxilium* as a technical term,[64] but not one hitched to much of a *theory* about how it works. *Auxilium* is a technical term, in the pragmatic sense that it usually does the same work. Like "infusion," it always marks the spot where God intervenes — powerfully, sovereignly, redemptively — in human acting. But also like "infusion," it is an *x* that marks the spot where God intervenes. It marks this spot much as the Barthian word "event" does. A theory would only obfuscate the simplicity of the claim, Here God acts. This claim is a mystery in the strict sense, an act of God that surpasses human understanding not because it is absurd, like evil, but because it is dazzlingly *good*. God's *auxilium* is a mystery, as if it were "too good to be true": that God acts in us, in such a way that we act. It is part of God's mercy and justice, that God gives us to participate in good works — all God's work — so that we are not left out of our salvation, but involved in it. In *auxilium*, God non-competitively bears, carries, moves, engages our wills.[65] As Richard Norris has written in another context, "What makes God *different* from every creature . . . is . . . precisely what assures his direct and intimate *relation* with every creature."[66] That is, this intimacy is what a first cause exercises, and what secondary, creaturely causes lack. Or as Aquinas's non-Aristotelian predecessors would say, God "influences" creatures not by force but so that God *flows into* them, *in-fluere*.[67] The correct translation is not "help," a word that truthfully expresses God's courtesy toward and non-violation of human beings, but which remains far too weak. A better translation is "engagement." There is no good human act without God's ongoing, eventful engagement of it. Of such acts God's act is causative. If human agency is also causative, that is precisely by God's gracious granting of an analogy between our goodness and God's, a participation which is already a share in God's own life and agency, since only God is self-standingly good, and human beings are good only in leaning upon God. The gracious and unexacted event of God's grant of such an analogy or share is God's *auxilium* or engagement of human beings in God's act.

For the Spirit's engagement of human beings in the Trinity's act of prayer when they "on account of weakness do not know how to pray," see the Epilogue.

---

64. I have been confirmed in this impression by a word study by my student Michael Lockaby.

65. For a general statement of this principle, see Tanner, *God and Creation*, esp. pp. 46-48.

66. Richard A. Norris, Jr., *God and World in Early Christian Theology* (New York, N.Y.: Seabury, 1965), pp. 84-86. Norris actually applies the description to Irenaeus.

67. Jacob Schutz, "Influentia," in *Surnaturel: une controverse au coeur du thomisme au xxe. siècle,* by Institut Saint Thomas d'Aquin, a special issue of *Revue thomiste* 102 (Toulouse: École de Théologie, 2001).

5 Ascension and Pentecost

"While he blessed them, he was carried up into heaven. . . .
Suddenly a sound came from heaven like the rush of a
mighty wind, and there appeared to them as tongues of fire,
distributed and resting on each one of them. And they were
all filled with the Holy Spirit" (Luke 24:51 and Acts 2:2-4)

As the Son rises like fire into the heavens, so the Spirit descends like fire upon
the disciples.

The problem I'm trying to solve appears in (say) Barth: that there's nothing
the Spirit can do, that the Son can't do better. On the other hand, you can't
separate the Spirit from the Son: then you land in unitarianism. The trick is
to do what Athanasius does, in *Contra Arianos* III or *Letters to Serapion on the
Holy Spirit,* and speak of the Son and the Spirit always together and always
distinctly. One way to ensure you do this is to look at biblical passages where
the Son and the Spirit *interact:* if they are interacting, then they must be together and distinct. So we have been looking at Annunciation, baptism,
Transfiguration, and resurrection. So far so good.

That procedure seems to have a very significant defect, however. Pentecost
is the feast of the Spirit. But Pentecost does not take place in the life of Jesus.
If I leave out Pentecost, a book on the Spirit is incomplete. If I put it in, the
Spirit seems to float free of the New Testament narratives about Jesus. Of
course the Spirit rests on the body of the Son, in the disciples, but that's not
elegant. If that's *all* that Pentecost means, it sounds Bultmannian — the crucifixion happened to Jesus, and faith happened to the disciples, as a kind of
sociological compensation for a failed hope. Furthermore, I have little to say
about the Ascension.

There is a second problem with my approach, according to specialists in
the Fourth Gospel. John displays the pattern that Jesus must leave in order for
the Spirit to come. So a John specialist might think my procedure of keeping

the Son and the Spirit together works only for the Synoptics — of which, if you are a John specialist, you might be suspicious.[1]

I want to incorporate that pattern, but call it interaction nevertheless. The pattern is one of retiring and invitation and sending, what Julian of Norwich would call God's courtesy. It describes an interaction, rather than avoids one. I claim that the relation between Son and Spirit portrayed in Jesus' farewell discourse in John just *is* an interaction — because it follows a pattern of bidding and waiting and courtesy whereby Jesus reverses Adam's grasping of divinity in the apple by "counting divinity not a thing to be grasped," and keeps choosing to receive what he already has anew from the Spirit. So Jesus knows how to wait, and how to turn over what he has to another — that is part of knowing how to receive — and that, in turn, is part of what he is talking about in the Farewell Discourses.

That is also what he *enacts* when, in Luke/Acts he departs (Ascension) before the Spirit arrives (Pentecost). Just because they happen as two different events, does not mean they are unrelated. They exemplify rather than undermine the pattern. If so, it turns out the two scenes or feasts that trouble this account — Pentecost and Ascension — belong together. It is not that Pentecost lacks the Son, and Ascension lacks the Spirit, but rather that they form a particularly good example of how the Son defers to the Spirit, in order to receive a gift. In both the Farewell Discourse of John and the Ascension-Pentecost drama of Luke/Acts, Jesus cedes place to the Spirit. But this is just what Jesus does in his characteristic humility and forbearance: in John and in Luke/Acts he counts divinity, and the Spirit, not things to be grasped, and in so doing reverses the grasping of Adam. In going to his death and in going to his Father, Jesus humbles himself and awaits the Spirit. Thus the relation of Jesus and the Spirit is not mechanical and automatic but personal and gratuitous. So too Jesus makes room for the Spirit to gift him with renewed life for his mortal body (Rom. 8:11) after his crucifixion, and renewed life for his churchly body (at Pentecost) after his ascension. In this case, the Messiah of the Jews receives the gift of the Gentiles unexpectedly from the Spirit.

The two feasts are related not only in my procedure. Indeed the early church celebrated the two together.[2] Fifty days of Paschal rejoicing culminated in Pentecost, and the Easter rising was imagined as one continuous mo-

---

1. I owe this objection to Ronald Piper.

2. See, for example, Thomas J. Talley, *The Origins of the Liturgical Year,* 2d ed. (Collegeville, Minn.: The Liturgical Press, 1986), pp. 57-69. For an alternate view, see the appendix in J. G. Davies, *He Ascended into Heaven* (London: Lutterworth, 1958).

tion from hell to the right hand of the Father, in which Jesus' last sojourn on earth represented an episode or elaboration.

Even after the church began to distinguish Pentecost from Easter and later Ascension from Pentecost, programs of decoration continued often to treat Ascension and Pentecost as a matched pair. An art historian has written that

> Polyptych icons often arrange the Dodekaorton scenes [scenes of the twelve most important feasts] in interesting ways — it is never casual what is over what, what is next to what, and what occupies on one leaf the position that something else occupies on another.[3] The little church of Asinou on Cyprus balances the Ascension in the bema vault with the Pentecost in the western vault;[4] St. Nicholas tes Steges on Cyprus of the 11th century places the Ascension on the north side and the Pentecost on the south side of the bema vault;[5] the Katholikon of Hosios Loukas near Delphi places the Pentecost in the bema vault where most churches place the Ascension;[6] San Marco in Venice and the Apostles' Chuch in Constantinople used the Pentecost and the Ascension in two of their five domes.[7]

A Western example — suitable, like programs of church decoration, for contemplation and anagogic practices of prayer — would be the Ascension and Pentecost on facing pages in a sixteenth-century French book of hours.[8]

What is sure is that this pairing frequently and significantly occurs; what the pairing means as a pneumatological statement is open to speculation: ascent and descent; departure and arrival; embrace of the congregation between trinitarian persons; the catching up of the congregation through their liturgical life into the life of the Trinity. If the *sursum corda* recalls the Ascension, and the epiclesis repeats the Pentecost, those would be speculative but appropriate ways in which what one hears and what one sees help to con-

3. For examples see Konstantinos A. Manaphes, ed., *Sinai: Treasures of the Monastery of Saint Catherine* (Athens: Ekdotike Athenon, 1990).

4. Andreas Stylianou and Judith A. Stylianou, *The Painted Churches of Cyprus: Treasures of Byzantine Art* (London: Trigraph for the A. G. Leventis Foundation, 1985), pp. 121-22; Marina André Sacopoulou, *Asinou en 1106 et sa contribution à l'iconographie,* Bibliotheque de Byzantion, 2 (Bruxelles, Éditions de Byzantion, 1966).

5. Stylianou and Stylianou, *The Painted Churches,* p. 55.

6. Otto Demus, *Byzantine Mosaic Decoration: Aspects of Monumental Art in Byzantium* (New Rochelle, N.Y.: Caratzas Bros., 1976).

7. I owe this paragraph to an email from Annemarie Weyl Carr. More examples appear in Marcell Restle, *Byzantine Wall Painting in Asia Minor* (Greenwich, Conn.: New York Graphic Society, 1967).

8. Musée de la Renaissance, château d'Écouen, France. See figs. 6-7.

struct the congregation as a liturgical body moving into God by taking on the identity of God's child in the community of God's Spirit. In the eucharistic celebration that such images surround, the Spirit descends on the bread and wine to make them the incorporable body and blood of the one who ascends, so that she can lift up with and after him those who eat the flesh and drink the blood of the Ascended One.

Theologians might associate Pentecost with the life (or death) of Christ for typological reasons, too.[9] If in Christian typology and liturgy (if not in the Gospel of Matthew) the crucifixion is regularly associated with Passover, so that the Easter acclamation is "Christ our Passover is sacrificed for us," then Pentecost ought to be associated with the feast that comes fifty days after Passover, namely Shavuoth. Historians of liturgy make this connection routinely.[10] But it shows up only rarely among theologians. Perhaps — to speculate — this is because the West, at least, tends to oppose the Spirit and the letter, and Shavuoth is among other things the feast of the handing down of the law. If the contrast of Spirit and law is misleading, however — if the law is a structure that liberates, and a delight to walk in; if Paul can speak of a "law of the Spirit of life" and James of a "perfect" "law of liberty"; if the indwelling of the Spirit habituates the soul to virtue — then the association of the descent of the law with the descent of the Spirit is appropriate rather than contrastive, a recollection rather than a reversal. Many characteristics of the Spirit appear, therefore, in the biblical descriptions of Shavuoth. It gathers the community in recognition of difference: "your male and female slave, the Levites resident in your towns, as well as the strangers, the orphans, and the widows among you" (Deut. 16:11).[11] It gathers the community in celebration of God's gifts; it is the feast of first fruits. And it gathers the community in celebration of God's liberation: it "celebrates the plentiful harvest of a free people."[12] Shavuoth, like Pentecost, is a feast of radical inclusion of the Gentiles in the care of the God of Israel: "When you reap the harvest of your land, you shall not reap to the very edges of your field, or gather the gleanings of your harvest; you shall leave them for the poor and for the alien: I am the LORD your God" (Lev. 23:22).[13] This concrete provision for the care of Gentiles becomes crucial to the story of Ruth, the Moabite, one of the Gentile women picked out in

9. I owe this paragraph to Aaron Riches, "The Event of Passover, the Diversity of Pentecost," unpublished typescript.

10. E.g., Talley, *Origins of the Liturgical Year*, pp. 57-59.

11. Riches, "The Event of Passover," p. 2.

12. Riches, "The Event of Passover," p. 3.

13. Riches, "The Event of Passover," p. 3.

Matthew's genealogy of Jesus, who gleans in the fields after Boaz, whom she calls her *goel,* her redeemer.

In the Johannine passages in which Jesus says that he must leave for the Spirit to come, and in its Lukan enactment in Ascension and Pentecost, Jesus pries open the very interval that Barth had let close. He insists on a space, a time between himself and the Spirit. The Spirit takes time, and grants a history — a history that can graciously last longer than a single life. Jesus trusts enough to leave; the Spirit grants him a church. Jesus must go to his Father to complete his work; the Spirit may add to it. We opened this book by complaining that an interval had closed up. We end it by observing that the New Testament narratives require an interval left open, both in John and in Luke/ Acts. They require the interval between Ascension and Pentecost as the interval in created space and time between the Son and the Spirit. Again Athanasius sees the pattern as one of a gracious superfluity; here he speaks of Easter and Pentecost, but Ascension only improves the point: "After Easter comes the feast of Pentecost which we shall welcome, one feast after the other, to celebrate the Spirit already with us in Christ Jesus."[14] Feast upon feast: it is not a question of sufficiency but of superfluity, of the peculiar resources of created time for celebration and variation. The intratrinitarian interpenetration of Son and Spirit becomes their economic interaction. And here that interaction reveals itself to insist on waiting and expectation, on delay for more, on a musical pause or rest, on a Sabbath also in the trinitarian taxis. Pentecost like Shavuoth comes after seven times seven days, or a week of weeks, as the Sabbath of Sabbaths.

Pentecost, the most activating of feasts, brings us back to the soft paradox that God is a Mover unmoved, whose pure act is perfect rest; that the Spirit comes to "rest" on God's actively becoming human, and in so doing begins to incorporate humanity into the unceasing activity of God's triune rest. The Spirit who comes on the Sabbath of Sabbaths is the Spirit therefore who sanctifies time and gives diverse human beings a history. Their history is not opposed to their deification, but enacts, celebrates, and practices it.

The Spirit's storied interactions with Christ tell us something about how God enters time, and as human befriends it, at incarnation, baptism, transfiguration, and resurrection. Christ befriends time by becoming human at the conception by the Spirit. He confirms that role humanly, in time, by submitting himself to the guidance of the Spirit at his baptism, the beginning of his ministry in time, and, over a period of forty days, to the Spirit's driving him

14. Athanasius of Alexandria, *Festal Letters* 14:6 (PG 26:1422), quoted in Cantalamessa, p. 189.

into the wilderness to be tempted. Christ displays time-friendly virtues in the course of his life, primarily a lack of anxiety about it: his ministry starts late and ends early, and he is willing to undergo death: in these concrete ways he counts timelessness not a thing to be grasped, but humbles himself, giving the initiative over to the Spirit, already at his baptism, but especially by his death, so that over great stretches of time, much longer than a human life, the Spirit can give additional unexpected gifts of people and holiness to the Son. Only by retiring from the scene, and sending the Spirit, can the Son pass on his ministry without grasping time, without seeking to live forever; only by withdrawing on behalf of the Spirit can the Son put death behind him. The Son gives his life in trusting the Spirit before all Israel has come in, allowing himself to "fail" as Messiah, and the Spirit gives the unexpected and peculiar gift of the mostly Gentile church.

The Spirit bears witness perhaps most obviously in the Upper Room, where tongues of fire appear over the apostles now able to speak in tongues. Not only does speaking in tongues evidence the Spirit's work, because human beings are getting taken up into the Spirit's proper work of bearing witness in many and various ways. But the tongues of fire also perform the witness's deictic work of pointing out and marking. For this reason fire becomes one of the chief hallmarks of the Spirit's witness, the witness to the witness as it were.

Fire descending from heaven is a counter-intuitive image. Earthly fire burns upward. The descent of the Spirit as fire is paraphysical. The ascent of the fire from human beings is its naturalized result. The descent of fire with the Spirit enables human ascent with fire in the Spirit, and after Christ.[15] The descent of fire on Sodom and Gomorrah destroys Gentile hostility; the descent of fire in the upper room invites Jews and Gentiles to a common hospitality.

In the Syriac liturgies, baptism and Eucharist are both sacraments by virtue of imparting the Spirit's fire working paraphysically in a wet medium. By uttering the epiclesis, according to a poem by Balai, "the priest kindles fire"[16] even in wine. Fire in the wine and in the womb: if the Son ascends, it is like fire, and if the Spirit descends it is with fire. In Christ's image human beings

15. This paragraph occurred to me while reading an unpublished paper by Keith Starkenburg.

16. Sebastian P. Brock, *The Holy Spirit in the Syrian Baptismal Tradition*, The Syrian Churches Series, vol. 9 (Poona, India: Anita Printers, 1979; 2d ed., 1998), p. 29, citing *S. Ephraemi Syri, Rabulae Episcopi Edesseni, Balai aliorumque opera selecta*, ed. J. J. Overbeck (Oxford: Oxford University Press, 1865), p. 252; translation in Kathleen McVey, "On the Dedication of the Church in Qennishrin," *Aram Journal* (Oxford) 5 (1993): 359-67.

may also ascend, with and therefore like fire. Indeed, they ascend where the fire is, with the paraphysical fire-bearing elements, the water and the wine. This again reverses the fall, since the angel of death guarding the Garden of Eden had a fiery sword. "God drove out the human being; and at the East God placed the cherubim, and a flaming sword which turned every way, to guard the way to the tree of life."[17] But now that Christ will not descend from the cross, reversing Adam's grasp, the fire too gives access rather than denying it.

Suppose the pair of Ascension and Pentecost furnishes an objection to my thesis in this way: At the Ascension Jesus takes his body away, so that the Spirit cannot rest upon it; at the Pentecost the Spirit comes down, away from the body of Christ.

On the contrary. At the Ascension Jesus goes up, with his humanity, to complete its deification. At the Ascension human nature ascends to be with the Father, to enjoy the trinitarian life. Without it — Calvinists argue[18] — the communion of the human being with the Trinity would be incomplete, because Christ would not have gone before to prepare a place for human beings, indeed for human bodies. In the same way, at Pentecost, the Spirit descends as a foretaste of heaven, to rest by anticipation on the bodies that will be deified. In the same way, at Pentecost, the Spirit descends to be in advance with those who will be with the Father, who already begin to enjoy the trinitarian life. Without it — trinitarians ought to say — the Trinity's embrace of the human being would be too narrow, because the Trinity would not have opened itself wide enough to find all human experience already within it, from the harrowing of hell to the session at the right hand of the Father. At the end of any human way stands Christ, whether that way leads to hell or heaven. The harrowing of hell makes Sodom internal to the community of Abraham's visitors, the trinitarian persons who come to embrace the Gentiles. The Spirit, therefore, may rest in the church and anywhere on earth, *without* departing from Christ, *without* exiting the trinitarian communion. The distance between Christ and the Spirit, between Ascension and Pentecost, between heaven and earth must not be seen as absolute, when it is the purpose of the incarnation to cross and embrace it. The distance between Christ and the Spirit, Ascension and Pentecost, heaven and earth is being crossed and embraced. It is becoming a measure not of the infinite distance between creature and Creator, but of the even more infinite activity of the Trinity in incorporating creation

---

17. Gen. 3:24.

18. See now Douglas Farrow, *Ascension and Ecclesia: On the Significance of the Doctrine of the Ascension for Ecclesiology and Christian Cosmology* (Grand Rapids: Eerdmans, 1999).

in its bosom, into its life. The space between Ascension and Pentecost measures not the distance of a departure, but the breadth of an inclusion. Christ receives from the Spirit the freedom to return to the Father with his human nature, and the Spirit gives to the Son the expansion of his own body even when it is with the Father — across extent, duration, and circumstance. If in the Incarnation the Son bids the Father to give him a body by the Spirit, then in the Ascension the Son presents the Father with a body, so that in the Spirit those with bodies may be present to the Father. The Spirit does not cease to cross boundaries, because the Son returns to the Father. The Spirit does not cease to act, because the Son takes his seat. The Spirit does not cease to expand her embrace, because the Son ascends with his humanity. On the contrary: Because the Son has ascended with his humanity, his humanity partakes in the Father's infinite extent, which the Spirit can inhabit. Because the Son sits upon the throne, his humanity partakes in the Father's infinite holiness, which the Spirit can distribute. Because the Son returns to the Father with his humanity, it partakes in the Father's infinite reconciliation, which the Spirit can diffuse. The space between Ascension and Pentecost does not divide the body of Christ from the descent of the Spirit, but opens it out to include more, more, and takes it up to pull higher, higher, as the fire of the Spirit also spreads and leaps.

About-Face

If you have turned to this section looking for conclusions to take away, and without having read Part II, consider how odd that is. Would you turn to the ends of other narratives looking for conclusions — *David Copperfield* or *Pride and Prejudice?* This is an About-Face, because it looks back where we have been.

In Part II, I have sought to portray the Spirit as a character interacting with the Son and the Father in a story. We know this character in her actions, rather than by conceptual analysis. If she is anonymous, as writers like Florensky and Lossky suggest, her anonymity turns out not to be the anonymity of an abstract unknown, but the difficulty and the desire of knowing a concrete person. If she is superfluous, her superfluity turns out to be the gratuity that gives grace and beauty in her interaction with the Son, who through her is allowed to receive what he already has so that others who do not have can share it.

In the resurrection, the Spirit allows the Son to count divinity not a thing to be grasped, but to be received. Because of the Spirit, the Son can be a Messiah who fails, who is crucified, who can rely on Another to advocate for him. The Spirit responds with an unexpected gift, the gift of the Gentiles, who through the Spirit receive what the Jews retain. Thus the Spirit forms human beings into the shape of Christ, who also receives from another what he possesses by right. By life in the Spirit Jews and Gentiles need to receive from one another so that the promise to Abraham might be fulfilled that by him all the nations of the earth should be not curses but blessings for one another.

At the Annunciation, the Son bids the Father to receive a body from the Spirit, so that those with bodies can receive the Spirit from the Son. The

Spirit invokes Mary for the Son to become incarnate, so that a priest may invoke the Spirit for bread and wine to become the Son. This is an exchange of gifts that shows a certain appropriateness in retrospect, but could not be predicted in advance. Like all totemic series, it can be recognized but not anticipated.

In baptism, too, the Son submits to receive from the Spirit the holiness he already enjoys. Because of the Spirit, the Son can be the Holy One who receives his holiness also at the descent of Another. The Spirit responds by descending also upon others who are baptized, who receive from the Spirit a holiness that they, unlike the incarnate Son, do not already enjoy.

In the transfiguration, the Son prays and the Spirit overshadows him, so that when other human beings pray the Spirit may catch them up into the prayer by which alone God may be engaged, the prayer of bidding and gratitude that the Trinity lives.

In the ascension and Pentecost we see the Son living in the Spirit by bidding and withdrawing and waiting, choosing again in confidence to receive, that others may share in the reception.

There is a pattern of action here that can be recognized, as I said, but not predicted. It is action in character, not by necessity and not by reduction to a function. It is a pattern that dies if reduced to statement, that lives rather in narrative and in typology, which is to say, in the incorporation of others into its pattern. We may call it the resting of the Spirit on the Son, if by that we mean not that the Spirit is passive, but that the Spirit is active on the Son who bids and chooses to receive. Medieval authors render the Son and even the Father receptive in giving them receptacles — wounds, wombs, and other orifices — which delight to be filled. In that playful or flirtatious but not needy demand, other human beings may, by the Spirit's innovation, come to be included and received. The Spirit may rest upon the Son, if she is as passive as fire and as still as the wind, as stable as water and as contained as oil. She rests like a bird. She gathers others as she alights.

The resting that incorporates moves up and down an analogical ladder. It characteristically incorporates others into the resurrection, the womb, the transfiguration, and so on. It even works cosmically to incorporate matter. In resting on the Son the Spirit befriends matter, so that Adam's scorn of matter for giving his pretension the lie is overcome, reversed, and turned — *felix culpa* — to ironic good. In resurrection and ascension, in the Stylite and the sacraments, the body says no longer to Adam, "You are a creature not divine by right," but to the second Adam, "You are a creature divine with the Spirit." In separating the Spirit from matter, Christians — especially Protestants — have abstracted the Spirit from the bodies in which God gives Godself to be perceived and manifested.[1] Each of the bodies on which the Spirit rests depends analogically on the body of Christ: the body of Christ in the church, the body of Christ in the Christian, the body of Christ in the sacramental element. In each case the Spirit befriends the body, because it is the body of Christ: in each case the Spirit gives a body to Christ, because Christ bade a body by the Spirit from the Father, that those with bodies might also receive the Spirit. The pattern of the annunciation is that the Spirit invokes Mary to give a body to the Son, a body with which the Logos could provide itself, but which it chooses to receive. The pattern of the baptism is the that the Spirit invokes the Baptist to baptize the Son with a baptism he does not need, but receives for the sake of humanity, just as he receives the Spirit that he already enjoys, also for humanity's sake. The pattern of the transfiguration is that the Spirit for humanity's sake overshadows a body that needs no beatification, in order that human beings who are destined for beatification might satisfy the bodies that lack and yearn for it. The pattern of the resurrection is that the Spirit dwells in the mortal body of the ever-living One, so that what he chooses to receive from the Spirit can belong to other mortals too. The pattern of befriending and descending on the body is not separate from the Incarnation, but the Spirit's innovative and superfluous gift in the Incarnation, grace on grace. What does the Spirit have to give the Son? What the Son delights to receive from the Spirit: the annunciation of his body, the baptism of his body, the transfiguration of his body, the resurrection of his body. Because this body is the body of the Logos, it structures other human beings and the whole world. Because this Spirit is the Creator God, the Giver of Life, it announces and sanctifies, transfigures and gives life to other human beings too and the whole world.

Son and Spirit cooperate in this. What if they could each do it all alone, since each is God? If the Persons sent by the Father cooperate in their missions, and if the works of the Trinity toward the world are indivisible, then why are we not back where we started — where one or the other is dispensable?

If either acted alone, they would not be enacting the trinitarian life. They would not be choosing to receive. They would not be opening up the space that gift-giving requires, the space of gratuity, of superfluity. They would not be enacting a pattern in which the Son chooses to receive what he has, so that others can receive what they lack. There would be, in short, nothing to join; in a word, no *koinonia*. Without *koinonia* there could be no *koinonoi* (II Pet. 1:4), no communers in the divine nature. Son and Spirit would not be drawing the

---

1. See Susan Harvey, "Embodiment in Time and Eternity: A Syriac Perspective," *St. Vladimir's Seminary Quarterly* 43 (1999): 105-30; here, p. 106.

world into the life of God, which the Father attracts by standing at the end of the Way, and the Spirit attracts by eluding our grasp. In enticing others she enlists them: first the Bride, the Church, and then the one who hears, and the one who thirsts:

> The Spirit and the Bride say, "Come." And let the one who hears say, "Come." And let the one who is thirsty come, let the one who desires take the water of life without price (Rev. 22:19).

"The one who desires": every person, every creature, every created thing, for "you open your hand and fulfill the desire of every living thing" (Ps. 145:16) and can raise up children even from the stones of the ground (Matt. 3:9).

The Spirit Rests on the Son in Those
Who Do Not Know How to Pray

Part II of this book began with an exegesis of Romans 8 under the aspect of the resurrection. It concludes here with an exegesis of Romans 8 under the aspect of prayer. Structurally, this section belongs at the end of the chapter on transfiguration — to those on whom the Spirit shines a Taboric light. Rhetorically, however, it belongs to the End — to those on whom the Spirit rests, because they have preceded us in facing it.

You might think that hesychastic and morally transformative versions of transfiguring prayer set a high bar. How are human beings to achieve this? On Christian terms God the Spirit can do anything christoform that she likes with human beings, even deify them; but is there no danger that transformative prayer will come to seem a human achievement, a "work" in the negative sense of the word? The Spirit protects against this, too, in that the Spirit prays "for" human beings, on their behalf, and by taking them up into a trinitarian prayer that is not originally their own, however much the Spirit may make it so. The pattern is that the *Spirit* changes them by prayer, not that they change themselves and earn the Spirit. The key is those "who cannot pray," as in Romans 8. It is the same Spirit who orchestrates the almost heroic prayer of the Son on Tabor, showing the most that can be made of human beings in praise; and who amplifies the apparently feckless prayers of Gentiles and the sick, people who are weak or corrupted or close to death, those who do not even know how to pray.

> Mysteries such as these are not merely theoretical and theological; they are thoroughly practical. It makes a great difference to the act of contemplation whether I see myself as an isolated subject, who, albeit assisted by God's grace, endeavors to understand something of the mysteries of revelation; or

whether, in faith, I have the conviction that my inadequate attempt to understand is supported by the wisdom of the Holy Spirit dwelling within me, that my acts of worship, petition and thanksgiving are borne along and remodeled by the Spirit's infinite and eternal acts, in that ineffable union by which all human doing and being has been lifted up and plunged into the river of eternal life and love. In this case, in a living faith, human inadequacy and ignorance are outbalanced by divine omnipotence and omniscience; it is part of the contemplative's act of faith to cling to this: "for we do not know how to pray as we ought, but the Spirit himself intercedes for us with sighs too deep for words," by calling Abba, Father, not somewhere outside or above us, but actually in us and from within us. This cry is heard by Him who "searches human hearts" [and] who "knows what is the mind of the Spirit." . . .[1]

Von Balthasar continues: "it is impossible to say what comes from the human being and what from God."[2] In this, von Balthasar suggests, the fruits of the Spirit resemble the fruits of a marriage, in which it is hard to say from which party they come, because the parties gradually come to inhabit one another. "Of its very nature, however, this fruit originates in the unspeakable 'mouth-to-mouth' interchange between the Spirit of God and the human spirit, a kind of kiss — *sapientia* comes from *sapere* [to taste] — in which, in faith, the human spirit experiences the distinctive essence of the divine wisdom (which is one with love)."[3] Indeed, the Bible speaks of Christians' "tasting the kindness of the Lord" and their having "tasted the heavenly gift, and become a partaker of the Holy Spirit, and tasted the goodness of the word of God."[4] "Perhaps the only natural analogy of our intimacy with divine truth is that of the union of the sexes."[5] This suggestion finds support elsewhere, too, and from both ends of the spectrum. A writer about the Trinity, Sarah Coakley, has pointed to the free use of sexual metaphors for precisely trinitarian forms of prayer in Origen's account of Romans 8 in his *De Oratione* — while a writer about sexual ethics, Mark Jordan, has pointed out that the spirituality of sex has no better model than prayer.[6]

If every human response to God is credited to God again in the Spirit,

1. Hans Urs von Balthasar, *Prayer,* trans. Graham Harrison (San Francisco: Ignatius, 1986), p. 76, translation slightly modified.

2. Von Balthasar, *Prayer,* p. 78, translation slightly modified.

3. Von Balthasar, *Prayer,* pp. 78-79, translation slightly modified.

4. I Pet. 2:3, Heb. 6:4-5; cf. Von Balthasar, *Prayer,* p. 81.

5. Von Balthasar, *Prayer,* p. 78.

6. Sarah Coakley, "Living into the Mystery of the Holy Trinity: Trinity, Prayer, and Sexuality," *Anglican Theological Review* 80 (1998): 223-32; Mark Jordan, *The Ethics of Sex* (London: Routledge, 2002), last chapter.

does that not destroy the human person's distinctive, personal response? Not if the Person of the Spirit is the very principle of distinctiveness in love, in which all human distinctiveness, to be distinctive, participates. "Our being indwelt by the Spirit of God 'which God gives us' (I Thess. 4:8) presupposes the trinitarian mystery at the heart of absolute Being: the wonder of the mutual indwelling *(circumincessio)* of the divine Persons in a way that does not restrict their personal distinctiveness."[7]

We turn to a distinctively personal case.

Victor Preller usually liked not so much to conceal the complications of his life from students, as to confuse students by revealing them. I remember my great surprise, as a sophomore at Princeton in the fall of 1981, at seeing a long, white strip of celluloid peeping out of Vic's shirt pocket. At that point I knew Vic chiefly as the teacher of a lecture course on approaches to the study of religion, a course that struck fear into the hearts of certain conservative Christians as a "faith-breaker."

"What's that?" I asked, nodding at the plastic strip.

"A collar," Vic replied coyly.

"What for?"

"For celebrating the Eucharist, of course." Vic often used some phrase such as "of course" or "didn't I tell you?" to forestall any more questions before surprise should dissipate.

Distancing maneuvers like the Prelline "of course" were conspicuous by their absence when Vic told me[8] after his bout with throat cancer that he had experienced being lifted up on the prayers of his congregation into the prayer of the Spirit, who prays for those who on account of weakness do not know how to pray as they ought, with sighs and groanings too deep for words (Rom. 8:26). He described this experience as the indwelling of the Spirit, not on his own account (he was too weak, he said, to form the words of the Lord's Prayer, or even the intention to pray), but on the account of others — on account of the faith of the church — and as a proleptic participation in the life of the Trinity, whereby the Spirit catches Christians up into the relationship of the Father and the Son by crying "Abba!" on their behalf (Gal. 4:6; cf. Rom. 8:15-16). Prayer is possible because a certain bidding and graciousness and gratitude takes place already among the Persons of the Trinity, and the Spirit incorporates human beings into that non-Maussian exchange.[9]

---

7. Von Balthasar, *Prayer*, p. 76, translation slightly modified.

8. In April 1998 — distinct from the pneumonia that killed him.

9. See Adrienne von Speyr, "Prayer in the Trinity," in her *World of Prayer*, trans. Graham

We did not discuss how such an experience might be articulated in the terms of the end of Preller's *Divine Science and the Science of God,* where he speaks of the intellect as being "seized by God,"[10] and beatitude as the seizure by the love of the Trinity[11] — or how that seizure makes no exception to the rule that prayer and experience happen through the "ordinary" practices of the church, such as teaching and preaching, since "faith comes by what has been heard" (Rom. 10:17).[12]

Nor did we discuss how such an experience might change or leave unaltered one's reading of Thomas Aquinas or one's use of Wittgenstein. Certainly Vic would have continued to regard such an experience as possible (without ceasing to ascribe it to the Spirit) only on the basis of social practices already well under way, and therefore as a mental, linguistic, and bodily one, or in Thomistic terms, a habit. It was Vic who first pointed out to me Thomas's suspicion of rapture, an "experience" that, because it took the soul out of this world — out of the shared world of society and language — was *in principle* incommunicable to others and therefore of little or no use to sacred teaching.[13] If Aquinas did not deny it outright, that was not only from high regard for scripture, but also because he believed such an "experience" produced nothing stably linguistic enough to deny. Accordingly, Vic did not experience this being caught up as a rapture in the incommunicable sense but as something for which the community and its practices had given him script in advance — language and experience one integral gift — and one that depended on the community not only for its expression but for its very existence. For it was on the prayers of his friends, whether in or abstracted from words, that the Spirit lifted him up.

That Victor Preller performed the life of the Spirit already and habitually before, after, and apart from that experience; that such a life was constituted in a linguistic, communal, bodily practice, including bowing and kneeling and "that funny bit of business on your chest";[14] and that such a life was

---

Harrison (San Francisco: Ignatius, 1985), pp. 28-73. That the trinitarian exchange of gift and gratitude grounds an economy different from that described in Mauss is the burden of John Milbank, "Can a Gift Be Given?" *Modern Theology* 11 (1995): 119-41.

10. Victor Preller, *Divine Science and the Science of God: A Reformulation of Thomas Aquinas* (Princeton: Princeton University Press, 1967), p. 242, citing A. Hayen, *La communication de l'acte de l'être d'après Saint Thomas d'Aquin* (Paris: De Brouwer, 1957).

11. Preller, *Divine Science and the Science of God,* p. 264, in the context of the trinitarian discussions of pp. 254-61.

12. Preller, *Divine Science and the Science of God,* pp. 230-37, 269, citing Aquinas's commentary on that verse.

13. Preller, *Divine Science and the Science of God,* pp. 192-94, citing *ST* I.88.3.

14. The "business of the self-crosser" comes up for characteristically self-ironizing discussion in Preller, *Divine Science,* pp. 7-8.

fleshed out in the sacraments, the collar playing hide-and-seek in his breast pocket: those features were no source of conflict with quasi-mystical experience, but prevenient and incarnate grace. They confirmed his dictum that grace, as a gift that does not violate human nature, is always habitual. Even infused grace, which does not (logically) originate in a habit, nevertheless *issues* in a habit. From Vic's experience, too, a habit emerged seemingly *de novo:* Vic said that the years after his recovery from throat cancer were filled with a sense — a habitual sense, a more or less settled, if waxing and waning disposition — of grateful delight, a delight in (for example) springtime flowers, and thus somewhat at odds with a previous sense (I might add) of burden, unease, and winking cynicism. It was as though he found himself no longer a *Preller* (in German, a fraud, cheat, humbug),[15] if not yet a victor. Now I have just said both that this transformation of Vic's habits had roots in communal practice, and that it emerged seemingly *de novo:* how can that be? I don't think Vic would have found that much of a paradox: In the work of the Spirit, the practice of gratitude was a habit of others before it was a habit of Vic's.

We did not discuss, as I said, how such an experience, one excellently susceptible of Wittgensteinian analysis, might have changed or deepened Vic's reading of Aquinas on the Spirit.[16] And yet the conversation leaves some clues about how to go on. For Aquinas, as for Wittgenstein and for Vic, the work of the Spirit is to be sought in the practices of the community, not because the Spirit is *reduced* to matter or community, but because the Spirit could not be received by human beings, for whom nothing can be in the mind not first in the senses, except through matter. Indeed one might think that for Aquinas as for much of the Western tradition such a reduction threatens. For Aquinas, as for many other Western theologians, the main treatment of the Spirit does not mention the Spirit much, but proceeds under a lower-case, common noun, namely grace. And yet Aquinas leaves the way wide open to read the tractate on grace as one about the Spirit, because he names it "The New Law," the one Paul calls "the law of the Spirit of life in Christ Jesus" (Rom. 8:2), the one that the Spirit writes on the fleshy tablets of the heart (II Cor. 3:3) — biblical tags that open and set up Thomas's account.[17] This phrase of Paul's, adopted so prominently and programmatically by Thomas, also introduces the very chapter, Romans 8 — astute readers will already have noticed — in

---

15. He never mentioned the German sense of his surname, but given his psychology and his love of German it can hardly have escaped his notice.

16. At best implicit in *Divine Science.* The one explicit mention appears on p. 260.

17. Rom. 8:2 appears in the first article of the tractate on grace, at I-II.106.1c, and the writing of laws on the heart is ascribed to the Spirit in a quotation from Augustine in the same place. II Cor. 3:3 appears in the next article at I-II.106.2 *ad* 3.

terms of which Vic described the Spirit's intercession. And this phrase of Paul's, in accord with the emphasis common to Thomas and to Vic, frames the apparently non-linguistic "too deep for words" activity of the Spirit in terms of "law" and "life," terms that recall the rules and forms of life in which alone such an experience, according to Wittgenstein and Vic, can come about. What would it mean to interpret Aquinas's account of grace generally, and not just quasi-rapturous experiences, in terms of the Holy Spirit's dwelling in the heart, catching the human being up into the intratrinitarian life through concrete, bodily — that is, habitual — experience? What if, that is, we recast the tractate on grace without the use of that word, in order to display the Spirit come to rest on a body, and issuing therefore in habit?

At the risk of explaining the obscure by the more obscure, I note a comparison between post-Augustinian talk of grace and post-Fregean talk of meaning. Like meaning, "grace, for the Christian believer, is a transformation [of a form of life] that depends in large part on knowing yourself to be seen in a certain way: as significant, as wanted."[18] As Aquinas would put it, grace is the meaning that God bestows, by which God arranges not primarily words, but states of affairs *(res)* or forms of life *(habitus)* to signify.[19] Like "meaning" in Wittgenstein's account, "grace" is a concept that took on a life of its own as its function of helping in controversy or clearing a space for debate was forgotten. As analysis of meaning went endlessly round and round after Frege attended to *Sinn* and *Bedeutung,* so too grace arose as a subject of analysis after the Pelagian controversy in the West.[20] After Pelagius, "grace and liberty . . . are transformed into two mutually exclusive concepts which then have to be reconciled, as if they were two objects exterior to one another."[21] After Frege, meaning, too, seemed to be a thing exterior to the discourse that enacted it. Both grace and meaning raise questions about the rules of a language-game, or in indigenous medieval terms, about the *modus loquendi theologorum.*[22] Both

18. Rowan Williams, "The Body's Grace," now in Eugene F. Rogers, Jr., ed., *Theology and Sexuality: Classic and Contemporary Readings* (Oxford: Blackwell, 2002), pp. 309-21; here, p. 311.

19. I.1.10. The idea that *logos,* small "l," might be translated in a christocentric anthropology as a form of life occurred to me while reading John Boswell's introduction to Chris Glaser, *Uncommon Calling* (Louisville: Westminster John Knox, 1988), now reprinted as "Logos and Biography," in Rogers, *Theology and Sexuality,* pp. 356-61, here, pp. 359-61.

20. For a typical, pox-on-both-houses account of Protestant and Catholic controversies about grace from an Eastern Orthodox theologian, see Vladimir Lossky, *Mystical Theology of the Eastern Church* (Crestwood, N.Y.: St. Vladimir's Seminary Press, 1976), pp. 197-99.

21. Lossky, *Mystical Theology,* p. 198.

22. It would be interesting to trace the *Wirkungsgeschichte* of that phrase or associated ideas from Luther through Dilthey to see whether Luther's thought about theological speech has in fact any historical influence on Wittgenstein, or whether they have simply an interest in common. I

grace and meaning can become a suspect *tertium quid*. In both cases, the way forward is sometimes to omit rather than obtrude the troublesome term.[23]

Raising anew the question of the proper *modus loquendi theologorum* or rules of the theological language-game about grace and the Spirit, Robert Jenson has recently posed it as an alternative, "grace or the Spirit." Quoting Augustine, Jenson notes that "The Holy Spirit's gift is nothing other than the Holy Spirit."[24] Noting that "It is, to be sure, an audacious doctrine," Jenson quotes Augustine again joining the indwelling of the Holy Spirit to charity in the heart: "Therefore the love *(dilectio)* which is of God and which is God is properly the Holy Spirit; by him that love of God *(Dei caritas)* is diffused in our hearts by which the whole Trinity indwells us."[25] With odd exceptions like Luther and Edwards, Jenson finds that "The doctrine was *too* audacious for subsequent theology," becoming an "option" in Peter Lombard's *Sentences,* which asked (rather than affirmed) whether "the Holy Spirit is himself the love . . . by which we love God and the neighbor."[26] Although Jenson admits the point of it,[27] Thomas's insistence that charity must (also) be our own possession, rather than the Holy Spirit *and nothing else* becomes suspect.[28] Is the alternative "grace or the Spirit" a useful distinction, or a failure of nerve? Does the language of grace "betray an impersonal conception of the Spirit"?[29]

In Thomas Aquinas, the discussion of the Holy Spirit and the human being proceeds mostly in terms of grace, but the scheme is still visible by which the Spirit is interior to ("indwells") the bodily habits that enact it. Indeed, the more Latin, less King James word for the Spirit's interiority to the body is even more telling: The Spirit quite precisely and explicitly in-habits it.[30] Can

---

have often wondered, for example, whether George Lindbeck could not have replaced all the points in *The Nature of Doctrine* made by reference to Wittgenstein with points made by reference to Luther. The result would perhaps prove more persuasive to some, and less persuasive to others.

23. For more, see Jeffrey Stout, "What Is the Meaning of a Text," *New Literary History* 13 (1982): 3-8.

24. Augustine, *De Trinitate* 15.36, at Jenson, *Systematic Theology* I (New York: Oxford, 1997), p. 148. Thanks to Fergus Kerr for reminding me of this discussion.

25. *De Trinitate* 15.32, very slightly modified from Jenson's translation.

26. Jenson, *Systematic Theology,* pp. 148-49, quotes Lombard, *Sentences* 1.d.xvii.2 and cites Luther, *WA* 1:224-28 and his own book on Edwards, *America's Theologian* (New York: Oxford, 1988), pp. 65-78.

27. Jenson, *Systematic Theology,* p. 149, esp. n. 22.

28. II-II.23.2.

29. Jenson, *Systematic Theology,* p. 149.

30. "Habitare," *ST* I.43.3. For more, see D. Juvenal Merriell, *To the Image of the Trinity: A Study in the Development of Aquinas' Teaching* (Toronto: Pontifical Institute of Medieval Studies, 1990), pp. 80-94 and 226-36. For Preller's account, see *Divine Science,* pp. 255-59.

you do without the language of grace altogether? Not quite. As with the language of meaning, sometimes you need it to get around certain other problems. Are there places in the discourse where it distracts? Yes, on the evidence of centuries of controversialists who have been so distracted. Can Thomas get along without it for long periods where he might otherwise use it? Yes, in his biblical commentaries.

In his *Commentary on Romans,* chapter 8, Thomas comments in context upon the verse from which the so-called tractate on "grace" takes its structural place and its proper name.[31] Thomas entitles his treatment in the *Summa* the *"Nova Lex,"* or New Law. Structurally, therefore, he places it at the end of the tractate on Law, the external regulation of human acts, as apparently opposed to their internal source, or the virtues. But since the New Law is the Law of the Spirit (Rom. 8:2) which is written on the heart,[32] the New Law caps the treatise on Law by overcoming the distinction between the interior and exterior springs of human action. The Spirit moves the heart *from the outside* and *most internally,* since it is a feature of God's transcendence of creatures to be more internal to them than they are to themselves.[33] Historically, it may be in commenting or preparing to comment upon this passage that Thomas hit upon the placement and title of the so-called treatise on grace: a placement and title that display the possibility of seeing the Spirit as the rule or form of the new life.[34]

The chapter in Romans is about the Spirit from beginning to end. It opens with the identification of "law" with the "Spirit," so foreign is it to Augustinian and Lutheran oppositions between those terms, which owe much, of course, to other bits of Paul. But here Paul has cast the law not as the *nomos* or *Gesetz* that accuses the conscience but as Torah, the law that the righteous person "delights to walk in."[35] The chapter in Thomas's commentary begins

31. Thomas Aquinas, *In Romanos,* in *Super epistolas S. Pauli lectura,* 8th rev. ed., ed. Raphael Cai (Turin: Marietti, 1953). Hereafter *In Rom.* with verse and Marietti paragraph number.

32. Which Thomas frequently quotes from Jer. 31, as in his commentary on Rom. 8:2 and elsewhere.

33. Kathryn Tanner, *God and Creation: Tyranny or Empowerment?* (Oxford: Blackwell, 1988), pp. 44-48 and Richard A. Norris, Jr., *God and World in Early Christian Theology* (New York: The Seabury Press, 1965), pp. 84-86.

34. This is admittedly a conjecture for which my evidence is circumstantial. According to the best datings known to me, Thomas was at work on the *Summa* I-II (which ends with the tractate on grace) in 1271, and on his second *Commentary on Romans* — the one we have — between 1271 or 1272 and 1273. Cf. the appendices in Jean-Pierre Torrell, *Saint Thomas Aquinas,* vol. I, *The Person and His Work,* trans. Robert Royal (Washington, D.C.: Catholic University Press, 1996).

35. So Rom. 8:4 recalls the Psalms, e.g., Ps. 1:1-3: "Blessed is the one who walks not in the counsel of the wicked . . . ; but delights in the law of the Lord, and on that law meditates day and

with talk of grace, because Thomas can hardly help but think of grace as counterpart to "law," and he is perhaps working out how well the Augustinian discourse about grace can be eliminated in favor of the Romans 8 discourse about the law of the Spirit by which one prospers, by which the Spirit "inhabits" the heart (Rom. 8:9, 11). For the chapter from which Thomas takes the title and structure of his so-called tractate on grace never uses the word. By the middle of Thomas's commentary on the chapter — by the time he comes to the passage about the Spirit praying for those who cannot form even the words of the Our Father — he has accordingly so conformed his exposition to Paul's language that the language of grace disappears.[36]

The Vulgate of Romans 8:1 unavoidably lands Thomas in the controversies over grace. For it translates the Greek *katákrima,* "there is now no condemnation," with the technical term *damnatio.* Thomas finds himself squarely in a tradition of commentary in which "having" grace makes all the difference between salvation and damnation — even if Paul's context specifies Jews and Gentiles. Although Paul is not in fact delivering a disquisition on "grace" as term of art and disputed question, it takes Thomas a while to notice.

Still, it's surprising how fast Thomas emerges from the briar patch in which the Latin had landed him. Already by the middle of commenting on the second verse he has found the plain air of a discourse in which the Trinity meets the Torah without the mediation of a third term:

> In "For the law of the spirit," law can mean in one way the Holy Spirit, in this sense: The law of the spirit means the law, which is the Spirit; for law is given for this, that by it human beings be led to the good, whence even the Philosopher says, that the intent of the lawgiver is to make the citizens good, which indeed human law accomplishes, only announcing what ought to be done; but the Holy Spirit inhabiting the mind not only teaches what ought to be done by illuminating the intellect about things to be done, but also inclines the affect toward acting rightly. "For the Paraclete, the Holy Spirit, which the Father will send in my name will teach you all things" [John 14:26], with respect to the first point, "and urge you to all things," with respect to the second, "whatsoever I will have told you." In another way, "the law of the spirit" can mean the proper effect of the Holy Spirit, namely faith operating by love, which of course also teaches interiorly about things to be

---

night. That one is like a tree planted by streams of water, that yields its fruit in due season, and its leaf does not wither. In all that he does, he prospers."

36. For other instances in which Thomas changes his vocabulary to conform to Paul, see Otto Hermann Pesch, "Paul as Professor of Theology: The Image of the Apostle in St. Thomas's Theology," *The Thomist* 38 (1974).

done. And according to this reading the law of the spirit is called the New Law, which is either the Holy Spirit itself, or [what] the Holy Spirit does in our hearts. "For I will give my law in your gut and I will write it upon your heart [Jer. 31:33]."[37]

The law of life either is the Spirit, or the effect of the Spirit habituating the human being. Law and the Spirit are one, as in Torah, and Spirit issues in habit. We could not wish for a lovelier statement. Thomas even has the good judgment to quote a passage from John naming all three persons of the Trinity, intimating that the true law, the one that succeeds in leading human beings toward the good, is already a participation in that ruled community that is the trinitarian fellowship.

By the time the commentary arrives at the passage to which Vic referred, Thomas has emerged even farther from a discourse of grace into a discourse of the Spirit and human infirmity, in the context of impending death.[38] As in Vic's experience — had he read this passage? — the Lord's Prayer is the prayer we cannot pray.[39] The language of grace disappears because human agency is too bare and the Spirit too present.

The Spirit still does not replace or violate human beings. Thomas's language is of "help" and "prayer." Not that they pray for help: that prayer is the result of help. The language of "help" implies that there are still two. The language of "prayer" is that rational *dependence* upon another rational person or Person; specifically, it is still a learned, communal, linguistic prayer that the Spirit prays for human beings; the Spirit does not enrapture them, but it is a human thing that the Spirit does for them. The Holy Spirit simply *helps* (*adjuvat*). It does not even particularly help human beings to do something, as if they and the Holy Spirit were two creatures on the same level, two hands pulling on one rope. Instead, the *adjuvare* of the Holy Spirit appears absolutely, that is, without qualification. The help of the Spirit is global: it holds creatures in being; indeed, it *assumes* them.[40] In this passage of support at greatest need, the language of grace falls away, and the language of the Spirit is just as audacious as anyone could wish.

It approaches, perhaps, the audacity of glory: the Spirit, in crying "Abba!" in sighs too deep for (this-worldly) words makes human beings capable of the divine Word, incorporates them into Christ's intratrinitarian address to the

37. *In Rom.* 8:2, ##602-3.

38. *In Rom.* 8:26, #687: "Dictum est quod per Spiritum Sanctum vivificabuntur nostra mortalia corpora, quando auferetur a nobis nostra infirmitas."

39. #690, for several paragraphs.

40. *In Rom.* #687 "Spiritus quoque elevit me, et assumpsit me," quoting Ezek. 3:14.

Father. Then indeed there is no need for the condescension of grace; human beings need no words if at last they possess the Word, God's own principle of intelligibility; they need no room of their own to act in, when they inhabit God's infinite roominess. Then they see God no longer by a form accidental to their nature, but by a participation become intrinsic; they see God by God's essence, or "as he is." Just that cannot, of course, be intelligibly communicated in this life, but is a radically eschatological matter.

As there is reputedly a linguistic and a mystical Wittgenstein, so there is assuredly a linguistic and a mystical Aquinas, and even a mystical Preller. If I may put his own words into his mouth, what he experienced was a *"quasi quoddam inchoativum* of a future intelligibility."[41] The piling up of qualifications was remarkable for Aquinas and noted by Preller with satisfaction. "A more guarded statement would be difficult to imagine: *quasi* is 'as if' language; *quoddam* is 'sort-of' language; and *inchoativum* signifies a first movement or 'a germ of a beginning.'"[42] So Aquinas practices the way of remotion; in piling up qualifications, he takes language away. About the light of glory, he keeps volubly silent by over-qualification. In the language of grace, too, Aquinas practices remotion, but now in a more positive way: The language of grace is inadequate to the Spirit, but (like "meaning") it is not dispensable. It has its uses. "Grace" marks a reserve — even a reticence about the Spirit — strictly appropriate to this life. The Spirit would blow our minds, or enrapture us; it must be passed over in silence.[43] But the language of grace does not silence human beings; rather it practices the reserve that alone permits language *in via*. The "Abba" that the Spirit cries is her Word *in patria*. That is why Vic could have applied to himself the words with which he closes *Divine Science:* he remained "in a kind of shadow of ignorance *(quadam tenebra ignorantiae),* by which ignorance, insofar as it pertains to this life, we are best conjoined to God *(optime Deo coniungimur)* . . . and this is the cloud in which God is said to dwell *(habitare)*."[44] Indeed this experienced ignorance was one by which, he might have said, God habituated and indwelt him, so that, well conjoined, he would not have been wrong to suspect in himself what he asserted of others, "a kind of beginning, as it were" of beatitude.[45]

41. Preller, *Divine Science,* p. 269.

42. Preller, *Divine Science,* p. 239, quoting the Latin from *In Heb.* 11, 1 and the definition from Roy Deferrari, *A Lexicon of St. Thomas Aquinas* (Washington: Catholic University Press, 1948), *s.v. inchoativus.*

43. Preller, *Divine Science,* pp. 193-94, citing I.88.3.

44. Preller, *Divine Science,* p. 271, quoting *In Sent.* I.vii.1.1.

45. Preller, *Divine Science,* p. 269.

Sources Cited or Consulted

For the convenience of general readers and scholars trained in modern Christian thought, I have listed ancient and modern titles together, and I have mostly but not consistently listed English translations first, where available, followed by the edition in the original language, if cited. Although Syriac and Russian sources appear to make it possible to follow up the notes, I do not read those languages myself.

I have marked with an asterisk (*) items that reward further reading.

Abbreviations

ANF   *The Ante-Nicene Fathers.* Ed. Alexander Roberts and James Donaldson. Reprint ed. Grand Rapids, Mich.: Wm. B. Eerdmans Publishing Company, 1983. Available online at http://www.ccel.org/fathers2.

CSEL   *Corpus Scriptorum Ecclesiasticorum Latinorum.* Vienna, 1866-.

NPNF   *A Select Library of the Nicene and Post-Nicene Fathers of the Christian Church* [First series]. Ed. Philip Schaff et al. Reprint ed. Grand Rapids, Mich.: Wm. B. Eerdmans Publishing Company, 1983. Available online at http://www.ccel.org/fathers2.

NPNF2   *A Select Library of the Nicene and Post-Nicene Fathers of the Christian Church.* Second series. Ed. Philip Schaff et al. Reprint ed. Grand Rapids, Mich.: Wm. B. Eerdmans Publishing Company, 1983. http://www.ccel.org/fathers2.

PG   *Patrologia Graeca.* Ed. J. P. Migne. Paris: Migne, 1857-66.

PL   *Patrologia Latina.* Ed. J. P. Migne. Paris: Migne, 1844-91.

Abdisho bar Brika. In *Woodbrooke Studies: Christian Documents in Syriac, Arabic, and Garshuni.* Edited and translated with a critical apparatus by Alphonse Mingana and with introductions by Rendel Harris. 7 vols. Cambridge: W. Heffer & Sons, 1927-34.

Acharya, Francis, ed. *Prayer with the Harp of the Spirit: The Prayer of the Asian Churches.* 4 vols. Vagamon, India: Kurisumala Ashram, 1982-86.

Acta Conciliorum Oecumenicorum. Ed. Edvardus Schwartz. Berlin: De Gruyter, 1935.

Addai and Mari — the Anaphora of the Apostles: A Text for Students. With Introduction, Translation, and Commentary by Bryan D. Spinks. Bramcote, Nottinghamshire: Grove Books, 1980.

Alexiou, Margaret. *After Antiquity: Greek Language, Myth, and Metaphor.* Ithaca, N.Y.: Cornell University Press, 2002.

Alison, James. *Faith beyond Resentment: Fragments Catholic and Gay.* New York: Crossroad Publishing Company, 2001.

Amadeus of Lausanne. *Magnificat: Homilies in Praise of the Blessed Virgin Mary by Bernard of Clairvaux and Amadeus of Lyon.* Trans. Marie-Bernard Saïd and Grace Perigo. Cistercian Fathers Series 18. Kalamazoo, Mich.: Cistercian Publications, 1979. *Homiliae octo felicis memoriae Amadei episcopi Lausannensis de laudibus beatae Mariae.* Ed. G. Bavaud. Sources chrétiennes, 72. Paris: Editions du Cerf, 1960.

Ambrose of Milan. *The Holy Spirit.* In *Theological and Dogmatic Works.* Translated by Roy J. Deferrari. The Fathers of the Church series, vol. 44. Washington, D.C.: Catholic University of America Press, 1963.

————. *In Lucam 7.* In *Corpus scriptorum ecclesiasticorum latinorum 32/4.*

————. *De obitu Valentiniani.* Ed. O. Faller. CSEL 73, 1964.

Ambrosiaster. *Commentarius in epistulas paulinas.* Ed. Heinrich Joseph Vogels et al. CSEL 81/1-3, 1966-69.

Anaphorae Syriacae. 6 vols. in 2. Rome: Institutum Pontificium Studiorum Orientalium, 1939-.

Anonymous. "Ancient Paschal Homily." *Sources Chrétiennes* 27.

Anselm of Canterbury. *Why God Became Human.* In *A Scholastic Miscellany: Anselm to Ockham.* Ed. and trans. by Eugene R. Fairweather. Library of Christian Classics, vol. 10. Philadelphia: Westminster Press, 1956.

Arnaiz, Ioseph. "Maria Sponsa Spiritus Sancti (Lc. 1,35)." *De Beata Maria in evangelis synopticis. Maria in Sacra Scriptura,* vol. 4. Rome: Pontificia Academia Mariana Internationalis, 1967.

Arranz, Miguel, ed. *L'Euchologio costantinopolitano agli inizi del secolo XI: hagiasmatarion & archieratikon (rituale & pontificale): con l'aggiunta del Leiturgikon (messale).* Rome: Pontificia Università Gregoriana, 1996.

Arranz, Miguel. "Les prières de la Gonyklisia ou de la Génuflexion du jour de la Pentecôte dans l'ancien Euchologe byzantin." *Orientalia Christiana Periodica* 48 (1982): 92-123.

Assemani, Giuseppe Luigi. *Codex liturgicus ecclesiae universae . . . occidentis & orientis.* 4 vols. in 13. Reprint ed. Westmead, Hampshire, 1968-69.

Athanasius of Alexandria. *Festal Letters. PG* 26.

————. *On the Incarnation of the Word.* In *Christology of the Later Fathers.* Ed. Edward R. Hardy. Library of Christian Classics, vol. 3. Philadelphia: Westminster Press, 1954.

————. *The Letters of Saint Athanasius concerning the Holy Spirit.* Translated with Introduction and Notes by C. R. B. Shapland. New York: Philosophical Library, 1951.

————. Orations against the Arians. NPNF2, vol. 5.

Augustine. *Commentary on the Psalms.* In NPNF 8.

————. *Confessions.* Trans. Albert C. Outler. Philadelphia: Westminster Press, 1955.

———. *De Trinitate.* Trans. Stephen McKenna. Fathers of the Church, 45. Washington, D.C.: Catholic University Press, 1963.

———. *Homilies on the Epistle of John.* In NPNF 7. *In Epistolam I Joan.* PL 35.

———. *On the Letter and the Spirit.* In NPNF 5.

———. *Sermo* 128, "In natali Domini." PL 39.

Ayres, Lewis. "The Fundamental Grammar of Augustine's Trinitarian Theology." In *Augustine and His Critics.* Ed. Robert Dodaro and George Lawless. London: Routledge, 2000.

———. *Nicaea and Its Legacy: An Approach to Fourth-Century Trinitarian Theology.* Oxford: Oxford University Press, 2004.

———. "On Not Three People: The Structure of Gregory of Nyssa's Trinitarian Theology as Seen in *Ad Abblabium: On Not Three Gods.*" *Modern Theology* 18 (2002): 445-74.

Baal, J. van. "Offering, Sacrifice and Gift." *Numen* 23 (1976): 161-78.

Baker, Anthony. "Making Perfection." Ph.D. dissertation, University of Virginia, 2004.

Balai. In *S. Ephraemi Syri, Rabulae Episcopi Edesseni, Balai aliorumque opera selecta.* Ed. J. J. Overbeck. Oxford: Oxford University Press, 1865.

Balthasar, Hans Urs von. *Elucidations.* Trans. John Riches. San Francisco: Ignatius, 1998.

———. *Explorations in Theology III: Creator Spirit.* Trans. Brian McNeil. San Francisco: Ignatius Press, 1993.

———. *Herrlichkeit: Eine theologische Äesthetik.* 3 vols. in 7. Einsiedeln, Switzerland: Johannes-Verlag, 1961-69. *The Glory of the Lord: A Theological Aesthetics.* Ed. John Riches and Joseph Fessio. 7 vols. San Francisco: Ignatius Press, 1982-89.

———. *Prayer.* Trans. Graham Harrison. San Francisco: Ignatius Press, 1986.

———. *Presence and Thought: An Essay on the Religious Philosophy of Gregory of Nyssa.* Trans. Mark Sebanc. San Francisco: Ignatius Press, 1995.

———. *Theodramatik.* 4 vols. in 5. Einsiedeln: Johannes-Verlag, 1973-83.

Bar Hebraeus. *Bar Hebraeus's Book of the Dove.* Trans. A. J. Wensinck. Leyden: E. J. Brill, 1919.

Barnes, Michel René. "Eunomius of Cyzicus and Gregory of Nyssa: Two Traditions of Transcendent Causality." *Vigiliae Christianae* 52 (1998): 59-87.

Barth, Karl. *Come Holy Spirit.* Grand Rapids: Eerdmans, 1978.

———. *Dogmatics in Outline.* Trans. G. T. Thompson. London: SCM Press, 1949.

———. *Epistle to the Romans.* 6th rev. ed. Trans. Edwin C. Hoskyns. London and New York: Oxford, 1933.

———. *The Holy Spirit and Christian Life: The Theological Basis of Ethics.* Trans. Birch Hoyle. Louisville: Westminster/John Knox, 1993.

———. *Die Kirchliche Dogmatik.* 4 vols. in 13. Zürich: Evangelischer Verlag/Zollikon: 1932-70. ET: *Church Dogmatics.* 4 vols. in 13. Trans. G. W. Bromiley et al. Edinburgh: T&T Clark, 1936-75.

———. *Kurze Erzählung des Römerbriefes.* Munich: Christian-Kaisar-Verlag, 1956. ET: *Shorter Commentary on Romans.* London: SCM and Richmond: John Knox, 1959.

———. *A Late Friendship: The Letters of Karl Barth and Carl Zuckmayer.* Trans. Geoffrey Bromiley. Grand Rapids: Eerdmans, 1982. Original in Karl Barth, *Briefe 1961-1968. Gesammtausgabe: Briefe,* vol. 5. Ed. Jürgen Fangmeier and Hinrich Stoevesandt. Zürich: Theologischer Verlag, 1975.

Basil of Caesarea. *On the Holy Spirit.* Crestwood, NY: St. Vladimir's Seminary Press, 1980.

Basile de Césarée. *Homélies sur l'Hexaéméron.* Ed. and trans. Stanislas Giet. Paris: Éditions du Cerf, 1949.

Bauerschmidt, Fritz. "Michel de Certeau and Theology." *Modern Theology* 12 (1996): 1-26.

Bavel, Tarsicius J. van. "The Anthropology of Augustine." *Milltown Studies* 19/20 (1987): 25-39.

Beck, Edmund. "Le baptême chez S. Ephrem." *L'Orient Syrien* 2 (1956): 111-36.

———. *Die Theologie des Hl. Ephraem in seinen Hymnen über den Glauben.* Studia Anselmiana, n. 21. Vatican City: Libreria Vaticana, 1949.

Bedjan, Paul, ed. *Homiliae selectae Mar-Jacobi Sarugensis.* 5 vols. Paris and Leipzig: Otto Harrassowitz, 1908-10.

Benedict. *The Rule of St. Benedict in English.* Ed. Timothy Fry. New York: Vintage Books, 1998.

Bernard of Clairvaux. *Homilia in laudibus Virginis Matris.* In *Sancti Bernardi Opera* IV. Ed. Jean Leclercq and H. Rochais. Rome: Editiones cistercienses, 1966. *Homilies in Praise of the Blessed Virgin Mary.* Trans. Marie-Bernard Saïd. Kalamazoo, Mich.: Cistercian Publications, 1993.

Bettenson, Henry, and Chris Maunder, eds. *Documents of the Christian Church.* 3rd ed. Oxford: Oxford University Press, 1999.

Boethius. *Consolatio philosophiae.* Ed. James J. O'Donnell. 2d ed. Bryn Mawr, Pa.: Bryn Mawr College, 1990. *The Consolation of Philosophy,* trans. Richard Green. New York: Macmillan, 1962.

Boguslawski, Steven Chrysostom. "Aquinas' Commentary on Romans 9–11." Ph.D. dissertation. Yale University, 1999.

Boismard, M. E. *Comment Luc a remanié l'évangelie de Jean.* Paris: J. Gabalda, 2001.

Bosch, David J. *Transforming Mission: Paradigm Shifts in Theology of Mission.* Maryknoll, NY: Orbis Books, 1991.

Boswell, John. "Introduction" to *Uncommon Calling.* By Chris Glaser. Louisville: Westminster John Knox, 1988. Reprinted as "Logos and Biography." In *Theology and Sexuality.* Ed. Eugene F. Rogers, Jr. Oxford: Blackwell Publishers, 2002.

———. *Same-Sex Unions in Premodern Europe.* New York: Villard Press, 1994.

———. *The Kindness of Strangers: The Abandonment of Children in Western Europe from Late Antiquity to the Renaissance.* New York: Vintage Books, 1990.

Boulnois, Marie-Odile. *Le Paradoxe trinitaire chez Cyrille d'Alexandrie: Herméneutique, analyses philosophiques, et argumentation théologique.* Paris: Institut d'Études Augustiniennes and Turnhout: Brepols, 1994.

Bouyer, Louis. *Eucharist: Theology and Spirituality of the Eucharistic Prayer.* Translated by Charles Underhill Quinn. Notre Dame, Ind.: University of Notre Dame Press, 1968.

Bowlin, John R. *Contingency and Fortune in Aquinas's Ethics.* Cambridge and New York: Cambridge University Press, 1999.

Braaten, Carl, and Robert Jenson, eds. *Union with Christ: The New Finnish Interpretation of Luther.* Grand Rapids: Eerdmans, 1998.

Bray, Gerald, ed. *Ancient Christian Commentary on Scripture.* New Testament vol. 6, *Romans.* Downers Grove, Ill.: InterVarsity, 1998.

Brightman, F. E., ed. *Eastern Liturgies, Being the Texts Original or Translated of the Principal Liturgies of the Church*. Piscataway, N.J.: Gorgias Press, 2002. Facsimile reprint of *Liturgies Eastern and Western*, vol. I, Eastern Liturgies. Oxford: Clarendon Press, 1896.

Brock, Sebastian P. "Baptismal Themes in the Writings of Joseph of Serugh." In *Symposium Syriacum 1976*. Ed. Arthur Vööbus. Rome: Pontificium Institutum Orientalium Studiorum, 1978.

——. "A Brief Guide to the Main Editions and Translations of the Works of Saint Ephrem." *The Harp: A Review of Syriac and Oriental Studies* (Kottayam, India) 3 (1990): 1-29.

——. *A Brief Outline of Syriac Literature*. Baker Hill, Kottayam, Kerala, India: St. Ephrem Ecumenical Research Institute, 1997.

——. "The Holy Spirit as Feminine in Early Syriac Literature." In *After Eve*. Ed. Janet Martin Soskice. London: Marshall-Pickering, 1990.

*——. *The Holy Spirit in the Syrian Baptismal Tradition*. 2d rev. and enlarged ed. Poona, India: Anita Printers, 1998.

——. *The Luminous Eye: The Spiritual World Vision of Saint Ephrem*. Rev. ed. Cistercian Studies Series, 124. Kalamazoo, MI: Cistercian Publications, 1992.

——. "Mary and the Eucharist: An Oriental Perspective." *Sobornost* 1 (1979): 50-59.

——. "The Mysteries in the Side of Christ." *Sobornost* 7 (1978): 462-72.

——. *Spirituality in the Syriac Tradition*. Moran Etho Series No. 2. Kerala, India: St. Ephrem Ecumenical Research Institute, 1989.

——. *Studies in Syriac Spirituality*. The Syrian Churches Series, vol. 13. Poona, India: Anita Printers, 1988.

——. "Studies in the Early History of the Syrian Orthodox Baptismal Liturgy." *Journal of Theological Studies*, n.s., 23 (1972): 16-64.

——. *Syriac Studies: A Classified Bibliography (1960-1990)*. Kaslik, Lebanon: Parole de l'Orient, 1996.

Brock, Sebastian P., trans. *The Harp of the Spirit: Eighteen Poems of Saint Ephrem*. 2nd enlarged ed. San Bernardino, Calif.: Borgo Press, 1983.

Brock, Sebastian P., ed. and trans. *The Church's Bridal Feast: A Syriac Hymn for Epiphany*. Parallel Syriac and English. Oxford: The Jericho Press, 1992.

——. *The Syriac Fathers on Prayer and the Spiritual Life*. Cistercian Studies Series, no. 101. Kalamazoo, Mich.: Cistercian Publications, 1987.

Brown, David. "Trinitarian Personhood and Individuality." In *Trinity, Incarnation, and Atonement: Philosophical and Theological Essays*. Ed. Ronald J. Feenstra and Cornelius Plantinga, Jr. Notre Dame, Ind.: University of Notre Dame Press, 1989.

Bulgakov, Sergei. *Philosophy of Economy: The World as Household*. Trans. and ed. Catherine Evtuhov. New Haven: Yale University Press, 2000. Russian: *Filosofia Khoziastva*. Moscow: Put', 1912. Reprinted New York: Chalidze Publications, 1982.

Bulgakov, Sergii. "The Economic Ideal." In *Sergii Bulgakov: Towards a Russian Political Theology*. Ed. Rowan D. Williams. Edinburgh: T&T Clark, 1999. Russian: "Ob ekonomicheskom ideale." In *Ot marksizma k idealizmu*. St. Petersburg, Tvo "Obschchestvennaia Pol'za," 1903. Reprint Frankfurt a. M.: Posev, 1968.

Bulgakov, Sergius (Serge Boulgakof). *Le Paraclet.* Trans. Constantin Andronikov. Paris: Aubier, 1944.

Bulgakov, Sergius. *The Bride of the Lamb.* Trans. Boris Jakim. Grand Rapids: Eerdmans and Edinburgh: T&T Clark, 2002.

———. *The Comforter.* Trans. Boris Jakim. Grand Rapids, Mich.: Eerdmans, 2004.

———. *Svet nevechernii* [*The Unfading Light*]. Moscow: Put', 1917. Reprint Westmead, England: Gregg International Publishers, 1971. French translation: *La lumière sans déclin.* Trans. Constantin Andronikof. Lausanne: L'Age d'Homme, 1990.

Burgess, Stanley M. *The Holy Spirit: Ancient Christian Traditions.* Peabody, Mass.: Hendrickson Publishers, 1984.

———. *The Holy Spirit: Eastern Christian Traditions.* Peabody, Mass.: Hendrickson Publishers, 1989.

Burns, J. Patout, and Gerald M. Fagin, eds. *The Holy Spirit.* Message of the Fathers of the Church, 3. Wilmington, Del.: Michael Glazier, 1984.

Burrus, Virginia. *Begotten, Not Made: Conceiving Manhood in Late Antiquity.* Stanford, Calif.: Stanford University Press, 2000.

———. "Queer Father." In *Queer Theology.* Ed. Gerard Loughlin. London: Routledge, forthcoming.

Butler, Judith. "Contingent Foundations." In *Feminist Contentions: A Philosophical Exchange.* Edited by Seyla Benhabib et al. London and New York: Routledge, 1995.

Bynum, Caroline Walker. *Jesus as Mother: Studies in the Spirituality of the High Middle Ages.* Berkeley, Calif.: University of California Press, 1982.

Cabasilas, Nicholas. *The Life in Christ.* Translated by Carmino J. deCatanzaro. Crestwood, NY: St. Vladimir's Seminary Press, 1974.

Calvin, John. *Commentary on the Epistle to the Romans.* Trans. Francis Sibson. Philadelphia: J. Whetham, 1836. Repr. LBS Archival Products, 1990.

———. *Institutes of the Christian Religion.* Ed. John T. McNeill. Trans. Ford Lewis Battles. 2 vols. Library of Christian Classics, vols. 20-21. Philadelphia: Westminster, 1960.

Cantalamessa, Raniero. *Come, Creator Spirit: Meditations on the* Veni Creator. Trans. Denis Barrett and Marlene Barrett. Collegeville, Minn.: The Liturgical Press, 2003.

———. *Mary: Mirror of the Church.* Trans. Frances Lonergan Villa. Collegeville, Minn.: The Liturgical Press, 1992.

———. *Il mistero della Trasfigurazione.* Milan: Ancora Editrice, 1999.

———. *Lo Spirito Santo nella vita di Gesù: il mistero dell'unzione,* 2d ed. Milan: Editrice Ancora, 1983. A shorter version is translated as *The Holy Spirit in the Life of Jesus: The Mystery of Christ's Baptism.* Collegeville, Minn.: The Liturgical Press, 1994.

Cary, Phillip. "On Behalf of Classical Trinitarianism: A Critique of Rahner on the Trinity." *The Thomist* 30 (1992): 365-406.

Casurella, Anthony. *The Johannine Paraclete in the Church Fathers: A Study in the History of Exegesis.* Beiträge zur Geschichte der biblischen Exegese. Tübingen: J. C. B. Mohr (Paul Siebeck), 1983.

Cavanaugh, William. *Torture and Eucharist.* Oxford: Blackwell Publishers, 1998.

Certeau, Michel de. "La Rupture instauratrice." In *La Faiblesse de croire.* Ed. Luce Giard Paris: Seuil, 1987.

————. "The Weakness of Believing: From the Body to Writing, a Christian Transit." In *The Certeau Reader*. Ed. Graham Ward. Oxford: Blackwell, 2000.

Chidester, David. *Savage Systems: Colonialism and Comparative Religion in Southern Africa*. Charlottesville and London: University Press of Virginia, 1996.

Clément, Olivier. *The Roots of Christian Mysticism: Text and Commentary*. Trans. Theodore Berkeley. London: New City, 1993.

*Coakley, Sarah. "Charismatic Experience: Praying 'In the Spirit.'" In *We Believe in the Holy Spirit*. By the Church of England Doctrine Commission. London: Church House Publications, 1991.

————. "The Eschatological Body: Gender, Transformation and God." In *Powers and Submissions*. Oxford: Blackwell Publishers, 2001.

*————. "Living into the Mystery of the Holy Trinity: Trinity, Prayer, and Sexuality." *Anglican Theological Review* 80 (1998): 223-32.

————. "Traditions of Spiritual Guidance." In *Powers and Submissions: Spirituality, Philosophy and Gender*. Oxford: Blackwell, 2002.

————. "The Trinity, Prayer, and Sexuality: A Neglected Nexus in the Fathers and Beyond." *Centro Pro Unione Bulletin* (Rome) 58 (2000): 13-17

*————. "Why Three? Some Further Reflections on the Origins of the Doctrine of the Trinity." In *The Making and Remaking of Christian Doctrine: Essays in Honour of Maurice Wiles*. Sarah Coakley and David A. Pailin, eds. Oxford: Oxford University Press, 1993.

"La Colombe et l'Agneau: Méditation sur le Christ et l'Esprit." Par un moine de l'Église d'Orient. *Contacts* (Paris) 15 (1963): 5-33.

Congar, Yves. *I Believe in the Holy Spirit*. Trans. David Smith. New York: Crossroad, 1997.

Corbin, Michel. *Le Chemin de la théologie chez Thomas d'Aquin*. Paris: Beauchesne, 1974.

*Cyril of Alexandria. *Commentary on the Gospel according to Saint John*. Trans. P. E. Pusey and T. Randell. 2 vols. London: Rivington, 1874-85.

————. *De recta fide ad Theodosius*. In *Acta Conciliorum Oecumenicorum*. Ed. Edvardus Schwartz. Berlin: de Gruyter, 1935.

————. *Select Letters of Cyril of Alexandria*. Ed. and trans. Lionel Wickam. Oxford: Oxford University Press, 1983.

*Cyril of Jerusalem. *Catechetical Lectures. Lectures XVI-XVIII. On the Article, And in one Holy Ghost, the Comforter, which spake in the Prophets, etc.* NPNF2 vol. 7.

Dabney, D. Lyle. "Why Should the Last Be First? The Priority of Pneumatology in Recent Theological Discussion." In *Advents of the Spirit: An Introduction to the Current Study of Pneumatology*. Ed. Bradford E. Hinze and D. Lyle Dabney. Milwaukee, Wis.: Marquette University Press, 2001.

————. *Die Kenosis des Geistes: Kontinuität zwishcen Schöpfung und Erlösung im Werk des Heiligen Geistes*. Neukirchner Beiträge zur Systematischen Theologie, Bd. 18. Neukirchen-Vluyn: Neukirchener Verlag, 1997.

Daley, Brian. "The Fullness of the Saving God: Cyril of Alexandria on the Holy Spirit." *The Theology of St. Cyril of Alexandria*. Ed. Thomas G. Weinandy and Daniel A. Keating. London and New York: T&T Clark, 2003.

————. "Nature and the 'Mode of Union': Late Patristic Models for the Personal Unity of

Christ." In *The Incarnation: An Interdisciplinary Symposium on the Incarnation of the Son of God*. Ed. Stephen T. Davis, Daniel Kendall and Gerald O'Collins. Oxford: Clarendon Press, 2001.

Daniélou, Jean. *The Bible and the Liturgy*. University of Notre Dame Liturgical Studies, vol. 3. Notre Dame, Ind.: University of Notre Dame Press, 1956.

———. *The Theology of Jewish Christianity*. Translated by John A. Baker. London: Darton, Longman, & Todd, 1964.

Davies, J. G. *He Ascended into Heaven*. London: Lutterworth, 1958.

D'Costa, Gavin. *Sexing the Trinity: Gender, Culture and the Divine*. London: SCM, 2000.

Deferrari, Roy J. *A Lexicon of St. Thomas Aquinas*. Washington: Catholic University Press, 1948.

Del Colle, Ralph. "The Holy Spirit: Power, Presence, Person." *Theological Studies* 62 (2001): 322-41.

Demus, Otto. *Byzantine Mosaic Decoration: Aspects of Monumental Art in Byzantium*. New Rochelle, N.Y.: Caratzas Bros., 1976.

Denzinger, Heinrich, and Peter Hünermann. *Enchiridion Symbolorum*. 37th ed. Freiburg im Breisgau: Herder, 1991.

Didymus of Alexandria. *On the Trinity*. PG 39.

Doran, Robert. *The Lives of Simeon Stylites*. Kalamazoo, Mich.: Cistercian Publications, 1992.

Durkheim, Emile. *The Elementary Forms of the Religious Life*. New York: Free Press, 1965.

Ephrem the Syrian. Armenian Hymn no. 49. *Patrologia orientalis* 30.

———. *Hymns*. Trans. Kathleen McVey. Classics of Western Spirituality. New York: Paulist Press, 1989.

———. *Hymns on Epiphany*. In NPNF, vol. 13.

———. *Hymns on Faith*. In *Select Works of St. Ephrem the Syrian*. Trans. J. B. Morris. Oxford: John Henry Parker and London: Rivington, 1897.

———. *Hymns on Paradise*. Translation and Introduction by Sebastian Brock. Crestwood, NY: St. Vladimir's Seminary Press, 1990.

———. *Hymns on Unleavened Bread*.

———. *Hymns on Virginity*. In *Hymns*. Trans. Kathleen McVey. Classics of Western Spirituality. New York: Paulist Press, 1989.

———. *Nisibene Hymns*, no. 50. *The Harp of the Spirit: Eighteen Poems of St. Ephrem*. Ed. Sebastian P. Brock. Studies Supplementary to *Sobornost*. Society of St. Alban and St. Sergius, 1983.

———. *Select Works of S. Ephrem the Syrian*. Trans. J. B. Morris. Oxford: John Henry Parker and London: Rivington, 1897.

Episcopal Church (USA). *The Book of Common Prayer*. New York: Church Hymnal Corporation and the Seabury Press, 1979.

*Evdokimov, Paul. *L'Esprit Saint dans la tradition orthodoxe*. Paris: Éditions du Cerf, 1969.

———. "Panagion et Panagia." In *Le Saint-Esprit et Marie*. Bulletin de la Société Français d'Études Mariales, 26. 2 vols. Paris: Éditions P. Lethielleux, 1969.

———. *The Sacrament of Love: The Nuptial Mystery in the Light of the Orthodox Tradition*.

Trans. Anthony P. Gythiel and Victoria Steadman. Crestwood, N.Y.: St. Vladimir's Seminary Press, 1994.

Evtuhov, Catherine. *The Cross and the Sickle: Sergei Bulgakov and the Fate of Russian Religious Philosophy, 1890-1920.* Ithaca, N.Y.: Cornell University Press, 1997.

Farrow, Douglas. *Ascension and Ecclesia: On the Significance of the Doctrine of the Ascension for Ecclesiology and Christian Cosmology.* Grand Rapids, Mich.: Eerdmans, 1999.

Ferraro, Giuseppe. *Lo Spirito Santo nel quarto vangelo: I commenti di Origene, Giovanni Crisostomo, Teodoro di Mopsuestia e Cirillo di Alessandria.* Orientalia Christiana Analecta, 246. Rome: Pontifical Oriental Institute, 1995.

Feuerbach, Ludwig. *The Essence of Christianity.* Trans. George Eliot. With an introductory essay by Karl Barth and a foreword by Richard Niebuhr. New York: Harper and Row, 1957.

——. *Die Philosophie der Zukunft.* Ed. H. Ehrenberg. Stuttgart: Fromanns, 1922.

**Florensky, Pavel. *The Pillar and Ground of the Truth.* Trans. Boris Jakim. Princeton: Princeton University Press, 1997. Original: *Stolp I utverzhdenie istiny.* Moscow: Put', 1914.

Fowl, Stephen. "How the Spirit Reads and How to Read the Spirit." In *Engaging Scripture: A Model for Theological Interpretation.* Oxford: Blackwell Publishers, 1998.

Frei, Hans W. *The Identity of Jesus Christ: The Hermeneutical Bases of Dogmatic Theology.* Philadelphia: Fortress Press, 1975.

Gaca, Kathy L. *The Making of Fornication: Eros, Ethics, and Political Reform in Greek Philosophy and Early Christianity.* Berkeley: University of California Press, 2003.

Galavaris, George. *Bread and the Liturgy.* Madison, Wis. and London: University of Wisconsin Press, 1970.

Gero, Stephen. "The Spirit as Dove at the Baptism of Jesus." *Novum Testamentum* 18 (1976): 17-35.

Goar, Jacques. *Euchologion, sive Rituale Graecorum complectens ritus et ordines divinae liturgiae, officiorum, sacramentorum. . . .* 2d ed. Venice: Typographia Bartholomaei Javarina, 1730. Reprint Graz: Akademische Druck- u. Verlagsanstalt, 1960.

Gospel according to Philip. In *Gnostic Scriptures.* Ed. Bentley Layton. New York: Doubleday, 1995.

Gratian. *Decreta.* In *Corpus iuris cononici,* vol. 1. Ed. Aemilius Friedberg. Graz: Akademische Druck- und Verlagsanstalt, 1955.

Graves, Charles. *The Holy Spirit in the Theology of Sergius Bulgakov.* Geneva: World Council of Churches, 1972.

**Gregory Nazianzen. *Orations XL-XLI. On Holy Baptism. On Pentecost.* Translated by Charles Gordon Browne and James Edward Swallow. NPNF2, vol. 7.

*——. *Theological Orations. Oration V. On the Holy Spirit.* In *Faith Gives Fullness to Reasoning: The Five Theoloical Orations of Gregory of Nazianzen.* Trans. and ed. by Lionel Wickham and Frederick Williams. With introduction and commentary by Frederick W. Norris. Leiden and New York: E. J. Brill, 1991.

Gregory of Nyssa. *Commentary on the Song of Songs.* Translated with an Introduction by Casimir McCambley. The Archbishop Iakovos Library of Ecclesiastical and Historical Sources, 12. Brookline, MA: Hellenic College Press, 1987.

————. *On the Holy Spirit.* NPNF2, vol. 5.

*————. *To Abblabius: On Not Three Gods.* In *Christology of the Later Fathers.* Ed. Edward R. Hardy. Library of Christian Classics, vol. 3. Philadelphia: Westminster Press, 1954.

Griffith, Sidney. Review of *La Trinité divine chez les théologiens arabes.* By Rachid Haddad. Beauchesne Religions 15. Paris: Beauchesne, 1985. In *Theological Studies* 48 (1987): 176-79.

Gross, Jules. *La divinisation du chrétien d'après les pères grecs.* Paris: J. Gabalda et Cie., 1938.

Guerric d'Igny, Fourth Sermon for Palm Sunday, *Sermons* 2:212-14. ET in *Liturgical Sermons.* Trans. the monks of St. Bernard Abbey, 2:77-78.

————. 2d Sermon for Annunciation. In *Sermons.* Source Chrétiennes, 166. Série des Textes Monastiques d'Occident, 31.

Hall, Pamela. *Narrative and the Natural Law: An Interpretation of Thomistic Ethics.* Notre Dame, Ind.: University of Notre Dame Press, 1994.

Halleux, André de. "'Hypostase' et 'Personne' dans la formation du dogme trinitaire." *Revue d'histoire ecclésiastique* 79 (1984): 313-69.

————. "Personnalisme ou essentialisme trinitaire chez les Pères cappadociens? Une mauvaise controverse." In two parts. *La Revue théologique de Louvain* 17 (1986): 129-55 and 265-92.

Hapgood, Isabel Florence, ed. and trans. *Service Book of the Holy Orthodox-Catholic Apostolic Church, Compiled, Translated, and Arranged from the Old Church-Slavonic Service Books of the Russian Church, and Collated with the Service Books of the Greek Church.* 6th rev. ed. Englewood, N.J.: Antiochian Orthodox Christian Archdiocese, 1983.

Harrison, Verna E. F. "Receptacle Imagery in St Gregory of Nyssa's Anthropology." *Studia Patristica* 22 (1989): 23-27.

Harvey, Susan Ashbrook. "Embodiment in Time and Eternity: A Syriac Perspective." *St. Vladimir's Seminary Quarterly* 43 (1999): 105-30

————. "Feminine Imagery for the Divine: The Holy Spirit, the Odes of Solomon, and Early Syriac Tradition." *St. Vladimir's Seminary Quarterly* 37 (1993): 111-39.

————. "St Ephrem on the Scent of Salvation." *Journal of Theological Studies,* n.s., 49 (1998): 109-28.

————. "The Sense of a Stylite: Perspective on Symeon the Elder." *Vigiliae Christianae* 42 (1988): 376-94.

*————. "The Stylite's Liturgy: Ritual and Religious Identity in Late Antiquity." *Journal of Early Christian Studies* 6 (1998): 523-39.

*————. *Scenting Salvation: Ancient Christianity and the Olfactory Imagination.* Berkeley, Calif.: University of California Press, 2006.

Hauk, Friedrich. *Das Evangelium des Lukas.* Leipzig: Scholl, 1934.

Hauschild, Wolf-Dieter. *Gottes Geist und der Mensch: Studien zur früchristlichen Pneumatologie.* Beiträge zur evangelischen Theologie, Bd. 63. Munich: Christian-Kaiser-Verlag, 1972.

————. *Die Pneumatomachen. Eine Untersuchung zur Dogmengeschichte des vierten Jahrhunderts.* Ph.D. dissertation, Universität Hamburg, 1967.

Hausherr, Irénée. "'New Theologian' Means 'New St. John.'" *Orientalia Christiana* 9 (1927): 98-210.

Hayen, A. *La communication de l'acte de l'être d'après Saint Thomas d'Aquin.* Paris: De Brouwer, 1957.

Hayes, Christine E. *Gentile Impurities and Jewish Identities: Intermarriage and Conversion from the Bible to the Talmud.* Oxford: Oxford University Press, 2002.

Helmer, Christine E. "Gott von Ewigkeit zu Ewigkeit: Luthers Trinitätsverständnis." *Neue Zeitschrift für systematische Theologie und Religionsphilosophie* 44 (2002): 1-19.

———. "Luther's Theology of Glory." *Neue Zeitschrift für systematische Theologie und Religionsphilosophie* 42 (2000): 237-45.

Hilary of Poitiers. *De Trinitate.* In NPNF2, vol. 9.

Hinkle, Christopher. "A Delicate Knowledge: Epistemology, Homosexuality, and St. John of the Cross." *Modern Theology* 17 (2001): 427-40.

Hinze, Bradford E., and D. Lyle Dabney, eds. *Advents of the Spirit: An Introduction to the Current Study of Pneumatology.* Milwaukee, Wis.: Marquette University Press, 2001.

Hippolytus. *Apostolic Tradition.* In *The Treatise on the Apostolic Traditions of St Hippolytus of Rome.* Ed. Gregory Dix and rev. Henry Chadwick. London: SPCK, 1968.

Holl, Adolf. *The Left Hand of God: A Biography of the Holy Spirit.* Trans. John Cullen. New York: Doubleday, 1998.

Holl, Karl. *Amphilochius von Ikonium in seinem Verhältnis zu den grossen Kappadoziern.* Tübingen: J. C. B. Mohr (Paul Siebeck), 1904.

Hütter, Reinhard. "The Church as Public: Dogma, Practice, and the Holy Spirit." *Pro Ecclesia* 3 (1994): 334-61.

———. *Suffering Divine Things: Theology as Church Practice.* Trans. Douglas W. Stott. Grand Rapids: Eerdmans, 1999.

Ignatius of Antioch. *Letter to the Ephesians.* In *Early Christian Fathers.* Ed. Cyril Richardson. New York: Touchstone Books, 1995.

Irenaeus of Lyon. *Against Heresies.* In *Irenaeus of Lyon.* Ed. and trans. Robert M. Grant. Early Church Fathers series. London: Routledge, 1990. *Adversus Haereses.* In *Irénée de Lyon: Contre les Hérésies.* Ed. A. Rousseau. Sources Chrétiennes, vol. 100. Paris: Éditions du Cerf, 1965.

Isaac of Nineveh. *Mystical Treatises.* Trans. A. J. Wensinck. Amsterdam: Koninklijke Akademie van Wetenschappen, 1923.

———. *Discourse XXII.* In *Mar Isaacus Ninivita de Perfectione Religiosa.* Ed. P. Bedjan. Paris and Leipzig, 1909. ET in *The Syriac Fathers on Prayer and the Spiritual Life.* Ed. and trans. Sebastian P. Brock. Cistercian Studies Series, no. 101. Kalamazoo, MI: Cistercian Publications, 1987.

Jackson, Pamela E. *The Holy Spirit in the Catechesis and Mystagogy of Cyril of Jerusalem, Ambrose, and John Chrysostom.* Ph.D. dissertation. Yale University, 1987.

Jacob of Serugh. *Homiliae selectae Mar-Jacobi Sarugensis.* Ed. Paul Bedjan. 5 vols. Paris and Leipzig: Otto Harrassowitz, 1908-10.

Jennings, Willie James. "Reclaiming the Creature: Anthropological Vision in the Thought of Athanasius of Alexandria and Karl Barth." Ph.D. dissertation. Duke University, 1993.

Jenson, Robert W. *America's Theologian.* New York: Oxford University Press, 1988.

————. "Beauty." *Dialogue* 25 (1986): 250-54.

*————. "The Holy Spirit." In *Christian Dogmatics*. Ed. Robert W. Jenson and Carl E. Braaten. 2 vols. Philadelphia: Fortress, 1984.

————. "Liturgy of the Spirit." *The Lutheran Quarterly* 26 (1974): 189-203.

————. "A Space for God." Unpublished typescript.

————. *Systematic Theology* I. New York: Oxford University Press, 1997.

————. *The Triune Identity*. Philadelphia: Fortress Press, 1982.

————. *Unbaptized God: The Basic Flaw in Ecumenical Theology*. Minneapolis: Fortress Press, 1992.

————. *Visible Words: The Interpretation and Practice of Christian Sacraments*. Philadelphia: Fortress, 1978.

*————. "You Wonder Where the Spirit Went." *Pro Ecclesia* 2 (1993): 296-304.

Jerome. *In Isaiam*. Ed. M. Adriaen and F. Glorie. CSEL, 73.1. Turnhout: Brepols, 1963.

John Chrysostom. *The Epistle to the Romans*. NPNF 11.

John of Damascus. *The Orthodox Faith*. Trans. Frederic Chase. New York: The Fathers of the Church, Inc., 1958.

John the Elder (Sabah)/John of Dalyatha. *Letter 12. On Prayer*. In Sebastian P. Brock, *The Syriac Fathers on Prayer and the Spiritual Life*. Kalamazoo, MI: Cistercian Publications, 1987. Original in R. Beulay, *La collection des lettres de Jean de Dalyatha. Patrologia Orientalis* vol. 39, fasc. 3. Paris and Turnhout: Brepols, 1978.

Johnson, Kelly F. *The Fear of Beggars*. Notre Dame, Ind.: University of Notre Dame Press, 2005.

Johnston, George. *The Spirit-Paraclete in the Gospel of John*. Cambridge: Cambridge University Press, 1970.

Jordan, Mark D. *The Ethics of Sex*. London: Routledge, 2002.

————. *The Invention of Sodomy in Christian Theology*. Chicago: University of Chicago Press, 1997.

Kadushin, Max. *Worship and Ethics: A Study in Rabbinic Judaism*. Evanston, Ill.: Northwestern University Press, 1963. Repr. Westport, Conn.: Greenwood, 1978.

Kattenbusch, Ferdinand. *Die Entstehung einer Christlichen Theologie: Zur Geschichte der Ausdrücke theologia, theologein, theologos*. Libelli 69. Darmstadt: Wissenschaftliche Buchgesellschaft, 1962.

Kearns, Cleo McNally. "The Scandals of the Sign: The Virgin Mary as Supplement in the Religions of the Book." In *Questioning God*. Ed. John Caputo et al. Bloomington, Ind.: Indiana University Press, 2001.

Keller, Catherine. *Face of the Deep: A Theology of Becoming*. London: Routledge, 2003.

Kermode, Frank. *The Sense of an Ending: Studies in the Theory of Fiction: With a New Epilogue*. Oxford and New York: Oxford University Press, 2000.

Kilby, Karen E. "Perichoresis and Projection: Problems with the Social Doctrines of the Trinity." *New Blackfriars* 81 (2000): 432-45.

Küng, Hans. *Justification: The Doctrine of Karl Barth and a Catholic Reflection*. 2d ed. Philadelphia: Westminster, 1981.

Laminski, Adolf. *Der Heilige Geist als Geist Christi und der Gläubigen: Der Beitrag des*

Athanasios von Alexandrien zur Formulierung des trinitarischen Dogmas im vierten Jahrhundert. Leipzig: St. Benno-Verlag, 1969.

Lampe, G. W. H. *God as Spirit.* The Bampton Lectures, 1976. Oxford: Clarendon Press, 1977.

**———. *The Seal of the Spirit: A Study in the Doctrine of Baptism and Confirmation in the New Testament and the Fathers.* 2d ed. London: SPCK, 1967.

Ledogar, Robert J. *Acknowledgment: Praise Verbs in the Early Greek Anaphoras.* Rome: Herder, 1968.

Levenson, Jon D. "Resurrection in the Torah." *Reflections* 6 (2003): 2-29.

———. *The Death and Resurrection of the Beloved Son: The Transformation of Child Sacrifice in Judaism and Christianity.* New Haven: Yale University Press, 1993.

Liddell, Henry George; Robert Scott; and Henry Stuart Jones. *A Greek Lexicon.* Oxford: Clarendon Press, 1996.

Lindbeck, George. "The Church." In *Keeping the Faith: Essays to Mark the Centenary of "Lux Mundi."* Ed. Geoffrey Wainwright. London: SPCK, 1989.

———. *The Nature of Doctrine: Religion and Theology in a Postliberal Age.* London: SPCK and Philadelphia: Fortress, 1984.

Lison, Jacques. *L'Esprit répandu: la pneumatologie de Grégoire Palamas.* Paris: Éditions du Cerf, 1994.

Loewe, Raphael. "Potentialities and Limitations of Universalism in Halakah." In *Studies in Rationalism, Judaism, and Universalism in Memory of Leon Roth.* Ed. Raphael Loewe. London: Routledge & Kegan Paul and New York: The Humanities Press, 1966.

Lossky, Vladimir. *In the Image and Likeness of God.* Ed. John H. Erickson and Thomas E. Bird. Crestwood, NY: St. Vladimir's Seminary Press, 1974.

———. *Mystical Theology of the Eastern Church.* Crestwood, NY: St. Vladimir's Seminary Press, 1976.

Lot-Borodine, Myrrha. *La déification de l'homme selon la doctrine des Pères grecs.* Paris: Éditions du Cerf, 1970.

Loughlin, Gerard. "Sexing the Trinity." *New Blackfriars* 79 (1998): 18-25.

———. *Telling God's Story: Bible, Church, and Narrative Theology.* Cambridge and New York: Cambridge University Press, 1996.

Luther, Martin. *Disputatio contra scholasticam theologiam. Martin Luthers Werke.* Weimarer Ausgabe, vol. 1.

Macarius. *Spiritual Homilies.* In *Pseudo-Macarius: The Fifty Spiritual Homilies and the Great Letter.* Ed. George F. Maloney. Classics of Western Spirituality, 75. New York: Paulist Press, 1992.

Mackinnon, Donald. "Atonement and Tragedy." In *Borderlands of Theology and Other Essays.* Philadelphia and New York: J. B. Lippincott, 1968.

———. "The Evangelical Imagination." In *Religious Imagination.* Ed. James P. Mackey. Edinburgh University Press, 1986.

———. "Incarnation and Trinity." In *Themes in Theology: The Three-Fold Cord: Essays in Philosophy, Politics and Theology.* Edinburgh: T&T Clark, 1987.

Magliola, Robert. *On Deconstructing Life-Worlds: Buddhism, Christianity, Culture.* Atlanta, Ga.: Scholars Press, 1997.

Maguire, Henry. *Earth and Ocean: The Terrestrial World in Early Byzantine Art.* University Park, Pa.: Pennsylvania State University Press, 1987.

Mahé, J. "La sanctification d'après saint Cyrille d'Alexandrie." *Revue d'histoire ecclésiastique* 10 (1909): 475-80.

Manaphes, Konstantinos A., ed. *Sinai: Treasures of the Monastery of Saint Catherine.* Athens: Ekdotike Athenon, 1990.

Mangina, Joseph. "*Christus pro nobis* and Participation in God." In *Karl Barth and the Christian Life: The Practical Knowledge of God.* New York: Peter Lang, 2001.

Mannermaa, Tuomo. *Der im Glauben gegenwärtige Christus. Rechtfertigung und Vergottung.* Hannover: Arbeiten zur Geschichte und Theologie des Luthertums, 1988.

Marshall, Bruce D. *Trinity and Truth.* Cambridge and New York: Cambridge University Press, 2001.

Martin, Dale B. "Heterosexism and the Interpretation of Romans 1:18-32." *Biblical Interpretation* 3 (1995): 332-55.

Martin, David. *Tongues on Fire: The Explosion of Protestantism in Latin America.* Oxford: Basil Blackwell, 1989.

Martinelli, Paolo. *La Morte di Cristo come rivelazione dell'amore trinitario nella teologia di Hans Urs von Balthasar.* Milan: Editoriale Jaca Book, 1995.

Martyrius (Sahdona). *The Book of Perfection.* Ed. A. de Halleux. *Martyrius (Sahdona): Oeuvres spirituelles,* vol. III. *Corpus Scriptorum Christianorum Orientalium* 252, Scriptores Syri 110. Louvain, 1965. ET: Sebastain Brock, ed. and trans. *The Syriac Fathers on Prayer and the Spiritual Life.* Cistercian Studies Series, no. 101. Kalamazoo, Mich.: Cistercian Publications, 1987.

Maximus the Confessor. *Ambiguum 7: On the Beginning and End of Rational Creatures.* In *On the Cosmic Mystery of Jesus Christ: Selected Writings from St Maximus the Confessor.* Trans. Paul Blowers and Robert Louis Wilken. Crestwood, N.Y.: St. Vladimir's Seminary Press, 2003. Greek, PG 91:1068D-1101C.

———. *The Church's Mystagogy.* In *Selected Writings of Maximus the Confessor.* Trans. George Bertholt. New York: Paulist Press, 1985.

McCarthy, David Matzko. *Sex and Love in the Home.* London: SCM, 2001.

McFague, Sallie. *Metaphorical Theology: Models of God in Religious Language.* Philadelphia: Fortress, 1982.

McIntosh, Mark A. *Mystical Theology: The Integrity of Spirituality and Theology.* Oxford: Blackwell Publishers, 1998.

McPhee, John. *Oranges.* New York: Farrar, Straus & Giroux, 1967.

Meredith, Anthony. "Gregory of Nyssa and Plotinus." *Studia Patristica* 17 (1982): 1120-25.

Merriell, D. Juvenal. *To the Image of the Trinity: A Study in the Development of Aquinas' Teaching.* Toronto: Pontifical Institute of Medieval Studies, 1990.

Metéos, J[uan]. "L'action du Saint-Esprit dans la liturgie dite de s. Jean Chrysostome." *Proche-Orient Chrétien: Revue d'études et d'informations* 9 (1959): 193-208.

Milbank, John. "Can a Gift Be Given? Prolegomenon to a Future Trinitarian Metaphysic." *Modern Theology* 11 (1995): 119-41.

———. *Theology and Social Theory: Beyond Secular Reason.* Oxford: Blackwell Publishers, 1990.

Mitchell, Louis J. *Jonathan Edwards on the Experience of Beauty.* Studies in Reformed Theology and History, n.s., 9. Princeton: Princeton Theological Seminary, 2003.

Monloubou, Louis. *La prière selon saint Luc: Recherche d'une structure.* Paris: Éditions du Cerf, 1976.

Moore, George Foot. *Judaism.* 3 vols. Cambridge, Mass.: Harvard University Press, 1927.

*Moore, Sebastian. *Jesus the Liberator of Desire.* New York: Crossroad, 1989.

Moshe bar Kopha. *Commentary on the Liturgy.* In *Two Commentaries on the Jacobite Liturgy.* Ed. R. H. Connolly and H. W. Codrington. London, 1913.

Murray, Robert. *Symbols of Church and Kingdom: A Study in Early Syriac Tradition.* Cambridge: Cambridge University Press, 1975.

Nickelsburg, George W. E., Jr. *Resurrection, Immortality, and Eternal Life in Intertestamental Judaism.* Cambridge, Mass.: Harvard University Press, 1972.

Niditch, Susan. *Prelude to Biblical Folklore: Underdogs and Tricksters.* Urbana, IL: University of Illinois Press, 2000.

Norris, Frederick W. *Faith Gives Fullness to Reasoning: The Five Theological Orations of Gregory Nazianzen.* New York: E. J. Brill, 1991.

*Norris, Richard A., Jr. "Trinity." Forthcoming in a volume to be edited by Mark MacIntosh.

———. *God and World in Early Christian Theology.* New York: The Seabury Press, 1965.

Ochs, Peter. *Peirce, Pragmatism and the Logic of Scripture.* New York: Cambridge University Press, 1998.

O'Donnell, James J. "In Him and under Him: The Holy Spirit in the Life of Jesus." *Gregorianum* 70 (1989): 25-45.

Opsahl, Paul D., ed. *The Holy Spirit in the Life of the Church.* Minneapolis, Minn.: Augsburg, 1978.

Origen. *De Oratione.* In *Origen.* Trans. Rowan A. Greer. New York: Paulist Press, 1979.

Ortiz de Urbina, Ignacio. *Patrologia Syriaca.* Rev. ed. Rome: Pontificiale Institutum Orientialium Studiorum, 1965.

Ott, Wilhelm. *Gebet und Heil: Die Bedeutung der Gebetsparänese in der lukanischen Theologie.* Munich: Kösel-Verlag, 1965.

Peeters, P. *Bibliographica Hagiographica Orientalis* 10:1121-26. Brussels, 1910, repr. 1954.

Péguy, Charles. *The Porch of the Mystery of the Second Virtue.* In *Oeuvres poétiques complètes.* Paris: Gallimard, 1975.

Perl, Eric David. *Methexis: Creation, Incarnation, Deification in Saint Maximus Confessor.* Ph.D. dissertation. Yale University, 1991.

Pesch, Otto Hermann. "Paul as Professor of Theology: The Image of the Apostle in St. Thomas's Theology." *The Thomist* 38 (1974).

Peter Lombard. *Sentences. Magistri Petri Lombardi Parisiensis episcopi Sententiae in IV libris distinctae.* 3rd ed. ad fidem codicum antiquiorum restituta. Grottaferrata: Editiones Collegii S. Bonaventurae ad Claras Aquas, 1971-81. 2 vols. in 3.

Peura, Simo. *Mehr als ein Mensch? Die Vergöttlichung als Thema der Theologie Martin Luthers von 1513 bis 1519.* Helsinki: University of Helsinki, 1990.

Peura, Simo, and Antti Raunio, eds. *Luther und Theosis: Vergöttlichung als Thema der abendländischen Theologie.* Helsinki: Luther-Agricola Gesellschaft and Erlangen: Veröffentlichungen der Luther-Akademie Ratzeburg, 1990.

Philoxenus of Mabbug. *On the Indwelling of the Holy Spirit.* In *The Syriac Fathers on Prayer and the Spiritual Life.* Ed. and trans. Sebastian P. Brock. Cistercian Studies Series, no. 101. Kalamazoo, Mich.: Cistercian Publications, 1987. Original in A. Tanghe, ed., "*Memra* de Philoxène de Mabboug sur l'inhabitation du Saint Esprit," *Le Muséon* 73 (1960): 39-40.

Photios I, Patriarch of Constantinople. *The Mystagogy of the Holy Spirit.* Translated by Holy Transfiguration Monastery. No place. Studion Publishers, 1983.

Preller, Victor S. *Divine Science and the Science of God: A Reformulation of Thomas Aquinas.* Princeton, NJ: Princeton University Press, 1967.

Prenter, Regin. *Spiritus Creator.* Translated by John M. Jenson. Philadelphia: Muhlenberg Press, 1953.

*Prestige, G. L. *God in Patristic Thought.* London: SPCK, 1952.

Provatakes, Thomas M.. *To Hagion Pneuma eis ten orthodoxon zographiken.* Thessalonike, 1971.

Radner, Ephrem. *The End of the Church: A Pneumatology of Christian Division in the West.* Grand Rapids: Eerdmans Publishing Company, 1998.

Rajewsky, Michael. *Euchologion der orthodox-katholischen Kirche aus dem griechischen Original-Text mit durchgängiger Berücksichtigung der altslavischen Übersetzung ins Deutsche übertragen.* Vienna: L. C. Zamarski & C. Dittmarsch, 1861.

Restle, Marcell. *Byzantine Wall Painting in Asia Minor.* Greenwich, CT: New York Graphic Society, 1967.

Richard of St. Victor. *De Trinitate.* In *The Twelve Patriarchs: The Mystical Ark, Book Three of the Trinity.* Trans Grover A. Zinn. New York: Paulist Press, 1979.

Riches, P. Aaron. "The Event of Passover, the Diversity of Pentecost." Unpublished typescript.

———. "On Robert Jenson's Critique of the Spirit in Barth." Unpublished typescript.

Rogers, Eugene F., Jr. "The Eclipse of the Spirit in Karl Barth." In *Conversing with Barth.* Ed. John McDowell and Michael Higton. London: Ashgate, 2004.

———. "The Mystery of the Spirit in Three Traditions: Calvin, Rahner, Florensky: Or, You *Keep* Wondering Where the Spirit Went." *Modern Theology* 19 (2003): 243-60.

———. "Narrative of Natural Law in Thomas's Commentary on Romans 1." *Theological Studies* 59 (1998): 254-76.

———. "The Ransom of Isaac." *Journal for Scriptural Reasoning* 1:2 (2001/02). At http://etext.lib.virginia.edu/journals/ssr/.

———. "Same-Sex Marriage and the Trinity." In *Authorizing Marriage.* Ed. Mark Jordan. Princeton, N.J.: Princeton University Press, 2005.

———. *Sexuality and the Christian Body: Their Way into the Triune God.* Oxford: Blackwell Publishers, 1999.

———. "Supplementing Barth on Jews and Gender: Identifying God by Anagogy and the Spirit." *Modern Theology* 14 (1998): 43-81.

———. "Theology in the Curriculum of a Secular Religious Studies Department." In *Re-*

flections on the Study of Religion. Edited by Jeffrey Stout and Randall Balmer. Princeton: N.J.: Princeton University Press, forthcoming.

————. *Thomas Aquinas and Karl Barth: Sacred Doctrine and the Natural Knowledge of God.* Notre Dame, IN: University of Notre Dame Press, 1995.

Rogers, Eugene F., Jr., ed. *Theology and Sexuality: Classic and Contemporary Readings.* Oxford: Blackwell, 2002.

Romanos the Melodist. *Kontakia of Romanos, Byzantine Melodist.* Translated and annotated by Marjorie Carpenter. 2 vols. Columbia, MO: University of Missouri Press, 1970. *Hymnes.* Ed. José Grodidiers de Matons. Sources Chrétiennes 109-110. Paris: Éditions du Cerf, 1965.

————. *Kontakia: On the Life of Christ.* Translated with an Introduction by Ephrem Lash. San Francisco: HarperCollins, 1995. *Hymnes.* Ed. José Grodidiers de Matons. Sources Chrétiennes 109-110. Paris: Éditions du Cerf, 1965.

Rorem, Paul. "Moses as the Paradigm for the Liturgical Spirituality of Pseudo-Dionysius." *Studia Patristica* 18 (1989): 275-79.

Rosato, Philip J. *The Spirit as Lord: The Pneumatology of Karl Barth.* Edinburgh: T&T Clark, 1981.

Rouner, Andrew. "Persona Non Grata." Ph.D. dissertation. The University of Virginia, 2004.

Rutherford, Janet E. "Praying the Trinity in Diadochos of Photike." Paper delivered at the Fourth Irish Patristics Conference, Maynooth, Ireland, 1999.

Saber, Georges P. *La théologie baptismale de Saint Ephrem.* Kaslik, Lebanon: Université de Saint-Esprit de Kaslik, 1974.

Sacopoulou, Marina André. *Asinou en 1106 et sa contribution à l'iconographie.* Bibliotheque de Byzantion, 2. Bruxelles, Éditions de Byzantion, 1966.

Samuel, Mar Athanasius Yeshue. *The Sacrament of Holy Baptism according to the Ancient Rite of the Syrian Orthodox Church of Antioch.* Hackensack, N.J.: A. Y. Samuel, 1974.

Scheeben, Matthias Joseph. "The Mystery of the Most Holy Trinity." In *The Mysteries of Christianity.* Translated by Cyril Vollert. St. Louis: B. Herder Book Co., 1951.

Schiller, Gertrud. *Iconography of Christian Art.* Trans. Janet Seligman from the 2d German ed. 2 vols. Greenwich, Conn.: New York Graphic Society, Ltd., 1971.

Schmeman, Alexander. *For the Life of the World.* 2d ed. Crestwood, N.Y.: St. Vladimir's Seminary Press, 1998.

————. *Of Water and the Spirit: A Liturgical Study of Baptism.* Crestwood, N.Y.: St. Vladimir's Seminary Press, 1974.

Schmidt, A. V. C., ed. *The Vision of Piers Plowman: A Complete Edition of the B-Text.* London: Dent, 1978.

Schork, R. J. *Sacred Song from the Byzantine Pulpit: Romanos the Melodist.* Gainesville: University of Florida Press, 1995.

Schutz, Jacob. "Influentia." In *Surnaturel: une controverse au coeur du thomisme au xxe. siècle.* By Institut Saint Thomas d'Aquin. Special issue of *Revue thomiste* 102. Toulouse: École de Théologie, 2001.

Schweitzer, Albert. *The Quest of the Historical Jesus.* Ed. John Bowdin. Trans. W. Montgomery et al. Minneapolis: Fortress Press, 2001.

Severus. *Homily 43 on John 1:16. Patrologia Orientalis* 84-86.

Shellard, Barbara. *New Light on Luke: Its Purpose, Sources, and Literary Content.* London: Sheffield, 2002.

Sherwood, Polycarp. *The Earlier Ambigua of Saint Maximus the Confessor and His Refutation of Origenism.* Studia Anselmiana 36. Rome: Herder, 1955.

Siman, Emmanuel-Pataq. *L'expérience de l'Esprit par l'Église d'après la tradition syrienne d'Antioche.* Théologie historique 15. Paris: Beauchesne, 1971.

Skeat, Walter W. *Langland's Vision of Piers Plowman: The Vernon Text; or Text A.* EETS, 28. London, 1867.

———. *The Vision of William concerning Piers the Plowman.* Oxford: Oxford University Press, 1886.

Smith, D. Vance. *Arts of Possession: The Middle English Household Imaginary.* Minneapolis, Minn.: University of Minnesota Press, 2003.

———. *The Book of the Incipit: Beginnings in the 14th C.* Minneapolis, Minn.: University of Minnesota Press, 2001.

Smith, Jonathan Z. *Map Is Not Territory: Studies in the History of Religions.* Leiden: Brill, 1978.

Sonderegger, Katherine. *That Jesus Christ Was Born a Jew: Karl Barth's "Doctrine of Israel."* University Park, Pa.: Pennsylvania State University Press, 1992.

Soskice, Janet Martin. "Trinity and Feminism." In *The Cambridge Companion to Feminist Theology.* Ed. Susan Franks Parsons. Cambridge: Cambridge University Press, 2002.

———. "Trinity and the Feminine Other." In *Explorations in Catholic Theology.* Ed. Geoffrey Turner and John Sullivan. Dublin: Lindisfarne Books, 1999.

Soulen, R. Kendall. *Christian Theology and the God of Israel.* Minneapolis: Fortress, 1996.

———. "YHWH the Triune God." *Modern Theology* 15 (1999): 25-54.

Speyr, Adrienne von. *The Birth of the Church: Meditations on John 18–21.* Translated by David Kipp. San Francisco: Igantius Press, 1991.

———. *The Word Becomes Flesh: Meditations on John 1–5.* Translated by Lucia Wiedenhöver and Alexander Dru. San Francisco: Igantius Press, 1994.

*———. *The World of Prayer.* With a foreword by Hans Urs von Balthasar. Trans. Graham Harrison. San Francisco: Ignatius Press, 1985.

Spinks, Bryan. "Vivid Signs of the Gift of the Spirit? The Lima Text on Baptism and Some Recent English Language Baptismal Liturgies." In *Living Water, Sealing Spirit: Readings on Christian Initiation.* Ed. Maxwell E. Johnson. Collegeville, Minn.: The Liturgical Press, 1995.

Staab, Karl. *Pauluskommentare aus der griechischen Kirche aus Katenenhandschriften gesammelt.* Münster: Aschendorf, 1933.

*Staniloae, Dumitru. "The Procession of the Holy Spirit from the Father and His Relation to the Son, as the Basis of Our Deification and Adoption." In *Spirit of God, Spirit of Christ: Ecumenical Reflections on the Filioque Controversy.* Ed. by Lukas Vischer. Faith and Order Paper 103. London: SPCK and Geneva: World Council of Churches, 1981.

*———. *Theology and the Church.* Crestwood, N.Y.: St. Vladimir's Seminary Press, 1980.

———. "The World as Gift and Word." In *Orthodox Dogmatic Theology,* vol. II. Trans. Ioan Ionita and Robert Barringer. Brookline, Mass.: Holy Cross Orthodox Press, 2000.

Stout, Jeffrey. "What Is the Meaning of a Text?" *New Literary History* 13 (1982): 3-8.

*Stowers, Stanley K. "Does Pauline Christianity Resemble a Hellenistic Philosophy." In *Paul beyond the Judaism/Hellenism Divide*. Ed. Troels Engberg-Pedersen. Louisville, London, Leiden: Westminster/John Knox, 2001.

*———. *A Rereading of Romans: Justice, Jews, and Gentiles*. New Haven and London: Yale University Press, 1994.

———. "A Response to Richard Hays' 'What Is Real Participation in Christ?'" Unpublished typescript.

Strawson, P. F. *Individuals: An Essay in Descriptive Metaphysics*. London: Methuen, 1964.

Stylianou, Andreas, and Judith A. Stylianou. *The Painted Churches of Cyprus: Treasures of Byzantine Art*. London: Trigraph for the A. G. Leventis Foundation, 1985.

*Swete, Henry Barclay. *The Holy Spirit in the Ancient Church. A Study of Christian Teachings in the Age of the Fathers*. London: Macmillan and Company; reprint, Grand Rapids: Baker Book House, 1966.

———. *The Holy Spirit in the New Testament*. Repr. ed. Eugene, Ore.: Wipf and Stock, 1998.

*Symeon the New Theologian. *The Discourses*. Trans. C. J. de Catanzaro. New York: Paulist Press, 1980. *Catéchèses*. Ed. Basile Krivochéine. Trans. Josephe Paramelle. Sources chrétiennes 113. Paris: Éditions du Cerf, 1965.

Taft, Robert F. *A History of the Liturgy of St. John Chrysostom, Vol. V: The Precommunion Rites*. Orientalia Christiana Analecta 261. Rome: Pontificio Istituto Orientale, 2000.

———. *The Liturgy of the Hours in East and West: The Origins of the Divine Office and Its Meaning for Today*. Collegeville, Minn.: The Liturgical Press, 1986.

Talley, Thomas J. *The Origins of the Liturgical Year*. 2d ed. Collegeville, Minn.: The Liturgical Press, 1986.

Tanner, Kathryn. *God and Creation: Tyranny or Empowerment?* Oxford: Basil Blackwell, 1988.

*———. *Jesus, Humanity, and the Trinity*. Edinburgh: T&T Clark and Minneapolis: Fortress, 2002.

———. *Theories of Culture: A New Agenda for Theology*. Minneapolis: Fortress, 1997.

Theodoret of Cyrrhus. *Eranistes* II. Ed. G. H. Ettlinger, 40: 20-21.

Thomas Aquinas. *The Commandments of God*. Trans. L. Shapcote. London, 1937. *Collationes in decem praecepta*. In *Opuscula theologica*. 2 vols. Turin: Marietti, 1954.

———. *Commentary on Matthew. Super Evangelium S. Matthaei lectura*. 5th ed. Turin: Marietti, 1951.

———. *In Romanos*. In *Super epistolas S. Pauli lectura*. 8th rev. ed. Ed. Raphael Cai. Turin: Marietti, 1953.

———. *Commentary on the Harmony of the Gospels. Catena aurea in quatuor Evangelia*. Turin: Marietti, 1953.

———. *Saint Thomas Aquinas' Commentary on the Gospel of Saint John*, Part I. Trans. J. A. Weisheipl and F. R. Larcher. Albany, N.Y., 1980. *Super Evangelium S. Ioannis lectura*. 5th ed. Turin: Marietti, 1952.

———. *Summa contra gentiles*. Trans. English Dominican Fathers. London, 1934. Latin ed. P. Caramello. 3 vols. Turin: Marietti, 1961-67.

————. *Summa Theologiae. Summa Theologica.* Trans. English Dominican Fathers. 5 vols. Reprinted by Thomas More Publishing, 1981. Latin (Leonine text). 4 vols. Turin: Marietti, 1963.

Thompson, John. *The Holy Spirit in the Theology of Karl Barth.* Allison Park, Pa.: Pickwick Publications, 1991.

Thorsteinsson, Runar M. *Paul's Interlocutor in Romans 2: Function and Identity in the Context of Ancient Epistolography.* Stockholm: Almqvist & Wiksell International, 2003.

Torrance, Thomas. *The Trinitarian Faith: The Evangelical Theology of the Ancient Catholic Church.* Edinburgh: T&T Clark, 1997.

Torrell, Jean-Pierre. *Saint Thomas Aquinas.* 2 vols. Vol. I: *The Person and His Work.* Trans. Robert Royal. Washington, D.C.: Catholic University Press, 1996.

Uthermann, Karl-Heinz. "Theologian." In *Oxford Dictionary of Byzantium.* 6 vols. Ed. Alexander Kazhdan et al. New York: Oxford University Press, 1991.

Vaschalde, Arthur Adolphe, ed. *Philoxeni Mabbugensis tractatus tres de trinitate et incarnatione.* 2 vols. Corpus Christianorum, Scriptores Syri, 9-10. Louvain: L. Durbecq, 1955.

Vischer, Lukas, ed. *Spirit of God, Spirit of Christ: Ecumenical Reflections on the Filioque Controversy.* Faith and Order Paper 103. London: SPCK, 1981.

Volf, Miroslav, and Maurice Lee. "The Spirit and the Church." In *Advents of the Spirit: An Introduction to the Current Study of Pneumatology.* Ed. Bradford E. Hinze and D. Lyle Dabney. Milwaukee, Wis.: Marquette University Press, 2001.

Wacker, Grant. *Heaven Below: Early Pentecostals and American Culture.* Cambridge, Mass.: Harvard University Press, 2001.

Wakefield, Gordon. "John Wesley and Ephraem Syrus." *Hugoye: Journal of Syriac Studies* 1 (1998). http://syrcom.cua.edu/Hugoye/Vol1No2/HV1N2Wakefield.html.

Weinandy, Thomas G. *The Father's Spirit of Sonship: Reconceiving the Trinity.* Edinburgh: T&T Clark, 1995.

Welch, Claude. *In This Name: The Doctrine of the Trinity in Contemporary Theology.* New York: Charles Scribner's Sons, 1952.

Welker, Michael. *God the Spirit.* Translated by John F. Hoffmeyer. Minneapolis, Minn.: Fortress Press, 1994.

Wells, Christopher. "Aquinas and Jenson on Thinking about the Trinity." *Anglican Theological Review* 84 (2002): 345-82.

Wesley, Charles. *Hymns for the Nativity of Our Lord.* Facsimile ed. Madison, N.J.: Charles Wesley Society, 1991.

Wilken, Robert Louis. "*Spiritus sanctus secundum scripturas sanctas:* Exegetical Considerations of Augustine on the Holy Spirit." *Augustinian Studies* 31 (2000): 1-18.

William of St. Thierry. *Meditative Orations.* In *The Works of William of St. Thierry* 1: *On Contemplating God.* Trans. Sister Penelope. Cistercian Fathers Series 3. Spencer, Mass., 1971. Latin: PL 180.

Williams, Anna Ngaire. *The Ground of Union: Deification in Aquinas and Palamas.* New York: Oxford University Press, 1999.

Williams, Rowan D. *Arius: Heresy and Tradition.* 2d ed. London: SCM, 2001.

————. "Barth on the Triune God." In *Karl Barth: Studies of His Theological Method.* Ed. Stephen Sykes. Oxford: Clarendon Press, 1979.

*————. "The Body's Grace." In *Theology and Sexuality: Classic and Contemporary Readings.* Ed. Eugene F. Rogers, Jr. Oxford: Blackwell Publishers, 2002.

*————. *Eucharistic Sacrifice: The Roots of a Metaphor.* Liturgical Study No. 31. Bramcote, Nottinghamshire: Grove Books, 1982.

————. *A Ray of Darkness.* Boston: Cowley Publications, 1995.

————. "A Response." In *Essays on Eucharistic Sacrifice in the Early Church.* Bramcote, Nottinghamshire: Grove Books, 1984.

————. "*Sapientia* and the Trinity: Reflections on the *De Trinitate.*" In *Collectanea Augustiniana: Mélanges T. J. van Bavel.* Ed. B. Bruning, et al. Leuven: Leuven University Press, 1990.

————. "Word and Spirit." In *On Christian Theology.* Oxford: Blackwell Publishers, 2000.

Winkler, Gabriele. "Ein bedeutsamer Zusammenhang zwischen der Bekenntnis und Ruhe in Mt 11,27-29 und dem Ruhen des Geistes auf Jesus am Jordan. Eine Analyse zur Geist-Christolgie in syrischen und armenischen Quellen." In *Studies in Early Christian Liturgy and Its Context.* Variorum Collected Studies Series 593. Aldershot, U.K.: Ashgate, 1997.

*————. "Eine bemerkenswerte Stelle im armenischen Glaubenserkenntnis: Credimus et in Sanctum Spiritum qui descendit in Jordanem proclamavit missum." *Oriens Christianus* 63 (1973): 130-62.

————. "Further Observations in Connection with the Early Form of the Epiklesis." In *Studies in Early Christian Liturgy and Its Context.* Variorum Collected Studies Series 593. Aldershot, U.K.: Ashgate, 1997.

————. "The Original Meaning of the Prebaptismal Anointing and Its Implications." *Worship* 52 (1978): 24-45. Reprinted in *Living Water, Sealing Spirit.* Collegeville, Minn.: Liturgical Press, 1995.

*Winslow, Donald F. *The Dynamics of Salvation: A Study in Gregory of Nazianzus.* Cambridge, Mass.: The Philadelphia Patristic Foundation, 1979.

Wyclif, John. *De civili Dominio.* Ed. Reginald Lane Poole. London: Wyclif Society, 1885.

Wyschogrod, Michael. "A Jewish Perspective on Karl Barth." In *How Karl Barth Changed My Mind.* Ed. Donald McKim. Grand Rapids: Eerdmans, 1986.

Yeago, David. *The Faith of the Christian Church.* Columbia, S.C.: Lutheran Southern Theological Seminary, n.d.

Zizioulas, John D. *Being as Communion: Studies in Personhood and the Church.* Crestwood, N.Y.: St. Vladimir's Seminary Press, 1997.

Index of Names and Subjects

Index of Scripture References